*Dieter Rehder, Aachen, utilizes motifs from the
Liber floridus of Canon Lambert of Saint Omer
(Herzog August Bibliothek Wolfenbüttel,
Cod. Guelf. 1 Gud. Lat. 2°):
the first four glorifications of the church
("Voces Ecclesiae")—cedars of Lebanon,
palm of Kedesh, cypress from Mt. Zion,
rose of Jericho.*

KURT ALAND

A HISTORY OF CHRISTIANITY

Volume 1
From the Beginnings
to the Threshold of the Reformation

Translated by James L. Schaaf

FORTRESS PRESS   **PHILADELPHIA**

92201

Library of Congress Cataloging in Publication Data

Aland, Kurt.
  A history of Christianity.

  Translation of: Geschichte der Christenheit.
  Includes index.
  Contents: v. 1. From the beginnings to the threshold of the Reformation.
  1. Church history. I. Title.
  BR145.2.A413 1985   270   84–47913
  ISBN 0–8006–0725–2 (v. 1)

9032D84   Printed in the United States of America   1–725

Contents

CHRISTIANITY IN THE MIDDLE AGES

CONTENTS

VOLUME 2

Preface

CHRISTIANITY IN THE REFORMATION

I. Fundamental Considerations

    1. Destruction of the Unity of the Church?
    2. The Motives for the Expansion of the Reformation
    3. The Reformation's Motives and Its Course
    4. The "Lesser" Reformers
    5. The Reformation as an All-European Phenomenon
    6. The "Left Wing" of the Reformation
    7. The "Copernican Revolution"

II. The Reformation of Martin Luther

    1. Martin Luther's Beginnings
    2. The Beginnings of Martin Luther's Reformation
    3. From the Leipzig Debate of 1519 to the Diet of Worms of 1521
    4. The Beginnings of the Church's Reorganization
    5. The Year 1525 and Its Effects
    6. Developments to the Diet of Augsburg in 1530

CONTENTS

Translator's Preface

It is a pleasure to present this translation of Kurt Aland's *Geschichte der Christenheit* to the English-speaking public. In an age oriented toward the future, the study of one's past becomes more and more imperative. Nowhere is this truer than in the church. As churches begin to come closer together in their life and work, the study of church history is particularly rewarding in helping us to understand the present as well as the past.

This volume clearly grew out of oral presentations in the university lecture hall. The translator has attempted to preserve that original character. It is to be hoped that readers will be able to visualize themselves sitting in Professor Aland's classroom and learning from his long experience as a student of the history of Christianity.

Kurt Aland, who was born in Berlin in 1915, is Professor of Church History and New Testament Textual Research at the University of Münster in Westphalia. Best known for editing recent editions of Eberhard Nestle's *Novum Testamentum Graece,* he has also written extensively in the field of New Testament studies and Reformation history. One of his earlier works was translated into English by the present translator as *Four Reformers: Luther, Melanchthon, Calvin, Zwingli* (Minneapolis: Augsburg Publishing House, 1979).

Special thanks are owed to my wife, Phyllis, for her work in typing the manuscript, to my former colleague, Professor Hans Schwarz, for reading the translation and offering many helpful suggestions, and to my assistant, Diane L. Dater, for her careful proofreading.

Columbus, Ohio   JAMES L. SCHAAF
September, 1984

Preface

This book has grown out of lectures which we in the enterprise of teaching theology title "Outline of Church History." But it is directed not only to students of theology and theologians but also—in fact, really—to the "laity," that is, to all those, regardless of their church membership, who are interested in the history of Christendom *(Christenheit)* and want to know what has happened in this history and what forces have determined its development from the beginning to the present. Therefore we will often speak differently than in the usual presentations. As much as is in our power, the endless variety of details will be reduced to the absolutely essential, and, in addition, we shall attempt to make clear the significant effect the past has had on the present. Thus the reader will surely note that the text, which attempts to use generally understandable language, has grown out of lectures; much of it has been smoothed out for the printed version—but not all of it, precisely in order to preserve its clarity.

The references found in the text and the index will assist the reader's understanding. Not infrequently (especially in the early period) a theme or a personality will be treated under various aspects, and only in the conclusion will there be a complete view. The accompanying chronological tables are intended to assist readers in seeing the course of events from generation to generation and allow them to see things that were happening contemporaneously. Here is where facts and dates will be rather thoroughly introduced; if the reader concentrates on the material in boldface type, that should suffice to give a picture of the development of the decisive factors. It is not the knowledge of historical details which is important, but understanding the contexts in which they belong. In order to explain them, this book attempts to develop the major themes in a new way. Therefore, it is possible that corrections in detail will need to be made on the basis of specialists' criticism. It has always been a risk to attempt a total presentation of the church's history. In view of the many extremely specialized works that exist, the task is greater today than ever, even for one who has worked deeply in the sources, not only in ancient church history, but also in the Reformation and modern periods—not to mention that I can only hope that all errors in the original have been removed in this (which, if I remember correctly, is now the sixth) version of the manuscript. None of this should deter us from risking a general presentation of church history, so that we might attempt to stem the frightening decline of historical consciousness and the knowledge about Christianity among theologians and people both inside and outside the church.

The translation of the second volume, which deals with the period from the Reformation to the present (for details see the Contents on pp. viii–x) is almost completed, so I have reason to hope that it will soon appear. For this volume I must thank B. Köster for assisting extensively with the final editing of the manuscript and preparing the index and my colleague, James L. Schaaf, for undertaking the difficult and painstaking work of translating it.

KURT ALAND

Münster (Westphalia), March 28, 1980

A HISTORY OF CHRISTIANITY

Volume 1

THE BEGINNINGS OF
CHRISTIANITY

1

The Argument with Paganism

1. PAGAN FAITH AT THE TURN OF THE AGE

In order to obtain a vivid overview of the religious surroundings in which Christianity emerged, we might wish for a map of world religions—such as exists today—from which we might see the geographical and statistical spread of the various types of belief. The preliminary work for such a map has been done. Archaeology has located the sites of ancient temples; as an example, there are maps which indicate all the known sites where Mithra was worshiped. But only some of the cultic locations of that age can be confirmed; many have vanished without leaving any traces behind them. And even if we could locate on a map the sites of all the temples and places of worship of that age and add to it all the Jewish communities then in existence, such a map would still lack something decisive. The philosophical schools and intellectual movements of those centuries cannot be geographically contained. In addition, there is the fact that it is virtually impossible to have statistical information about the adherents of that age's competing forms of religion. So there will never be a map comparable to those of our present religious atlases which can give us a complete view of the religious forms of that time. But even a glimpse at the existing maps and surveys gives us a strong impression of the great number of cultic sites in that age, as do the manifold literary witnesses which we possess. Even a walk through one of the preserved temple areas such as Paestum, or through one of the ancient cities which has been brought to light from the debris of the past such as Pompeii, or even a walk through the Roman forum, not to mention such a religious center as Delphi, shows most impressively that in no way did Christianity emerge in a vacuum but rather came into a world that in many ways was occupied with the question of religion and offered a profusion of answers to that question. And none of these cults, none of these forms of religion, none of these philosophical schools and

3

movements of that age was prepared to surrender to Christianity without a fight. This is the first thing we must establish here.

It is correct, as has been stated again and again, that the traditional belief in the pagan gods had in this period largely lost its power. It is correct that even Augustus's reestablishment of this pagan belief signified only a restoration, an attempt to hold to what was really outmoded and transfuse it with new power. It is also correct that skepticism particularly dominated the faith of the upper classes of that time with the demoralizing effects that accompany skepticism at any time. All of that is true. But if we were to let our view of the religious context of early Christianity be dominated by this, as often happens, we would be forced into fatal and erroneous judgments. We need only look at the end of the fourth century, at a time when Christianity had long since triumphed over governmental opposition and had won the powerful patronage of the emperor, until it was finally declared the official religion of the empire. At that time we see that paganism, which has lost the battle against Christianity—and it knows that it has lost—nevertheless continues to defend its position stubbornly and gives no thought to abandoning its opposition to Christianity, notwithstanding all the laws and prohibitions issued by the new Christian emperors. The Roman city prefect and rhetor Symmachus, one of the most illustrious personalities of the late fourth century, attempted again and again to have the altar of victory reestablished in the Roman Senate and renewed his attempt with each new emperor. He did it with such eloquence and skill that his great opponent, Bishop Ambrose of Milan, had to use every means at his disposal to prevent Symmachus's success. Symmachus did indeed belong to the upper class, but he spoke not only for these educated and wealthy circles, since behind him stood broad classes of people. Despite its external triumph, the church needed a very long time until it could break down the inner resistance of the pagan populace. A sizeable portion of the simple people in the rural areas had until very recently closed itself off to Christianity. The change noticeably took place in the fifth century when the Germanic tribes moved into the Western Roman Empire. These German people were Christians, but because they were Arians, the Catholics in the conquered provinces of the Roman Empire resisted them. The classes which, for whatever reason, previously had held to their traditional paganism, now turned away from it to the Catholic church, because to them the Catholic church with its opposition to the conquerors was the last protector of the ancient Roman ways, the last representative of the Roman Empire against the barbarism. It was at

4

that time that Catholicism first became a unifying bond and a characteristic symbol of the Roman populace.

36MWhen we speak of the vitality of pagan belief in the ancient age, we must not overlook paganism's intellectual struggle with Christianity. Obviously paganism made extensive use of the power of the state, as long as it was available to it in its struggle with Christianity. This was seconded by Judaism which, as is well known, played an especially active role in the persecution of Christians in the ancient world. But paganism and Judaism fought against Christianity not only with outward means, but also carried out an intellectual and a religious struggle against it. The arguments used in this struggle were not only the primitive ones which were used chiefly before and during the time of the persecutions to inflame the authorities and the populace to action against the Christians. Here they spoke not only of the Thyestean meals, that is, that human flesh was eaten in the Christian assemblies, of the oedipal immorality of the Christians, that is, that Christians practiced incest at their worship services, and of similar things, but they also argued against Christianity in an intellectual way. Celsus (see p. 36) in the second century and Porphyry (see p. 420) in the third century offer examples of this. They attack the authority of the New Testament and the authority of the entire Bible with arguments that sound quite modern. At the end of the eighteenth century, Lessing's publication of the so-called Wolfenbüttel Fragments created an extraordinary sensation and led to an embittered feud between Lessing and Goeze, the chief pastor in Hamburg. *Fragmente des Wolfenbüttelschen Ungenannten* ("Fragments of an unnamed Wolfenbüttler") is what Lessing titled his collection in order to cover the tracks that might lead to its author, Reimarus, from whose manuscript *Apologie oder Schutzschrift für die vernünftigen Verehrer Gottes* ("Apology or defense for the rational worshipers of God") Lessing had taken these fragments. What Lessing was here publicizing in Reimarus's fragments was nothing other than a renewal of the attacks on Christianity already made by Celsus and Porphyry. These arguments, found as early as the second and third centuries, are still with us today. Again and again we meet them and, because of the errors made over and over again by the church and theology, these arguments still bring results today in such matters as the authority of the Bible, because the laity have been trained in a wrong interpretation of the Bible, especially of the New Testament.

The vitality of paganism in the ancient world can be documented in many sources. The ancient writers and philosophers, as well as those of late antiquity, furnish an abundance of material as proof of this. But there is also a very simple way to observe the vitality of paganism— merely read the Acts of the Apostles. Here contemporary pagan belief is presented in the most impressive way. Acts 17 takes us into the metropolis. Here we read how Paul wandered through Athens and found the city full of images of the gods. His sermon on the Areopagus attracted attention because people thought he wanted to proclaim new gods, a new faith. This attention was based on a skeptical curiosity. When Paul began to speak about the resurrection, they no longer took him seriously, and only a few were willing to hear any more from him. Here we see confirmation of the continuing existence of the old belief in the gods, as well as the interest in religious questions, even if skepticism has affected its health in the big city. The story of Lystra in Asia Minor in Acts 14 brings us to a small village. Here we have a report of Paul's healing a man crippled from birth. When the people see this, they cry out in Lycaonian, that is, not in Greek, but in the vernacular: "The gods have come down to us in the likeness of men!" They still think it possible for gods to descend from heaven, take on human form, and display their power. "Barnabas they called Zeus, and Paul, because he was the chief speaker, they called Hermes." The priest of the temple of Zeus in front of the city brings sacrificial animals and garlands and, along with the people, wants to sacrifice to them. Only with difficulty can they prevent it.

In Acts 19 we read how the silversmith Demetrius in the large city of Ephesus can assemble a mob of people because—as he claims—Artemis has been injured by Paul's preaching and her worship endangered by the new faith. Naturally, local commercial interests play a role in this, but such a mob action is still possible only if the people are convinced that this is an insult to their god, an insult to their religious sensitivities. In the same chapter we find the report of seven Jews who functioned as itinerant exorcists. As they tried with the assistance of Jesus' name to exorcise an evil spirit from a man, the possessed man attacked them as punishment for misusing the name. This impressive event resulted in a public burning of magical books by their owners. And these were not only pagans who participated but, according to Acts, also Christians in great numbers confessed that they were guilty of magic (and doubtless are even to the present day). In the last chapter of Acts we read this about Paul's stay in Malta: Those who are shipwrecked are warming themselves by a fire. Paul also is gathering wood for it. But along with the bundle of sticks, he picks up a serpent which bites him as he places the wood on the fire. It hangs on his hand, visible to all. The inhabitants of the island, seeing this, exclaim in fright that this Paul must be a murderer who has incurred the wrath of the gods. If the sea was not able to devour him, the serpent will bring him the death he deserves. The gods are conceived of as living beings who pursue evildoers with their vengeance. Paul shakes off the serpent into the fire, and the observers wait for him to swell up and fall over dead. When this fails to happen, they change their minds and declare that Paul is a god.

These are the reports we have in Acts. Naturally the question arises whether what is reported in Acts really happened exactly this way in the places reported, at the times reported, and under the circumstances reported. The invincible skepticism with which these reports are not infrequently confronted does not detract in this context from their value as sources. The author of Acts was certainly aware of the critical judgment of his contemporaries. They were in a position to judge whether the depiction of the situation of the contemporary world around A.D. 80–90 in which Acts was written agreed with what they knew from their own perception. This is at least (although in reality it is much more; our "invincible skepticism" comes to a certain extent from a hypercritical attitude which goes far beyond what is the rule in classical philology and ancient history) typical truth that we find in these reports, and that is what counts here. When we later turn to a consideration of the cults which dominated the world at the time Christianity set out to conquer that world, we can stress and briefly consider them only in typological fashion, and we must do so chiefly from the standpoint of what these forms of belief meant for the wide masses of the populace.

When we seek to explain the reasons for the rapid expansion of Christianity during the first four centuries, we must first of all direct our attention to the ordinary people. Early Christianity won the greatest portion of its adherents from this group. That can be seen plainly from the testimony of Paul in 1 Cor. 1:26–29, which is all the more trustworthy since it is mentioned only in passing: "For consider your call, brethren; not many of you were wise according to worldly standards, not many were powerful, not many were of noble birth; but God chose what is foolish in the world to shame the wise. God chose what is weak in the world to shame the strong, God chose what is low and despised in the world, even things that are not, to bring to nothing things that are, so that no human being might boast in the presence of God." The early Christian congregations took an overwhelming number of their members from the poor, lowly, uneducated classes. The testimony of the pagan Celsus from the end of the second century confirms this, as does ancient church history. Even at the beginning of the third century such a large, important, and wealthy congregation as Rome chose as its bishop Callistus from the slave class, although his previous life story had run a very complicated course (see pp. 151–56). It selected him in definite opposition to a representative of the educated and wealthy class, Hippolytus (see pp. 152–53), and in so doing had to put up with a schism in the church.

Naturally, we must not—as has happened earlier and still happens today in many circles—turn Christianity into a religion of the proletariat, a religion of the oppressed who flee to this faith in order to find in it a compensation for the way the world has mistreated and misused them. Those who hold this view have not read Paul correctly. He does not say that in the church there are no powerful ones, no wise ones, none who have possessions, but rather that there are not many of them. And Acts—once again taken as representative—also shows us that from early on there were not only people from the lowest classes who belonged to the Christian church, but there were also members of the middle class, even the upper middle class, and very early we even find members from the upper classes in the church. But there are only a few, and the higher one goes on the social ladder the fewer there are. Their number did increase in the course of time, but even into the fourth century the educated, rich, and influential upper class generally kept its distance from Christianity, at least in the West. Therefore it is important, when we inquire about the reasons for the spread and the victory of Christianity over late antiquity, to pay special attention to the ordinary people.

When we now attempt to categorize the religiosity and worship practices of that time according to various types, we must first speak about the old anthropomorphic conceptions of the gods as we know them from Homer, from mythology, from the *Sagen des klassischen Altertums* ("Sagas of classical antiquity"), as Schwab titled his well-known collection, or from similar sources. The old faith in the gods is still very much alive in the period which we are considering. Everywhere the temples of the preceding age stand in their old glory. The construction of temples has not ceased, but rather new temples are continually being built to honor the old gods. The festivals of the gods are regularly being celebrated; the gods are offered the prescribed sacrifices, just as always. Naturally this veneration of the old gods—as Homer, for instance, depicts it—has changed completely for the educated, insofar as they take their faith seriously. They can no longer enter directly into this cultic anthropomorphic understanding which has so much that is inappropriate for divinity, or even creates offense. But nevertheless, the educated remain faithful to the old cults of the god. They signified a reality for them just as they do for the common folk. This takes place partially because the public repudiation of these cults of the gods could have very detrimental consequences, for they are closely connected with public life and most highly regarded by the simple populace. But it was not for these reasons alone that they maintained the old cult of the gods, but rather because the educated had the possibility of reinterpreting these divine figures and through allegorical consideration could fill the old outlines with new contents. They made a great deal of use of this, just as they identified the old figures of the gods with the new gods who at that time were coming into the picture in great numbers. And finally the members of the educated and wealthy class had the possibility of finding in the old gods only varied personifications of the one divine being who controlled the fate of the world. For them, therefore, there were various ways not only of remaining true externally to the old cult of the gods, but affirming it inwardly as well. Even the ordinary people made use of the varied possibilities of allegorical interpretation, of identification of the old with the new gods. In general one must say, however, that for them the cult of the gods in its old form was much more real than it was for the upper class, since for them the old gods were more reasonable, tangible, vivid, and intimate than the philosophical doctrinal formulations which had meaning especially for the educated. Here we see the first type of contemporary faith.

We meet the second type in the veneration given to the wave after wave of new forms of gods and new forms of faith which came to the attention of people of that time as the Roman Empire expanded toward the East. The greatest extension of the Roman Empire took place in the first century before Christ and the first century after Christ, a fact that is often overlooked. At the threshold of the first century B.C., the Roman Empire was essentially confined to the West. In Africa the area around Carthage had already been conquered for a long time, and behind it extended the allied Numidian Empire. But this eastern boundary of the Roman Empire was located only in western Asia Minor; therefore, with the exception of a small portion of Africa, it included only European territories. Not until the first century B.C., that is, under Pompey, Caesar, and Octavian, did Rome's rule expand significantly eastward into Asia Minor, did Syria become a Roman province, and all of North

Africa came to Rome. In the first century A.D. the Roman Empire achieved the boundaries which we generally associate with it. In the West it included all of Europe including the province of Britannia; then the boundary ran along the Rhine and Danube, in places extending beyond these rivers, then included Greece and the entire Balkans, thus virtually surrounding the Black Sea. Then it included the Roman provinces of Armenia, Assyria, and Mesopotamia; it extended past Syria, Judaea, the provinces of Arabia, Egypt, and the African coastal areas back toward the West, until the circuit was completed at the entrance to the Mediterranean. Naturally we must concede that the Roman Empire's relations with the East did not first begin at that time. Even the old Roman Empire was in many ways connected with the East through commercial and cultural relations, and in addition also included the East in its sphere of political influence. But it was in the last pre-Christian and in the first Christian century that the significance of the East came to the fore. When this happened essential changes took place in the areas of intellectual life, chiefly in the area of religion.

The beginnings of the influences of Eastern religion extend back into early times. As early as the Second Punic War, that is, the end of the third century B.C., the holy rock of Magna Mater was brought to Rome at the order of the sibyls. At the time of Cato (beginning of the second century B.C.) we already find Syrian soothsayers in Rome, and in the following centuries the mystery religions already have adherents in the West. But when the sources speak about mystery religions at that time they do so only in connection with reports about persecutions of these mystery religions, and this remains true until the turn of the age. Again and again we hear, for example, that the sanctuaries of Isis in Rome were destroyed: in the years 58, 53, 50, 48 B.C., and so it continues. Very early, therefore, there were outposts of the Eastern forms of religion in Rome, and the state fought emphatically against them. Not until the first century of our age did the situation change. Emperor Augustus (30 B.C.–A.D. 14), like his predecessors, issued laws against the oriental religions. But in these laws it becomes clear that the emperor did not take these oriental forms of faith very seriously. He thought that the Eastern religions could be attacked at their root by the religious renewal of his age, and one need only wait until they died out completely. In this Augustus was fundamentally wrong. It is true that as early as the year 19 B.C. a bloody persecution of the adherents of Isis took place in Rome, but by 38 we see Emperor Caligula (37–41) constructing a temple to Isis on the Campus Martius, and at that time we already find an Isis festival on the calendar. Step by step the mystery religions now press forward. Under Emperor Claudius (41–54) the veneration of Attis is permitted. Domitian (81–96) not only greatly enlarged the temple of Isis in Rome, but also confirmed the veneration of Adonis. Under Hadrian (117–38) the veneration of Isis reached its high point. Commodus (180–92) had himself consecrated in the Mithras mystery. Caracalla (211–17) made a pilgrimage to Egypt in order to study the religion there, and finally when Heliogabalus became emperor in the year 218 the advance of the Eastern religions toward Rome was brought to everyone's attention in an obvious manner.

Before becoming emperor, Heliogabalus was a priest of the Syrian sun-god in Emesa. He now brought the holy rock of this sun-god with him to Rome. With a great deal of ceremony the rock was transferred to the city. The emperor personally accompanied the wagon, walking backward before it with his eyes fixed on the relic, and now officially and ceremonially connected this god with the city. He was offered a bride, at first an old Roman goddess whom he scorned, and instead chose a Carthaginian-Phoenician moon-goddess, whose marriage with him was celebrated in frenzied festivals. The mystery religions were finally worthy of the imperial court. If that was the way it was in Rome, we can imagine approximately how things must have been in the rest of the empire. In these mystery religions, which now permeated the entire empire, the real piety of the earlier age lived. They bore various names according to their different central figures: Orpheus, Demeter, Cybele, Attis, Mithras, Isis, to mention only a few.

In their areas and practices of worship, the mystery religions are completely different from one another, and they also are capable of development from time to time and are not always the same. They can adopt new customs and abandon old usages. But the nucleus of these mystery religions is always the same: at their center stands a divine or semidivine figure, a god who has become human or a human who has become divine, with whom the believer enters into fellowship, either through cultic washings or through cultic meals. Through these, the believer participates in this god. God becomes human in him, the believer; he, the adherent of the mystery, becomes divine. With this formula, all these mystery religions can be described. The cult is directed to the individual believer, but at the same time it creates a close fellowship among all who are consecrated in it. Thus, a believer significantly often joins not only one mystery religion, but belongs to several at the same time. This he does because he is attempting to gain the power of not just one god, but trying to combine as many deities as possible in himself, to multiply their power in himself at the same time in order in this way to participate completely in the Soteria, the salvation, which stands at the center of these mystery religions. In these mystery religions, which spread in the Roman Empire simultaneously with the Christian faith, we have the first great competitors of Christianity, so that it has been claimed, as we shall discuss later (see pp. 22–27), that Christianity has an inner essential connection with these mystery religions.

Alongside these mystery religions are the philosophical schools which underwent an essential change in the centuries we are considering. For the mystery religions had an influence on these schools so that philosophy developed at this time from a pure theory of knowledge to a total *Weltanschauung*. The philosopher is now not only a thinker and a teacher, but also a physician and a spiritual counselor.

Ethics now receive increasing attention in philosophical teachings, ethics which not only give fundamental guidelines but also discuss and make decisions in great detail about individual questions such as education, marriage, and the like. The question of religion now also plays an essential role in these philosophical schools. In this context, seldom is the old religion of the people characteristically cast completely aside. It can remain in force because one reinterprets it either mystically or pantheistically or even rationalistically. Philosophy, so it is thought, is mirrored in the secrets of the mystery religions so that both can be combined. Thus it is possible that ecstasy, something that is quite antithetical to philosophy, can now become a constituent part, even the crowning glory of philosophical systems. Some of these philosophers and philosophies appear to be very close to Christianity. For example, the Stoic Seneca (see p. 129) was considered a secret Christian because of his writings and a voluminous correspondence with the apostle Paul was attributed to him. And in fact some of these philosophies did exercise a very great influence on Christianity. The formulation of not a few theological and dogmatic views in the second century, for instance, is inconceivable without Middle Platonic thought and its influences. Neoplatonic thought then continued to affect most strongly the history of theology and the history of the church, for example, with Augustine, (see p. 209). And in other places so many contacts and parallels may be found that we can understand why some people a generation ago sought to emphasize not only Christianity's closeness to these mystery cults but also to these philosophical schools, and that some went so far as to deduce and explain the existence of essential parts of Christianity not only from the mystery religions but also from the influence of the philosophical schools. Today we recognize—or we should recognize—that these contacts on which the previous generation placed such great emphasis are chiefly external and that the parallels between Christianity and the philosophies of the early centuries only seem to be parallels. For these philosophical schools live from a completely different spirit, from a completely different understanding of existence than Christianity. They grow out of completely different roots and strive to attain completely different goals, about which we shall speak in the next section where we discuss the reasons for Christianity's triumph over these cults.

If these philosophical schools were changing in the centuries under consideration, the reason for this is that the world view in that age was decisively changing. That is an additional factor which must be considered if we wish to understand the religious development of the first centuries. Originally the earth was viewed as a disc in which the continents were surrounded and limited by water. Above the water were the heavens, so that the world resembled something like a dome. The heavens touched the earth everywhere, and in them dwelt the gods whose kingdom was thus closely connected with the earth. They were conceived of as being enthroned on Olympus, a mountain hidden by clouds; even today the traveler through Greece who views Mount Olympus notes that the peak is regularly obscured by clouds. If it is so that the gods lived on this mountain, their relationship to the earth posed no problem. We find this connection between the gods and the earth and its people (most often with the female segment of the human race) in ancient mythology in very different ways, but always in most graphic forms which we do not want to repeat here. This world view—people upon the earth, gods above the earth, the realm of the dead ruled by the gods of the dead under the earth—is now abandoned; the earth floats freely in space, around it orbit the planets, and over them hover the heavens with their fixed stars. It is here that the gods are now enthroned; consequently they are far removed from the earth. Between the gods, the divinity, the divine power, or however one expresses it, and humankind lies an intermediate world divided into spheres. These are ruled by beings between man and god.

There are varied consequences that grow from this change in world view, consequences whose roots extend not only to philosophical, but also to religious perceptions. For how shall one now conceive of the activity of the gods and their influence on earthly events, if they are so far distant from them and from human beings? It is no longer conceivable (at least in principle) that the gods might come to the earth in person, but they can affect the earth and its people only through the power that proceeds from them. But now it is not only the gods who work in earthly events, but also the powers of the stars, the powers of the intermediate beings from the spheres between heaven and earth. Thus the influence of the gods is relativized and, even more importantly, the gods become abstract conceptions.

The old, colorful, vivid world of the gods evaporates. The new world of the gods, the divinity, the divine power, just to repeat these expressions, can play a role in philosophy. One can find the way to the gods through mysticism; but for the ordinary person, who cannot or only with great difficulty can follow this path of philosophy and also the way of mystical ecstasy, access to these new conceptions of the gods becomes very difficult. He can no longer conceive of a direct connection to them. He has access to them only if the gods personify themselves, whether in rocks, monuments, amulets, or sacred animals. But even then the possibility of finding a personal relationship with these gods is very limited, and this relationship is the real heart of every religion. Only the path of prayer remains, but prayer rises into a void, and there is no a priori guarantee of its success. So from prayer one turns to magic, to sorcery. The spiritualization of the gods, their abstraction, which signified a powerful advance in comparison to the old anthropomorphic conceptions, finally did not lead to a higher development of the conception of the gods, but—seen by the great masses—to a decline. The gods were not spiritualized, but were rather turned into things. And they also became less powerful. For, as we have said, the new gods could not enter directly into the events of the world and change them. This world and what happens in it was subject to strict unchanging and unchangeable laws. The only thing that a person might do, aside from prayer and magic, would be to study the laws which control both the world and the gods in order to accommodate himself to them and thus make these laws as useful as possible.

It was also a decisive shock to the popular religion that in the new world view there was no room for a realm of the dead. As always the ordinary person—even to the present day—holds to this conception, for it is a comforting thought to know that under the earth below his feet the dead are resting. In the new world view there no longer was any room for the realm of the dead. So they sought an alternative solution by simply naming a portion of the heavens Hades, and what previously had been said about the realm of the dead below the earth was now predicated of this new Hades in heaven. But, understandably enough, this achieved no great success. Another solution was sought in the development of the conception that souls after death ascend into heaven. At that time originated the conception of the journey of souls into heaven which still influences us today. This conception was completely worked out in Gnosticism (see p. 95). The soul, that is, the divine portion of a person, ascended after death from earth to the deity. In doing so, according to the view of late Gnosticism, it had to pass through the various spheres which lay between earth and the deity. That naturally presupposed that it was satisfactorily equipped for this journey. First of all, it had to know the passwords that were in effect in the various spheres. And in addition the soul had to be created in such a way that it could pass through these spheres.

Either it had to be already cleansed from all dross which adhered to it, or the dross had to be so insignificant that it would fall away from it as it passed through the various spheres, for the basic belief of the time, about which we shall speak in more detail (see pp. 36–39), was that nothing impure could enter into the pure divinity. Again we recognize a spiritualization of the old conceptions, something that appears to mean an unmistakable advance. But again this sort of spiritualization is very difficult for simple people to understand, and thus we see that for the simple person the spiritualization paradoxically leads anew to a crude reproduction of these conceptions.

Let us summarize: the old world of the gods has gone. If one looks at the laws which support this world, if one observes the impressive new system of the world directed by providence, then one can no longer simply harmonize it with the gods of the old mythology. It is only possible if one thinks of the many gods about whom the poets and philosophers spoke as mirrors of the one highest god who created the world. But this highest god is transcendent; he is absolutely elevated over the world, that is, he is separated from this world. There is no access to him; there is no way from impure humanity to the highest purity, to God.

A bridging of this gap can be found in the conception of mediating gods, of beings who rule the various spheres between divinity and humanity. They are variously named; some talk of Aeon, the god of fate, some of the Demiurge, and some of Helios, the sun-god.

The most successful and powerful of these was the figure of Helios, the sun-god, who was virtually the official ruler of the empire in the third century. The worship of the sun apparently came from Syria but quickly spread throughout the entire world, doubtless because of its vividness to the masses. For this god could be seen. Every morning he rose anew in the east; then, drawn by the four horses—thus he was visualized—he drove majestically through the heavens; he gave power and life to all. Not only could this god be seen, but his salutary effect could be felt quite tangibly, and thus people turned to him. In addition this cult also enjoyed official support, apparently because the emperors found it practical for sanctioning their demands and desires. So the veneration of Helios, the *Sol Invictus,* increased more and more, and the cult of the sun developed into one of the major truly international religions which competed seriously with Christianity far into the Christian Era. It was not merely in the third century that the cult of the sun enjoyed a special significance, but it maintained its force far into the fourth century. For example, in the arch of Constantine, erected by the Senate in the year 315 to honor the Emperor Constantine after his victory over Maxentius in Rome, a portrait of the sun-god can be seen in one of the portals. It has even been claimed that belief in the *Sol Invictus* was the real religion of Constantine. It is doubtless false to claim this for Constantine's entire life. It is naturally possible that the cult of the sun had meant something significant to Constantine prior to his attraction to Christianity, for there was—and we can document this from various sources—the possibility of a direct transition from belief in this sun-god to the Christian faith. Some time ago an especially vivid witness of this was found, and in a place no less significant than underneath St. Peter's Cathedral in Rome. Excavations revealed a cemetery from late antiquity and in it the actual or supposedly historical grave of the apostle Peter. This cemetery was closed and covered over by Constantine for the construction of St. Peter's Cathedral, so that everything remained intact. In addition to individual graves (the apostle's grave is located in the paupers' section of the cemetery) there is a whole row of family tombs for wealthy families. In these family tombs it seems that Christians were also buried, for example, at least in the final use of the so-called Julian Mausoleum. Either this family itself had converted to Christianity or a Christian family later took over the mausoleum, for here we find mosaics of unmistakable Christian content. For example, here is a picture of Jonah being cast into the sea. This is a motif which is seen again and again in the paintings of the catacombs and Christian mosaics, for it was seen as a symbol of the Christian hope of the resurrection: Just as Jonah was saved from the belly of the fish, so the dead will rise after a stay in the grave. In these mosaics a shepherd is pictured. What he bears on his shoulder cannot be absolutely identified, but apparently it is a sheep. Also there is a fisherman who is casting a line on which one fish bites while another flees. Although the good shepherd is not only a Christian symbol, the Christians nevertheless at this time made the greatest use of it and the fish is *the* Christian symbol. The sign of the fish served as a cryptogram, that is, a veiled confession of Christianity, for in Greek the word fish is ΙΧΘΥΣ, and this word was understood as the abbreviation of Ἰησοῦς Χριστός Θεοῦ Ὑιός Σωτήρ ("Jesus Christ, God's Son, Savior"). If a Christian painted or scratched the image of a fish on a house or a wall, he intended thereby to make a confession, and not a few of the passersby would know that this meant a witness and an invitation to Christianity. All of these mosaics in the tomb of the Julians give evidence of the Christian confession of the family, at least in its last generation. Now we find here—and this is the reason for this long story—a domed mosaic as the crowning point of the artistic decorations. It depicts Helios with the sun-chariot. But we may not really call him Helios any longer, for although the sun-god is here traditionally depicted in the chariot with four horses, the rays which surround his head are formed in such a way that this Helios wears a nimbus with a cross in it. Either we have here a camouflaged representation which simultaneously reveals, as well as conceals, a Christian confession, understandable in the time of persecution, or this mosaic represents some kind of mixed and transitional religious form between the sun cult and Christianity which we must assume existed at the turn from the third to the fourth century. These mixed forms facilitated the transition to the Christian faith from the cult of the sun, which, together with the cult of the emperor (about which we must now speak), was one of the most serious opponents of Christianity.

The imperial cult began for the Roman Empire in the first century B.C., grew further in the first century of the Christian Era, and continued to develop more and more, both in its conception and in the number of its adherents, until the other cults receded behind this cult of the emperor and it became the real opponent of Christianity. Again and again in the accounts of the persecutions we find this conflict with the imperial cult. For what was demanded of Christians was that they sacrifice before the emperor's image and venerate his divine power. Because they refused, they died a martyr's death.

We can most clearly trace the advance of the imperial cult in Asia Minor. From the imperial age on, here generally only temples for the ruler were constructed, no longer ones for the old gods. This cult of the ruler grows from a twofold root. It originated in Greek culture, but it received its decisive forms in the Orient. Greek culture recognized no intermediate forms between God and man. Here there is a connection between God and man, generally in the way we have already mentioned (see p. 13), but man can develop beyond his form of existence: One is reminded of the heroes, of the demigods, of the conception of "Theios Aner." On this basis the Greeks possess the theoretical possibility of venerating a ruler as God. But this theoretical possibility develops into a real one when the Eastern conceptions are added, according to which the ruler from ancient times signified a representation and personification of the deity. As early as the time of Alexander the Great, these two elements came together in the East, but it is not until the first century B.C. that we see the idea of a divine emperor also spreading in the Roman Empire. This begins with Caesar and then under Augustus develops significantly until in the first century of the Christian Era all the emperors claim this supreme achievement for themselves. It was possible in the age of Augustus to overcome the strong old Roman prejudice against divinization of the emperor. While in the Eastern Roman Empire the emperor was venerated as a god along with the *Dea Roma,* the goddess of Rome, in the West it was only the genius of the emperor, an abstraction, his *pax, felicitas, clementia,* and the like that were worshiped. Only after his death, so it was thought, could the emperor be raised to a *divus,* that is, divinized, and this only through the action of the Senate. Under Augustus the decisive change took place. A whole century before him the empire had been ravaged by civil war, by famine and suffering; for a whole century there was no end to the shedding of blood and general insecurity. Now under Augustus all of that was over. Peace, a united government, order, law, and justice took the place of war, murder, assassination, anarchy, destruction, and arbitrariness. These circumstances affected the people's consciousness; during the generation prior to the appearance of Christianity in the world people felt themselves redeemed. This is the only word that can be used to characterize this age. A wave of enthusiasm, a high religious mood swept through the empire. In Vergil's Fourth Eclogue we find eschatological formulations that sound almost Christian: themes of paradise are revealed to the human race. Everything which makes for the misery of the present will soon be at an end and the emperor is initiating this change. There is a documentary expression for this religious enthusiasm in the inscription on the calendar in Priene: The Senate had announced a prize for the person who proposed the best way to honor the emperor, who best could find a way to express in words what this emperor meant for humanity. The proconsul received the prize, a golden laurel wreath. We can do nothing but quote what he wrote:

> It is difficult to say whether the birthday of the divine emperor has brought more joy or profit; we do right to honor him as the beginning of the universe, not according to the origin of everything, but according to the benefits. For everything was collapsing and leading to disaster. He re-established it and gave the world a new appearance, a world which wished its own destruction if the emperor had not been born as a blessing to all. Therefore we rightly see in him the beginning of life and existence; what was born to sadness he gave a goal and an end.

In this vein it continues. At the conclusion it is proposed that the beginning of the new year should be transferred to the birthday of the emperor, a proposal that received enthusiastic support. The god's birthday, so the order establishing it proclaims, was the first message of joy which went out from him to the world, or more precisely, the first evangel, the first good news. We can see the sort of powerful effects that issued from the Augustan Age. The formulations that are used here are so close to Christianity that the Christians of the ancient world had no qualms about interpreting Vergil's words as a pagan prophecy of Jesus.

Naturally this high mood of the Augustan Age did not last. The blossoming of the empire was only brief, and a time of decay followed it. But despite this, or perhaps because of it, the emperors after Augustus especially promoted the cult of the emperor. Augustus's personality and achievements created the presuppositions for the cult of the emperor. While Augustus's person carried the institution, the following emperors let themselves be carried by the institution. They willingly promoted the cult of the ruler and soon demanded it from their subjects. The imperial cult now became the inner adhesive which held the disparate Roman Empire together. The external adhesive was the army, government, commerce, and similar things. What was lacking in this empire, however, which in the first Christian century had annexed in the East so many different elements, was a real national identity. There was no common culture in East and West, so that the veneration of the emperor, or to put it more precisely, the veneration of the emperor's divine mission of maintaining peace, became the means of amalgamating the very different inhabitants of the Roman Empire into a community. Naturally this veneration of the emperor had its limits. In Rome, of course, but also in other places among the decisive classes of the empire, one had very definite notions about the deficiencies of the current divine emperor. Even outsiders would regularly become conscious that this emperor was god only in a very relative manner. For the one who today was most venerated and adored might tomorrow be killed. Then his monuments would be defaced, his statues would be toppled, and in his place his murderer would now be highly honored. That took place again and again, and for this reason from its outset the imperial cult was subject to a certain relativization. Yet we must observe that the farther away one got from Rome the less this came into the general consciousness. And in addition one could certainly hope, if one emperor had not appropriately evidenced himself as divine, that his successor might possess the necessary qualities. Here is not where the real limits of the imperial cult lay. The fact that the personality of an emperor did not meet the demands was of less significance in the process of relativization than the fact that there was no individual relationship possible with this deity, that what was lacking was that personal relationship to him which people at every time—especially the ordinary people—needed in relation to a god.

The various forms of faith of the early centuries appear something like this (just to give an outline): the faith in the old gods, the mystery religions, the philosophical schools, the sun worship, the imperial cult. All of these forms of faith we can now see in the most varied combinations, for one of the foremost characteristics of these forms of faith is that they did not exclude one another but could all exist side by side. All these philosophies, all these cults, all these forms of belief could be reconciled. An individual could for himself, in any way he considered it appropriate, construct a synthesis or an amalgamation of them. Naturally the accents would be different. Just to repeat, the simpler a person is, that much greater for him will be the significance of the belief in the old gods. The more educated a person is, that much more will he turn to abstract philosophies, perhaps even to mystical conceptions. Nevertheless, we observe in one respect how the ordinary person as well as the educated one goes beyond what we have previously said: With both groups the belief in fate, astrology, magic, interpretation of dreams, and everything that is associated with these played an extraordinary and continually increasing role. This is evidence of the insecurity of people in spite of, or perhaps because of, the numerous cults which were available to them. The fact that an adherent of the mysteries enrolled not only in one mystery religion but in several at the same time points in this direction. A person felt isolated, insecure, and searched for stability, for comfort, for help, for security even in times when the empire was enjoying good fortune and prosperity, and still more so in the periods when it seemed that the empire was collapsing and the insecurity of the individual appeared in the face of war, plague, and the like. And that was more and more the case as time continued.

In the new world view the stars attained a new significance, so that people attempted to assure their favor. The exceptional role which astrology played in this time had as its presupposition the idea that everything that took place in heaven had a consequence on earth, or that whatever took place on earth only mirrored what had taken place in heaven. The stars determined the history of the world as well as individual events, the fate of nations as well as that of the individual. So people attempted to learn these laws in order to conform their lives to them. The professional astrologer assumed an extraordinarily high position. Augustus announced the results of his horoscope, and a few years later Tiberius officially appointed a court astrologer. Oracles also played an ever-increasing role. It is true that there had always been oracles and places where oracles could be consulted. The ancient world was full of very prominent locations of oracles; we need only think of Delphi. But these old locations of the oracles—and that is something that is characteristic of this age—have now been practically abandoned. They are mistrusted because they have so frequently and so obviously been in error. Since there were only a few, the fulfillment or nonfulfillment of the oracles they uttered could be precisely examined. This was no longer possible for now there are countless proclaimers of oracles. In every street, on every corner we find merchants of oracles who proffer all kinds of oracles—oracles from consulting the alphabet, oracles from casting lots, and everything imaginable. There was nothing that could not be used to try to discern the time and its signs. The interpretation of dreams was also a part of this. It now developed into a science, and every dream, no matter how obscure, could be scientifically interpreted and could be claimed to have some significance for a person's life.

All of this could have significance only because people believed that here they found a connection with the powers that controlled their lives. With these oracles and the interpretation of dreams, people believed they could discern the secret laws of life and the world. With prayer and with magic they thought they could influence the powers behind them. We have an extraordinarily vivid amount of material on this subject, for obviously there were books of directions for performing magic. In these books of magical formulas there are prayers about everything and for everything, for assistance in swindling, for success in love, for the misfortune of a rival suitor and so forth, although in order not to skew the picture, we must also observe that not only are there prayers for these purposes, but also for peace, for the health of the soul, for salvation, and for purity. Magic was performed with everything possible and for everything possible; in doing so people characteristically attempted to involve all the gods in their magic. Many formulas begin: "I implore you, demon, whoever you are," and then follows a long list of gods, known and unknown, through which one attempts to form as many new special combinations of letters as possible in order to include all the gods and summon their aid.

Only when one includes everything about which we have spoken— belief in the old gods, mystery religions, philosophical schools, veneration of the sun, the imperial cult, belief in oracles, and magic—can one have an approximate conception of the beliefs of the age during which Christianity entered the world. The decisive question is now: by what means was Christianity in a position to triumph over these competing forms of faith which were in every respect, both in the number of their adherents as well as in the external power they possessed, far superior to it?

2. THE REASONS FOR CHRISTIANITY'S TRIUMPH OVER PAGAN BELIEFS

Various answers have been given to the question of how Christianity could be in a position to win out over the competing forms of faith, even though in every respect its competitors exceeded it in membership as well as in resources. A generation ago, some scholars often conceived of Christianity as a mystery religion and thought that it triumphed over the other mystery religions because it took from them what was most decisive and effective and formed it into a new whole. It was believed that this could be documented with the example of Paul. Even a superficial comparison between the mystery religions and Christianity would show—so they argued—that Christianity simply expressed the same things as the mystery religions, but in a different way. In both of them God was venerated as the Lord with whom a believer desired to become one. In both of them the nucleus of everything was the cultic legend of a dying and rising god. This agreement was supposed to extend to a liturgical use of the cultic drama and to the adoption of external formalities. Everything served as proof for this; for example, we have the following quotation: "Just as Sabazios blessed the faithful with a peculiar gesture of three fingers extended and the other two closed, in the same way within the Christian church does a Western Catholic bishop still bless the people." In such a view Christianity became a syncretistic religion, an expression of the religious needs of the early centuries. In distinction to this view there immediately arises the question I think decisive: If Christianity was only *one* of the contemporary expressions of the same thing, why then did it triumph, and why did the other religions disappear even though they enjoyed the support of the state, even though this government persecuted Christianity so fiercely and tenaciously?

Again and again we must put the greatest emphasis possible on asking such methodological questions. A great deal of academic theology is conceived and flourishes in an ivory tower but cannot be maintained when we subject it to the complete reality of the past. When we see a hypothesis presented, it is therefore advisable to do what we also recommend for the scholars who originate it but have forgotten to do in their joy of discovery, that is, to step back three paces and ask ourselves: is this possible, does it agree with what we otherwise know, is it logical, does it have a *Sitz im Leben* in the contemporary period? There is no sense in producing theories without testing them this way, even though we see it happening again and again. These kinds of solutions cannot endure in the long run, no matter how great an impression they may make on a certain age and no matter how many people accept them.

If Christianity were only one of the contemporary religious expressions for the same thing, there could be no explanation of why it triumphed over its numerous rivals and why the others disappeared, even though for centuries Christians were repeatedly subjected to severe persecutions and the other faiths enjoyed all the official support of the state. Some have thought, adding one illogical statement to another, that the others were disunited and Christianity was a united power. This is true neither in the ivory tower nor in real life. Aside from the fact that Christianity was not a "power" until the third century, the facts are clearly established: no matter how divided the non-Christian world was, no matter how the philosophical schools—to take one example—argued among themselves, they all were still united in their opposition to Christianity. The notion that Christianity is to be identified with the mystery religions and derived from them cannot be maintained. An impartial, precise comparison between the mystery religions and Christianity proves again and again the same thing as a comparison between early Christianity and the philosophical views of the period: there are things that correspond, similarities, and parallels, but they are only so on the surface. The most we can say is that there are certain themes in the mystery religions which also appear in Christianity and which someone might claim Christianity adopted from them. But what happens to them is completely different. The chief concern is just as antithetical as are the ways of realizing this concern.

The most significant work on this subject is the two-volume history of Greek religion by Martin P. Nilsson in the series *Handbuch der Altertumswissenschaft* ("Handbook for the Study of Antiquity") (1961). We certainly cannot accuse Nilsson of being too close to Christianity and having too great a sympathy for it, but nevertheless his investigation of the mystery religions and their relationship to Christianity has a fundamental significance. He begins with a comprehensive definition: "The ideas usually ascribed to the general theology of the mysteries can be summarized under very few themes: death and resurrection, rebirth and becoming a child of god, enlightenment and redemption, divinization and immortality." Then he discusses each of these concepts and explores what they mean in the mystery religions and in Christianity. Over and over again he reaches the conclusion—to summarize it at the outset—that in each case the only thing the mystery religions and Christianity have in common is the term, but that the things that really matter are fundamentally different. Let us begin with the resurrection. It is true that in the mystery religions god dies and rises again. Attis and the numerous other fertility gods which were venerated in that age die at the end of summer when winter arrives. But they die repeatedly and reappear each year, so here we cannot speak about a real death and a real resurrection. In the cultic legend of Attis it is said: "Take comfort, god is safe," but he has not risen, he has only departed and will come again in the spring when nature lives anew. Or instead of the cult of Attis, let us take the Osiris cult. Each year in October and November the Osiris festival is celebrated, and the god's death is depicted in passion plays. Osiris, who is wedded to Isis, leaves his home in order to proclaim wisdom to other regions as well. Typhon and seventy-two other gods form a conspiracy, and when Osiris returns they imprison him in a box and throw it into the Nile. Isis wanders sadly throughout the land searching for him until she finally finds the box with the body washed ashore near Byblos. When Isis wants to retrieve the one who was lost and now has been found, Typhon cuts the god into fourteen pieces. Isis searches for them and painstakingly reassembles them. Thus the god rises again. This legend of the god who dies and rises again is depicted in the cultic festival. But still we must inquire why the god rises. It is not to assume rule or power over humanity, but to become the ruler of the underworld. Here death is mentioned, and this death is a real death, but nevertheless it is different from the Christian concept of death, not to speak of the way the resurrection is mentioned here, something that is totally different from that for which Christians hope.

Or let us look at rebirth, at palingenesis. This is not only the central doctrine of Christianity, but also of the mystery religions. In them, in order to be reborn, a person undergoes complicated rites. The adherent of a mystery religion crouches in a pit covered with a grill and on this grill a steer or ram—it varies in the different cults—is slaughtered. The blood of the sacrificial animal runs down into the pit and covers the person crouching in it. It bathes him externally, but he also drinks it in order to become clean inwardly as well as outwardly. The god who is represented in the steer or the ram purifies the believers with his blood so that they can begin a new life. This is the way numerous cults present and conceive of rebirth. What is now the relationship between the person who has been reborn and the god who has purified him? The mystery religions also speak about father and son, that is, that every believer becomes a child of god and participates in him. But the decisive thing here, as in other matters, is that a person's way to divinity proceeds from below to above. The person rises to god; he begins to follow the way to god when he lets himself be consecrated in the mystery cult in the prescribed manner, but from then on he must go it alone. Except in the mythological tales (see p. 13), it is never true that god descends from above so as in love to draw a person up to himself.

The mysteries also speak about Soteria, about Apolytrosis, about salvation, about redemption. They use the same words as Christianity but the differences in their meaning are characteristic. With this ceremony of dedication a new life begins for the adherent of the mystery, but the new life looks completely different than it does in Christianity. In order to be brief and unbiased I cite Nilsson: "There is a great deal of talk about immortality and making one immortal without really clarifying what immortality is supposed to be." There is the bodily resurrection which ancient paganism decisively rejected. It is quite typical that in Athens on the Areopagus, Paul failed in the moment when he began to speak about the Christian understanding of the resurrection. Rather, it was the immortality of the soul that was cultivated in various ways, an immortality of the soul by which the dead person either went directly to a blessed life in another world (understood in a relatively materialistic fashion) or reached it via a route that led through purification and punishment, conceived of in various fashions. In the final analysis paganism and the mystery religions surrendered in the face of death. For pagans, death meant the end of things, whereas the Christians could nevertheless seek death, even though fully aware of its consequences, because they knew of a complete bodily immortality in which the body will not be a continuation of this present earthly body, but a change for it, as Paul puts it in 1 Corinthians 15.

Nilsson deals with all the rest of the concepts of the mystery religions which need not concern us here; again and again he comes to the same result, that the correspondences and parallels between Christianity and the mystery religions are purely external. In addition, we dare not overlook what seems to me a decisive point of view. The various mystery religions doubtless have a great deal in common, both in their general concerns as well as in their details. But if we attempt to reconstruct *the* mystery religion on this basis it will be purely a construction that never really existed that way. What really existed were the individual concrete mystery religions which, despite all their similarities, were considerably different from one another. If we want to compare Christianity with the mystery religions we will have to compare it with real ones. The presuppositions of the attempts of our predecessors, however, were based on this reconstructed (or rather, constructed) abstract mystery religion. If we attempt to compare it with Christianity or to reconcile it, then we are comparing things which cannot be compared or reconciled, for what we have is a historical reality over against a figment of our imagination.

This methodologic impossibility, as we have said, did not prevent the preceding generation from doing this and also has not prevented today's theologians from joining this chorus. One might even say that this belongs to the almost suicidal tendency we see again and again in academic theology of attempting to explain Christianity, wherever possible, on the basis of everything else, but not from itself. Not only is this true in this case where some writers attempt to explain the phenomenon of Christianity on the basis of a fabricated mystery religion or on the basis of philosophy; we find it happening over and over again in the past, and not merely in the generations which have gone before us, but in our own time as well. In the previous generation the Mandaeans were discovered, and some rejoiced that now they had finally found the key to the mysterious phenomenon of "Christianity." We hear little anymore about the Mandaeans, and for good reason—the clever theories and claims were untenable—but they still exist in the background and await a renaissance. Then Qumran and the writings of the Essenes were discovered, and once again some rejoiced that now we could finally explain Christianity.

That sort of thing happens all the time. For example, when some people wanted to explain the phenomenon of monasticism in the ancient church they were prepared to journey to the most distant spots, both in time and place. They found the preliminary stages of monasticism in the cult of Serapis, or they looked at Philo's Therapeutae, or Buddhism furnished the model, or the ancient Celts were brought into consideration. But they were not prepared to ask if monasticism might not really be explained without difficulty on the basis of the fundamental principle of Christianity and the presuppositions which can be observed in the early centuries within Christianity. Sometimes we have the impression that theologians are inclined to recognize only that as historic and Christian which, in spite of all their efforts, they cannot explain in some other way. For them this is only a last resort. Before adopting this conclusion, as we have said, they go to Egypt, or to India, or to Gaul, but never to the early history of Christianity itself. A great deal could be said about this, but let us return to other answers given to the question about the reasons for Christianity's victory.

They are just as improbable. For example, some people have gone even farther than those who see in Christianity a mystery religion or an amalgamation of the most effective forces in the mystery religions, and have maintained that Christianity triumphed because it did the best job of combining the most valuable elements in the religiosity of late antiquity. That may sound impressive, but it is also created in an ivory tower. Proof for this sort of deliberate assimilation of the best elements of all cults—for the amalgamation of the most promising elements in the religiosity of late antiquity, for their consolidation into a higher unity in Christianity—can be found neither in the history of Christianity's beginning, nor can such a thesis be harmonized with what we know about Christianity's development in general. This attempt at a solution has no *Sitz im Leben*; it is divorced from historical reality.

This also goes for those who believe that Christianity was the religion which was best suited to be an ally of contemporary learning, and this is the reason Christianity triumphed. This also has nothing to do with historical reality. Opposed to this is Paul's testimony, along with everything else we know about the early history of Christianity. Only those who do not seriously concern themselves with the recognition of historical facts can hold to this sort of interpretation. The education of the early centuries was marked with the stamp of paganism, and it remained so up to the decline of late antiquity. It is true that Clement of Alexandria and Origen attempted to combine pagan educational presuppositions with Christianity, but Clement of Alexandria was alone in this, and it is no coincidence that normally his works are extant in only a single manuscript. Origen also failed in his attempt to blend ancient education with Christianity; finally he was excluded by the church. In the time of the persecution of the fourth century, when Julian excluded Christians from the faculties of the schools and universities, they attempted to create a substitute for pagan literature—for the writings of the poets and philosophers—and replace them with a purely Christian form of education. From its outset this attempt was doomed to failure. Until the end of antiquity all Christians had to work through the pagan educational system on their way to all higher callings, what today we would call the higher schools and universities. In so doing they were always confronted with the question of how they might reconcile this educational system, deeply marked with pagan mythology and paganism in general, with Christianity, which was completely antithetical to it. A Christian did not live in league with the pagan educational system, but in opposition to it. Accordingly, after its victory the church was only too willing to do away with this pagan literature in education; only with difficulty could Basil the Great and other educated church fathers prevent the exclusion of pagan literature.

It is somewhat different with the claim that it was the superiority of its moral teaching that led Christianity on its way to victory over the other religions. There is no question that the ethics of Christianity were superior to the ethics of the contemporary world. That was true in theory and even in practice as well. The moral conduct evidenced by Christians in their daily life and the social establishments created by the Christian churches impressed people, even those who were enemies of Christianity, and certainly won many over. But those who deduce the victory of Christianity from the superiority of its moral teachings or the moral activity displayed by Christians are looking only at the outside of things. Ethics were not the real content of Christianity, only the result of Christian faith.

There is definitely some truth to the attempt at an answer which Nilsson presents. He shows again and again that the forms of faith of the ancient world (whether the continuation of the cult of the ancient gods, or philosophy, or the mystery cults, or the religion of the sun, or the imperial cult) all lacked real vividness. These forms of faith were too

28

abstract for simple people who made up a very high percentage of the populace at that time. For the people on the street they were not sensible enough, nor comprehensible enough. Thus, they could not relate to these forms of faith in their full scope, and therefore they had no real and permanent effect, while Christianity, according to Nilsson, offered the ordinary people what they were seeking. It is true that in Christianity God is also transcendent and is enthroned in heaven, but here is a God who also appeared on the earth to humankind. In the sacraments one can find direct access to him; in his commandments one finds guidance for a moral life. Nilsson believes that Christianity presented a healthy reaction to the philosophical and religious development of antiquity and thus triumphed among the majority of the people, with those who were not satisfied with the other teachings, philosophies, and religions. Even Neoplatonism failed because it could not gain access to the ordinary person, while Christianity decidedly pursued this access from the very beginning. Thus Christianity, after a period of difficulties and restrictions, enjoyed an unstoppable victory march in the later period of the ancient world.

There is a great deal to be said for this view; not without reason have I emphasized this point of view over and over. But I believe that we cannot explain the course of this development from this view alone. A philosophy, a teaching, a religion can never conquer and rule the world if it is a philosophy, a teaching, a religion only for the ordinary person, but it will succeed only if it can win for itself the leading figures as well as the masses. Perhaps we may pointedly claim: winning the leaders is almost more important than winning large masses. For when one has won the intellectual upper class then so much activity will flow from it that the ideas which it holds will finally—in the course of one or several generations—spread throughout the masses as well. This is the way it has happened with many movements—the Enlightenment, for example. It was first conceived of by a few solitary thinkers, objected to in various ways, then popularized and adopted by the educated middle class, and from there—in a much more simplified and vulgar manner—finally came down to the masses, where to a large extent it still dominates to the present day. What was special about Christianity was that it was in a position to win the common people as well as the intellectual upper class.

Characteristic of this is the report that the Apologist Justin (cf. p. 130) gave about his own development shortly before the middle of the second century. What he presents took place about the middle of the first half of

29

that century. He writes about it in Chapter 2 of his *Dialogue with Trypho:*

> Being at first desirous of personally conversing with one of these men [the famous philosophers], I surrendered myself to a certain Stoic; and having spent a considerable time with him, when I had not acquired any further knowledge of God (for he did not know him himself, and said such instruction was unnecessary), I left him and betook myself to another, who was called a Peripatetic, and as *he* fancied, shrewd. And this man, after having entertained me for the first few days, requested me to settle the fee, in order that our intercourse might not be unprofitable. Him, too, for this reason I abandoned, believing him to be no philosopher at all. But when my soul was eagerly desirous to hear the peculiar and choice philosophy, I came to a Pythagorean, very celebrated—a man who taught much of his own wisdom. And then, when I had an interview with him, willing to become his hearer and disciple, he said, "What then? Are you acquainted with music, astronomy, and geometry? Do you expect to perceive any of those things which conduce to a happy life, if you have not been first informed on these points which wean the soul from sensible objects, and render it fitted for objects which appertain to the mind, so that it can contemplate that which is honorable in its essence and that which is good in its essence?" Having commended many of these branches of learning, and telling me that they were necessary, he dismissed me when I confessed to him my ignorance. Accordingly I took it rather impatiently, as was to be expected when I failed in my hope, the more so because I deemed the man had some knowledge; but reflecting again on the space of time during which I would have to linger over those branches of learning, I was not able to endure longer procrastination. In my helpless condition it occurred to me to have a meeting with the Platonists, for their fame was great. I thereupon spent as much of my time as possible with one who had lately settled in our city—a sagacious man, holding a high position among the Platonists—and I progressed, and made the greatest improvements daily. And the perception of immaterial things quite overpowered me, and the contemplation of ideas furnished my mind with wings, so that in a little while I supposed that I had become wise; and such was my stupidity, I expected forthwith to look upon God, for this is the end of Plato's philosophy.

At the conclusion of a long and difficult journey toward the attainment of wisdom, truth, salvation, Soteria, Justin thinks that he is now near his goal. He goes walking along the beach and meets an old man with whom he has a conversation which he then describes in Chapters 3—7 of his work. At the very outset Justin is disarmed by this old man, for his discussion partner values "deed" and "truth" more than "word," that is, reality more than purely theoretical discussion, the practical reality of the thing recognized, and the possibility of doing it more than philosophers' hairsplitting. During the continuing discussion Justin is shown that pagan philosophy in general is deceitful and foolish. The prophets of the Old Testament, understood not in the Jewish sense of the word, but interpreted by Christ and referring to Christ, are the true source of wisdom, the source of truth. Thus Justin is converted to what he calls the "only dependable and salutary philosophy," to Christianity. We must not think derogatorily of this term, for Justin died a martyr's death for this "dependable and salutary philosophy." People have thought that Justin was driven exclusively by an intellectual curiosity. That may well have been the case for his pilgrimage through the various philosophical schools. But if these schools did not satisfy him, this is proof that Justin was driven not merely by an intellectual curiosity, but that he wanted more. He wanted an entire solution, a solution for all humanity. He wanted the certainty of Soteria. The philosophers also spoke this way, but Justin considered what they had to offer unworthy to be compared to Christianity. According to his testimony, Christianity gave a perfect solution, certainty, and security in a completely different measure than did all the pagan philosophies and all the pagan cults.

Another who was concerned about striving for this certainty was Cyprian, a man who belonged not only to the intellectual, but also to the wealthy upper class. At the end of the first half of the third century he was brought to Christianity and records this in his writing *Ad Donatum* ("To Donatus"). Here he speaks first about his own conversion and then turns his consideration to conversion to Christianity and the nature of conversion in general. He describes its course: suddenly, once for all in conversion a person discards what he has either had from birth or what, on account of habit and custom, has taken deep root in him. Even he, Cyprian, in his life before baptism was imprisoned "by very many errors," so that he would not have believed that he could ever be free from them. In his despair over the possibility of any improvement, he would have resigned himself to the burdens which adhered to him like roommates without whom one cannot get along. Baptism not only washed away the debris of the past and "poured from above the light" into his purified breast and changed him into a new person in this second birth, but "the doubt was turned into certainty," what was previously dark became light, and what formerly appeared impossible to him, namely life in the Spirit without sin, not only now became possible but was even made easy. As a gift of divine grace the ability was given to him to live according to the commandments of Christianity and no longer to sin. As he continues to write he leads Donatus (and the readers of this work) to a high mountain in order to view the world. Compassion for the world and thankfulness that they have escaped from it will be the experience of all Christians as they observe it: brigands fill the highways and pirates the seas, war with its shedding of blood and its atrocities encompasses all continents, in the arena in the cities murder and cruelty are turned into virtues worth imitating, in the theater immorality is taught, in homes shamelessness rules, in the forum injustice and fraud dominate. These things for which people strive—power and honorable positions, wealth, governmental authority—are undermined by the fear of their loss; they are not a blessing, but a curse. Only "in the anchorage of the harbor of salvation"—Christianity, as Cyprian says—can a person find a "dependable rest for the soul," and an "unshakable and lasting security." Only faith lasts, only it gives imperishable treasures. Only here—Cyprian emphasizes it once again—can a person find the "lasting, unshakable refuge"; the world can do nothing more to him, he has triumphed over it.

These reports about the reasons for the change of faith of two members of the upper class are characteristically different. Justin's is typical for the East, and Cyprian's is typical for the West, for we can without difficulty associate Augustine's (see pp. 208–9) with Cyprian's. These reports about the reasons for a change of faith certainly show that Nilsson's attempt at an answer—regardless of how much truth there is in it—cannot be convincing for methodological reasons. In addition, there is the fact that Nilsson deals only with paganism. Along with almost everyone else who thinks about the reasons for the victory of Christianity, he views only paganism and forgets that alongside paganism there was Judaism, at least in the areas in which the development of Christianity was first significant. A discussion (which considers only paganism) of the question about the reasons for the victory of Christianity over the religions of the ancient world appears to me to be doomed to failure from the outset, both for methodological reasons as well as in reference to reality. Christianity spread in the train of Judaism. Acts definitely offers here the historical truth, regardless of how much we might discuss the details. When Paul comes into a city, he first goes into the synagogue and there preaches to the Jews. The synagogue is the natural center for him, for there he finds those who are interested in the subject. He only goes to the pagans when the Jews refuse to hear him, but even among the pagans he begins with those who have already developed a certain relationship to Judaism, with the proselytes who belong to the Jewish fellowship and therefore are more approachable with the questions presented by the Christian faith. Perhaps we can even say that among the presuppositions for the spread of Christianity in the early period, Judaism was a great deal more important than paganism. The only answer to our question that can be right, therefore, is one which explains not only why Christianity was able to triumph over the pagans, but also over the Jews. When we put the question in this way, completely new aspects are opened up. Certainly Judaism—especially Judaism of the diaspora of that time—had been strongly influenced by Hellenism. Yet we must not overrate these influences. Paul, in whom some scholars in the past frequently saw the prototype of Hellenistic Judaism, indeed grew up in Tarsus and doubtless became acquainted with Hellenism there. But Paul was nevertheless no Hellenist and certainly not a Gentile; rather he had gone at a very early age through the Pharisees' educational system in Jerusalem and thus belonged to the radical wing of Judaism at that time. Also, the stumbling block he found in Christianity was not Greek, but typically Jewish. For Saul the Pharisee, Christianity was not folly as it was for the Greeks, to use the characteristics which Paul mentions in 1 Cor. 1:23; "We preach Christ crucified, a stumbling block to Jews and folly to Gentiles," but Christianity for Saul the Pharisee was a completely Jewish offense. For the sake of this offense which penetrated deeply into his existence as a Jew and a Pharisee, he persecuted the Christian congregations. If we want to understand the stumbling block which Paul and the Judaism of his time found in Christianity, we must return to the message of Jesus.

Jesus preached judgment, indeed a judgment that would soon take place. That is shown by the way he associated himself with John the Baptist. Jesus' preaching is eschatological preaching which proclaims to humankind the nearness of God who will summon humanity before his judgment seat. On its face that was no stumbling block for the Jews, for that they knew already. But Jesus' preaching brought with it the decisive paradox that in this judgment it was not the righteous who will survive, but the sinners, if they recognize their sinfulness and give themselves into the hand of God. In the parable of the Pharisee and the publican in Luke 18:9–14 we see a typical way of presenting this paradox, but because of our Christian presuppositions we usually water it down in an inappropriate fashion. We see this Pharisee as someone who unjustly claims to be righteous and thinks that the publican is a sinner, but one whose sin appears to us to be less serious. For people at that time, however, the very words, "Pharisee" and "publican" clearly gave a different accent. The Pharisee in the parable is really presented as righteous. He has fulfilled all the demands which one could ever place

33

on a person, and, in fact, has done even more, while the publican is really a sinner with all the attributes which this term denoted in people's consciousness. The parable ends, as we know (Luke 18:14): "This man [the publican] went down to his house justified rather than the other [the Pharisee]." And then follows the application, and this application contains the real message of Christianity: "For every one who exalts himself will be humbled, but he who humbles himself will be exalted." It is no coincidence that the words, "The first shall be last, and the last shall be the first," are added again and again to the New Testament Greek manuscripts of the Gospels, even where they are not originally found.

The paradox of the message of Jesus and Christianity in general consists in the preaching of a judgment that is not an evidence of God's wrath, but of the love of God who in grace accepts man. When Luther spoke about the *justificatio impii,* that is, not about the justification of the sinner (for that word is really too weak), but of the godless, about the justification of those who according to all human standards are absolutely not worthy of it, then he was expressing the decisive thing in Christianity. This message of justification of the sinner, I believe, is what brought Christianity the victory over the "competing religions" of late antiquity. It is true that in Christianity man is also separated from God, just as in paganism, which speaks about a transcendent god who is infinitely distant from man. But in Christianity this God who is separated from man is still not far away, but near to him. And further: man does not rise by his own powers to God as in paganism, but God himself descends to man and graciously draws him in love to himself. This is just as foreign or offensive to the Jews as to the Greeks. According to Judaism, God is concerned with the righteous, not with sinners. Judaism did indeed succeed in struggling to reach the point where it did not necessarily draw conclusions from a person's conduct on earth about his status with God, as it had originally done. In distinction to its earlier belief, Judaism later believed that it was possible that things might go badly for the righteous on earth and might go well on earth for the wicked, as is expressed in the Book of Job. But still the conclusion expressed in Job is characteristic (Job 42:10–17). Here we are told how Job, after suffering everything described, is rewarded by God:

> And the Lord restored the fortunes of Job, when he had prayed for his friends; and the Lord gave Job twice as much as he had before. Then came to him all his brothers and sisters and all who had known him before, and ate bread with him in his house; and they showed him sympathy and comforted him for all the evil that the Lord had brought upon him; and

each of them gave him a piece of money and a ring of gold. And the Lord blessed the latter days of Job more than his beginning; and he had fourteen thousand sheep, six thousand camels, a thousand yoke of oxen, and a thousand she-asses. He also had seven sons and three daughters. . . . And in all the land there were no women so fair as Job's daughters; and their father gave them an inheritance among their brothers. And after this Job lived a hundred and forty years, and saw his sons, and his sons' sons, four generations. And Job died, an old man, and full of days.

Thus ends the Book of Job. The entire majesty of the statements of the book is here destroyed, and this is no coincidence, for this epilogue—whether a later addition, whether original—reverts to the common Jewish view that things go well on earth for those who are pious. If they have to suffer misfortune, they can do so much more easily because they know that it is only a transitional phase which will be followed by an even greater reward.

We do find in Judaism the beginnings of a deeper understanding. For example, in 4 Esdras (8:36) God is addressed: "You reveal your righteousness and goodness, O Lord, by showing mercy on those who have no store of good works." But this thought immediately recedes. The angel dismisses the seer: he should not concern himself with sinners, since they lack good works, but he should rejoice in the glorious lot of the righteous. That is the normal attitude of Judaism in general. When we look up and assemble words such as these in 4 Esdras or in the prophets—and there are a great many of them—we get an ivory tower picture of Judaism, not a picture that corresponds to the reality of that time. For example, under Paul's influence we understand the law too easily and too obviously as a burden imposed upon the Jew. But that is not the normal relationship of the Jew to the law; for the Jew, the law is an order established by God. For him the law meant a special gift to the people of Israel, a distinction of which Judaism was proud and in which it rejoiced.

The whole offense which the Jews took on Jesus and his message is expressed in the term which they ascribe to him: "A companion of publicans and sinners." When we read Luke 13, we find here the normal conception of contemporary Judaism, which was also the disciples' general idea, as well as Jesus' position, which is completely opposite. This is the story of the Galileans and the tower in Siloam:

There were some present at that very time who told him of the Galileans whose blood Pilate had mingled with their sacrifices. And he answered them, "Do you think that these Galileans were worse sinners than all the other Galileans, because they suffered thus? I tell you, No; but unless you repent you will all likewise perish. Or those eighteen upon whom the tower in Siloam fell and killed them, do you think that they were worse offenders than all the others who dwelt in Jerusalem? I tell you, No; but unless you repent you will all likewise perish."

All people, no matter how good and righteous they appear, no matter what they do, are in the same ominous condition. Especially those who consider themselves righteous suffer from the wrath of God in a completely different way from those who are aware of their sin. If we compare this with the story about the man born blind in John 9, we can see how here the point of the story is somewhat different, and how the Gospel of John begins at a different place than do the synoptics, which are much closer to the historical situation of the time and to Jesus' original message. Jesus passes by a man blind from his birth. His disciples question him about the man, and their question is characteristic of the disciples' attitude and typical of the attitude of contemporary Judaism: "Rabbi, who sinned, this man or his parents, that he was born blind?" The question is completely in line with the presupposition of Judaism at Jesus' time. But when Jesus answers: "It was not that this man sinned, or his parents, but that the works of God might be made manifest in him," that is, when Jesus does not really answer the disciples' question but explains that the man born blind serves to demonstrate Jesus' power (in the story he is directed to wash in the pool of Siloam and then he receives his sight), this is a typical way the Gospel of John alters the parallel reports of the healings in the Synoptic Gospels and no longer accords with the real situation at the beginning of Christianity.

Just as Jews took offense at the message of Christianity, so also did paganism. Celsus, the most significant anti-Christian polemicist of the second century, has already been mentioned (see p. 5). If we read his attack on Christianity, the *Alethes Logos,* the "True Word," from the second half of the second century, we will find here with all clarity this offense which educated paganism took at the fundamental conception of Christianity. Celsus writes: "Every other religion accepts only honorable people, educated, irreproachable, but Christians passionately seek the dregs of society, as if God were the head of a band of thieves who assembles criminals around himself, and as if it were something terrible to have committed no sin." Naturally this is a distortion by pagan polemics, but the substance is very clear. The same thing Celsus says, we find among all pagan writers of that time: God, the divinity, deals with pure people, not with sinners. If people are sinners and have committed sin, then they must be freed from this sin in order to find a relationship with God. God does not forgive sin, but expects that a person appear before him free from guilt. God can give hints about how a person can free himself from this sin. Various ways are open to the believer. He can be absolved in the mysteries, he can become free of his guilt by confessing it, but nothing more—from God's point of view—can be done. The thing that ascends to God, according to the teaching of the mystery religions as well as later in Gnosticism, is that part of a person which is pure and divine. But this divine part in man must also first be cleansed from all impurity adhering to it if it is to rise to God and enter into God. We have already spoken about how the doctrine of mature Gnosticism taught that people shed the impurities which adhered to them while ascending through the various heavenly spheres (see p. 15). If they had so many impurities that they could not be removed by this process of ascension, they would have to return to earth. They would have to be reincarnated and then during their second life (or third, or as many as it might take) prepare as best they can for purity so that the next time, assisted by this path of purification, they could ascend through the spheres to God. Here we see the distinction between Jesus' message and the views of contemporary Judaism and paganism in their full clarity— and not only the difference between Jesus' message and paganism and Judaism, but also the difference between Paul's message and the religions of his time. For despite all the developments which the proclamation of the Synoptic Gospels received in Paul, both of them essentially agree; they both possess the same nucleus.

Let us take Rom. 3:22–23 as an example. We are so accustomed to this text that we no longer sense its newness, the differentness, the powerful force which it carried at that time: "For there is no distinction, since all have sinned and fall short of the glory of God, they are justified by his grace as a gift, through the redemption which is in Christ Jesus." This verse provides not only the theme of Romans, but also the center of Paul's message which is decisively at one with Jesus' message. If Paul had been asked to describe in one sentence the way in which Christianity related to the religions of the surrounding world, he would have given the answer already mentioned (see p. 33) in 1 Cor. 1:23: "But we preach Christ crucified, a stumbling block to Jews and folly to Gentiles." What Christianity teaches was foolishness for the educated Greek of that time, something which could not even be discussed because it was so far beneath what an educated person would expect. It was completely impossible for the pagan of that time to imagine how the divinity, that divinity which is infinitely elevated and infinitely distant from humankind, could come to earth. But even if one could conceive of this, it was completely unthinkable for the pagan that this divinity would do that in Palestine—the end of the world—and take the form of a human of the lowest classes, and even die in what has to be termed the most miserable fashion possible. That simply could not be ascribed to divinity. Such a teaching was so ridiculous that it just could not be taken seriously. If we were to attempt to take it seriously, we would be blaspheming God.

That is the foolishness. And for Jews that which Christianity proclaims is a stumbling block whose magnitude we can now see clearly in Saul's reaction to the message: his intellectual struggle against the new teaching did not bring him to agree with it; rather he turned to a bloody persecution of those who were preaching the new message because they had to be exterminated for the glory of God. What we have in Jesus' death is the real death of a real man under the most aggravating and humiliating circumstances. And this death and its circumstances are reported about God's messengers, and not only about God's messengers, but about God himself. And for the Jews this stumbling block was not an offense only because of the outward circumstances, but it extended to the very depths of faith. For who is it who brought this messenger of God to the cross? The people, naturally, the rulers of this world. But the people, as well as this world's rulers, were only tools, they did not act on their own, they did not know what they were doing. When the *kyrios* (Lord) was nailed to the cross, that happened not only with God's permission, but through God himself. In a completely different way than for the Greeks, but with the same—perhaps even greater—acuteness the Jews are faced with the insoluble paradox that we find the greatest expression of God's love and grace in the greatest wrath and the most severe punishment. Here the concept of God is destroyed for the Jews; here the law is destroyed, that orderliness which God himself gave his people in the beginning. That is the real offense which Judaism and the Jewish Saul took at Christianity. This is the reason for the passionate struggle of Judaism against Christianity, the reason for the passionate struggle of Saul against Christianity, until this Christianity then overcame him. I believe that the decisively characteristic marks of Christianity lie here. Here we find its nucleus, the thing that distinguishes it from the religions of late antiquity. And here we also find the reasons for Christianity's victory over the other religions of its time. Christianity is the proclamation of God's grace for sinful humanity. In Christianity God, man, sin, and redemption were and are understood completely differently and much more deeply than in everything else which then—

and also now—preached salvation for humanity and in which people then—and also now—sought their salvation. Christianity put the questions differently and gave different answers; Christianity even eliminated all the questions or at least raised them to a completely different level than did the other religions. Therefore, Christianity was able to gather in all those who were not satisfied with the answers which their age and the religions and philosophical systems of that age gave for their questions. The example of Justin is symptomatic (see pp. 29–31).

All in all, there were at first only a few people, but things depended on them. When they were won over, things really happened. Thus Christianity triumphed over the other religions, despite the powerful position these religions had always possessed, despite the support which they received from the state. Now obviously this victory did not come by itself. What we have previously said describes only the *potential* of the Christian message. If it were to be effective, this message would have to be brought to the people, and further developments depended upon the measure in which that took place. That happened for the Christians of the early age in a way that has become completely foreign to us today in Europe. In the early period, the "second calling" of every Christian was to be a missionary. The "full-time" missionaries—the greatest of them was Paul (we shall speak about the details in the next chapter [see pp. 47–49])—founded congregations in cities where they visited for a few days, a few weeks, or at most a few months. But these initial congregations had only a limited number of members. And after the departure of the "full-time" missionaries, at least until their next visit or permanently, these Christians were alone and dependent on their own resources. If the congregation were to grow, it would need the missionary activity of all its members. This took place in the proclamation of the new faith and in the resistance to attacks made on it; but also it happened through attacks on beliefs of others. It was not difficult to attack the old belief in the anthropomorphic gods, for here mythology provided plenty of points of attack, not only with its juicy details, but in general. Not only were the scandalous stories told not worthy of divinity, but not even of being pulled down into the human sphere as such. It was also relatively easy to demonstrate the questionableness of the mystery cult and the new religions coming from the East (for the immoralities often connected with these forms made the argumentation easier). And what could the members of the sun cult or the imperial cult answer when they were accused of worshiping the creature instead of the creator? Where was the life-giving power of the sun during the winter? Why was the emperor's divinity not able to prevent sickness and death, his own as well as others'? How could a god be killed, and even in such a way that his murderers or the people behind them could enthrone themselves as a god and as his successor? How did it happen that the Roman Empire, instead of being protected by the divinity of the emperor in order to increase or at least remain stable, was continually being attacked by barbarians and reduced in size? How was it possible that the empire that stood under the protection of a divine emperor could be visited by plagues and economic disaster? The argumentation was even easier against astrology, the interpretation of dreams, and magic.

In view of the fact that Christian congregations were recruited for the most part from the simple people this argumentation must have proceeded on a rudimentary plane, but because it was addressed to the conceptual ability of people who were also simple it must have sufficed. What it depended on was the ability of the one arguing to convince and the existential way in which the missionary's conviction was introduced. In their life style Christians showed themselves different from those around them. We dare not underestimate the attractiveness of this difference in daily ethics or what we might simply call living in accordance with the Ten Commandments (not in the way we interpret them, but rather in the exposition given them in Luther's Small Catechism many centuries later). What was decisive was that Christians were prepared to put all their possessions and their lives on the line for their faith. *Sanguis est semen Christianorum*, blood is the seed of the Christians, is what Tertullian triumphantly declared, and not without reason. For even the greatest skeptic, the most convinced pagan, had to wonder about the stubbornness with which Christians persevered in their faith, even to the martyr's death.

There is much more that could be said, but we must stop here. In conclusion it may be enough to ask the question: what Christians today are missionaries for their faith in their immediate surroundings, in their neighborhood, at their jobs, the way the Christians of the early age were? The so-called pietists, the members of the Free churches, and the Salvation Army (about whom today's "enlightened" Christians chuckle) are, and there are the members of the sects: the Mormons and the Jehovah's Witnesses. This sheds light on the distance between the present day and the early period.

Let us return to the early age. That Christianity in its contacts with the pagan world accepted some things from it cannot be denied, but in some ways Christianity was influenced by its environment and in some ways was independent from this environment. That was the case not only in the beginning, but remained so in the later centuries and has lasted to the present day where only the order has changed. Sometimes Christianity goes ahead and drags the tenor of the time behind itself, and sometimes the tenor of the time predominates and pulls Christianity after it. In the Middle Ages Christianity took the lead, but in the modern age it lags behind, even in theological schools in which many people today see the epitome of our theological activity. They are decisively dependent upon philosophical ways of thought and systems which come from outside. Certainly in the final analysis these stem from Christianity and cannot be conceived of without Christian preparatory work and apart from Christian thought, but they are nevertheless concepts which come from outside the Christian sphere. The theology of hope, just to choose an extreme example, takes its catchword from the atheist Bloch.

Christianity has always stood in a reciprocal relationship with the work and advancement of the human spirit; that cannot be otherwise, and anyone who attempts to make a negative judgment about Christianity on this basis does not recognize the laws of history. If Christianity used all the means available to late antiquity in order to make itself understandable, that was legitimate. For it is necessary that old ideas must be thought through anew and expressed anew with the means of the present age. For example (and we could also choose other examples), it was not demeaning to Christianity when a generation ago some believed that the Christian dogma was formulated in the first centuries under the influence of the Greek spirit, as Harnack expressed it. We have to separate the kernel from the shell. Even Paul said that we have this treasure in earthen vessels (2 Cor. 4:7). The decisive thing in Christianity was not taken over from the surrounding world, but originated in opposition to it and was proclaimed in opposition to it. It is correct when Bultmann speaks about the mythological ideas of the first century in which Christianity has come to us. And his claim is also justified that we dare not absolutize these mythological ideas. But here we must also not confuse kernel and shell—the indispensable kernel of revelation and the transitory shell of the forms in which it is expressed. The question is only whether it is possible, as Bultmann demands, to disregard completely the forms of expression of the first century and whether demythologization, regardless of how justified its fundamental concern, really helps us. For we must certainly be clear that we can never directly and never completely express the totality of Christianity, that we must always speak in pictures, that we can only stammer when we want to describe the reality of God and his actions. Speaking in pictures belongs to Christianity and to its theological expressions, and to the theological expressions of all ages just as much as it does to the theological expressions of the twentieth century—even those made by Bultmann—and perhaps precisely then when it thinks it is rid of them. The theological expressions of our time will be judged by later generations to be just as time-conditioned, as "mythological," just as dependent upon cosmological and other conceptions of the age, as those of the first century appear to us. In addition, when we once critically examine the measures with which demythologization is carried out at least in some places, we see that we cannot ignore the question of whether modern rationalism is not sometimes active here, a rationalism that attempts—justifiably so—to do away with antiquated forms, but in doing so exceeds the limits and together with these antiquated forms also does away with the unantiquated contents which are never out-of-date.

It is understandable when a Christian sees a confirmation of the truth of Christianity in the fact that in late antiquity it triumphed over all religions of the then-known world, despite the improbability of this victory, and then draws distinctive consequences for the later epochs. Today we can no longer do that so straightforwardly as earlier centuries did, because we have a different impression of the non-Christian religions than that age did. The situation has changed very drastically since the appearance of Islam. From the seventh century on, Islam not only spread with astonishing rapidity, but it has also made inroads in areas which Christianity had never been able to reach. And it frequently triumphed in the struggle with Christianity and led important territories which once belonged to the heartlands of the Christian church to Mohammed's faith: North Africa, Egypt, Asia Minor, where to the present day, despite many attempts, it has not been possible to regain these territories from Islam and re-Christianize them. Where Islam and Christianity struggle with one another for souls, whether in Africa or Asia, Islam is frequently the winner, and the missionary activity among Islamic peoples belongs to one of the most difficult and least successful activities of mission in general. In addition, there is the fact that in the course of centuries other religions whose adherents number in the hundreds of millions have come to our attention, so that Christianity, when taken over against all of these religions, is in a minority. This minority character of Christianity will increase in the next decades, simply because the birthrate in Asia and Africa far exceeds that in Europe, North America, Australia, and so forth. Despite these statistics, there is no doubt for the believing Christian that Christianity will eventually triumph over these religions. But there is no question that this will not be the case in this generation, as the Americans once thought and demanded. In fact, when we look at the present statistics of births and religious allegiance and how they will most probably develop, I would like to say—in fact, with certainty claim—that some people perhaps doubt that this goal is at all attainable. They think—justifiably—that the expansion of Christianity is proceeding too slowly; they think—justifiably—that the number of members of the other religions is increasing too rapidly. So it is hardly surprising when their confidence not only about the task of winning the world for Christianity is shaken, but also their confidence in Christianity itself. They are close to resignation, to being satisfied with the pluralism of the various forms of faith and what goes with them. But if we look for the reason for this development in Christianity as such and not in ourselves—this we must say with simple clarity—then we are uncovering only reasons for the negative development. Looking for causes in the Christian faith and not in our own shortcomings is naturally the simplest solution. It is the most comfortable thing to do, to ascribe the guilt to Christianity and not to ourselves. But if we act this way we are closing our eyes to reality. The victory of Christianity in late antiquity over the competing forms of faith was rooted in its superiority to them, but it was accomplished by the sacrificial missionary activity of the early Christians and the earnestness with which they embodied the Christian message. That is what is lacking today, for the fact that Christianity is just as superior to the religions competing with it today, as it was in the early age, needs no real proof. Naturally the blame for this belongs not only to us, but we are the heirs of our parents and ancestors who without question for centuries did not devote the necessary sacrifices to carrying out the missionary command, "Go therefore and make disciples of all nations." But this is no excuse. Today we are not even in a position to make the people of our own nation disciples of Christ; we only compound the sins of our parents and ancestors and suffer the same condemnation they do, even more so. Things can only change when Christianity itself changes. The accusation cannot be directed at Christianity, the accusation is directed at us. If we expended only a portion of the missionary power which early Christianity possessed, the situation today would look completely different. So much for this chapter which has dealt with the reasons for Christianity's victory over the religions of that time and necessarily has had to conclude with a few general observations.

II

The External History of Early Christianity

1. THE SPREAD OF CHRISTIANITY

If we want to study the history of Christianity's spread in the early period, we have (like all the ages before and after us, whether laity or clergy, students or professors) only one document—the Acts of the Apostles. We have to read this, naturally comparing it to and supplementing it with Paul's epistles, if we want to get a picture of the early history and the spread of Christianity during its first generation. We have already mentioned (see p. 7) that contemporary scholarship, especially in Germany, is dominated by "invincible skepticism" (that is a direct quotation) when it comes to interpreting Acts. It is quite true, of course, that Acts is not a history book in the modern sense, but the report of Christianity's spread in the early period which it abbreviates in the light of a definitely biased perspective. But I believe that this "invincible skepticism" goes too far—anyway, it is not widely shared outside the German-speaking countries—and that at least among works of this type—to return to what we have said previously—Acts possesses a completely different sort of historicity than we often believe. If we judge Acts by the usual standards which ancient historians and classical philologists apply to similar investigations, there are certainly many aspects of this skeptical view which we cannot share.

When we summarize all the material that we have to consider for the beginning of Christianity, the following picture presents itself: the first Christian community was located in Jerusalem, but did not limit its activity to that locale, apparently from the very beginning conducting missionary work more than we previously assumed. In Acts we have a report about the missionary journeys of Peter. This is introduced in 9:32 with the phrase: "Now as Peter went here and there among them all. . . ." This purports to give a report of Peter's missionary travels. But

45

in Acts 9 and 10 only three places are mentioned—Lydda, Joppa, and Caesarea. Here we see the abbreviated character of the report in Acts. This does not contradict what I said about Acts' historicity and about the typical nature of its truth, but rather only underscores it. The reports of Peter's journeys are not the only indication that the original congregation in Jerusalem, generally interpreted too much as being confined to Jerusalem, did carry out mission work, but there is other evidence of such missionary activity as well. For example, Saul was given authority by the Sanhedrin to persecute Christians in Damascus (9:2). I believe that in this activity of Saul we receive an indirect picture of the missionary activity that proceeded from Jerusalem, not just the mission work of the Hellenists, that is, that the Damascus congregation, for example, was founded by missionaries from Jerusalem. It even appears that Peter developed a widespread missionary activity. For when we read in 1 Corinthians about the existence of a party of Cephas in Corinth, we can really explain its origin only on the basis of the work of Peter himself or of Peter's followers or pupils. The party of Paul in Corinth originated because Paul worked there. There was a party of Apollos there because Apollos carried out mission work there. The party of Cephas must also have some similar sort of concrete origin. On the basis of these and other reports, some scholars have even developed the thesis that Peter, after his rejection by Paul in Antioch, became a rival of Paul and his missionary activity and subsequently followed him everywhere in order to lead those whom Paul had won to Christianity back to Jewish Christianity. If this theory is correct, Peter would be behind a great percentage of the difficulties Paul encountered in the course of his missionary activity and because of which he occasionally failed, as shown in the catastrophe of the Galatian congregations. This theory would explain a great deal; for example, it would give us an answer to the question we must still ask: why did Peter really go to Antioch? what led him there? And if the dispute with Paul mentioned in Galatians 2 occurred there, following which messengers sent by James arrived, we must also ask: what really brought them there? why did Peter then go to Rome? what brought him there? The stay of Peter and his death in Rome are historic facts. If Peter traveled to Rome, it was certainly because he saw a task there; if Peter traveled to Rome, it was certainly not as a "tourist," but because he wanted to do mission work there. And when Paul in 1 Cor. 9:5 says that "the other apostles and the brothers of the Lord and Cephas" are "accompanied by a sister as wife," he certainly means on their journeys—not pleasure trips, but missionary travels. Thus we would come to congregations in Spain, about which we have already spoken (see p. 47), chiefly in southern and western Spain. We meet Christian congregations around 180 as far as the border of Germany in the area of present-day Trier and Cologne. We find Christian congregations in Numidia, in the territory around Carthage; we can document Christian congregations in Cirenaica; we see Christian congregations in Egypt, in the Nile delta as well as farther upstream; and finally we find a territory in and around Edessa that is already widely Christianized. All of this is new territory.

We are relatively well informed about some of the new congregations. That is true for the congregations in Gaul. Here Irenaeus worked around the year 180 (see p. 130). However, we learn relatively little from his writings about the congregations which he served as bishop. The main source of our knowledge is the report of a persecution of the congregations in Lyons and Vienne around 180, which is preserved because Eusebius included it in his history of the church. Here we receive an extraordinarily powerful impression of the vitality of Christianity in these congregations, of its power to resist persecution. The report of the congregation in Lyons, characteristically sent to Asia Minor, is one of the most impressive documents of the early history of Christianity. From Irenaeus's theological significance we can draw conclusions about the high level of Christianity in southern Gaul, but we still know nothing about the origin of these congregations, when and by whom they were founded. The same is true for the congregations in the area of present-day Cologne and Trier and the congregations in Africa, both those in the area around Carthage and those in Cirenaica. (Characteristically, the oldest report we have of these congregations is the report of the martyrdom of Christians in Scillium in 180.)

The same thing is true for the origin of Christian congregations in Egypt. All the reports about them available to us are legends, created from the brief comments in Acts. Mark is made into Egypt's missionary, some talk about Luke and Barnabas, others mention Apollos. Even a New Testament manuscript from the fifth century, the Codex Bezae Cantabrigiensis, claims that Apollos became a Christian in Egypt and was taught Christianity there. But this is pure fantasy. The only thing that is certain is that there were Christians in Egypt very early and that these Christians must not have been few in number. We first see Christianity in Egypt appearing around the year 200, and this appearance comes suddenly making a great impression. At that time the head of the congregation in Alexandria was Bishop Demetrius who had the intention of extending a single episcopal organization throughout the entire

a much more vivid picture of the early history of Christianity than the usual exegesis offers us. However, we cannot be absolutely sure; the role of Peter, for example, like so many other things in this early period, remains shadowy.

In any case, it is true that the measures used in Jerusalem to stamp out Christianity, now that Christianity was beginning to be more and more distinguishable from Judaism, really helped to further the spread of Christianity and in fact may possibly have created the real impetus for its spread. The execution of Stephen and the persecution of his followers drove them out of Jerusalem; compelled by the external circumstances, they now developed a widespread missionary activity in Palestine and Syria. Their activity in Antioch took on special significance, not merely because an especially large congregation developed here—Acts 11:26 reports that it was here that the followers of the new faith were first called Christians—but primarily because this was the place where Paul began. Paul undertook his missionary activity not as an independent missionary, but as an emissary of the congregation in Antioch. Paul now gives Christianity a worldwide scope. Not only does he carry out missions in Syria and Cyprus and Asia Minor, but also goes to Europe. He works in Macedonia and Achaia, then goes to Italy, even perhaps to Spain. We are in the dark about this activity of Paul in Spain. We know for certain only that he planned to make a missionary trip to Spain, as he clearly mentioned in Romans. We definitely know also that there already were Christian congregations in Spain in the second century. We know nothing about the history of their origin, so we are inclined to believe that there must be a connection between Paul's intention to travel to Spain and the origin of the early congregations there, especially since there are indications that what is said about Paul in Acts 28 is not an account of the end of his life. At least it appears possible that Paul may have been set free once again after the imprisonment described there.

Two observations about this missionary work of Paul are necessary. Acts abbreviates the account of Christianity's spread. That we have already said. In the first part it deals almost exclusively with Peter. In the second part it is dominated almost exclusively by a presentation of Paul's activity. This is definitely something intentional, but just as indisputably an abbreviated description of what took place at that time. And this abbreviation goes even further. Certainly Paul was the missionary who incomparably towered above all his contemporaries. But we dare not forget that numerous missionaries besides Paul were important for the spread of Christianity in the early age. They also did their part for what—when we consider the external circumstances—was the almost inconceivable rapidity of Christianity's spread. Occasionally they become visible to us in Acts; we must assume that the very few whose names we know represent many others, and that those named are only types of the various ways Christianity spread in the early age. We hear about Barnabas, the Levite from Cyprus, who first collaborated with Paul but then broke with him and began his own missionary work—work about whose results Acts tells us nothing, although certainly his work could not have failed to bear some fruit. Then we read about Apollos who apparently comes from a completely different world of thought than Paul and Barnabas and, as we conclude from the brief comments here and in 1 Corinthians, was at home in a world of thought similar to Philo. In addition, there are the so-called Hellenists whose missionary activity apparently goes beyond the reports in Acts and, for example, to which can be attributed the establishment of the Roman congregation. These should all be seen as types of the various styles of Christian mission at that time in addition to the Pauline one.

A second thing we must not forget is that Paul was not alone but had a circle of helpers around him who contributed to the success of his mission. At least some of them were not mere helpers, but, as we can conclude from the references in Acts and the Pauline epistles, were significant and independent missionaries. This is true for Timothy and Titus, for example, who are nebulous figures for us, even though (or perhaps because) pastoral epistles are allegedly addressed to them. The pastoral letters which purport to give Timothy and Titus elementary instructions are in fact directed to Paul's missionary assistants, to people who are on the level of beginners in the Christian ministry, something that these men certainly were not, judging by what we can conclude indirectly from 2 Corinthians. Here Paul reports the deep-seated disagreement in the large Corinthian congregation which was threatening to lead to a catastrophe similar to that we observed for different reasons in Galatia. Paul himself went to Corinth in an attempt to overcome the opposition to him on the spot. But he failed in this attempt. Then Paul sent Timothy, apparently because he believed that Timothy might be able to accomplish what he had been unable to do. But Timothy also was unsuccessful. Then finally Titus went to Corinth and accomplished what Paul and Timothy had not been able to do, to bring about a reconciliation between the congregation and the apostle and its reestablishment under his authority. Naturally it was a help to Titus that in the meantime

those causing the ferment in the congregation had been subdued and the prudent leaders had once again gotten the upper hand. But what we can see from the way Paul acted is that Timothy and Titus were not mere helpers, not just apprentices in Christian mission; they definitely belong among the masters. And from time to time we also find reports about independent organizers of congregations, such as Epaphras, who apparently organized several congregations on his own in Lycia and then brought them into the Pauline circle.

Until the end of the second century, Christianity in the East remained within the boundaries Paul drew for it. If we want to learn about the details of this, we must still use the two-volume work by Adolf von Harnack, *Die Mission und Ausbreitung des Christentums in den ersten drei Jahrhunderten* ("The mission and expansion of Christianity in the first three centuries"), the fourth edition of which appeared in 1924 and now has been republished in an unaltered reprint because no one is in a position to continue it. The maps contained in this work condense what Harnack presents in his thoroughly researched investigations. On the map showing the spread of Christianity in the year 180, he has identified all the locations where reports indicate Christian congregations existed at that time.

First we find Christianity in several places in Palestine, although there can be no doubt—in contrast to a widespread opinion—that the significance of the Palestinian congregations decisively declined after the catastrophe of Jerusalem in the year 70. We find Christian congregations in Asia Minor, especially numerous along the western coast, but also on the southern coast; we find Christian congregations on Cyprus, on Crete, in Achaia, in Macedonia, chiefly in the eastern section opposite Asia Minor, that is, in areas which are familiar to us from Paul's missionary journeys. Generally we find only the names which we know from Acts and—in Asia Minor—from the Apocalypse; only a few places and areas of expansion are known beyond these. These are explained by the missionary activities of the old Pauline congregations. The Christian congregations established by Paul did not confine their work to their own territory, but also carried out missionary work in their immediate surroundings.

In Italy we find only a few congregations: Rome, Puteoli, Naples, Ravenna. Of these only Ravenna is not mentioned in Acts. But from here we enter new territory: we find congregations in Sicily, especially in Syracuse. We can confirm that Christian congregations existed in Gaul: in Lyons and Vienne, and also in the Rhone estuary. We find Christian

country. At that time the catechetical school in Alexandria already existed which from its organization, which apparently took place only shortly before, enjoyed very significant teachers. Pantaenus was the first, then came Clement of Alexandria (see p. 141), and then the school reached its heights under Origen (see pp. 141–51). We know nothing about the time before this. The papyri which have been discovered indicate only that there must have been Christian congregations here very early at the latest around A.D. 100. The oldest witness to the history of Christianity is Papyrus 52 which contains a fragment of John 18. This papyrus definitely comes from Egypt and was written around 125, perhaps even earlier. This brings us, as far as the writing of John is concerned, back before the turn of the century, for none of the canons of historical probability allow us to see in P^{52} the first copy made of the Gospel of John (which certainly did not originate in Egypt). We must rather assume a certain period of time for the gospel to spread as far as Egypt; therefore, it was most probably written some thirty years earlier than the papyrus. But it is not the only witness. We possess the famous Chester Beatty Papyri and the Bodmer Papyri that all come from the period around 200 or shortly thereafter and must have originated in congregations which not only possessed a great number of members but also enjoyed an amazingly high level of learning (as the texts accompanying the papyri prove). If, on the one hand, we can establish the existence of quite a few Christian congregations in Egypt in the early second century, and, on the other hand, note that we hear nothing of these Christian congregations until almost a century later, the only way this silence can be explained is that these second-century congregations in Egypt must have stood outside the larger church. Apparently they possessed Gnostic character; this is why the official church in other territories paid no attention to them. Not until the "orthodox" portion of the Egyptian church, which was in fellowship with the larger church, became large and strong enough did people begin to notice this part of the church and thus the entire Egyptian church.

It was different with Edessa. Eusebius even reports for us an exchange of correspondence between Abgar of Edessa and Jesus himself. Abgar writes to Jesus, asks him for healing from his illness and offers Jesus his protection, and Jesus replies. Naturally the mention of these letters has nothing to do with historical facts. It can be traced to a confusion between Abgar V, who ruled at the time of Jesus, and Abgar IX, who ruled 179–216 and was a Christian. People knew about a Christian Abgar and that an Abgar ruled at the time of Jesus, and this story of an exchange of letters originated because they identified the two. But—and this is the important point—at the end of the second century not only had the court come to confess Christ, but the entire territory was Christianized, at least to a great extent (the first state church is not found in the fourth century, therefore, but here in Edessa at the end of the second century!). And this area also produced people of extraordinary significance, which is not lessened even though they later left the church: among them are Bardesanes, the significant teacher of a Gnostic Christendom whose influences extended to Mani and later times, and possibly also the apologist Tatian, who performed the great undertaking of producing the Diatessaron, that is, the collation of the four Gospels into a unified account. It is definitely probable, or perhaps we should more cautiously say that it is possible, that Edessa was a missionary center for the East. In any case Christianity came early to Assyria, extended along the Persian Gulf, and possibly also reached India early, as the legend says which claims that the apostles Bartholomew and Thomas did mission work in India. This cannot be proved. But, as usual, legends contain a kernel of truth: the legendary part could be the activity of the apostles Bartholomew and Thomas, but the factual part is the early existence of congregations in this area. That is the way Christianity had spread by about A.D. 180.

The second map in Harnack's work depicts the extent of Christianity around 325. People have tried to determine how great the percentage of Christians in the Roman Empire could have been at that time—at the time of the Council of Nicaea. They have come to widely differing answers. The estimates range between eight percent, which would be one-twelfth, and fifty percent. Certainly neither statistic is correct. If we take eight percent, this may at best pertain to the earlier period. In a frequently quoted statement, Origen declared that there were not many Christians in relation to the total population. If that is true (and we are right to be skeptical because Origen was here minimizing things for apologetic reasons), that can at best pertain only to the beginning of the third century, since from the middle of the third century we have the trustworthy statement of a pagan writer that the Christians were more numerous than the Jews. Apparently at that time the number of Christians already exceeded one million. At the beginning of the fourth century, Eusebius said that the Christians were the most numerous of all people. That is possible and would not be a contradiction of the preceding, for the Christians were included as a single group in the entire empire in comparison to the other forms of religion and individual

tribes. The number of Christians has been estimated—all of these figures, we must add, are only very rough approximations—at about three
to four million in the time around 325. In the year 312 there were about
900 bishoprics in the East and approximately 800–900 bishoprics in the
West. These figures could perhaps lead us to conclude that there were
about the same number of Christians in East and West, since the number
of bishops was the same. Nothing could be further from the truth; rather
the strength of Christianity was still in the East. Christianity's spread was
very uneven. We find areas in which Christians did in fact number as
much as half of the populace. There were at that time individual cities
and villages which were completely Christianized. In this connection, we
must note in passing, Christianity had become a religion of the cities.
Paul consciously began his missionary activity in the cities, preferably in
the large cities. But there were, as we coincidentally learn from the
reports of persecutions, also smaller places where no one but Christians
lived. There were even whole stretches of countryside in which no
pagans lived anymore. All of that was true in the East. But there were
also areas in which Christian congregations were a rarity; there were
vast stretches of countryside, whole provinces, in which no Christian
congregations existed, perhaps not even individual Christians, this
chiefly in the Western Roman Empire.

If we want to describe the extent of Christianity in the fourth century,
we can, along with Harnack, proceed by looking at four categories. The
first includes the territories in which Christianity made up almost half
the inhabitants and in any case had already far surpassed all the other
cults. To the second category belong the other territories in which
Christianity had won a considerable portion of the populace, among the
third are numbered the areas and provinces in which Christianity was
less widely found, and the fourth category then includes the areas in
which Christianity was spread very thinly or could hardly be found. Not
a few provinces, just to repeat what we have said, belonged in this final
category. The areas included in the first category are all located in the
East. All of Asia Minor belongs to it, along with Armenia, including
Edessa. In addition, there is the area of Thrace which lies directly
opposite Asia Minor, and Cyprus. Here about half of the populace is
Christian; this is where Christianity had its main strength.

Then come the areas in which Christianity already had won a significant portion of the populace. This begins in Syria and then follows the
coast through the province of Phoenicia in a stretch which becomes
narrower the farther it goes. To this second category belong the Nile

Delta, a narrow coastal territory in the north of Cirenecia, the territory around Carthage with its Numidian hinterland, and the south of Spain and the Spanish coast extending up toward Gaul—it is striking that Christianity is especially widespread in the coastal areas. In Gaul we then find relatively many Christians in the Rhone estuary. In Italy the second category includes only Rome, the area around Naples, small parts of Sicily, and the eastern coast of Italy along the Adriatic Sea, from up as far as Venice down to the south, as well as the area along the western coast of Greece. The eastern coasts of Achaia and Thessaly also belong in this category of lands in which Christianity had to a certain extent gained a foothold. In all other areas it is spread very thinly, so that Harnack believed—somewhat too glibly—that we could exclude them without difficulty from a presentation of Christianity's early history. Here belong all the territories not previously mentioned.

What conclusions can we draw from these facts? The first, which we cannot sufficiently emphasize, is this: the strength of Christianity in the first centuries was in the East, not in the West. Because of our ancestry and the impression of the role which the West later played, we instinctively have the impression that Christianity always had its strength in the West. We just cannot talk this way. In the early centuries, Christianity had not simply its numerical strength, but also its essential strength in the East. The decisive events of church history, at least in the first two centuries, took place in Asia Minor. It is true that Rome soon came to play a relatively important role, but not on its own, rather only because the people from Asia Minor went to Rome; they believed that if they gained the support of the imperial capital they could attain a decisive advantage. This is true for Marcion, it is true for the Monarchians at the end of the second century, and it is also true for the Apologists. In this way Rome clearly attained a significance in the theological disputes, but—just to repeat ourselves—not an original significance, but a derived one. Rome's own significance lies in the area of practical church affairs. Here is where, as far as we can tell, the creed was first formulated, or, to put it more precisely, here is where a preliminary form of the Apostles' Creed originated. Apparently here is where the canon (insofar as it was fixed at the time) was fixed in writing. Here the bishop's office was decisively developed further, as were many other things. We shall speak about them when we come to the internal history of Christianity. For centuries Rome made no independent contribution to theology. The theologians who might have been in a position to do so— Hippolytus at the beginning and Novatian at the middle of the third century—were not accepted by the Roman congregation, and when they aspired to the bishop's office were not elected and accordingly were forced into separation. When Constantine in 306 became ruler of Gaul and in 312 extended his dominion over Italy, the territory he ruled was only weakly Christianized in comparison with the East. This is true as far as the numbers are concerned, but more so as far as the status of Christianity's adherents is concerned. Many studies of Constantine's attitude toward Christianity simply overlook this fact. The only people who can say that Constantine converted to Christianity for political reasons are those who have no idea of the insignificant role Christianity played in the West, both numerically and in every other respect. In the East it was different indeed. But it is typical ivory-tower wisdom if we believe that it was for the sake of Christendom in the East that Constantine first attached himself to Christianity—so that he could prepare for the later conquest of the East. This overestimates Constantine's planning and underestimates the realities with which he had to deal. In Gaul, as well as in Italy, Constantine was at first a usurper; he stood in opposition to the central government and first of all had to secure his own position and pay careful attention to the political forces at work there. In 312 Constantine was occupied with many things, but not with preparing to conquer the East.

If we now consider the linguistic aspects of early Christianity and divide it into Latin and Greek portions, then the role which the West plays becomes even smaller. Even in the West the congregations, or at least the Christian theologians, speak and write Greek past the beginning of the third century. The reason why this Greek Christianity had such a superiority is very clear. In the East, in the Greek-speaking area, Christianity had existed from the early days, while a Latin-speaking Christianity developed much later. Not only was Greek the language of all educated people but the Old Testament, the Gospels, and the Pauline epistles could be read only in Greek. The writings of all the Apostolic Fathers, the writings of all the Apologists—in short, all Christian literature of the second century—was written in Greek. Not until the end of the second century did the use of other languages begin to develop. At that time the number of ordinary people who could no longer understand Greek apparently had grown in the congregations—the congregations in the West (both Africa and Italy), as well as the congregations in Syria and Egypt—so that people began to translate the New Testament into the vernacular. This is when the first non-Greek Christian literature appears. Tertullian (see pp. 130–31) wrote in Latin around 200; Bardesanes (see p. 52) wrote in Syriac. For Egypt we have no corresponding tradition, but we must assume that a similar development began about the same time or shortly afterward. It is true that Hippolytus (see p. 130) was still writing his works in Greek in Rome around 225, but about that time Greek must finally have disappeared from use in the Roman congregation, since Hippolytus was soon completely forgotten and had to be rediscovered in the sixteenth century.

2. THE SOCIAL STRUCTURE OF THE EARLY CHURCHES

When we begin to explore the sociological composition of early congregations, we must remember what we previously said about 1 Cor. 1:26–29 (see p. 7). We must assume that the picture painted by Paul here also applies to other Christian congregations of the time. Paul says that God has chosen what is foolish in the world, what is weak in the world, what is low and despised in the world, even things that are not. Christianity in the early period was found among the lower—we can almost say the "lowest"—classes of society. Here is where Christianity had its chief influence and from where most of its adherents came. Yet we must not interpret this one-sidedly in the sense of a proletarian Christianity—just to remind us of what we have previously said—for what Paul says is that not many wise according to worldly standards, not many powerful, not many of noble birth were called—not many, but still a few of the wise, powerful, and those of noble birth. Besides the large number of simple Christians, representatives of the middle and upper classes were found in the early churches. Acts gives us a whole list of names of people from these classes. But the majority of churches appeared just the way Paul described them in the first chapter of 1 Corinthians far into the third century. The pagan polemicists confirm this for us, and it is also indirectly confirmed by the Apologists, all of whom belong to the educated class and represent this upper circle in the churches. A congregation like Rome—rich, influential, large, and certainly numbering prominent people among its members—did not find it strange, as we have mentioned (see p. 8), that Callistus should be its bishop; in fact, the congregation chose this slave in express opposition to Hippolytus who not only belonged to the educated but also to the social upper class; and it chose him even though there had been several very turbulent episodes in Callistus's life. Of course, his biography comes to us from Hippolytus's pen, and doubtless an unchristian hate was directing that pen, but even if we discount all that, there still remains a great deal in Callistus's life which gives legitimate cause for offense to the usual standards of propriety, at least those which dominate Christian congregations today (and probably then as well).

A fundamental change can then be observed in this third century. We begin to see more and more representatives of the wealthy class and educated class streaming into the churches. The way for this was paved in the preceding generation. This can be seen in the writings of the second century, at first in the polemic directed against the members of the wealthy class. For example, the Epistle of James, which is to be dated at the beginning of the second century, in chapter 2 bitterly addresses the situation of a prominent rich man coming into the Christian worship service where he is treated better than other people. This indicates that there were at that time prominent and rich people in the church, even though they may have been exceptions. "Is it not the rich who oppress you, is it not they who drag you into court?" asks James 2:6. Even Paul himself, to go back beyond the turn of the century, complained about the grievances which arose because wealthy people belonged to the church. At the agape meals (see p. 74) in Corinth some of the wealthy had previously eaten at home before they came to the agape so they would not have to share at the communal meal with those who had nothing. Some even come, says Paul in 1 Cor. 11:21, to the agape while drunk. The passionate polemic of the Shepherd of Hermas against the rich shows that the position of the wealthy in the church was still disputed in Rome around the year 150. One of the rich people in the Roman church was Marcion, who, at the time of his reception, could give a gift of an extraordinarily large amount of money, which the church to its credit completely repaid when he left (something that later hardly ever happened)—proof that the Roman church at that time had considerable means.

Although rich people were an exception in the second century, around 200 the change became much clearer. The writings of Clement of Alexandria (such as the *Paidagogos* which gives the church moral guidance) can be understood only if we presuppose that if not the Alexandrian church as such, at least the circle to which Clement belonged and to which this writing was addressed consisted not only of educated people, but those who were wealthy, since the questions which concern Clement and his readers just do not exist for members of the lower social class. Clement wrote a work entitled *Quis dives salvetur?* ("What rich person can be saved?"). This writing serves practically as the justification for owning property, the justification for retaining the wealthy in the Christian church. In it Clement comments on the story of the rich young ruler, but the rich man is not given the same answer here as the rich young ruler received in the gospel, "Sell what you possess and give to the poor," but he matter-of-factly assumes that people not only own property, but that they can also keep it. They do not need to give it away to the poor, as the early age demanded; the gospel's requirement—according to Clement—was fulfilled if they simply did not fix their hearts on the riches they possessed. This change in the pericope's interpretation is not only characteristic, but it is even more characteristic that someone could write this sort of work and that it could enjoy wide circulation. If we look at the bishops of the third century, there we find not only Callistus (see pp. 151–52), but also Cyprian of Carthage (see pp. 31–32), Dionysius of Alexandria (see p. 103), and Paul of Samosata, to mention only these three. All three belong to the upper class and, as far as their ancestry and wealth are concerned, can be compared to any pagan in their diocese. They can even (as did Paul of Samosata) simultaneously hold high public offices. Thus the development is beginning in the third century which we see raised to its height in the person of Ambrose (see p. 4), who belonged to one of the most prominent families in the empire and was the governor of Milan. Members of leading families in the empire not only were Christian, but they even were leaders of churches and by their personalities gave a special prominence to these churches and a special weight to the decisions of these churches.

Perhaps Christianity very early gained influence at the very center of the imperial government, at the imperial court itself. In his letter to the Philippians, Paul sends greetings from Christians in Caesar's household. It is beyond doubt that Christians in the imperial household were certainly slaves, but when we say this the subject is not yet closed, for we know that slaves everywhere, especially in the imperial court, attained considerable significance. The history of late antiquity shows us that over and over. At the close of the First Letter of Clement (that is, shortly before A.D. 100), the messengers who are sent from the Roman church to Corinth are mentioned by name, and these names bring us once again into the circle of imperial servants, something that is certainly not coincidental. At that time, around A.D. 100, Christians were found not only among imperial slaves, but also among the immediate relatives of the imperial household. During Domitian's time, shortly before the end of the first century, the consul Titus Flavius Clement was executed and his wife Domitilla exiled because of their religious convictions which can be characterized as at least sympathetic to Christianity. Around A.D. 225 Marcia, the emperor's concubine, was a Christian. We learn this only incidentally in the context of the biography of Callistus which Hippolytus gives us. This Marcia had significant influence at court and used it to express concern about the freeing of imprisoned Christians. When the last great persecution of Christians broke out at the beginning of the fourth century, the emperor Diocletian first forced his wife and daughter to offer pagan sacrifices, obviously because it was at least suspected that they were adherents of Christianity. And we have members sympathetic to Christianity among the imperial family not only in the East but also in the West. One of the daughters of Constantius Chlorus, Constantine's father who ruled Gaul and Britain, bore the name Anastasia. Only Christians bore such a name. There is no other conclusion we can reach, therefore, than to say that this daughter of Constantius Chlorus (or, more probably, her mother who named her) was at least sympathetic to Christianity. There is no doubt that Christianity had climbed to the highest classes of the empire, even before its official recognition in the fourth century, and exercised considerable influence there. The report which Lactantius gives about the outbreak of Diocletian's persecution shows that Christianity had won a greater number of adherents not in the imperial family alone but also among the leading members of the imperial government. The immediate cause of the persecution's outbreak was the fact that attempts of the augurers to foresee the future in the entrails of slaughtered sacrificial animals were fruitless. These augurers blamed their failure on the presence at the sacrifices of too many people who made the sign of the cross, thus foiling their efforts. Since only the highest imperial officials took part in these sacrifices, there must have been Christians in the highest positions of the imperial government. As a requirement of their office they had to appear at the auguries; by making the sign of the cross they protected themselves against the demons they believed were active there, robbing them of their power.

Naturally we dare not draw too many far-reaching conclusions from these isolated reports, which—as we have said—have come to us quite incidentally. We must not go to the other extreme: people have wished to read into Paul's description a proletarian form of early Christianity. Someone might come and, on the basis of these reports, turn the Christianity of this later period into a religion of the influential, the wealthy, and the educated. That is wrong. The fact remains that the number of Christians, seen as a whole, becomes fewer and fewer the higher we climb on the social ladder of late antiquity. At the beginning of the fourth century the upper classes as such are still overwhelmingly oriented toward paganism, and this continues, especially in the West, through the fourth and into the fifth century. Even at the end of the fourth century the Roman Senate had numerous pagans among its members. The strength of paganism among the wealthy and educated classes was still strong in the fourth century. Constantine, for example, attempted to marry his children to Christians. But he found that difficult, because Christians could scarcely be found within the only stratum of society suitable for marriage to heirs of the ruling family. All in all, Paul's statement in 1 Corinthians holds true. Common people predominated in the Christian churches, yet within these churches members of the upper class, the wealthy, and the educated continued to increase the longer time went by.

3. THE POSITION OF WOMEN IN EARLY CHRISTIANITY

It is by no means superfluous to speak about the position of women in the church. Christianity, if we look at its official representatives, is today a male religion. Not only in the Catholic church and in the Orthodox church but even in Protestant churches it is exclusively men who hold all the offices. Women are excluded from them; the highest level they can attain in Catholicism and Orthodoxy is to be an abbess of a nunnery; in Protestantism it is to be a "female pastor," very seldom a member of an ecclesiastical governing body. In the Catholic and Orthodox churches this certainly will not change. Even among Protestant churches we cannot really say that men have made it very easy for women to attain the ministerial office. This is true for the office of pastor, and even truer for the higher steps of the ecclesiastical hierarchy; up to now we have never had a female superintendent or bishop, at least not in Europe. The sole exception so far has been that of the French Reformed congregations in Germany who at the end of 1979 chose a woman as their moderator.

But if we look at the daily life of the church we get a very different impression. If we attend a "normal" worship service (that is, not a special festival), we have the impression—among Protestants, but also among Catholics and Orthodox—that Christian congregations consist predominately of women. On this basis the participation of women in the church appears much greater than the official membership records indicate. In the early period the participation of women not only appeared larger than that of men, as it does today, but in fact was as great as, if not greater than, that of men. At least in the upper classes more women had become Christians than men, as we learn incidentally in Hippolytus's biography of Callistus which we have mentioned several times. These women are serious Christians and do not want to marry pagan husbands. The naturalness with which Paul in 1 Corinthians could assume "mixed marriages" existed had vanished. Christians wanted to make a Christian marriage. But, as a rule, these young, rich, and prominent Christian women in Rome could not find a husband in their circle because there were so few Christian men among the Roman upper class. Thus they were compelled to marry considerably beneath their station. That they also could not do—at least officially—because Roman marriage law provided that in such cases they would lose not only their status but also their property. They were helped out of this dilemma, according to Hippolytus's account, by obtaining sanction only from the church for their marriage with a Christian of a lower class, that is, a marriage that in the eyes of the state would be only a relationship without official character similar to marriage—a marriage of conscience, something which we are acquainted with in the modern period during the time of the Third Reich. After 1937 marriages between Christians and Jews were forbidden by law. Such marriages took place only in church but were not officially registered. Not many pastors had the courage to perform them, but they did occur. These marriages were not legally valid, but in the consciences of those who participated, this act—which was officially illegal and punishable—was a true marriage.

While it was not merely the number of women that was large in the early church, it was also their influence. It is true that no women belonged to the inner circle of the disciples, to the Twelve; this is the chief reason people oppose the ordination of women. And it is also true that no women belonged officially to the larger circle of the disciples (the Seventy, or—more accurately—the Seventy-two). But it is also just as obvious that women accompanied Jesus from the very beginning, that from the very beginning women were among his closest confidantes. We see this quite frequently throughout the Gospel accounts. Jesus was not only surrounded by men but by women as well. And in decisive ways these women distinguish themselves more than the men. At the cross it is women who stand around Jesus, not men, for they have all fled. It is not the disciples who first go to Jesus' grave, but the women. And the risen Lord first appears not to the disciples but to the women. There can be no doubt about all of this, for the simple fact that this tradition has been preserved for us indicates its factualness. The early period was definitely not an age that was friendly toward women, and these reports were preserved only because people could not do away with this old and fixed tradition.

This prominent position of women was characteristic not only at the time Christianity began, but it endured. The church in Jerusalem assembled in the house of Mary, the mother of Mark. The first Christian congregation in Europe originated in the house of a woman—Lydia, a seller of purple goods. And so it continues. Once again the factualness is indisputable, for the simple fact that this is reported to us again speaks for the absolute veracity of the tradition and the fact that it extends back to the very earliest beginnings. Moreover, these women not only placed their property at the disposal of the church but also played a role in the worship services. When Acts 21:9 tells about Philip's four daughters who prophesied, these four daughters are not only an oracle for household use, but, according to what we learn from Paul's letters about the organization of offices in the church, we may certainly assume that they also prophesied during worship services, that is, they participated in the ministry of the church. First Corinthians contains the well-known and oft-quoted passage which commands that "women keep silence in church." In 1 Cor. 14:33–35 we read: "As in all the churches of the saints, the women should keep silence in the churches. For they are not permitted to speak, but should be subordinate, as even the law says. If there is anything they desire to know, let them ask their husbands at home. For it is shameful for a woman to speak in church." This is what Paul demands in that place. However, this is not a description of actual circumstances in the Corinthian congregation, as people continue to suppose; rather it is only Paul's demand which is to be explained from the Jewish tradition in which he stands. At least in Corinth, women took an active part in the organization of the worship service, as this same epistle shows us. Paul describes things the way he wishes they were, not the way they are in reality. Paul also reports the real situation in the early period, as we see in 1 Cor. 11:5, where he says quite incidentally that "any woman who prays or prophesies with her head unveiled [that is, takes part in the church's ministry] dishonors her head—it is the same as if her head were shaven." People have often perceived these two passages as standing in opposition to each other and then decided (as New Testament scholars like to do) that one of them must be an interpolation, that is, something inserted later, because Paul could certainly have had only one opinion. No, we just cannot see this as an interpolation; it is only if we take the things exactly as they are presented that we can form a picture of the situation which really existed at that time. Women participated in the church's worship services. Paul made an attempt to oppose this, but he was forced to recognize the reality. In the New Testament we find women not only in serving roles, such as the deaconesses in Rom. 16:1, but also in the administration of the churches, even when men are available for these positions. We meet the couple Prisca and Aquila several times in Acts and in Paul's letters, and each time Prisca clearly stands above her husband—in the reference as well as in fact. She is discussed with such respect that Harnack believed that Prisca may even have been the author of the Epistle to the Hebrews. That certainly goes too far, but there can be no doubt that Prisca played a leading role in the church. She and Aquila further instructed Apollos in Christianity, they taught the disciples in Ephesus, and so on. When we go beyond the New Testament and look at the apocryphal literature (see pp. 128–29), then we often find a woman as a central figure of these writings, which were the early Christians' real reading material (Scripture was read in the worship service; at home people edified themselves with what we call the apocryphal writings). The much-read Acts of Thecla, from the second half of the second century, dealt with a woman about whose piety and sanctity all sorts of possible and impossible things were said, proof of what sort of reputation a woman could enjoy in the church at that time.

But we must quickly add that the position and reputation of women had already reached its peak. The decline was already beginning which was to lead to the complete exclusion of women from ecclesiastical offices and to their devaluation in Christians' consciousness—not only at this time but for all the subsequent centuries up to modern times. The opposition to a prominent position for women is obvious from the beginning, and it is just as obvious that this opposition stems from Judaism. We find it in Paul; we find it even more clearly—and thus we see how quickly it develops—in 1 Tim. 2:9, where it is established that (1) women should clothe themselves modestly and not adorn themselves with ostentatious hairdos, gold, or pearls, and (2) women should evidence their fear of God by their good works: "Let a woman learn in silence with all submissiveness. I permit no woman to teach or to have authority over men; she is to keep silent." The reason for this is important: "For Adam was formed first, then Eve; and Adam was not deceived, but the woman was deceived and became a transgressor." We find this reasoning again and again up until the late middle ages; in Erfurt during Luther's time the students had to thank God weekly in a morning prayer that they had not been born women, but men. What, then, can a woman now do to obtain salvation? First Timothy 2:15 answers this with utmost clarity: "Yet women will be saved through bearing children." Even this is not sufficient, however, for a woman will be saved not just by bearing children, but only "if she continues in faith and love and holiness, with modesty."

Here the opposition to the actual position of women in the Christian church is manifested—probably about the beginning of the second century, I should judge. It was the crises of the second century which brought victory to this opposition, for in the opposing churches—Montanism (see p. 94), as well as Gnosticism (see p. 95)—women enjoyed a significant position. That was what led to their ruin. In Montanism the prophetesses were equal in authority to Montanus; they did not simply speak for others but for themselves; they prophesied, and their oracles were regarded as a holy revelation. Gnostic teachers were also accompanied by women; it was no coincidence that Ptolemy wrote his famous letter to Flora. Thus in the struggle against Gnosticism as well as in the struggle against Montanism, the leading position of women in the church became suspect. Equating women with men in the ministerial office became a characteristic of those movements outside the church and opposed to it. Because of this, the opposition finally achieved the upper hand, especially since it could appeal to Paul's authority in 1 Corinthians and 1 Timothy.

In addition, this repression of women was encouraged by the ascetic movement which devalued marriage or even repudiated it entirely. This ascetic movement already enjoyed extraordinary strength in the second century, and then in monasticism, beginning at the end of the third century, encompassed the broadest circles. In addition to the ascetics we have an ever-increasing number of their admirers who want to adopt their principles without separating from the world. With this devaluation of married life was associated the devaluation of women as such—in fact, it contributed to it. Characteristic of this is Tertullian's expression in *De virginibus velandis* ("On the apparel of women") that it would be appropriate for a woman to dress in mourning because she was a descendant of Eve who had brought suffering upon the entire human race. This conception then influenced all the succeeding centuries. Only one woman was spared from this radical devaluation—to a certain extent as compensation for the low estate of all other women—and that was Mary, who from early on grew and grew in esteem and honor.

This devaluation of women unmistakably stands, as we have attempted to show, in contrast to the former equal status of women in early Christianity. What Paul has to say on this theme, after he has liberated himself from his inherited and acquired prejudice, can be found in Gal. 3:28: "There is neither Jew nor Greek, there is neither slave nor free, there is neither male nor female; for you are all one in Christ Jesus." Here is where the differences in ancestry, the differences in social position, and the differences in sex are taken up into a higher unity; here is where Christianity's real answer is given.

4. THE PERSECUTION OF CHRISTIANS

We began our chapter with an overview of the spread of Christianity (see pp. 45–56); an overview of the persecution of Christians must now follow as a necessary addition. The first sentence of this overview must be: the persecutions are as old as Christianity, as old as the Christian church; the second sentence must be: the persecutions are an indispensable component of the existence of the Christian church. In his work *Von den Konzilen und der Kirche* ("On the councils and the church"), Luther in 1539 spoke about the way we recognize the church. He enumerated seven marks: we recognize the Christian church (1) in that it has God's Word, (2) see it in the sacrament of baptism, (3) in the sacrament of the Lord's Supper, (4) in absolution, (5) in the ministerial office, (6) in that it publicly worships, prays, praises, and thanks God, and (7), says Luther, "the holy Christian people are externally recognized by the holy possession of the sacred cross. They must endure every misfortune and persecution, all kinds of trials and evil . . . in order to become like their head, Christ." Persecution is not only as old as Christianity, but persecution is also a genuine mark by which we are able to recognize the Christian church; something is lacking in the church if it lacks persecution, that is, genuine persecution. Luther then continues: "And the only reason they must suffer is that they steadfastly adhere to Christ and God's Word, enduring this for the sake of Christ." Only a persecution for the sake of Christ and the faith is a real persecution. Luther does not mean a nongenuine persecution, such as some Christians and some churches suffer because of their own fault. A pastor who, because of genuine German stubbornness, has a falling out with his brethren in office, the church authorities, and his congregation, and then has to bear the consequences, is not suffering a genuine persecution no matter how much he may complain about it. And the high church official—just to say this as well—who throws a stone into the pond and then is surprised that it creates waves and he himself gets wet from the drops or waves, is not suffering a genuine persecution. These are self-made persecutions. But about one thing we must be clear: if Christianity is without offense, if the world does not become irritated at it, if the world and Christianity appear to be at one, then something is not right with Christianity. We all long for the situation described at the end of the church's general prayer: "that we may lead a quiet and peaceable life in all godliness and honesty." That is everyone's dream, but we must be quite clear—just to repeat it—that this is not the perfect Christian existence. Those who are prepared to be Christians only on the condition that there will be no uncomfortable consequences for them, those who are not aware that Christianity demands from them a willingness to suffer genuine persecution and genuine suffering, have a Christianity that is incomplete; something decisive is lacking in it.

The persecution of Christianity is as old as the Christian church itself. The hatred of Judaism is what brought Jesus to his death; that much is certain, no matter how we may answer the complicated questions associated with Jesus' trial. Judaism also bitterly persecuted the apostles; that is just as certain, no matter what sort of problems the details of the presentations in Acts may offer. As soon as it became apparent that Christianity was about to separate from Judaism, or had already separated, Judaism persecuted Christianity with fervent hatred. Thus Stephen was killed and his followers were scattered. And when the instigator of this persecution (or at least one of them, for there must have been other instigators besides Saul) became a Christian, Judaism also bitterly persecuted him. After many confrontations which almost led Paul to his death, the Jews finally managed to secure his imprisonment in Jerusalem. It was no thanks to them that Paul left Palestine alive. This is the way it went, as we find it reported in Acts and coming through again and again in Paul's letters: Judaism bitterly persecuted Christians as long as possible. During all of late antiquity Jews and Christians—or, Judaism and Christianity—were bitter opponents. There is not only a body of literature which defends Christianity against paganism and attacks paganism, there is also a body of literature which defends Christianity against Judaism and attacks Judaism. (The most important work is Justin's dialogue with the Jew Trypho.) The reason that so little of this literature is preserved is that the later church no longer needed it. The writings of the Apologists also have mostly been lost and, if they are preserved, as a rule exist in only one manuscript, for precisely the same reason.

Judaism bitterly fought Christianity for religious reasons as long as it could. On the other hand, Christianity bitterly persecuted Judaism for religious reasons as soon as it was in a position to do so. In the entire ancient church a certain "anti-Semitic" attitude cannot be denied, and this "anti-Semitism" remained in Christianity through the centuries until the age of the Reformation and far beyond. Luther's work in 1543, *Von den Juden und ihren Lügen* ("On the Jews and their lies"), is only one of a lengthy series. People have occasionally referred to it, especially those who have no use for Christianity and the church and for whom Luther's attitude only serves as an excuse to misuse what Luther meant and said. The opposition of Christians to the Jews, of Christianity to Judaism, before the Reformation and after the Reformation until the beginnings of secularization was a religious opposition and had nothing to do with ethnic or even racial beliefs. Naturally we cannot deny that non-Christian motives and arguments played a frequent role in the medieval Jewish persecutions, especially financial considerations which often appear frightfully similar to those of the modern age. But these motives were secondary; the attitude of the Middle Ages was dominated by an opposition because of faith, not of blood; modern people have persecuted Jews because of their ancestry. And if Luther, who—speaking in a modern fashion—began as an outspoken friend of the Jews, uses his harshest words against the Jews in his later writings, this is because of his opposition to them for reasons of faith. Behind the attitude of those centuries is the ancient motif: the Jews nailed Christ to the cross, they persecute Christianity to the present day with the same hatred they had toward Christ, and, if they could, they would even today repeat the deeds they did then. In his old age Luther came to doubt the possibility of winning Jews to the Christian faith; this is the reason why he now attacked them, in contrast to his defense of them in his earlier years, when he still believed that Jews rejected the Christian faith only because it had never been proclaimed to them in the proper manner. But at the same time Luther said—and in even his severest and sharpest writings— to his dying day: the Jew who becomes a Christian is my dear brother. Modern anti-Semitism must be clearly distinguished from the opposition to Jews before the Reformation.

Naturally no one denies—and it cannot be denied—that Christians have paid back the Jews many times over for the persecutions the early church suffered, just as Christians did to the pagans. There are many things that have taken place in the history of the church which can in no way be excused and can in no way be justified. The Jewish persecutions before and even after the Middle Ages, along with the pagan persecution after the end of the fourth century, belong to the great debt Christianity owes which cannot be annulled. However, the modern Jewish persecutions did not originate with Christianity, but—we need only think of our own recent history—were initiated by a movement which proceeded simultaneously against Christianity and came from an anti-Christian position.

The persecution by Judaism paralleled the persecution of Christians by paganism until the state persecution came to the fore and became the exclusive external threat to the young church. In the eyes of Roman officials, Christianity in the early period certainly did not appear to be an independent body. For them Christianity, if they even considered it at all, was a new sort of Judaism. We do not know when the Roman state first noticed that in Christianity a new religion had originated, one which could not be ignored. Certainly the Jews would have used all methods possible to make this clear and to abolish the misunderstanding by which Christians could claim for themselves the protection of the law that Jews had gained through difficult struggles. According to Tacitus's account, it appears that the persecution by Nero in A.D. 64 assumed this distinction between Jews and Christians. But that is surely something that is projected backward from the time of Tacitus's report (around 100, that is, a generation later) and speeds up the events. Probably the independence of the new group remained unknown to the state at least as long as a generation after Nero. But as soon as the state clearly understood that here was something new and what this something new was, it began to persecute Christianity with severity.

This persecution of Christians did not begin, as we instinctively suppose, by the promulgation of a special law against Christians which provided definite penalties for holding the Christian faith, similar to theft, murder, and the like. Rather, for the state and its administrators, Christianity fell under the regulations issued about the supervision and suppression of forbidden organizations—under the laws issued for combating traitors. This meant that Christianity was to be supervised by the police—police which, we must understand, had systems and methods developed as thoroughly as those in any modern totalitarian state.

It is an error if we imagine that we are separated from the past by a great gulf. Outward circumstances certainly have changed, but in those things which are decisive, people of that time were just the same as people of today. In many contexts we can project the same motives and procedures which we observe today back into that earlier time. These police authorities acted brutally because they considered it necessary: either when they were prodded into it by a denunciation from the populace or when they considered it a practical political necessity; they acted most vehemently when an energetic provincial governor—or one who was especially devoted to the pagan faith—ordered them to because he believed it necessary to exterminate this Christian cancer in the body of the Roman Empire, at least as far as his influence extended. Thus up into the fourth century, Christians always found themselves in an exceptional circumstance, although there was no special law against them; for all practical purposes they were outside the law and subject to every arbitrary action. Only when we understand this can we explain the situation which we find in the ancient church: in some provinces things were peaceful, but at the same time Christians were attacked sharply in others. In one city nothing happens to Christians, in a neighboring city fierce persecutions simultaneously take place. There could be no explanation for this situation if—and this is something scholars have long discussed—a special law directed against Christians had been promulgated.

Up until the third century larger persecutions apparently did not occur; the persecutions were only local in nature. They were limited to individual communities, or even to one province, but did not extend beyond that. Only a few had a comprehensive nature. They begin, as far as we know, with Nero in the year 64 and then continue under Domitian in A.D. 95. Then they cease and do not resume until the third century. Despite all the victims they claimed, the persecutions under Nero and Domitian had only a limited effect, so that someone might say: why do Christians make so much of them? In the early period only very few people suffered the martyrdom to which so much attention is given, but ninety-eight percent of all Christians were never touched. That ignores the historical reality, for the reports we possess about the Christian persecutions are very incomplete. Despite the high honor in which martyrs were held by Christians—something that developed very quickly and led to the writing of martyr acts, then to celebrating the memory of martyrs on the anniversary of their death—far from all the martyr acts written were preserved. If even Eusebius's collection of martyr acts could be lost, we must assume that numerous other martyr acts of nameless authors were either destroyed or forgotten. Whenever a persecution broke out, it was first directed against the church building and the congregation's records. The church building was razed and all writings publicly burned. That is one thing, and the other is that it was by no means the case that every martyr's death was automatically recorded in a written report. Rather, the reports about Christian persecutions which we possess are only incidental lights in this darkness dominating the early period. Reports about martyrs or written accounts of their deaths (the so-called martyr acts) are not the rule but the exception. These writings originated only in situations to which people ascribed a major significance, either because of the number of martyrs, because of the circumstances of the martyrdom, or because of the person of the martyr. In numerous cases such a written account was simply never produced. The martyrdom of a single anonymous Christian or a small group in a far-distant place, in a remote province of the empire, as a rule enjoyed no literary record. That happened not only because the persecution often exterminated all the Christians, but also because very frequently there was no one there who possessed the literary skills necessary for such a task. And if such a writing were produced, its existence would be threatened anew in every subsequent persecution (see p. 77). Not only in every decade but in every year there would have been martyrs in the Christian church—sometimes here, sometimes there, sometimes in one province, sometimes in another—so that (just to repeat what we have already said) all Christians, especially in view of the arbitrary nature of police action, really had to reckon that they might at any time be brought before the judge and then executed or painfully punished because of their faith.

The fact of being a Christian itself sufficed for punishment. The *nomen ipsum* ("the very name"), the fact of a Christian confession, was enough. This is important in understanding the martyr acts and the trials of Christians. In the trial the judge determined nothing except whether the accused confessed Christ and did not inquire about details; in all the reports we possess this stereotype occurs over and over. The complaints which people raised against Christians, the charges which were made against them—which we shall mention soon (see pp. 71–74)—did not enter into the discussion. It was sufficient to establish that the accused confessed Christ. The judge then attempted—and this stereotype also recurs in the reports—to bring them to deny their faith and compel them to perform the sacrifice. If the accused denied Christianity, they were freed, but if they persevered, they were condemned. Again and again we have reports that Christians were freed as soon as they either cursed their Christian faith—that was the negative way of proving their innocence—or when they took the affirmative step of venerating the pagan gods (by which almost always what was demanded was not declaring allegiance to the territorial gods but to the imperial cult). As soon as Christians did that, they were freed. This is how easy it was for them to escape the danger which threatened them: they needed only to sprinkle a few grains of incense in the sacrificial flame burning before the emperor's statue—and correspondingly great was the temptation for Christians to apostatize, since there were gruesome punishments for those who persevered in their Christianity. If the Christians were Roman citizens, they would be beheaded; others were burned, they were crucified, they were sentenced to fight with wild animals in the circus, that is, to be eaten alive. Sometimes they were condemned to forced labor in the mines or forced into exile, something that sounds relatively harmless to us, but in the circumstances of that time it meant a sentence to a slow but sure death. Girls and women were sent into brothels and suffered whatever similar fates could be devised; all of this—just to repeat ourselves—only because they had made a Christian confession as such. Just the fact of confessing Christ was sufficient for the judge and the police authorities to condemn a person for a capital crime. Next to sacrilege, *atheotes* (that is, the godlessness), denial of God, and lese majesty—with which these trials basically dealt—all other accusations paled into insignificance.

In the daily argument between pagans and Christians—on the street, on the job—other things certainly played a role, namely, the concrete charges which the Apologists had to combat up until the beginning of the third century, when things quieted down. If we want to have a vivid conception of this, we must read the appropriate chapter in the dialogue *Octavius* by Minucius Felix. Here in a very few sentences is summarized—I would almost say in classical fashion—the accusations which the average pagan made against Christians. What is mentioned here must have happened countless times in arguments on the street, in speeches which Jewish or pagan agitators used to stir up the crowd. It played a decisive role if they wanted to stir up a Christian persecution or incite the mob to even sharper attacks against Christians. This dialogue *Octavius* was written about 200 or shortly thereafter. It begins with three friends—all lawyers, namely, the Christian Octavius from whom the writing gets its name, the pagan Caecilius, and the author—walking from Rome to the seashore at Ostia during the court's recess. Along the way they pass a statue of Serapis, which the pagan honors by blowing it a kiss. That causes a sharp comment from the Christian, the pagan is offended, and thus an argument over the true faith occurs when they reach their destination. Either this is fiction or it is a literary embellishment of what really took place; however, it possesses the sort of typical truth we saw in the reports of Acts. The pagan Caecilius first presents the pagan arguments against the Christians. At that time they were probably expressed countless times in this way, even if not so artfully: the Christians are

> a reprobate, unlawful, and desperate faction ... who, having gathered together from the lowest dregs the more unskilled, and women, credulous and, by the facility of their sex, yielding, establish a herd of a profane conspiracy, which is leagued together by nightly meetings, and solemn fasts, and inhuman meats—not by any sacred rite, but by that which requires expiation—a people skulking and shunning the light, silent in public, but garrulous in corners. They despise the temples as dead-houses, they reject the gods, they laugh at sacred things; wretched, they pity, if they are allowed, the priests; half naked themselves, they despise honors and purple robes. Oh, wondrous folly and incredible audacity! they despise present torments, although they fear those which are uncertain and future; and while they fear to die after death, they do not fear to die for the present: so does a deceitful hope soothe their fear with the solace of a revival.
>
> And now, as wickeder things advance more fruitfully, and abandoned manners creep on day by day, those abominable shrines of an impious assembly are maturing themselves throughout the whole world. Assuredly this confederacy ought to be rooted out and execrated. They know one another by secret marks and insignia, and they love one another almost before they know one another. Everywhere also there is mingled among them a certain religion of lust, and they call one another promiscuously brothers and sisters, that even a not unusual debauchery may by the intervention of that sacred name become incestuous: it is thus that their vain and senseless superstition glories in crimes.

In this account of Caecilius we perceive Christianity from the distorted viewpoint of an opponent. Much in Caecilius's polemic can be explained by the arcane discipline of the Christians, in which they kept the decisive elements of their faith and worship practices secret from the outside world. Thus people on the outside knew about them, about their practices and their doctrine, but never anything precise. At first the pagan notes that Christians have something to hide. There must be things among the Christians which they are ashamed to expose to the light of day, or else they would not so stubbornly keep silent about them. From the pieces of information which leaked out they justifiably construct a picture like Caecilius's, for people read their own existential understanding into things and work with the usual evil fantasy. On this basis they polemicize against Christians, from it they take their justification for persecuting Christians, and suppose that by stamping them out they perform a useful service to humanity and a work pleasing to the divinity. The report sent to Asia Minor about the persecution of 177–78 in Lyons and Vienne, which we have already mentioned (see p. 50), sheds a great deal of light on this subject. The persecution began with a boycott of Christians in the shops, in the marketplace, in all public institutions, on the street. That then developed into a riot and into a tumultuous arrest of a number of Christians. Most of them remained steadfast at their hearings, although a lesser number denied their faith. At the hearings there were no accusations against the Christians aside from the *nomen ipsum,* the very fact of being a Christian. Subsequently, the slaves of these Christian confessors were arrested. When threatened with torture, the slaves said whatever they were asked and confirmed everything of which the Christians were suspected. Now the passion of the mob was inflamed. The statements of the slaves—so people believed—proved the truth of what previously had been circulated only as a terrible rumor. As a result, they not only felt it necessary to extirpate Christians but believed they would be performing a meritorious work and contributing to humanity's moral purification in ridding the earth of these criminals, who were not worthy to have the light of the sun shine upon them.

> Nor, concerning these things [Caecilius explains], would intelligent report speak of things so great and various, and requiring to be prefaced by an apology, unless truth were at the bottom of it. I hear that they adore the head of an ass [crucifixes with asses' heads ridiculing Christianity have been found] that basest of creatures, consecrated by I know not what silly persuasion,—a worthy and appropriate religion for such manners. Some say that they worship the *virilia* of their pontiff and priest, [the source for this charge is probably the kneeling posture in which penitents made confession before the priest] and adore the nature, as it were, of their common parent. I know not whether these things are false; certainly suspicion is applicable to secret and nocturnal rites; and he who explains their ceremonies by reference to a man punished by extreme suffering for his wickedness, and to the deadly wood of the cross, appropriates fitting altars for reprobate and wicked men, that they may worship what they deserve.
>
> Now the story about the initiation of young novices is as much to be detested as it is well known. An infant covered over with meal, that it may deceive the unwary, is placed before him who is to be stained with their

rites: this infant is slain by the young pupil, who has been urged on as if to harmless blows on the surface of the meal, with dark and secret wounds. Thirstily—O horror!—they lick up its blood; eagerly they divide its limbs. By this victim they are pledged together; with this consciousness of wickedness they are covenanted to mutual silence.

It is obvious where this story originates—here we have a pagan distortion of the Lord's Supper. Bread and wine are offered to Christians as the body and blood of Christ. From eating the body and drinking the blood it is only a short leap to this story, which incidentally remarkably resembles some accounts of Jewish ritual murders which Christians spread further. Indeed, Christians later said the same things about their opponents of which the pagans at that time accused them. In horror Augustine, for example, reports exactly the same story which we find here in Minucius Felix with only minor changes about the Montanists. The nocturnal agape feasts, the assemblies of the congregation to eat a common meal which Paul described, are also objects of the partially informed pagan polemics. Caecilius continues:

And of their banqueting it is well known all men speak of it everywhere. . . . On a solemn day they assemble at the feast, with all their children, sisters, mothers, people of every sex and of every age. There, after much feasting, when the fellowship has grown warm, and the fervour of incestuous lust has grown hot with drunkenness, a dog that has been tied to the chandelier is provoked, by throwing a small piece of offal beyond the length of a line by which he is bound, to rush and spring; and thus the conscious light being overturned and extinguished in the shameless darkness, the connections of abominable lust involve them in the uncertainty of fate. Although not all in fact, yet in consciousness all are alike incestuous, since by the desire of all of them everything is sought for which can happen in the act of each individual.

These were some of the rumors which were spread about Christians at that time, so it is really no wonder that people who took them at face value broke into passionate attacks against Christians.

Up until the third century, these persecutions, no matter how frequently they occurred, were always local in character, as we have already said (see p. 69). After this, they extended throughout the entire empire and encompassed all Christians. They increase in number, as well as in length and intensity, something that can be explained by the increasing spread of Christians. The more numerous Christians became, that much more and that much more frequently did the police authorities notice them, that much more and that much more frequently did government officials—especially since the imperial cult was gaining significance at the same time—feel themselves obligated, if not to root out, at least to limit this faith. The first wave of persecution which encompassed the entire empire occurred significantly at the time of the thousandth anniversary of the Roman Empire, at a time when it encouraged the national consciousness as well as the traditional ancestral faith. This is the Decian-Valerian persecution, which gets its name from the emperors Decian and Valerian. It broke out in 250 and extended—albeit with interruptions—until 260, when it officially ended. After this persecution came a forty-year epoch of tranquillity, although this quiet was not uninterrupted by persecutions of lesser extent in quite different places.

Under Diocletian the persecution then broke out anew in even greater measure and in even greater sharpness. At the beginning of the fourth century, paganism undertook a final attempt to exterminate Christianity. This attempt proved fruitless, however, even though it was the personal desire of the emperors, especially the Eastern emperors, which continued to promote it. It is questionable whether Christianity even in the third century could still have been subdued by force; at the beginning of the fourth century it certainly had become impossible. In the year 303 the persecution began. In the year 311, after it had lasted that long with almost no interruptions, Galerius, the most enthusiastic persecutor of Christians, had to accept the facts and issue the Edict of Toleration of Nicomedia, the text of which indicates the sort of reluctance with which he did so, perhaps being forced by someone else—Constantine, perhaps. In this Edict of Toleration of Nicomedia the emperor declared that Christians should enjoy freedom from persecution. They had abandoned the religion of their fathers and had created laws according to their own opinions. Therefore, the emperors had attempted through various decrees to bring them back to the old order. But these decrees were unable to break the opposition of the Christians; rather, the result of the emperors' actions had only been that Christians now honored neither the traditional gods nor their own god. Therefore the emperors had decided to allow Christians to be Christians again; they could hold their assemblies again and rebuild their destroyed churches. However, this could take place only under the provision that they undertake nothing against public order in the empire, praying rather for the empire's welfare and its emperors. These were the terms of the edict, which concluded by stating that regulations for carrying it out would follow in instructions to the authorities.

That is the Edict of Toleration of Nicomedia of 311, with which at least in principle the persecution ceased. The Edict of Toleration of Milan of

313, about which we generally speak exclusively when we talk about the stopping of the persecutions, did not have the same fundamental significance. To a certain extent it represented only the situation which in principle had already come to pass in 311 through Constantine and Licinius in the western territories. Yet it is noteworthy how much more clearly and decisively it speaks. And it is also noteworthy that it goes far beyond what was achieved in 311. It not only assured Christians that they would be free from punishment, but it also declared that the Christian church had equal rights with pagan cults. It also ordered the return of confiscated property, regardless of who had come into possession of it in the meantime. If it were no longer in government hands, but had gone to private individuals, these private owners would have to restore the Christian property to its original owners; the state would undertake to compensate them for it. The Christians of the West, therefore, were handled in a much friendlier manner in the Milan Edict of Toleration; yet we must add that for them this was not something so fundamentally new. In the West, apparently in contrast to the East, the persecution of Christians probably ended before 312, the date of Constantine's victory over Maxentius. Constantine's father, Constantius Chlorus, the ruler of Gaul, apparently had only incompletely carried out the edicts about persecution, and even Christian historians either expressly report or intimate that Maxentius, Constantine's opponent in Italy, allowed Christians in Rome a relatively free hand.

In the West the great persecution apparently came to an end even before the Edict of Nicomedia, while in the East it continued even after the year 311. The Edict of Toleration of Nicomedia was not something that came from the rulers' inner conviction, but was merely a concession grudgingly given. Thus both the ruler, as well as even more so the subordinate authorities all the way down to the city magistrates, used every opportunity to continue the persecution of Christians. This situation lasted in the East, even though with interruptions, until the year 324. There were years in which Christians enjoyed a respite, but then the persecution was always renewed until at the end even Licinius became a persecutor of the Christians—the same Licinius who together with Constantine had originally supported toleration and freedom for Christianity. Licinius had risen to mastery over the East in various stages, just as Constantine had over the West. The third and fourth centuries were an age of powerful rulers aspiring to all-encompassing, if not totalitarian power. Diocletian's attempt to use a tetrarchy, that is, a painstakingly balanced system of four rulers, to prevent the earlier power struggles had failed. Out of all the Augusti and Caesars—after violent battles of almost everyone against everyone else—at the end only Constantine and Licinius remained. We might say that the conflict between them happened inevitably, despite all the oaths they swore, despite all the marriage alliances they concluded to secure the peace. Accordingly, Licinius now attempted, in distinction to Constantine, to gain support among the pagans and win or increase their sympathy for him by persecuting Christians. But he failed, was conquered by Constantine in 324, and lost first the rule, then—according to the laws of the time—despite all the assurances given him, finally his life. Christianity had "triumphed," as we like to say. But how did this "victory" now appear in reality?

5. THE "VICTORY" OF CHRISTIANITY

When the persecutions actually came to an end (in 312 in the West and in 324 in the East), Constantine did not find—as might have been supposed after the preceding persecutions—a broken or despairing church. It is true that the persecutions had taken their toll. We should have no illusions about the percentage of those who did not stand firm under persecution. The great persecutions, especially in the large cities, eliminated a multitude of Christians. This reduction extended also to the ranks of the clergy, even the bishops, for the provisions which had applied to theologians were especially severe. As soon as someone who held a church office handed over the Bible manuscripts from his church or his diocese to the police or the authorities, the Christians considered him just as much an apostate from Christianity as if he had sacrificed to the pagan gods. Not infrequently were Bible manuscripts surrendered, for the initial target of the pagan attack was always the church building and the ministers, whose names and addresses the police obviously knew well. Characteristically, the great persecution of 303 began in the capital of Nicomedia when a company of soldiers was sent to destroy the great church of the Christians opposite the palace; they quickly razed the church to the ground and at the same time burned the manuscripts they found there.

But the persecutions were not able to break the power of the church; instead, the Christian church was purified by the persecution of Diocletian and his successors and emerged from it with new strengths because the persecution rid it of those who were weak and indecisive. We see the church after 312 or 324 confronting the emperor with self-confidence.

We need think only of the appearance of the Donatists in North Africa (see p. 167); not only did they seek recognition from the emperor, they demanded it. When he did not fulfill their wishes, they were not intimidated, but continued to repeat their demands, even though one synod after another rejected them as unjustified. They also attempted, when the emperor refused to agree with them, to influence his decisions in their favor by inflaming the passions of the people. When that also did not help and the emperor finally sent troops, a revolt broke out in Africa.

That is the one aspect. The church self-confidently confronted the emperor. But it also formed an alliance with the emperor—with the state—which grew stronger from decade to decade. There are reasons for this which go back to the beginnings of Christianity. In the first three centuries there existed for Christians not only the necessity of maintaining loyalty to the state but also the necessity of agreeing with the state. Obviously Christians could not affirm the form which paganism gave to the state and the emperor who demanded divine veneration of his person—in the final analysis, the state's own self-understanding. But nevertheless they regarded this pagan state as their own. They always prayed for the emperor and for the state, even when emperor and state persecuted them. The positive statements of the New Testament about the state must be seen against the background of persecution by this state; thereby they gain a special character and special importance. This is true not only for Romans 13, where Christians are exhorted to obey the higher powers (to use this old expression)—the governing authority in all its manifestations down to the very last police officer, down to the very last civil servant; it is also true for the other writings of the New Testament, of which the most detailed is the First Epistle of Peter. We read in 1 Pet. 2:13–17:

> Be subject for the Lord's sake to every human institution, whether it be to the emperor as supreme, or to governors as sent by him to punish those who do wrong and to praise those who do right. For it is God's will that by doing right you should put to silence the ignorance of foolish men. Live as free men, yet without using your freedom as a pretext for evil; but live as servants of God. Honor all men. Love the brotherhood. Fear God. Honor the emperor.

This attitude toward the state exhibited in the New Testament continued in the years following. We find a long prayer for the emperor and the state in the First Letter of Clement (that is, about 95), although this letter was written immediately after a bloody persecution or even during a bloody persecution of the church in Rome. Again and again Christians attempt to achieve a positive relationship with the state, but again and again the state fiercely repulses them. This explains how Christians could have a high regard for the emperors who did not persecute Christianity, and how they could interpret all these emperors' statements in some positive fashion, carefully collect and preserve them, and hold them in high esteem—sometimes even viewing these emperors as secret Christians. If the victorious Constantine had maintained even a neutral attitude toward Christianity, that would have been sufficient for Christians to see him in a new light and assure for him the honor, even the love of these Christians. But Constantine did a great deal more than this. At the very least (to express ourselves very cautiously), he awakened among the Christians the impression not only that he tolerated the new faith but that he was prepared to encourage it. Thus he received the overflowing adoration of Christians. The dam was broken; the pent-up wave of loyalty flowed out over the empire and the church of the fourth century. Only when we presuppose this mind set can we understand some of the things that happened in theological and ecclesiastical affairs at that time; we shall speak about them later (see pp. 192–94). It is very easy, as people always do, to measure dogmatic orthodoxy by what the bishops in particular and the church in general did, and then severely criticize both. Indeed, it is almost the fashion in theology today to condemn Bishop Eusebius of Caesarea and others. But this can be done only if we ignore the historical circumstances and are prepared to dispense with a real understanding of the past which could justify such a judgment.

The events under Constantine signified a new beginning. Constantine postponed his confession of Christianity until he was on his deathbed; not until he was dying—on May 22, 337—was he baptized. We have to admit that during his entire lifetime he did not visibly burn his bridges to paganism behind him. With Constantine's sons the situation changes. Although Constantius, for example, also was not baptized until he was on his deathbed, Constantine's sons still took an active interest from the very beginning in the internal affairs of the church. But what is here important is that they proceeded just as actively against paganism. Constantine had refrained from doing that; with his sons the turning away from paganism became clearer virtually from year to year. These emperors not only wanted to be Christians themselves but also wanted to force paganism out of its previous position. In both of these intentions they enjoyed support among what was now an extensive Christian populace.

For a time it appeared as if this development might be reversed. That took place under Julian, who assumed the rule of the empire in the year 361. As soon as he came from Gaul to take the field against Constantius, it became clear that Julian would attempt to reverse the religious politics of the last fifty years, especially the last twenty-four years since Constantine's death. Everywhere along Julian's way to the East closed temples were opened, destroyed temples were rebuilt, and the building of new temples begun. The emperor demonstrated before the eyes of all that he did not regard his traditional office as *pontifex maximus*—the supreme priest (which the Christian emperors before him had not given up either)—as an empty formality, but as a genuine obligation. But this lasted only for a few years, and in 363 Julian fell in battle against the Persians. This pagan restoration was only a brief episode. Even if Julian had reigned longer, if he had had more time for his attempt to turn back Christianity and renew paganism's dominance, he would not have been able to reverse the development which had taken place since Constantine. There is no doubt of this. For Julian, paganism was a living force, and he also enjoyed the enthusiastic support of the highest educated class. But the emperor still had great difficulties in finding a sufficient number of priests for the newly opened temples, especially a priesthood which satisfied his moral and religious demands. He had to devote a great deal of effort to get the available pagan priests to measure up at least partially to these demands. And, above all else, the masses of the populace were not interested in Julian's attempt at restoration. They had no understanding for the revival of the pagan cults, even in places where the people had not yet adopted the Christian confession; in fact, there they passively and sometimes very actively dragged their heels. Julian's attempt at restoration came too late; his intention of reversing the developments of centuries was in vain. The laboriously revived paganism was no longer a match for a Christianity which in the meantime had become aware of its strength and position.

What were the reasons that led Julian to attempt a pagan restoration? How could paganism have become a vital force for Julian? He was baptized as a Christian, he was raised as a Christian, he had occupied the office of a lector in the church. There are no reasons to assume that this was only hypocrisy. Christianity apparently fell apart for Julian when he realized the contradiction between the words of Constantine's sons and their actions. These emperors, who considered themselves the champions of Christianity, had murdered Julian's entire family after Constantine's death in order to secure their own succession to the throne. Julian escaped this bloodbath only because Christian priests hid him. At that time he was only a child. Thus it took some time until he clearly understood who was guilty of this murder and that the emperors themselves had ordered this assassination, and that it was not simply a crime committed by soldiers, as the official account stated. When that became clear to him, Julian's Christianity crumbled

In addition, there was the fact that in his education he had had a deep encounter with Greek thought. At that time, every Christian in his normal studies—as we have stated (see p. 28)—was led through pagan literature and the writings of the old philosophers and poets. Countless others read and interpreted these pagan writers during their studies, just as Julian had done, but for them the myths and the Greek religiosity they contained was only something external. Julian was inwardly moved by them. Julian had himself been initiated into the mystery religions (note that this was in the first half of the fourth century, decades after the Edicts of Toleration of Nicomedia and Milan)—first in the cult of Mithras, then in the Eleusinian mysteries, and then in the cult of Cybele, just as we previously mentioned about adherents of the mystery religions (see pp. 11–12). The piety of the mystery religions affected him ever more deeply. He then combined their teachings and views with contemporary philosophical wisdom, that is, with Neoplatonism. To this he added the cult of the sun. With these assumptions Julian could then reinterpret the old gods and the old mythology and make it his own. Thus Julian—and this is why we speak about him here—is to a certain extent a confirmation of what we previously said (see pp. 21–22) about the amalgamation of the varied components of the religiosity of late antiquity and pagan faith of the early centuries into a new entity. All of this really lived in Julian; for him it was the source of strength from which he drank. But in the middle of the fourth century there were only very few people like him. This is why the pagan restoration collapsed immediately after Julian's death. The rulers following him were Christians again, and they immediately restored Christianity to its old position. They first proceed cautiously against paganism, but already under Julian's successor Valens (364–78), the Neoplatonists—Julian's compatriots—were energetically being persecuted in the East. This took place for the same reasons people earlier persecuted Christians. The Christian state considered these Neoplatonists hidden and secret, and therefore a group dangerous to the empire, as always a reason for persecuting them with all means possible.

In the year 380 the Edict of Theodosius (379–95) was issued for the entire empire over the names of all the emperors. It stated:

> It is our desire that all the various nations which are subject to our clemency and moderation, should continue in the profession of that religion which was delivered to the Romans by the divine Apostle Peter, as it hath been preserved by faithful tradition; and which is now professed by the Pontiff Damasus and by Peter, Bishop of Alexandria, a man of apostolic holiness. According to the apostolic teaching and the doctrine of the gospel, let us believe the one deity of the Father, the Son, and the Holy Spirit, in equal majesty and in a holy Trinity. We authorize the followers of this law to assume the title of Catholic Christians; but as for the others, since, in our judgment, they are foolish madmen, we decree that they shall be branded with the ignominious name of heretics, and shall not presume to give to their conventicles the name of churches. They will suffer in the first place the chastisement of the divine condemnation, and in the second the punishment which our authority, in accordance with the will of heaven, shall decide to inflict.

In this edict of 380, paganism was excluded as a matter of course, and everyone was required under penalty of law to adhere to the Christian faith—and not just the Christian faith in general, but to all of its details. It had to accord with the faith of Rome and Alexandria and must possess definite dogmatic contents (the dogmatic formulas used here were ones which accorded with the current phase of the Arian controversy, then coming to an end). Other Christian groups and opposing churches—what the edict called heretics—were threatened with persecution by the state.

The state church has come, and it encompasses everyone in the Roman Empire. This is the way it looks when we read this law, and this is also the way it is usually interpreted. But, in my opinion, we must be careful not to read too much into this edict of 380. It is quite obvious that it did not have the validity which it claimed, since we see that paganism continued to exist, something that according to the text of the law was really impossible. This law was no different than many others before it. For there had already been a whole series of laws issued against paganism. Apparently Constantius in 341 had already forbidden all pagan sacrifices under penalty of death. Again and again temples were destroyed or converted to secular uses. When this happened, the Christians or the civil authorities occasionally displayed their malice when, for example, a pagan temple was converted into a house of prostitution.

Christianity took the same revenge on paganism that paganism had earlier taken on it. Nevertheless, the sacrifices still continued. All the edicts only seemed to limit the existence of paganism, and did not seriously threaten it. The severe punishments which threatened everyone who persevered in the pagan faith were apparently never employed, or only in exceptional cases—at least not everywhere and not in every case. Apparently it was impossible because the number of pagans concerned was too great for people to proceed against them as they always threatened—as in their hearts they certainly would have liked to do. The edicts against paganism up until 380 and shortly thereafter did not describe the actual reality; they only expressed wishes.

When we look at the face of things, it appears that the events of the earlier centuries are repeated, only with the participants reversed. Earlier, Christianity was one of the forbidden groups, but this prohibition had no real effect. Persecution could only limit the expansion of Christianity and hinder its progress, but not stop it. Now they continually proscribed paganism, but the effect of these prohibitions was very limited; the measures which they took against the temples did reduce their number, but were not sufficient to abolish the temples and stamp out belief in the pagan gods. It thus appears that this development is proceeding like the earlier one. But if we look more closely, it becomes clear that things are now different than they were during the persecution of Christianity in the previous centuries. Paganism at that time did not possess the inner power which the Christian church had had in the first three centuries, which would have enabled it, despite persecution by the state and its authorities, to maintain its size—even, in spite of all oppression, to continue to expand. Paganism did remain alive, but in the course of the fourth century its power waned, so that after the turn of the fifth century there was no longer any doubt that paganism was finally and irrevocably heading for destruction.

In the last twenty years of the fourth century some decisive things happened. After the basic declaration in the edict of 380, Theodosius issued a new edict in 381, the text of which was closely related to that of the earlier one. Sacrifices were forbidden and only temples with artistically valuable decorations could remain open; this the edict declared, just like the earlier one had done. This law might have been fated to remain just as ineffective as the emperor's earlier orders saying almost the same thing, had there not been in the East a high Christian official who took it upon himself to put it into effect. This is similar to what took place at earlier times, even at the beginning of the fourth century, when pagan officials attempted to gain popularity with the people and at the same time special notice from their superiors by being especially zealous in persecuting Christianity. On his own initiative this Christian began to close temples, without being specifically commanded to do so by the imperial authorities. He was covered by the edict and officially was doing only what the emperor had ordered, but in fact he went far beyond what the emperor believed could be accomplished by this edict. And this official achieved results. The Christian clergy applauded his action, just as earlier the pagan groups in the populace had greeted the measures against the Christians. The initiative of this official soon slackened, but bishops and monks now continued his measures on their own.

As long as the governor was behind it, the pagans acquiesced. When the Christians took such action themselves, the pagans resisted. In Alexandria, the pagan populace, their feelings cut to the quick, rose up against their oppressors. The outbreak of resistance did not lead the Christians to discontinue their measures against the religious monuments of the pagans, but was rather countered in 391 by an extensive Christian reprisal against the pagan resistance. The Christians felt themselves challenged and a popular tumult resulted in which the populace, incited by bishops, monks, and priests, destroyed all the temples and images of the gods in the city, above all the huge temple of Serapis in Alexandria and the monumental statue of Serapis itself. The destruction of this statue of Serapis had extraordinary consequences, just as did Boniface's felling the Oak of Thor in the Middle Ages. (The Oak of Thor was the image of god. Anyone who chopped down this oak, it was believed, would be immediately punished by the deity with death. When Boniface, however, did not die, the Germanic people had one of the foundations of their faith destroyed and they abandoned the old faith.) The destruction of the statue of Serapis had the same significance in the consciousness of paganism in the East in the fourth century. In the amalgamation of various conceptions of the gods, Serapis had achieved a central position. He was considered the preserver of the world and his statue in Alexandria was a representation of this function. At that time people throughout the East believed that the destruction of Serapis's statue would be accompanied by the immediate destruction of the world. When the Christians in Alexandria actually did destroy it during the riot and the anticipated end of the world did not occur, this was a severe blow to paganism's inner confidence in the East.

Thus Theodosius in 391–92 could issue new laws, which prohibited pagan sacrifices and provided the severest penalties for even entering a temple. These laws were not just on paper but were actually enforced with ever-increasing severity. It is clear: the old age is ending, the first period of Christianity is coming to its conclusion. Starting in a corner of Palestine, Christianity had spread throughout the entire Roman Empire, despite all the attempts to stop it. In so doing it surpassed and conquered all the rival religions, one after another, until the number of Christianity's adherents outnumbered those of all other cults and philosophical schools. This took place relatively early. Even when Christianity in a province may have won over only twenty-five percent of the populace, it was often the strongest religion in that province, for the substantial majority of non-Christians were divided into numerous cults and beliefs. It is obvious from the way in which Christianity increased that among its members were also some who did not live up to the demands of the new faith. There can be no doubt that the moral level of Christianity dropped when its numbers increased. As early as the third century, the demands, which even in the second century unquestionably applied to individual Christians, were clearly reduced. But the Christian persecutions, which we are accustomed to seeing as something only negative, still had a very positive result for the church. They prevented the number of lax and unsatisfactory Christians from becoming too large. These were the first Christians to weaken during the persecution and deny their faith. Even at the beginning of the fourth century, Christians were still filled with vital faith and were totally prepared to sacrifice themselves for this faith.

At the beginning of the fourth century, the church, after great sacrifices, achieved equality with the other cults and religions of the time. Now, at the end of the fourth and beginning of the fifth centuries, we see Christianity about to displace all other forms of religion and to claim dominance over the souls of all people. This does not mean claiming dominance over the empire. Not until the next period of church history—the Middle Ages—is the claim of dominance over the secular sphere raised. For a long time this was nothing more than a mere claim; not until well along into the Middle Ages—in the second period—was dominance over the secular sphere more or less completely realized.

Thus we come to the end of this chapter, which has dealt with the external history of Christianity from the beginnings up until about the year 400. The only thing still necessary is just a comment about the frequently used term "Constantinian Age," which is either ending or is already at an end. What is meant by this very common expression is that *today* the age of the state church is at an end or is coming to an end. That is an indisputable fact; we need say nothing about it. But when this term is used in connection with the Constantinian age, it is wrong. The Constantinian age was far removed from a Christian state church. Under Constantine the Christian church can in no way be given this label. Even under Constantine's sons it was only on its way to becoming a state church, and still under Theodosius (that is, at the conclusion of the fourth century), this state church was mostly a theory. It was proclaimed, indeed repeatedly proclaimed—there is no doubt about that—but it had not yet proceeded so far as to include all the inhabitants of the empire. Under Constantine the church had achieved nothing more than freedom from persecution, equality with the other cults in the empire, and also the goodwill and powerful encouragement of the ruler. Perhaps Constantine could have done more—we could even say that Constantine certainly would have liked to do more—but consideration for the pagan portion of the populace caused him to hold back. If he had not done that, the support for his rule over the empire, which he had achieved only after many struggles, would have been shaken. We must keep this in mind if we want to have a correct understanding of the fourth century and the early history of Christianity.

III

The Internal History of
Early Christianity

An account of ancient church history which attempts to present in one sweep the development from the beginnings until the end of the fourth century must first address itself to the external development—as we have done here—but then must immediately amplify it by considering the internal development of Christianity during this period, and to a certain extent must fill it out from within. It is obvious that this can be done only with broad strokes, so that some things can be mentioned only incidentally or merely hinted at; but we shall include everything in order to develop a picture which is not only understandable and one that we hope will also be memorable, but also one that is complete. These are our premises.

1. WANING OF EXPECTATIONS OF THE END

If we attempt to summarize the internal development of Christianity in the early centuries, we discover a decisive turning point in the second half of the second century. The second century is not only a watershed, but here there is also something decisive for the development of the Christian church. In a manner of speaking, what comes before the end of the second century can be called the "prehistoric" age of Christianity. Up until the middle of the second century, and even later, Christians did not live in and for the present, but they lived in and for the future; and this was in such a way that the future flowed into the present, that future and present became one—a future which obviously stood under the sign of the Lord's presence. It was the confident expectation of the first generations that the end of the world was not only near, but that it had really already come. It was the definite conviction not only of Paul, but of all Christians of that time, that they themselves would experience the return of the Lord. In 1 Thessalonians 4, we see that the church was already upset about the fact that some Christians had died before the last day came, but Paul's conviction that those still alive will experience his return is not shaken. When the trumpet of the Lord sounds, so 1 Thess. 4:16–18 states, those who have already died, as well as those who are still alive, "shall be caught up together . . . in the clouds to meet the Lord in the air," and thus be with the Lord forever. Also, the Apocalypse of John, written about the year 96, still contains this eschatological expectation in an unchanged and unbroken form. To a certain extent, the words of Rev. 22:12 can be taken as the title of the Apocalypse: "Behold, I am coming soon, bringing my recompense." In the original text, the Greek work used is $\tau\alpha\chi\acute{\upsilon}$, and this does not mean "soon," in the sense of "sometime," but rather "now," "immediately." Therefore, we must understand Rev. 22:12 in this way: "I am coming now, bringing my recompense." The concluding word of Rev. 22:20 is: "He who testifies to these things says, 'Surely I am coming soon.' " Here we again find the word $\tau\alpha\chi\acute{\upsilon}$, so this means: I am coming quickly, immediately. This is followed by the prayer: "Amen. Come, Lord Jesus!" These words are a summary of the contents of Revelation, which uses continually new images to paint the coming of the Lord. The Apocalypse expresses the fervent waiting for the end within the circles in which the writer lived—not an expectation that will happen at some unknown point X in time (just to repeat this), but one in the immediate present. Naturally, people can retort that this fervor has something of the character of a pledge about it and desires to utilize all its power to bring about something that it secretly sees endangered by the possibility of delay. But no one will be able to deny that the writer of Revelation— and its readers—are utterly devoted to the coming Lord.

If we browse through the writings of that period, we observe that this expectation of the end continued. Today New Testament scholarship widely assumes that the expectation of the Parousia comes to an end with the Gospel of Luke, but I believe this is not only a one-sided interpretation of Luke's Gospel, but also does not give sufficient attention to the development in the time after Luke's Gospel. It is one of the decided weaknesses of New Testament scholarship in general that it limits itself to the twenty-seven books of the New Testament and does not consider contemporary literature—the Apostolic Fathers and the New Testament Apocrypha. If it were to do this, some of its results would look different. It is true that at that time there was already something which people call "present eschatology": in and with Christ judgment has come, in and with the decision for or against him occurs

God's acceptance or rejection of a person—now, not first in the future. The Gospel of John presents this present eschatology impressively enough. But we see that the "future eschatology" (that is, the traditional expectation of the end) has not been abandoned in the fact that, even in this comprehensive present-oriented conception of John's Gospel, the expectation of the future resurrection intrudes several times. A whole series of passages in John's Gospel expresses a future expectation of the end, something which simply cannot be harmonized with his fundamental conception of present eschatology. This is proof that the piety of the church was so strong at that time that in various places it modified the eschatological world view of John, which was so cogent in itself. If we carefully observe the first evangelists, we shall see that Luke has indeed developed the eschatological concepts further, but even he does not alter those statements of Mark which can be explained only on the basis of a vital expectation of the Parousia. Such a theory of a general cessation of the expectation of the Parousia around the year 80 will immediately appear unacceptable to historians who study the second century, for they will see how preaching about the imminent end of the world in the second half of the second century can be found not only in all of Asia Minor, but has adherents everywhere throughout the church, although the official church forcefully opposed Montanism which considered itself the proclaimer of the expectation of the imminent Parousia. The phenomenon of Montanism is explicable only if we assume that belief in an imminent end of the world and an imminent return of the Lord was still extraordinarily strong in the church. Perhaps the fire at that time did not burn as brightly as before, perhaps ashes were already covering it, but the first breath of wind was sufficient to fan the embers into flame anew. In fact, we also find in the writings of the first half of the second century sufficient evidence to indicate that the expectation of the Parousia was by no means at an end then. In any case, it persisted in the church, even among theologians. People in no way followed John's line everywhere, but the expectation of the Parousia was proclaimed in a way which appeared quite similar to that of the first three evangelists. At the end of the *Didache* ("The teaching of the twelve apostles"), from the time shortly after 100, there is, for example, an apocalyptic chapter which corresponds completely in its outline to the Synoptic apocalypse in Mark 13 (and the parallel chapters in the other Synoptic Gospels); here we can only very cautiously say that it uses the same words, but that its content is imperceptibly in the process of change. Even chapter 16 of the *Didache* can be correctly understood only if we assume that the expectation of the Parousia was a living reality. It is quite similar to the Epistle of Barnabas, which was written a little later than the *Didache,* where we read: "The day is near in which everything will perish together with the evil. The Lord and his recompense are near."

However, another development is taking place at the same time. We read in 2 Peter, for example, about doubters in the congregation who question the promise of the Lord's return in view of the fact that they claim that everything has remained the same since the beginning of the world. It is characteristic enough that doubters should appear, although their doubt is probably not directed toward the Parousia itself, but toward the expectation that it is soon to occur. More important than this report about the doubters, which in 2 Pet. 3:3 should be understood as an indication of the last days, is the answer 2 Peter gives. Here we read in 3:10: "But the day of the Lord will come like a thief." This is a word we meet in the Gospels, where it is used to indicate the suddenness and unexpectedness of this return. In 2 Peter it is used to emphasize the impossibility of setting a time for the event. Indeed, it says that Christians can hasten the coming of that day of the Lord by leading a life of holiness and godliness (3:11, 12). The writer of 2 Peter also declares that God is not shortening his promises, and he declares it emphatically in 3:9. But when he adds that with the Lord one day is as a thousand years, and a thousand years as one day (3:8), and further says that the Parousia has not yet occurred because of God's forbearance with Christians so that none should perish but all reach repentance (3:9), then it becomes clear that, to the author of 2 Peter and to the circles which he addressed, the imminent expectation of the end is not only in the process of disappearing, but has already virtually vanished. We cannot say for sure when 2 Peter was written, although it was probably A.D. 130–40. All exegetes—Protestant as well as Catholic—are unanimous in agreeing that 2 Peter is the last writing of the New Testament. In the Second Letter of Clement, written about 150, this is even clearer. In 2 Clement we find a quotation from an unknown work which also speaks about doubters, saying: "We already heard this a long time ago at the time of our fathers; but we have waited from day to day and have seen nothing of it." This writing, which 2 Clement cites, is certainly a great deal older than 150, for we find almost the same quotation in 1 Clement, written about 95. It is questionable if the expressions of this earlier writing, which was probably a Jewish work, originally referred to the coming of the Messiah (this would not be the only time the Apostolic Fathers took a quotation out of its context and used it for a purpose completely different from its original one). At any rate, in both 1 Clement and 2 Clement, the quotation unmistakably refers to the return of the Lord. The doubters are repudiated by the image of a vine. Even the vine, so 2 Clement says, must endure several stages of development before producing ripe grapes. Second Clement then follows the quotation with this warning: "So we shall not doubt, but persevere in hope; we will await the kingdom of God at all times, for we do not know the time of God's appearing." When we compare this statement of 2 Clement with the one 1 Clement used following the same quotation more than fifty years earlier: "Truly, quickly and suddenly his decree will be fulfilled to which also the Scripture bears witness: 'He will come quickly and not delay,' " it becomes clear that doubt about the imminent occurrence of the Parousia has increased and that the expectation of the imminent end is declining. Again and again the old expressions echo. They echo apparently almost unchanged, but doubt about the imminence of the Lord's return is increasingly mixed with them until around the middle of the second century when the Shepherd of Hermas thinks he has found a solution and expresses it with great thoroughness and emphasis: the Parousia—the Lord's return—has been postponed for the sake of Christians themselves. If the Lord were to come today, he would find Christians spotted by sin. After receiving grace and becoming pure in baptism, they have not kept themselves pure but have been entrapped by this world and have been soiled by it. In this way the construction of the tower has been interrupted—the church is symbolized by the image of building a tower, when it is completed, the last day will arrive. All the stones which are not blameless are removed from this tower, are laid aside, and subjected to a process of purification, that is, Christians are offered the possibility of a second repentance. By this repentance they can free themselves from their stains and can be remade into blameless stones for building the church, or created anew. The building of the tower has not been stopped; it is only temporarily suspended. Therefore—and this is the warning of the Shepherd of Hermas, on account of which the entire work was really written—do good works for your purification, for if you delay too long, the construction of the tower may be finished and you will not be included as stones built into it.

The thought of a postponement of the Parousia appears all through 2 Clement, just as it does all through 2 Peter, but here it is expressly mentioned for the first time. Thus, about the middle of the second century, a decisive turning point occurs—one which can be compared in significance to all other great turning points, including the Reformation.

Obviously, we cannot fix this turning point precisely at the year 150, for it took a while until the thought caught hold everywhere. But a development does begin with the Shepherd of Hermas which could not be stopped—a development at the end of which we stand today. As soon as the thought of a postponement of the Parousia was uttered once—and indeed not only incidentally, but thoroughly presented in an entire writing—it developed its own life and power. At first, people looked at it as only a brief postponement, as the Shepherd of Hermas clearly expresses. But soon, as the end of the world did not occur, it was conceived of as a longer and longer period, until finally—this is today's situation—nothing but the thought of a postponement exists in people's consciousness. Hardly any longer is there the thought of the possibility of an imminent Parousia. Today we live with the presumption—I would almost say *from* the presumption—that this world is going to continue; it dominates our consciousness. Practically, we no longer speak about a postponement, but only seldom does the idea of the end of the world and the Lord's return for judgment even occur to us; rather, it is pushed aside as annoying and disturbing—in contrast to the times when faith was alive. It is very characteristic that in ages when the church flourishes, the expectation of the end revives—we think of Luther; we think of Pietism. If we judge our present time by its expectation of the future, our judgment can only be a very negative one.

For the early age, the thought of the postponement of the Parousia had a decisive significance. As long as the expectation of an imminent end reigned supreme, or was only slightly limited—as we see in the first and the beginning of the second centuries—everything which happens in the church and everything which the church does has only a more or less preliminary significance. Only when the imminent expectation of the Parousia diminishes, only when life is no longer lived in constant reference to the Last Day and no longer takes its direction from the Last Day, was an organization of the church as an institution even possible or necessary. This took place in the second half of the second century. This development ends with the formation of the early Catholic church, which to a certain extent provides the prototype for the church's later nature. This early Catholic church already possesses all the characteristics of a great church body, at least in preliminary form. All churches today go back directly to it. Here the number and extent of holy documents were definitely limited, at least in principle; here not only was the concept of the ministry formed, but also the office and its functions were firmly defined; here the confession of faith was fixed, and guarantees for the purity of the transmission of doctrine were sought and found.

2. THE ORGANIZATION OF
THE EARLY CATHOLIC CHURCH

The Presuppositions

The organization of the early Catholic church was accelerated by the crises which Christianity underwent at that time. It is certainly not correct to view these crises as the real causes for the formation of the early Catholic church. Rather, it was through this decline in eschatological concern that the prerequisite first existed for the entire development we observe in the second century, a development which made it necessary for the church, when confronted with internal crises, to continue to shape into a confession of faith the elements which it had possessed from the outset, to determine the extent of the sacred documents, and to organize the ministerial office and the apostolic tradition. All of these things took definite shape only in the middle of the second century (after the time when the expectation of an imminent end of the world ceased), but their embryonic beginnings go back to earliest times. When some New Testament scholars speak about "early Catholicism in the New Testament," they are definitely saying something that is correct—they mean these very early beginnings. But in doing so, they also run the danger of a misunderstanding, because what they frequently lack is a trustworthy presentation of how the early Catholic church really existed at the close of the second century. We can really speak about early Catholicism only after it is present in its well-marked and well-developed form, and we dare not project conceptions back into the early age which did not take shape until 120 years later.

There is no doubt that the beginnings exist at that time, for in 1 Clement we already find the concepts of the apostolic tradition: here we read that the Lord conveyed leadership in the church to the apostles, and they passed it on to the other clergy. But these beginnings would never have led to the so-called early Catholic church, if the decline in eschatological concern (see pp. 87–88) had not happened on one hand, and if the crises of the second century had not intervened on the other. When the church wanted to overcome the attacks from outside and the threatened destruction from within which we observe in the second century, it had to take the embryonic beginnings of the first century and develop the canon, develop the confession of faith, develop the ministerial office, and develop the conception of the apostolic tradition into their full-blown forms. Even in the first century, an early form of Gnosticism threatened to suck Christianity into the general process of religious amalgamation going on at that time. Colossians and Ephesians already struggle against this. But at that time Gnosticism's influence on Christianity was only in the earliest stages. Not until the second century did Gnosticism develop its first great systems (chiefly Basilides and Valentinus), and this Gnosticism attacked Christianity in full measure, so that here for the first time there was a real danger that Gnosticism might inwardly destroy Christianity. Gnosticism was also not the only movement with which the second century had to struggle. In addition to it there was Marcion, who attracted great numbers of people to an opposing church after he had failed in his attempt to establish his teachings in the church itself. In addition to these two, we find Montanism which originated in Asia Minor but accumulated numerous adherents, not just in its land of origin, but in Africa as well where it was even in a position to attract such a significant man as Tertullian among its followers.

At first, the Christian church was at a loss in confronting these movements. There can be no doubt about this. Only slowly did it learn how to defend itself. Its helplessness can be explained by the fact that the teachings and demands of these opposing churches were different from those of the church only in their final effect, not in their o gin, and very frequently not even in their form. For example, Montanus and the women associated with him appeared as prophets. The church was still acquainted with prophets in the second century; in principle, the claim of prophecy was still recognized at that time. Montanism declared that the message of Montanus and that of the women around him was that of the Paraclete, which Luther translates "Comforter," and the Revised Standard Version calls "Counselor." The Paraclete was promised in John's Gospel, and, according to John 14, would lead Christianity into perfect knowledge. What the Montanists essentially proclaimed was a message about the imminent end of the world. At that time Christianity also taught this concept. Therefore, Montanism appeared to be proclaiming and demanding the same thing as did the larger church. Of course, there were certain differences; for example, it was taught that the heavenly Jerusalem would descend as written in the Apocalypse, but that it would not take place in Jerusalem itself, but in Asia Minor. When Montanism demanded that Christians should prepare themselves for the imminent end of the world by undertaking special ascetic practices, that was completely in accord with ancient Christianity and must have sounded not only genuine but also exemplary to all Christians. Marcion built on the basis of the holy documents then in existence—on the Gospels. It is true that he limited their number to only one, Luke's Gospel, and also abbreviated it. But beside this Gospel were the epistles of Paul, which enjoyed high authority in all Pauline churches, and even beyond them. It is true that Marcion also abbreviated and revised these epistles of Paul, but since Luke's Gospel and the Pauline letters formed the true basis of the faith for him, the church had a great deal of difficulty polemicizing against this. Things looked different when Marcion deduced from these documents that the Old Testament God was really not the father of Jesus Christ, but the creator of this world, and that the creator of the world was sharply opposed to the highest God of love who had sent Jesus; therefore, the Old Testament should be condemned along with the God it proclaimed. Then it became easier for the church to polemicize against Marcion.

Finally, Gnosticism appeared with a variety of gospels and acts of apostles, which at least superficially were parallel to those transmitted by the church. At that time the church was acquainted not only with the four Gospels which later were incorporated in the canon, but in addition was familiar with and recognized—at least at first—a great deal of other gospels, the so-called apocryphal gospels. Thus, some Christians read the Gnostic gospels in good faith as a genuine gospel. In these Gnostic gospels, Jesus appears as the proclaimer of a new doctrine which leads to a higher knowledge, in comparison to which the gospel ordinarily taught in the church appeared to be only a preliminary step. God and world, flesh and spirit are to be sharply distinguished; the only thing valuable in humankind is the divine spark which originally shared in the divinity. With a very complicated cosmogony (see p. 37), Gnosticism attempted to explain how this portion of divinity became part of humankind; Jesus actually came to redeem only this portion of God in humankind, not humankind as such. He showed the divine spark the way to ascend to its origin. It was at this point that the church was first able to counterattack, as well as on the point of repudiating the Old Testament and its God (on which Gnosticism agreed with Marcion).

"Holy Scripture" in the Second Century

Not until the consequences appeared did it generally become obvious to Christians of that time that a foreign spirit was at work in these move-. ments of the second century. At first glance they all appeared genuine

95

and seemed to be only different forms of the same Christianity, which in the second century still had great varieties of expression. Thus, the church and Christians in the second century needed more definite and secure ways to evaluate the movements. Christians would have to be able to distinguish Christianity clearly and easily from Gnosticism, Marcionism, Montanism, and other groups which always emphatically claimed to present the true doctrine. The first thing that unmistakably had to be determined was what was—and what was not—revealed Holy Scripture. Gnosticism and Montanism offered something clearly positive in comparison to what the church at that time considered Holy Scripture: either the oracles of Montanus and the prophetesses and their own scriptures, or the Gnostic gospels and acts of apostles. Marcion, on the contrary, offered something negative that was just as clear: he eliminated three Gospels; he eliminated important statements of Luke and large parts of Paul's epistles. Thus it was essential to define the New Testament canon, to determine what did and did not belong to it, or at least to establish definite criteria about what could be accepted in the New Testament canon. In no way had this New Testament canon achieved the form at the end of the second century which we know; this did not come about until the fourth century. Much of what now is contained in the New Testament was still strongly disputed in the second century.

From the very beginning there was no doubt that the Old Testament had to be preserved. The Old Testament was not only the Holy Scripture of Jesus and the apostles, but also of the same Paul whom Marcion continually cited against the Old Testament. Quite simply, the Old Testament was *the* holy document of the time. Even until the third generation, whenever Christians were asked for written documents of their faith, without exception they unambiguously pointed first to the Old Testament. Until the middle of the second century—we shall soon speak about this (see pp. 97–98)—proof for the truth of the Christian faith was found in the Old, not in the New Testament. To put it bluntly, for the early Christians the Old Testament occupied the place the New Testament does for us. Therefore, we not infrequently find an interpretation of the Old Testament which we cannot follow, as well as ways of thinking which appear completely foreign to us. Christianity of the early second century just cannot be equated that easily with present-day Christianity; it cannot be measured with the same dogmatic criteria which we use today; it is an entity in itself and demands and deserves to be judged with its own criteria—just as all the early centuries do. We can ignore this, as has often been done, but then we must forgo an understanding of the past and any judgment about it. It is certainly easy to criticize the theology of that time, as we shall soon see with the example of 1 Clement, but we must not forget that 1 Clement was written during or immediately after a horrible persecution. For this faith—no matter how theologically incomplete it was—the members of the Roman church went to martyrdom and death. In the face of this, all criticism has to fall silent no matter how justified and necessary it may be.

As far as theological position is concerned, the beginnings of Christian literature appear different than we might imagine. For an example, let us take 1 Clement (as we promised), the earliest writing of the Apostolic Fathers, that group of writings alongside the New Testament whose later writings were not only contemporaneous with the New Testament, but in the early centuries were considered equal in importance to it. Several Bible manuscripts show that the Apostolic Fathers had the same status as the New Testament, even up into the fourth century and beyond. In 1 Clement, for example, the resurrection is mentioned, and proof for the truth of the Christian belief in the resurrection is introduced. But this does not happen in the way we might naturally assume, namely, by referring to the accounts of the resurrection in the Gospels. There is not even a reference to 1 Corinthians 15, although only a generation earlier Paul had worked for a lengthy time in the Roman church where 1 Clement originated. In spite of the nearness in time and the intensity with which Paul worked in Rome, we find 1 Clement proving the resurrection with the assistance of a natural theology which makes the modern theologian tremble: just as day surely follows night, and harvest follows sowing, so does resurrection follow the death of a Christian—this is the proof given here. Even pagan mythology is used extensively to prove the resurrection. Just as it is said that the phoenix comes to earth every 500 years, says 1 Clement, so the resurrection of Christians is also a reality. Only then, almost as an afterthought, is the resurrection proved with three brief Old Testament quotations, the convincing power of which would be seriously doubted by even the most allegorically inclined interpreter of Scripture in our generation. Especially noteworthy is the fact that these thoughts are not the thoughts of a lay theologian or a private individual. We are used to all sorts of this kind of thing; again and again in the modern age we find pamphlets and books in which the laity present their lay ideas which they believe will solve all the problems of early Christianity and Christianity in general. All people believe they are experts on this subject, no matter how deficient their knowledge and astuteness may be. Fortunately, as a rule these flourish only briefly, although frequently enough they create confusion.

But 1 Clement was not written by a private individual or a lay theologian, but by the leader of the Roman church and in its name. First Clement enjoyed not only the approval but even the admiration of the Roman church at that time and the following times, or else it would not have enjoyed what might be called canonical status for centuries. The Epistle of Barnabas even proves the entire Christian faith from the Old Testament. In it, as in all the other writings of the Apostolic Fathers, we find surprisingly few words of the Lord, not to mention quotations from the Gospels. Christ, the whole life of Christ, the whole work of Christ— everything is described on the basis of the Old Testament. Only occasionally is a word of the Lord added, and then we can only recognize with difficulty (or not even at all, so freely is it quoted) that it comes from the four Gospels which we possess—if it is even taken from the Gospels at all and does not originate in the oral tradition of the time. Sometimes it even comes directly from the apocryphal tradition. For the early church, Scripture was the Old Testament; the news about Jesus, Jesus' message, was transmitted orally alongside it.

The Pauline congregations provided a certain exception to this. For their scriptural authority, alongside the Old Testament they first had a letter or the letters which Paul had sent them. After the beginning of the second century, they also probably had the collection of the Pauline letters (already in existence in preliminary forms) in the form which is in the New Testament today (including the Epistle to the Hebrews, but excluding the pastoral epistles, which definitely did not belong to the first collection of the Pauline letters). Of all the New Testament writings, the letters of Paul existed earliest as a unified group, and their reputation grew very rapidly, so that by about 135, Polycarp—when he wanted to edify and exhort the church—offered in his Epistle to the Philippians almost a mosaic made up of Paul's words. Thus the letters are the first unified group of writings to exist alongside the Old Testament. However, as a spiritual and theological authority they ranked in third place. The words of the Lord (or the Gospels, insofar as they existed or were known then) were second in authority directly after the Old Testament; then came the letters of Paul.

The Gospels, insofar as they existed or were known—that is what we said. This deserves an additional comment: the four canonical Gospels were indeed first written during the years from shortly before A.D. 70 until 90–95. Of course, the tradition about the Lord's life and works essentially existed before that in an oral form. But obviously, from very early on, there were also written gospels. The transmission took place not only orally—this fact, true in itself, is today over-emphasized—but it also achieved a written form very early, even though this form has been lost to us today. The first verses of Luke's Gospel, for example, show that Luke is certainly not the first to undertake the composition of a gospel, but that numerous people before him had done something similar. Modern criticism with its skepticism has sometimes gone so far as to label this an exaggeration: "numerous" means perhaps only the Gospels of Mark and Matthew. But when we think of the number of individual traditions which lie behind those Gospels, and when we consider the number of so-called apocryphal gospels, of which we still have fragments, we soon become skeptical of this skepticism.

Paul apparently possessed a written collection of Jesus' words and had it with him on his journeys. He referred to it when he was concerned with making decisions on important questions and wanted to appeal to the authority of the Lord, as in 1 Corinthians, for example. And Paul could certainly not have been the only person who possessed such a written collection, such a "pre-gospel." The same sort of written collections originated in places and in times—both are important—when no eyewitness was available who could report about the Lord from personal experience. As eyewitnesses died, the number and extent of collections correspondingly increased, until finally the complete Gospels came into being.

Thus Mark's Gospel was written shortly before the year 70, and Matthew's Gospel not too long afterward. Luke's Gospel originated shortly before 80 (prudent scholarship will not allow us to date it very much later), and John's Gospel belongs to the time around A.D. 90–95. The late dating of these Gospels far up into the second century (which used to be considered so up-to-date and by which people judged a theologian's "scholarship," just as people on the other side measured a theologian's piety by whether he held the names ascribed to the individual writings as really "genuine") has become obsolete, and we hope will not return. These two methods of procedure have no support in the Reformation; they have no support in the ancient church; rather, they are a product of the time following the Reformation, chiefly a product of the nineteenth century—a false development about which we shall speak later.

The Gospels were obviously not written as a historical sourcebook with the thought in mind that they would be a documentary transmission of events to later times; they were written as a testimony of faith. The later times were of completely no interest for the writers of the Gospels and were completely outside their perspective, simply because of the eschatological consciousness that dominated that early period. The Gospels were written because the oral proclamation of eyewitnesses either was no longer available or was not available at the place where the Gospel in question was written. Thus the Gospels originated in isolation; in the area where it circulated each one formed *the* gospel.

It is characteristic that we find in both Acts and in Paul words of Jesus which are not in the Gospels, for example, 1 Thess. 4:15–17 and Acts 20:35. In addition, we note the way Paul frequently appeals to words of the Lord which we also do not find in the four Gospels. These words of Jesus in the New Testament outside the Gospels are only the final remnant of what was doubtless a very voluminous amount of material. The Gospels did not completely exhaust even the sources they used, as we see in the way Matthew and Luke select different material from the so-called Sayings Source (Q). In addition to what the four gospels report, a voluminous amount of words and deeds of the Lord was handed down. But all of it will have to be regarded as lost, unless some completely unexpected discovery is made. What was not included in the canonical Gospels or the other writings of the New Testament no longer exists for us. There are indeed a lot of so-called *agrapha* (literally, "unwritten"), which were not written down in the four Gospels. Again and again people have searched through this rich tradition in hopes of finding new material about the story of Jesus' life and new words of Jesus. In the nineteenth century such a collection was made; it numbered several hundred passages. But when the frost of historical criticism fell upon this bloom of early spring, it turned out that almost none of it could stand the test of genuineness. During the 1950s a well-known New Testament scholar attempted, in a frequently reprinted book, to collect genuine words of Jesus from the apocryphal tradition. At that time he came up with twenty-one of them. But even this number of twenty-one was set much too high. In later editions of the book, the number of "genuine" words of Jesus was reduced. Today, however, it is still much too high. At most, there are two or three of the so-called *agrapha* about which we might say with some certainty that they *could* be a genuine word of Jesus.

The rich tradition which existed beyond the four Gospels has been lost, and perhaps that did not take as long as we often think. If the report is dependable that Eusebius gives in his church history about Papias, who organized a collection of extracanonical materials—an interpretation of the Lord's words (see p. 100)—the essential extracanonical material was already no longer available around the year 150. What Papias tells about Jesus otherwise fits in completely with the rest of the nonhistorical apocryphal tradition, and has nothing to do with the historical life and the real teaching of Jesus. Here we find the same exaggeration, the same fantastic miracle stories as in the extracanonical tradition. In general, too much value is placed upon it, even by theologians who have in no way been discouraged by earlier disappointments. When the Coptic Gospel of Thomas was found among the papyri at Nag Hammadi, there were not a few who believed that here we possessed a text that would lead us back into the time before the Synoptic Gospels and which served as a source for them. It is true that the Gospel of Thomas—written in its Coptic form in the fourth century—in reality comes from a much earlier time and dates back to a Greek original. But we cannot speak about this Gospel of Thomas belonging to a time prior to the Synoptic Gospels. Even the Gospel of Thomas offers us, as a thorough investigation has shown—the literature on the Gospel of Thomas already includes several dozen volumes—nothing new, nothing trustworthy about a genuine tradition which goes beyond that which we have in the Gospels. The Gospel of Thomas can in no way be seen as a source for the Gospels; rather, it presents a reworking of Jesus' words in the Gospels by a Gnostic. Nor have any of the papyri discovered in the sands of Egypt given us any new material beyond the Gospels, that is, new material about genuine words of Jesus and trustworthy reports about his activity. Therefore, we should not expect that future discoveries will lead us any farther, although naturally we cannot exclude the theoretical possibility that perhaps some copy of an old collection of sayings which preceded the Synoptic Gospels might be found. But so far, the investigation of both the previously published papyri and the thousands of unpublished fragments has led to nothing of the kind.

We have established that the Gospels originated in the first century, in the period between shortly before A.D. 70 and 90–95. In this period (to deal briefly with the questions of chronology) Acts also belongs, while the letters of Paul himself come from the period earlier (the oldest of them, 1 Thessalonians, from the time around A.D. 50). But even those letters which were transmitted under Paul's name (for example, Ephesians and even Hebrews) were still written in the first century, except for the pastoral epistles. In addition, the Apocalypse belongs to the first century, though possibly—and this is pure theory—it had a preliminary form in the earlier period somewhere around 64. Perhaps 1 Peter also belongs in the first century and possibly also the Johannine letters. All the other New Testament writings come from the second century, either right from its beginning or the decades immediately after: James, the pastoral epistles, Jude, 2 Peter (this order corresponds to the likely chronology; in any case 2 Peter is the last writing of the New Testament). So much for this very brief account of the time of origin of the New Testament writings.

Now we turn to what is called their "genuineness," something that was much disputed in the nineteenth century. At that time, and sometimes also today, one of the criteria for determining whether someone possessed the right theology and the right piety was whether he considered these letters "genuine," that is, whether he believed that the writings came from the author whose name they bore. To make this very clear, let us take as an example the so-called catholic epistles (called this because they were written to the entire Christian church): James as well as Jude bore the names of Jesus' brothers; the two epistles of Peter, that of the apostle Peter; the epistles of John, that of the apostle John. Even in the nineteenth century the question of whether these designations of authorship were historically accurate was answered in the negative for all the letters. Except for a few outsiders, all contemporary New Testament scholars hold this opinion, which even today often causes offense in the church: the most famous names in Christianity are named here as authors, and none of these titles is "genuine"!

On the contrary, I would believe that even discussing the question of the "genuineness" of a New Testament writing by inquiring whether the name of its author is correctly stated is a sad story. Whoever asks such a question expresses the epigonic character not just of our age but of the church and theology of any age that poses such a question. We need only look at the early age of the church and the nonchalance with which it handled the so-called questions of genuineness, as well as all the so-called introductory questions, and then this will become evident. Even the history of the canon, about which we shall speak in the next chapter, shows us this emphatically. The "catholic epistles" had to struggle for a long time to achieve recognition in the church. 1 Peter and 1 John attained it only in the third century; for a long time there was no general recognition of James, 2 Peter, 2 and 3 John, and Jude in the church. If the early church had believed that the epistles really came from the authors whose names they bore, this would have been inexplicable. The early church operated with a completely different kind of freedom than the church today; what was significant for it was the content, not the name of the author of a New Testament writing. For example, Bishop Dionysius of Alexandria around 250 compared the Johannine writings with one another, just the way a modern New Testament scholar does— according to vocabulary, according to theological concepts, and so forth—and came to results that sound quite modern: the Revelation of John and the Gospel according to John could not have been written by the same person because of their vocabulary and theological conceptuality. We can accept these results directly, even though we do not share the premises with which this church father operated around the middle of the third century, for what really was behind what sounds so modern and impartial was a definite dogmatic and ecclesiastical concern of the age. However, this does not change the early church's freedom of judgment, which is mirrored in the history of the canon.

Even freer in judgment than the early church was the Reformation of Martin Luther. Luther's prefaces to the New Testament are given in Volume 35 of the American Edition of *Luther's Works* (we note in passing that these prefaces were written for members of congregations; they were reprinted in almost every edition of the German New Testament in the sixteenth and seventeenth centuries). In them we can see how far distant our age, which considers itself so modern, is from that of the Reformation. Luther really used modern methods and came to modern results. For example, he wrote in the Preface to Hebrews of 1522:

> In the first place, the fact that Hebrews is not an epistle of St. Paul, or of any other apostle, is proved by what it says in chapter 2, that through those who had themselves heard it from the Lord this doctrine has come to us and remained among us. It is thereby made clear that he is speaking about the apostles, as a disciple to whom this doctrine has come from the apostles, perhaps long after them. . . . Who wrote it is not known, and will probably not be known for a while; it makes no difference. We should be satisfied with the doctrine that he bases so constantly on Scripture. For he discloses a firm grasp of the reading of Scripture and of the proper way of dealing with them.

In the Preface to James of the same year, Luther writes: "However, to state my own opinion about it, though without prejudice to anyone, I do not regard it [the Epistle of James] as the writing of an apostle. . . ."

He also says about Jude in this same preface, that "no one can deny that it is an extract or copy of St. Peter's second epistle, so very like it are all the words." Today we would suppose that it is the other way around, that 2 Peter is dependent on James, but that is not the significant point— rather it is the determination that there is a connection between the two.

> He [James] also speaks of the apostles like a disciple who comes long after them and cites sayings and incidents that are found nowhere else in Scripture. This moved the ancient fathers to exclude this epistle from the main body of Scripture. Moreover the Apostle Jude did not go to Greek-speaking lands, but to Persia, as it is said, so that he did not write Greek. Therefore, although I value this book, it is an epistle that need not be counted among the chief books which are supposed to lay the foundations of faith.

Luther not only argues in a completely modern way and comes to completely modern results, but he also goes much farther than a contemporary New Testament scholar would go, at least as far as some "Modernist" theologians have gone, suffering fierce attacks for their work. If certain circles in the church today attack—even condemn— New Testament scholars for their critical method and their critical results, they will have to attack and condemn Luther even more strongly. Luther not only used historical criticism on the New Testament, but— what is much more significant—Luther established the decisive criterion for the "genuineness" and "nongenuineness" of New Testament writings, and he does this in complete opposition to many modern opinions. The author of a writing, whoever he is, declares Luther, is completely inconsequential; rather, what is decisive for their evaluation, as Luther categorically emphasized again and again, is whether a New Testament writing "proclaims Christ" *("Christum treibt")*. In the Preface to James mentioned above, he writes:

> All the genuine sacred books agree in this, that all of them preach and inculcate *[treiben]* Christ. And that is the true test by which to judge all books, when we see whether or not they inculcate Christ. For all of Scripture shows us Christ (Romans 3:22ff.) and St. Paul will know nothing but Christ (1 Corinthians 2:2).

And then come the words that at least every theologian should know: "Whatever does not teach Christ is not apostolic, even though St. Peter or St. Paul does the teaching. Again, whatever preaches Christ would be apostolic, even if Judas, Annas, Pilate, and Herod were doing it." Whatever preaches Christ is evangelical and apostolic, regardless of its author. The criterion for a book of the New Testament—indeed, for any book of the Bible—lies in its content, not in its title. If Judas, Annas, Pilate, or Herod had written such a book that proclaimed Christ, then it would be evangelical and could claim full recognition by all Christians. Judas betrayed the Lord; we need not mention the role Herod, Annas, and Pilate played in his death, or also the moral level of Herod. If any one of them had written a work which proclaimed Christ, it would be evangelical and apostolic, says Luther. This is how important for him the content was, and how unimportant the author's name on which we place so much emphasis. The New Testament writings are authoritative for us, not because of *who* wrote them, but because of *what* is written in them. I would maintain that this is the only way we can come to a genuine appreciation of the New Testament; any other criterion will lead us along human paths and cannot endure.

We need only observe the course of church history during the last centuries where we will find with clarity the devastating consequences that result from using such inappropriate criteria. It began in the time of Orthodoxy, repeated itself in a new way in the nineteenth century, and continues to our own day: the "genuineness" of the statements—the authority of the New Testament—had as its presupposition the fact that here apostles and eyewitnesses were speaking. Because of what the apostles were, what they had written had to be true, had to be valid. As soon as critical scholarship proved that this or that New Testament writing could not have been written by an apostle, the authority of its author collapsed; with the authority of the author, the authority of the New Testament writing collapsed along with it; and with the authority of the New Testament writing collapsed the authority of the church, which had claimed all this. It is an all-too-simple solution to blame everything on "unbelieving scholarship." The New Testament is read and studied not just inside the church but also outside the church. And the church cannot and dare not wait—and not only in this context, but for anything else—until others come and tell it what has long since been seen and should have been made known among its members.

In the nineteenth century, the work and the results of critical scholarship caused deep agitation among church members, for if they could not believe in the foundation of the church on which everything else was built, what else could they then believe? Of course, the genuine foundation of faith was not disturbed, but only a false foundation—nonetheless a false foundation which the church had proposed as the genuine one. The results of this were unavoidable, as is demonstrated by the movement of withdrawal from membership in the church in the nineteenth and twentieth centuries. If the church at that time had understood what it apparently even today cannot rightly understand—namely, how to create a genuine relationship between Christians and the New Testament, a genuine consciousness of the authority of Scripture—we would have been spared much of this.

We must additionally (and finally) ask the question: what has been achieved with the efforts to preserve the "genuineness" of the New Testament writings? It has destroyed more, even within the church, than it has preserved. If the catholic epistles really were written by the apostles whose names they bear and by people who were closest to Jesus (by James, the brother of the Lord; by Jude, James's brother; by the prince of the apostles, Peter; by John, the son of Zebedee; if the Gospel of John was really written by the beloved disciple of Jesus), then the real question arises: was there really a Jesus? Can Jesus really have lived, if the writings of his closest companions are filled with so little of his reality? The catholic epistles, for example, have so little in them about the reality of the historical Jesus and his power, that it suffices for James, for example, to mention Christ's name only in passing, and that 1 Peter limits itself to speaking only incidentally about Christ's suffering. Otherwise, these letters present Christian exhortations—a parenesis—which in many ways are connected with the parenetic literature of that time and even partially grow out of it. Or these writings, along with John's Gospel, present a unique theology which theologically reinterpret the figure of Jesus and raise it to a completely different level than we find in the first three Gospels, the so-called Synoptic Gospels, which doubtless are incomparably nearer to the historical Jesus.

When we observe this—assuming that the writings about which we are speaking really come from their alleged authors—it almost then appears as if Jesus were a mere phantom and that the real theological power lay not with him, but with the apostles and with the early church. These are the consequences that ultimately result from this sort of apologetics (even if it does not acknowledge these consequences, or if it itself is not even aware of them). In almost greater measure, this sort of apologetics comes to the same results as do Bultmann and the so-called Modernist theologians, which it passionately attacks. Bultmann and the history of tradition ascribe to the church the decisive activity in producing the Gospels. However, as a question of methodology—methodological questions, as we have emphasized, are often the decisive ones—we must ask where these congregations whose composition we know really obtained the intellectual and spiritual power, if we deny this power to Jesus himself. The modern apologists just do not see the consequences of what they are doing. They devote so much effort to saving the names of the authors of these epistles and gospels, and *perhaps* they do manage to save these names (for a limited circle, but not for everyone), but in so doing they definitely lose the real substance, that is, Jesus' reality and power. If we want to see a vivid picture, then we can imagine the eyewitnesses only the way Peter and John are portrayed in Acts 4. There the apostles stand before the Sanhedrin and are called to account for their preaching. They answer (4:20): "We cannot but speak of what we have seen and heard." The exegetes may explore whether this hearing before the Sanhedrin took place the way Acts reports or not, but that really has no significance for our purpose. The statement of Acts 4:20 expresses the reality of that time—typical truth, truth in the real sense. We can understand the statements of eyewitnesses and the eyewitnesses themselves only as having their own power (which we certainly should not regard as being too insignificant) absorbed by the power of Jesus, so that when they speak about Christianity—about Jesus, about his word, about his works—they are speaking by his power. When they take a stand on problems of their time, they can do that only by constantly referring to Jesus, by constantly appealing to him, and not in such a way as we see in the catholic epistles—as if Jesus were only a mere phantom from sometime in the past to which they could now attach and implant their own opinion which came from somewhere else.

We would completely misunderstand these explanations, if we were to derive a rejection or a depreciation of apologetics from them. Apologetics, correctly understood, is a churchly and also theological necessity, for there is an infinite amount of material in the church and theology from which people outside have drawn false impressions and which has prevented the respect and expansion of Christianity, indeed severely damaged it. There have always been attacks on the church and Christianity at all times; only the names under which they appear change. Before 1933 it was the so-called godless movement *(Gottlosenbewegung);* after 1933 it was all the different shades of the German-Christian movement *(Deutschglaube).* In addition, both then and today we have the sects. In place of the godless movement and the German-Christians *(Deutschglauben),* at present we have definite modern movements and some occasionally very prominent individuals who, for the same reasons as always, attack Christianity and the church, not infrequently with the assistance of church history. We should energetically oppose all of them.

This is the task of all Christians, especially of all theologians. Theologians who do not undertake it violate their office. This does not mean that they should go through the streets as itinerant preachers and say: may I help you with apologetics? And they should very carefully consider where they step in. Apologetics that sounds the alarm and blindly rushes in wherever it sees any smoke is an evil thing. In the first place, things are not always burning where there is smoke, and in the second place, not every fire is a dangerous one. Apologetics for apologetics' sake creates more harm than good. We cannot maintain something or defend it with all our power just because it once existed that way in the history of the church. We cannot defend mistakes and errors; rather, we can only abandon them and must do this with the public acknowledgment that they were mistakes and errors. If the church acts in any other way, it makes itself and its message unbelievable and causes irreparable damage. If modern people come to mistrust the church and its proclamation, how will the church get them to listen to what it has to say to them that is essential and irreplaceable?

The Origin of the New Testament Canon

We need only look at the history of the New Testament canon, and it will become clear that reality looks different than it appeared to the apologists of the nineteenth and twentieth centuries. It becomes even clearer when we look at the canon of not only the New Testament but of the entire Bible. Then we shall recognize that the unity of the canon, which is either silently assumed or proclaimed in the Christian church, just does not exist in fact. The Old Testament scholars seem to make it simple when they talk about the Old Testament canon as if there always were and still is a canon of the Hebrew Bible. That is a deception. It was not even true in the ancient church. The early church used the Septuagint, that is, the text and versions of the Greek Old Testament, not the text and versions of the writings in the Hebrew Old Testament. It is true that people in the ancient church frequently attempted to establish the Hebrew canon, but all of these attempts, which as a rule were undertaken by academic theologians, had only limited results. Even Augustine could not understand Jerome's attempt to establish the Hebrew text as a basis for the Old Testament; he pointed him to the Septuagint, which was entirely sufficient. And even in the modern period there is no canon of the Old Testament which corresponds to the Hebrew canon, not to mention one that is uniform for all churches, since they take completely different directions with regard to the so-called

Apocrypha. For the Roman Catholic church, ever since the decision of the Council of Trent in 1546, the Apocrypha are canonical; the Reformed churches emphatically reject them. The Lutheran and also the Anglican churches take a middle way; they believe that the Apocrypha of the Old Testament are "good and useful to read," as Luther said, but are not obligatory for faith.

The differences go so deeply that even the Orthodox churches, of whom we might sooner expect unity, do not possess a unified Old Testament. The Bible of the Russian Orthodox church is different, in regard to the accepted Old Testament books, from the Bible of the Greek Orthodox church. This relates only to portions, of course, but it sheds light on the situation.

So what remains of the unity of the canon, about which we instinctively speak, is only the New Testament. Here, in fact, all twenty-seven books with almost exactly the same textual composition are recognized by all churches—or more precisely, by all churches we know about, for even here there are exceptions about which we shall speak later (see p. 112). To us today this unity of the New Testament canon appears to be a matter of course. But it did not exist in the early church. The unity of the New Testament canon with its twenty-seven books, as all churches in Christendom today have them, was not achieved until the end of the fourth century as a result of a tedious and complicated process in a number of church provinces—and not even in all church provinces—until finally after several more centuries it was established almost everywhere.

This unity was reached in seven stages. The first stage of the development takes place between the time of Paul and the older writings of the Apostolic Fathers at the beginning of the second century. At this time, alongside the Old Testament stood the word of the Lord. It circulated orally but was already assembled into written collections of sayings from which people quoted. Toward the end of this first epoch, the Pauline letters (except for the pastoral epistles) already existed as a closed collection, just as did the Gospels, although these were not a closed collection, only individual writings. People also quoted from them and they were also read in the worship services without, however, being considered equal to the Old Testament.

The second stage of the development is characterized by the later writings of the Apostolic Fathers and Justin. It therefore lasts until A.D. 150. In addition to the previous authorities, the Old Testament and the words of the Lord, a new one appears: the group of the twelve apostles, in which people automatically included Paul (contrary to historical reality). People now appealed to these apostles as a closed group and to their instructions. Gradually the first New Testament writings developed into an authoritative position approaching that of the Old Testament: first came the Gospels, followed by Paul's epistles. Justin is the first writer who quotes from the Gospels in a way in which we can recognize their words (even though he does not call them Gospels, but "reminiscences of the apostles").

Around 150 the third stage of the development begins in which the formation of the canon as such sets in. Everything which takes place before 150 is only a preparatory step for this. The canon of the four Gospels is organized; the epistles attain a status which is equivalent in principle, but not in practice.

Around 200 the fourth stage is reached (with Irenaeus, Tertullian, and Clement of Alexandria). The canon of the four Gospels is completely recognized; beside it as a second group are the writings of the apostles. The nucleus of these writings of the apostles is the Pauline epistles, and to them are attached the first other apostolic epistles and, in the West, the Apocalypse. The reading of a writing in the worship service now conforms to its canonical validity. That automatically leads to the demand for excluding everything which does not possess this canonical validity from the readings in the worship services. And thereby something new begins, for previously this limitation did not apply. Rather, until now writings, the general validity of which was not recognized, could be read in the worship services.

The fifth stage of the development lasted throughout the entire third century and into the beginning of the fourth. Now 1 Peter and 1 John attained a firm, generally recognized position alongside the four Gospels and the Pauline epistles. 2 Peter, 2 and 3 John, James, and Jude are striving for this recognition, but with varying results. The church in both East and West is divided about recognizing or excluding them. What one diocese may accept among these letters can be completely rejected by another. In relation to Hebrews and the Revelation of John, however, the two areas of the church were completely different. The East received Hebrews and rejected the Apocalypse, while the West did exactly the opposite, and both did it with astonishing unanimity. This happened for theological reasons which can be clearly determined. In Hebrews the second repentance was condemned, something that in the West was of fundamental significance for building the church, and therefore it did not accept the canonicity of Hebrews. The East, under the influence of

Origen's theology, was offended at Revelation's presentation of the millennium. In addition, it was shocked by the experience of Montanism, so that for a long time it rejected the Apocalypse here.

Not until the middle of the fourth century did an agreement open up. Now the sixth stage of the development of the New Testament canon took place, the most significant one. Here we have the first official decisions of bishops which bore authoritative weight for entire provinces of the church and the first decrees of synods with official determination of the New Testament canon in the form in which we have it today. This sixth stage begins about 350 and lasts until the beginning of the fifth century. To it belongs Athanasius's famous thirty-ninth Easter letter. (At Easter the Alexandrian bishops wrote pastoral letters to their church, chiefly to inform them about the date of Easter which was difficult to calculate because it depended on the lunar calendar, and they took the opportunity to discuss current issues. In this context, in 367 Athanasius expressed himself about the canonical extent of the Bible.) In addition to Athanasius, Jerome and Augustine must be mentioned, who have the same importance for the triumph of the canon of twenty-seven books in the West as Athanasius has in the East. It appears that the church, after long hesitation, rapidly achieved a unified form of the New Testament canon in both East and West which has lasted up to the present day, one with a defined and equal content in all churches. But this impression is deceiving. Rather, it still took a long time until this uniform content, which we see being proclaimed everywhere around 400, was in fact accepted in all the provinces of the church. That is true even for the Latin church, where the whole structure strives for definite order. That Augustine had to argue with a presbyter, who allowed writings not accepted in the canon to be read in his worship service, may not have such great significance. But when Augustine himself in his later literary activity displays a clear reticence about Hebrews, whose acceptance into the canon he had encouraged and helped to achieve, it gives us pause. The decisions of the Western church around 400 were able to bring Hebrews into the canon, but it was really not accepted there for a long time more. Even around 550 Cassiodorus could find no Western commentary on Hebrews and therefore had to have Chrysotom's translated into Latin.

This throws light on the actual situation. But in addition, we should not overlook the fact that up until the seventh century, in some parts of the church either an abbreviated canon existed or people possessed an expanded canon through accepting apocryphal writings. Even in the

West, this decisive sixth stage of the reception of the canon of twenty-seven books was followed by a seventh. Not until this seventh stage did the canon of twenty-seven books really become the general property of the church. The seventh stage is seen even more clearly when we look at the Greek church. Here Athanasius's authority does have a significance similar to that of Augustine in the West. Nevertheless, it took a great deal of time and trouble until the canon of the twenty-seven books was generally recognized. At that time the Antiochene theological school recognized only two catholic epistles, 1 Peter and 1 John, and still continued to reject the Apocalypse. James came in very slowly alongside 1 Peter and 1 John, but only after 431 did opposition to the canonicity of 2 Peter, 2 and 3 John, and Jude gradually lessen. It took the Apocalypse even longer to take over completely in the East. That did not begin until about 500. The list of canonical books ascribed to Patriarch Nicephorus of Constantinople in the ninth century still included the Revelation of John in the same breath with the Apocalypse of Peter, the Epistle of Barnabas, and the Gospel of the Hebrews in the category of writings not generally received and experiencing opposition.

Even more negative is the picture in the Syrian church, which then was not on the fringe of contemporary events, but from its very beginnings until well into the fifth century belonged to the heartland of the early church. Here in the Syrian church until 400 the canon did not include the four Gospels, but a harmony assembled from the four Gospels, Tatian's Diatessaron. Of course the Gospels were known to the official church, but the Diatessaron was canonical. It took extraordinary measures (and burnings of manuscripts instigated by the church), until the Diatessaron was forced to the sidelines. In addition, all the catholic epistles and the Apocalypse were missing. Even the epistles of Paul present a different picture from the usual one. The Epistle to Philemon is missing, and in its place we find a writing of the Corinthian church, along with the so-called Third Epistle to the Corinthians as a reply. Finally, in addition, there are other apocryphal writings of the most varied types. Only very slowly did the situation change in this church: gradually the Diatessaron had to give way; James, 1 Peter, and 1 John were accepted, but still the four shorter catholic epistles, as well as the Apocalypse, were lacking. From the sixth century on, they came into use in the Western Syrian church, but it took many generations for this process. The Eastern Syrian church—the Nestorian church—preserved a canon without Jude and the Apocalypse. For the present day, this Nestorian church is at best only a hazy concept, yet all through the

Middle Ages it represented Christianity in all of Asia from Persia as far as China.

This—painted in broad strokes—is how the evolution of the New Testament canon appears. Yet we should not overlook the fact that the criteria used by the early church for receiving writings into the canon were not only insufficient but also often incorrect. If we want to summarize in one formula the external principles which played a role in selecting the canonical writings, we can only speak about a principle of no principles at all. We can study that in the Muratorian Canon, a canonical list from the end of the second century (so named after the librarian who discovered the manuscript in the eighteenth century and published it). Here every conceivable principle of selection is removed either expressly or implicitly, so I would at least believe. Here it is proclaimed that the writers of the canonical Gospels must be apostles; but Luke and Mark were not apostles, Luke not even an eyewitness. There are forgeries of apostles' writings, which obviously are rejected. But even writings the apostolic authorship of which was not doubted at that time, such as the Apocalypse of Peter, are not considered canonical by some, so the Muratorian Canon declares. Finally, the Wisdom of Solomon appears in the New Testament section of this list, completely breaking the context, first because it does not belong to the New Testament, and second because, according to the Muratorian Canon's statement itself, it was not written by Solomon himself, but by "friends to honor him." The further demand is made that writings must have been directed to the entire church to be accepted in the canon. But Paul wrote not only to individual congregations, something that might, although with difficulty, be fitted into this scheme, but several times also to individuals. The Muratorian Canon requires that the message must be unified, but at the same time it declares that the "principia" of the Gospels (does this mean their beginnings, which is more probable, or their principles?) are different. The single requirement that is really fulfilled is that canonical writings must be old. But even this principle continually has holes poked in it by errors in dating. This is the way it goes with the Muratorian Canon, and it would be the same with all other early canonical lists if they did not limit themselves to a mere listing of canonical writings but gave a commentary on them. The confusio hominum ("confusion of men") connected with the determination of the canon cannot be disputed by anyone who takes the trouble to look some into its history. But on the other hand, I would think, just as unmistakable is the providentia Dei ("providence of God"). Despite all the lack of principles, despite all the arbitrariness, despite all the errors—what the church has received in the New Testament stands on an incomparably higher level than all other early Christian literature. None of the writings of the Apostolic Fathers can even remotely compare with those of the New Testament. None of the so-called New Testament apocrypha can remotely be compared with what was accepted in the New Testament. It is characteristic that in the last generation, which brought to our attention either complete texts or thorough reports about many previously unknown writings from that early period, no one claimed that any of these newly discovered early Christian writings could claim canonical validity. That is how wide the gap is between what we know from the early age and what the New Testament offers. Even in their weakest sections, these writings possess the witness of the Spirit and power in a completely different fashion than all other early Christian literature.

The Rule of Faith

When we follow the process of the formation of the canon in detail, we can hardly avoid the impression that the second century really had no need of a canon. That sounds paradoxical. But if we once read the writings of that time in their context, this impression is almost unavoidable. That is all the more impressive, since this age has decisive significance for understanding all of church history and, moreover, for every modern consideration of systematic theology, right down to distinctive differences between churches. When we look for the final theological court of appeal which was responsible for receiving debatable writings into the canon, what we find is the norm of faith, the rule of faith (the *regula fidei,* the *regula veritas,* the *canon aletheias,* or however it was named). Against this rule of faith, this *regula fidei,* everything was measured, even the writings of the developing New Testament. Whether one of the numerous writings circulating under the name of an apostle could really be accepted by the church was finally decided by whether its contents agreed with *this* canon, with the *regula fidei.* Authorship by an apostle, age, and whatever other criteria there may have been—all were only provisional in comparison with this. What Eusebius relates in his church history about Bishop Serapion of Antioch is characteristic. This bishop visited Rhossus, a congregation in the vicinity of Antioch. Here people were accustomed to reading the Gospel of Peter in the worship services. Because there was doubt whether that was correct, they asked the bishop about it. He approved the reading, apparently because of the author's name, for he was not acquainted with the writing itself. Returning home, he obtained a copy of this gospel, read it, and immediately wrote a letter to Rhossus: reading the Gospel of Peter in worship services is forbidden and must cease immediately because of the errors found in this Gospel of Peter among the many correct things it contains. He included a list of the errors with the letter. In addition, the bishop announced his intention to return to Rhossus immediately, apparently in order to stamp out the roots of the error current in the congregation. Because of the author's name, he had agreed to its acceptance in the canon, but when he became acquainted with the writing's contents and measured them against the *regula fidei,* he had to change his mind.

Naturally this *regula fidei* stands in close relationship to Scripture. The *regula fidei* grew out of Scripture, insofar as it was received at the time, as a summary of the faith possessed by the church. But it is still not true that this *regula fidei* now served as a compendium, a short summary of the contents of Scripture. This is indeed what the late second century believed, yet it is unmistakable that the *regula fidei* goes back to the age of oral tradition, back to the earliest beginnings of Scripture. It was indeed influenced by Scripture, by Paul's epistles, for example, but then itself influenced Scripture and the content of its teaching, for example, the later catholic epistles. It presents the deposit of the developing faith possessed by the church. Its content accordingly changed, even when the words remained the same for a longer period of time or altogether. The formula attained life, indeed its real existence, only through interpretation. It presupposes a definite and continuously developing basic prior understanding, even though the *regula fidei* was only one of the normative points in which the church of the second century saw the pure doctrine being guaranteed. Alongside it were the many unbroken chains of holders of the episcopal office, theoretically extending back to the time of the apostles and—again theoretically—guaranteeing the unaltered transmission of the received faith and doctrine from one generation to the next. We can describe the sequence of meanings which the early church gave to the word "canon" as demonstrative of its ranking of values. It is not true, as we and even some New Testament scholars imagine, that people meant the canon of the New Testament when they spoke about "canon" in the early age; what they first meant was the *regula fidei.* It was the standard, the guiding principle of faith. Then people applied it to the decisions of synods, and finally, from the fourth century onward, it was used to designate the books of Holy Scripture which were authorized for churchly use.

If we want to obtain a clear presentation of the significance which the

115

regula fidei had in the second century, we must read Tertullian's writing *De praescriptione haereticorum* (which should be translated approximately "On the legal argument against the heretics"). It deals with the problem of how one should conduct an argument with heretics. The church at that time had learned that it was not possible to carry out a successful argument with the opposing churches on the basis of Scripture alone. They also appealed to Scripture, so that a discussion with them on the basis of Scripture went in circles and produced no results, especially because at that time what was and what was not to be included in Scripture had not been finally determined. Therefore, says Tertullian, one should not argue with heretics on the basis of Scripture, but at the very outset of the debate must ask the question whether this opposing church even has the right to appeal to Scripture. Obviously, the only answer can be that it does not have the right, since it does not belong to the community which has possessed the Scripture since ancient times. Here the concept of apostolic tradition plays a role. The writing's title already gives the essential information about its content. *Praescriptio* is a legal term: the argument by which people reject participation in a trial altogether, because it does not apply to them.

This writing of Tertullian will soon be eighteen hundred years old, but the problem with which it deals, as well as the answer which it gives, is quite modern. For example, let us consider the Jehovah's Witnesses or other groups, perhaps the Adventists. The writings of the Jehovah's Witnesses are teeming with Bible passages. Each member of this group commands a store of Bible quotations which anyone else can hardly match. Thus an argument with them necessarily goes in a circle. If we present one Bible passage, they have ten more available. Here it depends on the principles of the debate, as Tertullian required. For what the Jehovah's Witnesses present are only single verses of Scripture taken out of context and arbitrarily assembled into a new system which is absolutely foreign to Scripture. Just as typesetters select individual letters from their font of type in order to create words by assembling them however they wish, so the Jehovah's Witnesses assemble the Scripture passages they quote into a message which simply cannot be harmonized with what is decisive in the New Testament. It is quite characteristic, that among the voluminous and constantly growing literature of the Jehovah's Witnesses there is not a single commentary on even one single biblical book *as a whole*. The Jehovah's Witnesses are not in a position to produce *one book of the Bible as a whole,* or even just one chapter from it, in their support. They can construct their temple of ideas only by proceeding absolutely arbitrarily with individual quotations from the Bible—and this is especially important—from which the central statements of Scripture are excluded. That is the debate on principles which has to be carried on with them. Everything else is superfluous. Those who consider the historical-critical method of Bible interpretation a danger and carry on polemics against it should have frequent meetings arranged for them with the Adventists, the Mormons, or their like. Then they would see that the historical-critical method does not pose a danger—it is that only for a poorly instructed church—but is a completely essential safeguard, for only what proceeds on this basis can have any hope of success in a discussion with Jehovah's Witnesses, Adventists, and similar groups.

That was an excursus; let us return to the rule of faith with the question: where was the rule of faith of the second century, about which we have said so much, written down? There have been long debates about this, which we need not discuss here. All in all, we can definitely say: the *regula fidei* of the second century was given in the creed which, significantly, was just then attaining a formulation which was valid for larger areas. In the New Testament there were creedal formulas in great number and in rich variety. From the beginning there had been a confession of faith—for the statement: *"Kyrios Jesus"* ("Jesus is Lord") is already a Christian confession of faith—but this confession of faith was formulated in different ways in different churches and in the different New Testament writings. Not until the second century did a summary of this confession of faith gradually develop into a uniform, fixed form.

When we now look at the confession of that time, that original form of the so-called Apostles' Creed, the origin of which is placed in Rome about 170, we could object that this confession of faith really does not have the protective function and the significance which the second century ascribed to it, because it is limited to fundamental statements. But when we once compare it with the later confessional formulas, the complete Apostles' Creed or the Nicene Creed, we find the same facts there. There, too, the mesh of the text has holes that are large enough to let everything possible slip through. Even when we look at the Confessio Augustana, the Augsburg Confession of the Reformation, we find that even this confession's definitions are couched in such general language that, if we take the text literally, a great many things can be reconciled with it. That is true with Article 7 on the church, with the decisive Article 10 on the Lord's Supper, and in many other places. The effects of that *regula fidei* in the second century, the Apostles' Creed, the Confessio Augustana, and all confessional statements up to the present day—all rest on the prior understanding which lies behind them, on the interpretation connected with them, which the person using this confession or reading this confessional writing has in mind. The confession of faith of the second century can become a *regula fidei,* a norm determining everything, only as a result of the presuppositions transmitted to every Christian in baptismal instruction. This interpretation is what they have in mind as they recite this confession of faith. Only in this way can the *regula fidei* of the second-century church perform the service which it did for that church. And only in this way can that *regula fidei* do justice to general theological and ecclesiastical developments with their growing and changing demands. The text remains the same, but the understanding changes. The second century goes back to this *regula fidei* in struggling with other churches, and with its help can meet them successfully, even when these other churches are supported by a literature that, according to the claims of the time, appears to be justified in its appeal to canonicity.

The Apostolic Tradition and the Monarchical Episcopate

We have already mentioned (see p. 115), that in addition to appealing to the *regula fidei* there was also a third measure in the church of the second century for determining whether a newly organized church or a group which one might meet was really to be labeled as Christian. That was to refer to the origins of that group. Once again the presupposition for this was the revision of eschatological consciousness. When the expectation of an imminent end faded away, people began to think historically. They began to be concerned about their own history. They could not only plan for the future, but they were in a position to see themselves and their age as a continuation of the past. Every church did indeed possess a definite tradition: in addition to the leader of the church, people knew at least a few of his predecessors. In not a few cases people were even acquainted with the history of their church's founding from Acts and Paul's letters. That was the case in Judaea, in Syria, in Asia Minor, in Greece, and also in Rome. All of this combined into something new, and it became obvious that this historical perspective could offer decisive help. All opposing churches originated either in the present or only a brief time earlier. In those cases people could confirm the details of their historical origin: the Marcionite church had its beginning with Marcion whose biography was known to people in the second century. The Montanists went back to Montanus, and people possessed sufficient information about him and his prophetesses. The Gnostic schools could trace their history back only into the second century, at best to its beginning. All of these bore the names of founders whom people knew, while the Christian churches normally went back beyond the turn of the first century into the time of the apostles. If they were of more recent date, they were still connected with churches which did reach back into the first century, thus also participating in fellowship with the apostles. Only that which can trace its history back into the earliest time, either directly or through fellowship with churches which are able to document it directly, can be genuine. In this way the concept of apostolic tradition developed and along with it, apostolic succession.

In this context people sometimes proceeded quite liberally in building the chain of tradition, for historical thinking was still in its beginnings. Then, as now, historical thinking was also overlaid with wishes. For example, people in Rome were convinced that Peter and Paul had founded the church. They knew that both had worked in their city. That was the historical core; if two men that great had lived and worked in Rome, it was simply unimaginable that they had not founded the church. The idea that both of them first came to Rome after the church had already existed there for a longer time had no place in early Christian thinking, which in this case wanted to forge a connection between something they knew and the earliest and best-known men whose names they knew. Thus the author of the two epistles of Clement was naturally identified as the same Clement mentioned as Paul's co-worker in his epistles. And thus Peter's successor in Rome was identified as Linus from among those who had accompanied Peter, and so forth.

The fourth characteristic of this time also developed out of necessity, namely, the monarchical episcopate. In times which were threatened by so many dangers, when everything appeared to be disintegrating, *one* person belonged at the head of the congregation, not a committee. People quickly came to this conviction everywhere. A committee is always cumbersome; different opinions exist side by side, and because of human considerations the correct one does not always triumph. Here different sorts of powers struggle with one another, so that the power of the congregation is endangered. The best person who can be found must be placed at the head of the congregation, and he must also have complete authority to act. Thus, in the second century we see—in addition to the New Testament canon, in addition to the confession of faith or the *regula fidei*, in addition to the apostolic tradition—the monarchical episcopate developing, something that was foreign to the earlier age. The monarchical episcopate was a product of the second century.

3. DEVELOPMENT OF THE PRIESTLY OFFICE
AND THE HIERARCHICAL STRUCTURE

The earliest period knew nothing of the monarchical episcopate—this sentence must be placed emphatically at the head of this section, despite the significance it holds for certain claims. When Pope Paul VI greeted the World Council of Churches with the sentence: "I am Peter," the most this statement possessed was symbolical force and had nothing to do with historical reality. Peter died in Rome, but Peter was never bishop of that city and was certainly not a monarchical bishop. In the first century and the beginning of the second, the Roman church was led by a college of presbyters, as we learn reliably from 1 Clement which we have frequently mentioned. We can no more speak about an apostolic succession, by which Peter passed on the episcopal office by a laying on of hands, than we can about many other things. This idea was a product of the second century when the idea of apostolic succession inevitably developed from the concept or requirement of the apostolic tradition. Both existed only after the second half of the second century.

The sources are such that we can say this with certainty. In the beginning, as we reported (see pp. 45–47), there were three various types standing side by side: the first congregation, the Pauline congregations, and the non-Pauline Gentile Christian congregations. At the head of the first congregation stood the apostles as witnesses to Jesus' life and resurrection. A special significance among them belonged to James, Peter, and John—definitely in this order—the so-called apostolic pillars. We can see with certainty in the presentation of the New Testament that James the brother of Jesus, along with Jesus' entire family, had not believed in Jesus during his lifetime but had rejected him. Yet after Jesus' resurrection we find him not only among the disciples but at their head. Some have thought that here a sort of dynastic principle was at work, as in the rabbinic schools. That is possible and is supported by the fact that also after James's death we see members of Jesus' family at the head of the congregation, but it is in no way certain. However, James's conversion from an unbeliever to a Christian is decisive, and this transformation probably took place in the experience of the resurrection which Paul reports in 1 Corinthians 15 about James.

The organization of the Pauline congregations was different from that of the first congregation. Obviously Jerusalem also possessed a not insignificant authority for them, just as it did in the non-Pauline Gentile Christian congregations. But Jerusalem's authority was a great deal weaker than in the Jewish Christian congregations, where everything was decided and directed by Jerusalem. We also cannot say that Paul assumed the position in his congregations that Jerusalem had for the Jewish Christian congregations. Paul was indeed the spiritual leader of the congregations founded by him, but these congregations were still independent members of the body of Christ, and the real authority in them was Christ's spirit. Accordingly, we find in the Pauline congregations the charismatic offices of apostles, prophets, and teachers. Paul was only one of the apostles, even though he did claim central authority. The task of the apostle was the founding of new congregations, as well as traveling to nurture the congregations already in existence. We are relatively well informed about the prophets—purely coincidentally—because disputes had caused the difficulties in the Corinthian church which Paul discusses in 1 Corinthians 14. We know almost nothing about the teachers. We meet them now and then in the early time as individual personalities; we can only surmise that the institution of the catechetical school in Alexandria goes back to this office of teachers in the ancient church. It is certain, however, that all three offices were preserved into the postapostolic period, where they gradually declined. The *Didache,* a constitution for the church written about 100–120, lets us look directly at this process of the decline of charismatic offices. There are still the three, but the number of those holding these charismatic offices has declined, so that it is no longer normal to find them everywhere. The Spirit's blowing has declined, for not only has the number of these officeholders been reduced, but they sometimes have also been questioned by the congregation; thus, the *Didache* has to give characteristics by which people can judge not only the message but also the genuineness of the activities of the apostles, prophets, and teachers. There is no mention yet of real pseudoprophets, that is, representatives of the opposing churches. But soon they arise and add to the further decline of the charismatic offices. The fact that prophets and prophecy played such a great role in Montanism could have had no other result than to cause the congregations ultimately to doubt the prophetic institution itself.

In the place of these charismatic offices, what gradually enters is presbyters, bishops, and deacons. *Presbyteros* was probably first an honorary title for the first-converted or the preeminent members of the congregation. *Episkopoi* ("bishops") and *diakonoi* ("deacons") were designations for bearers of services voluntarily assumed—technical services necessary for maintaining an ordered congregational life, such as assembling the collection for Jerusalem in the early period. These functions probably existed from the beginning. But the bearers of these functions changed from time to time, for the tasks were not assumed permanently; in addition, in each case these functions were not their main tasks. But now when there were no longer enough apostles, prophets, and teachers, the church, in addition to those who performed purely technical functions and those who kept order, found it necessary to provide men who could undertake to preside over celebrations of the Lord's Supper, the proclamation of the Word, and the instruction. It was inevitable that what had previously been the secondary functions of the *episcopoi* and *diakonoi* took on primary character and at the same time expanded in content.

In this transitional epoch, the officeholders still had to be protected from disdain because they did not belong to the charismatics who in principle continued to enjoy the highest regard. The *Didache* expressly states that people should not despise bishops and deacons but regard them as highly as prophets and teachers. At that time they certainly still held these offices on a temporary basis, but it could not have been long until they assumed them permanently. First Clement informs us that around A.D. 95 the Corinthian congregation replaced all of its officeholders. A new group of officeholders was inducted on the basis of charismatic authority (or charismatic claims). Here we again catch a glimpse of the transitional period, in which the permanence of the office was not yet assured. But we just as clearly learn from 1 Clement the Roman congregation's opinion (and surely not only this congregation's), that anyone who performs his office irreproachably may not be removed from office. The offices are here considered to be undertaken permanently and they quickly become—as could take place in no other way as congregations grew—also full-time offices. Thus we find the three offices—*episkopos, presbyteros, diakonos* (*presbyteros* had now developed from an honorary title into a designation of an office)—in various groupings, but always—this is important to remember—as a council. It was only a question of time, a question of the special needs of the congregation, but naturally also a question of the personalities represented in this college, that one of them would take over the leadership, even before the function of actual direction was officially given to him. Such a development was inevitable. In this way the administration of the congregation gradually became organized everywhere under one officeholder. That took place in different ways, and in different congregations it also took different lengths of time, but it always led to the same result, and the crises and necessities of the second century accelerated this process. In the letters of Ignatius between A.D. 110 and 120, it appears that the monarchical episcopate (that is, the leadership of a congregation by one bishop, to whom the other officeholders are subordinate) already exists, and indeed it enjoys a reputation that could hardly be higher. For example, Ignatius exhorts the Ephesians to walk in accordance with the bishop's will. People should be as closely connected to the bishop as the church is with Jesus Christ and as Jesus Christ is with the Father.

These letters of Ignatius present us with a picture which is completely different from that which we know from other sources. If we compare the two, it appears that the letters of Ignatius must come from a later time; not exactly to their credit, Protestant patristic scholars frequently argued this way in the nineteenth century. But the solution is a different one: what Ignatius includes in his letters, as often in church history, is not a description of the real situation, but a demand. In fact, matters had taken a completely different course in the churches to which Ignatius addressed his letters, as their texts show clearly when we examine them more closely. Ignatius is greatly ahead of the actual development; not infrequently it took several generations until the monarchical episcopate was generally accepted. Not until the necessities of the second century became extremely urgent, did it take over everywhere. Thus, the conclusion of the first step was reached—the monarchical episcopate, the leadership of a congregation by one officeholder to whom the others, if there are any, are subordinate.

But no sooner was the monarchical episcopate once established, than the further development necessarily followed: it was inevitable that even in an area where several monarchical bishops existed alongside one another, sooner or later one of them had to take over the leadership of the entire province of the church. We can still trace this organization of church provinces and the hierarchical structure in individual places. For example, in Egypt (see pp. 50–51) around 200 we have Bishop Demetrius of Alexandria as the only bishop in the country. Alexandria, not only the largest congregation in the land, but apparently also the oldest, was originally not a single congregation, but the church in the city was made up of congregations in various parts of the city. At the head of these individual city congregations stood presbyters, who had a relatively independent relationship to the bishop up into the third and even into the fourth century. The bishop could exercise only limited influence over them; in Alexandria at that time he was only *primus inter pares* ("first among equals"). Demetrius made up for this by creating a network of dioceses throughout the entire country and placing at the head of each one a bishop who was directly subordinate to him. Thus, he established the powerful position which we see developing in Egypt in the bishop of Alexandria in the later centuries, especially the fourth and fifth centuries.

Alexandria probably did not stand alone in this development, but it was similar in other places, in Syria for example. Here we first have a monarchical bishop in Antioch; because he was the initial bishop and also had the largest congregation in the country, a position of leadership automatically came to him. He established other episcopal sees until the province of Syria was covered with a network of dioceses, at the head of which was the bishop of Antioch. Things were more problematic when several monarchical bishops already existed alongside one another, as was certainly the case in Asia Minor, as well as in Palestine and Greece. Then it took a longer process until the leadership of the entire church province came into the hands of one person. The person called to be the leader of the church province was then the bishop of the city which had the largest church and/or the most renowned history. In this way, clearly distinct areas of the church became established. With this the second stage came to a conclusion.

Then in the third stage one province of the church or one bishop surpassed all others, and in this way the larger churches of the West and of the East developed. In the West the bishop of Rome only seldom had serious opposition, although even here at certain times bishops of other cities were more influential than the bishop of Rome. At the time of Ambrose, for example, the bishop of Milan was at least equal to the one of Rome. But this circumstance was based exclusively on the person of Ambrose. Milan did retain a significant position after his death, but the danger of real opposition was past. It was the same in Africa during Augustine's time. Augustine at that time dominated not only the church of Africa, but that of the entire West, although he was not even bishop of the capital of Carthage, only the bishop of a provincial city. Augustine not only directed the bishop of Carthage, he not only dominated the synods of the African church, but also dominated the bishop of Rome whom he successfully opposed when Rome had a different opinion. But with Augustine's death that was over; in addition, the triumph of the

Vandals in Africa led to a catastrophe for the flourishing Catholic church, and finally destroyed any hope Carthage might have had of attaining a position alongside Rome, or even of only an independent relationship. Naturally, Rome also suffered much during the period of the Germanic attacks, but it still continued to remain—either officially or in a hidden way—the capital of the empire, at least the oldest and most respected city of the West; the church there was still the one with the claims of having been founded by Peter and Paul, the one which could lay claim to the promise given to Peter. Thus the development of the West into a united area of the church was accomplished relatively simply.

In the East, at first, the situation was a great deal more difficult. We have Jerusalem, Caesarea, Antioch, and a great number of other churches which go back into the earliest time, all of which could point to a splendid history and many great names. But the situation here changed quickly. Jerusalem declined considerably from its position because of the exodus of Christians into Trans-Jordan before the outbreak of the Jewish War, because of its destruction in A.D. 70, and even more because of the construction of the purely pagan Aelia Capitolina in the first half of the second century. Things were not much different in Asia Minor and Greece in the third and fourth centuries, although outstanding theologians were at work everywhere in these dioceses, everywhere in these church provinces. The position of leadership in the church of the East was assumed by Alexandria. This came to Alexandria first because of the extraordinary position Demetrius had created for the bishops of his church province. The bishops in the country were placed directly under the bishop of the capital; they obeyed—we can hardly express it any other way—every time he snapped his fingers. In the catechetical school in Alexandria, Egypt possessed a highly regarded center of theological education. From the end of the third century on, it was the heartland of monasticism, exemplifying the piety of the time. Of course, the monks, who were found throughout the country either as hermits or in monasteries, were difficult to deal with, for from the very beginning they stood in a certain opposition to the clergy. They felt themselves superior to those clergy who worked in the world and were entangled in worldly things. They had a certain tendency to regard the church and its hierarchy as superfluous for them and to separate themselves from the church. But when the bishop knew how to handle them correctly, they were of inestimable assistance for him. When the bishop called upon them to defend the true faith, the monks unhesitatingly rushed to him and placed themselves at his disposal, either to demonstrate loudly or forcibly to convince people who held different opinions. The use of a club soon became a significant part of the struggle not only with pagans, but also with theologians and congregations holding different opinions.

In addition, the history of the Egyptian church exhibits strong men: Athanasius in the fourth century, Cyril and Dioscoros in the fifth. It cannot be disputed that these men made use of every power available to them without being troubled by too many scruples. Even Athanasius was accused before Emperor Constantine of having a contrary-minded bishop murdered by his own bodyguard who carried out the bishop's every wish and command in a characteristically unscrupulous manner. The accusation is characteristic both for what they thought Athanasius capable of doing, as well as for the methods of his opponents. Athanasius's bodyguards saved him. They were immediately sent through the desert and brought the allegedly murdered bishop back to judgment from the remote monastery where he had been hidden (some resistance had to be overcome, both in the search and in the return).

Cyril played a decisive role at the Council of Ephesus in 431 and later at other synods. But when we look at the way these synods acted, then we can only say that they often played very loosely not only with the ecclesiastical rules of the game, but also with the rules that applied to the secular realm. The synod of Ephesus in 449, which was dominated by Dioscorus, was not called the "Robber Synod" for nothing. Even a shadow lies on the Council of Nicaea in 325, for here Constantine really exercised an inadmissible influence, or perhaps the bishops were too willing to bow to the emperor's influence and accepted theological statements to which they really could not inwardly agree. But what took place at Nicaea was only something minor compared to what took place at other famous ecumenical synods. Both in Ephesus in 431 and in Chalcedon in 451 we experience a disgraceful show, as bishops succumb to the power of the other side and loudly proclaim statements as the true faith, while only a few weeks earlier they claimed absolutely the opposite. This we mention only as a preface to our next chapter on the non-theological factors in church history (see pp. 143–69), which we must also examine if we desire to obtain a picture which corresponds to reality.

However, Alexandria's position was decisively weakened by the actions of its bishops; not a few of their triumphs were in reality Pyrrhic victories. Even as early as Athanasius's time, we see the theologians of the East opposing the theology represented by the Alexandrian bishop. That continued under Cyril and reached its height under Dioscorus.

When Bishop Dioscorus thought he had won the "victory" in Ephesus in 449, he ignored the previous alliance with Rome and the West, one of the decisive prerequisites for the previous position of Alexandria (and possibly also for its rise to dominance in the East). Now West and East join in fighting Alexandria's claims. Thus, this Egypt with its tight organization, with its great men, this Egypt which at that time appeared as a land of exemplary piety, was conquered in the struggle for leadership of the East by the youngest of all episcopal sees, namely, by Constantinople, which did not develop as a city—as a Christian church—until Constantine. The decisive cause for the decline of Alexandria was provided by Alexandria itself (see pp. 201–4). The second cause for its succumbing to Constantinople is to be found in non-theological factors. In Constantinople the rulers had their seat. Therefore they wanted to have the church in their capital rank above others. The emperors would have preferred for Constantinople to have first place altogether in the whole church. That was impossible, for Rome claimed that. So they attempted to place Constantinople at least second to Rome, in any case above all other episcopal sees in the East. Alexandria's bungled politics made that possible. By the middle of the fifth century the struggle had ended; Constantinople clearly had leadership in the East, just as Rome did in the West. Alexandria was now not only out of the race but led an existence on the fringes of the larger church, even in opposition to it (see pp. 203–4). The ultimate result of this development was the two great areas of the church, East and West.

Yet it was already obvious at the end of this third stage with its organization of two areas of the church, that the development was not at an end. Long before it actually came to a separation of the two, it was obvious that a division between East and West was inevitable. In the fifth century there was already evidence that the two great territories of the church were quite different. The inner alienation of the two proceeded rapidly; as the church entered the Middle Ages, it was completed (see p. 212). Everything that followed was only the logical consequence of this.

4. THE WRITINGS OF THE EARLY PERIOD

It is not possible to deal with the internal history of early Christianity without including its writings, which are the exclusive sources for our statements concerning its first centuries and from which we therefore must draw conclusions about the foundations on which the church built in later centuries. Our observation will limit itself to a few significant points, either examining or amplifying what we have said previously.

The Relationship Between East and West

As far as the New Testament is concerned, the only books we can even consider written in the West are Mark, Luke, Acts, Hebrews, and 1 Peter—nothing more. Everything else undoubtedly originated in the East, and most of these five writings just mentioned probably also belong to the East. Even most of the Apostolic Fathers come from the East. The West was the place of origin of 1 Clement, perhaps 2 Clement, and certainly the Shepherd of Hermas. Everything else comes from the East: probably 2 Clement and, in any case, the Epistle of Barnabas (with its allegorical interpretation of the Old Testament) and the *Didache* (that church constitution for early Christianity which carried forward in the time shortly after 100 that which we already see beginning in the pastoral epistles). Characteristically, the *Didache* had many successors because it continued to be necessary to adapt basic regulations for church life to the actual needs of the situation. The Epistles of Ignatius were written by the bishop of Antioch, the Epistle of Polycarp came from Smyrna in Asia Minor, and Papias also was from Asia Minor (he was the bishop of Hierapolis). It was the same with all the other writings of the early period.

The apocryphal literature, which at one time was exceptionally voluminous, was the literature which really edified people in the early period: the New Testament was officially read in the church, but the laity read the apocryphal books, insofar as they possessed the necessary requisites (they had to have money to buy the manuscripts, and they had to be "literary," that is, capable of doing more than just read and write; the latter was something which would not have applied to many Christians in the early age). This once exceptionally voluminous literature has been preserved for us only in fragments. This has to do with the development of the canon, which we have discussed (see pp. 108–14). A writing which the church officially excluded, which could not be read in the worship service, which was condemned by the church, circulated only for a limited time. The church even neglected its own writings which it no longer needed. If, for example, the writings of the Apologists and heretic fighters are only incompletely preserved, we cannot be surprised if we have only scraps today of what was once so rich an apocryphal literature. The Hebrew Gospel, the Ebionite Gospel, the Egyptian Gospel, the Nazarene Gospel—all of which played a prominent role in the ancient church—are preserved for us in such a fragmentary way that not only is the original form or the fundamental character of these gospels disputed, but even their very existence. Besides the fragments of these apocryphal gospels which may be compared to the canonical Gospels, we possess various other remnants of apocryphal gospel material.

For example, the Protevangelium of James, which tells us about Mary's childhood and which we previously knew only from late manuscripts, is now available to us as a whole in an early papyrus. In addition, from the find at Nag Hammadi we possess a complete fourth-century Coptic Gnostic library which, after very complicated negotations, is now available in facsimile and in a complete translation. Here we have available, in addition to numerous other important writings, a series of gospels about which we previously often knew only the titles: the Gospel of Thomas, the Gospel of Philip, and others. We therefore possess a much more complete understanding of the apocryphal gospels than previously, but everything we know today is only a small portion of that available to the ancient church.

In the subject matter treated by the canonical book of Acts, we have presentations, even if only fragmentary, of the life and work of almost all the apostles. The most famous are the *Acta Petri* ("Acts of Peter") and the *Acta Pauli* ("Acts of Paul"). We know about apocryphal letters of the apostles. Characteristically, these purport to fill in the obvious gaps in the New Testament. Thus, there is a 3 Corinthians, because it is clear in the Corinthian epistles that an epistle of Paul existed which has not been preserved. Thus, there is an Epistle to the Laodiceans, because Colossians says that Paul sent a letter to Laodicaea. But in addition to these works, there is also a writing such as the *Epistula Apostolorum* ("Epistle of the Apostles"), which records Jesus' conversations with his disciples after the resurrection. Among the apocryphal apocalypses we mention only the Apocalypse of Peter. All of this belongs to the literature of the East. The West also produced apocrypha, the previously mentioned correspondence between Paul and Seneca, for instance (see p. 12). We also see not a few apocryphal writings circulating in Latin translation, but the West is still far behind the East.

The situation with the Apologists is similar to that with the apocryphal writings. The Apologists all come from the East and have their intellectual homeland there. The first of them, Quadratus (about A.D. 130), comes from Asia Minor; Aristides (shortly thereafter), from Athens; Theophilus worked in Antioch; Athenagoras, also in Athens; and

Melito of Sardis represents Asia Minor. Until only recently we knew hardly anything about Melito. Eusebius preserved a few accounts of his life in his church history, a few fragments of his apology, and a list of his writings. Now in the early papyri we possess (and even in dual copies) one of Melito's Easter sermons, which opens up a new world for us. All of this, as we said, is literature of the East. The only Apologists who worked in the West were Justin and, at some times, Tatian. Nevertheless, they still remained Eastern writers. Tatian emphasized his Eastern origin; his opposition to Hellenism, especially to the Greek spirit, is unmistakable. Justin comes from Palestine; then he later received significant influences in Asia Minor (see pp. 29–31). As it went with Justin and Tatian, so it was with all the other famous names which we find in Rome in the second century. Marcion comes from the Black Sea area; the Monarchians, from Asia Minor, thus from the East. We have already emphasized (see p. 54) that they go to the West only because it holds promise for the success of their cause if they and their message can gain a hearing in Rome. Even in the third century, the most significant theologians of the West came from the East, for example, Hippolytus (see pp. 152–53). We know nothing certain about his origin, but at least we can say that Hippolytus either came directly from the East to the West, or at least he was marked by Eastern influence and lived in the Eastern intellectual world. Around 180, Irenaeus worked as a bishop in Gaul, but there can be no doubt about his origin in Asia Minor or the fact that he viewed it as his intellectual and spiritual homeland.

There are only a few exceptions to this rule that the early literature comes from the East. Among them are Minucius Felix and his Apology, from which we earlier quoted extensively (see pp. 72–74), and above all Tertullian. So far the question of which of the two is earlier remains unanswered. Did Minucius Felix write before or after Tertullian? Is he dependent on Tertullian (this is the more probable), or is Tertullian's Apology dependent on Minucius Felix? In any case, Minucius Felix belongs to the West, perhaps even to Rome (the conversation which we reported and which provides the framework for the entire writing does take place during a journey from Rome to Ostia). Minucius Felix doubtless performs an outstanding task, but Tertullian is infinitely more important for the West than he. Tertullian provided the West with the necessary prerequisites for translating the Bible into Latin; he created the Latin ecclesiastical language and made Latin capable of expressing Christian concepts and expression taken over from Greek. Tertullian was just as important for Western theological thought for many centuries to come. We find him already anticipating the controversies which troubled the fourth and fifth centuries. The results achieved after the long struggles of the Arian and Christological controversies were already expressed by Tertullian. In particular, that which the West contributed to these solutions is directly traceable to Tertullian. It has been asked how this was possible, and the usual answer given is that it was coincidental. Certainly this answer is incorrect, for this is too much to be a coincidence. Tertullian could not have developed these Trinitarian and Christological statements by chance. Perhaps they are the results of formal thinking, and Tertullian may not have comprehended the range and depth of the future questioning. But in any case, his statements were a result of conscious theological reflection.

However, Tertullian stood completely alone. Except for Minucius Felix, who was soon forgotten when his Apology was no longer needed, there was no one comparable to him. In addition, he ended up at odds with the church, from which he withdrew in 207 in order to join the Montanists (see p. 94). Thus, he lost his official standing in the Western church; at least the church in later times could no longer officially appeal to him. It had to suppress his name, even though it made great use of him—even directly, but most of all indirectly. We can study the church's direct use of him a generation later in Cyprian, the second most significant Western writer. Cyprian was indeed greatly dependent upon Tertullian; many of his writings sound just like repetitions of Tertullian's works. We know that he read them every day. But even Cyprian, no matter how much his writings mirrored Tertullian's thought, could not quote him directly.

Around the middle of the third century, once again an original Western theologian writing in Latin appears, Novatian. But the church also expelled him (see pp. 54–55). Thus, from the beginning of the second century onward, we see an independent Latin literature slowly arising, but for a long time its sole official representative remains Cyprian. Even Cyprian was not a writer in the real sense. For him, writing was only an occasional task. Cyprian understood himself as a bishop. He picked up his pen only when he wanted to give his thoughts the widest possible distribution. His writings were to carry his word, his advice, and his wishes to places which he could not personally reach. That was also true at the end of the fourth century with Ambrose, whose literary work indeed possesses a great significance but nevertheless was not the decisive thing he did.

In the third century we also have Victorinus of Pettau (in Styria!), the first exegete of the Western church. He wrote the first biblical commentaries in the Latin language. Victorinus certainly came from the East, so that when we go through the Western literature of the early centuries the only writers we still find are Arnobius and Lactantius. With both of them we are already at the beginning of the fourth century, that is, in the Constantinian age, into which Victorinus, who died in 304 as a martyr in the Diocletian persecution, also extends. And—this must be added—Arnobius was at best only a mediocre figure. His works have no special significance.

When we summarize by placing before us the names mentioned—Minucius Felix, Tertullian, Cyprian, Novatian, Victorinus, Lactantius, and Arnobius, that is, the entire literature of the large church in the Latin West—we once again observe that in the early period the West was absolutely surpassed by the East. It remained this way during the whole of the Arian and Christological controversies, that is, through the entire epoch we are considering until virtually its end. The theological controversies were raised in the East; the theological controversies were fought in the East. The theological decisions were made in the East, even if the West took part in these struggles and decisions, even if the synods which made these decisions met in the West. The theologians of the West did participate in the decisions of the time, but it was not a productive, creative participation. It might be said that they did not act, but were acted upon. For example, at the end of the second and the beginning of the third century we see the Monarchian controversies being transferred from Asia Minor to Rome (see pp. 190–91). In Monarchianism we have to deal with what might be called a prehistoric stage of the Arian controversy. It was an attempt to harmonize monotheism, Christianity's basic tenet, with the fact that Scripture speaks not only about God but also about Christ and the Holy Spirit. This problem was solved in a twofold way. Mostly, the solution was to label Jesus and the Holy Spirit as ways in which God appeared, as modes of divinity (therefore, modalistic Monarchianism). The divinity has different ways of appearing: as Father, as Son, as Holy Spirit. On the other hand, we have dynamistic Monarchianism (the Greek *dynamis* means power): God sends his spirit into the man Jesus and in this way changes him into Christ. Thus they maintained monotheism, but ran into difficulties with the problem of the Trinity. As the Monarchians came to Rome and taught this, the Roman church proved itself helpless in the face of this theology. This we learn from the statements of the Roman bishops of that time. Zephyrinus and Callistus were not in a position to argue with the Monarchians, let alone overcome them theologically and present a real solution to the problem. Only Hippolytus could do that, but Hippolytus came from the East, while the other two were (typical) representatives of the West.

Even if we look at Western theologians who really participated in the controversies of the time and took an independent part in them, as was the case with Hilary of Poitiers (ca. 315–67) in the Arian controversy, the reason for this is found in the fact that these theologians lived in the East and there gained a deeper understanding of the questions at issue. Hilary was banished to the East by Constantine. Here in the East he learned to comprehend the questions with which the Arian controversy dealt. Thus he could help not only his own church, but the church in general in solving the problems. The situation remained as we have described it throughout the entire period until the conclusion of the Christological controversy in which the *Epistula dogmatica*, the dogmatic tome of Bishop Leo I (440–61), attained great significance. The participants at Chalcedon in 451 acclaimed Leo's tome as a proclamation of orthodoxy and accepted it. Ever since, we find this tome mentioned again and again when people want to emphasize the West's theological achievement. For the 1500th anniversary of the Council of Chalcedon a three-volume anthology appeared (incidentally, a treasure trove of erudition), yet the real reason certainly was only to display the theological achievement of the West (and of a pope) in the ancient church. Yet even the tome of Leo, looked at carefully, is not an original theological achievement but in its nucleus only repeats the theological statement about the Trinity and Christology already given to the Western world by Tertullian (see p. 200).

Obviously, the longer these disputes continued, the more the West achieved a definite point of view. And the West performed very significant services in these controversies, for example, in maintaining the doctrine of the two natures against the East, which had been influenced by Monophysitism more than was permissible. But what the West represented was something it had inherited, not something it had achieved itself. What is to be credited to the West, as far as the internal development of the church in the early centuries is concerned, lies in another area: in church organization, in the ordering of ecclesiastical life. It is no coincidence that the power of the episcopal office was brought to its completion in Rome (by Callistus). It is no coincidence that the original form of the Apostles' Creed originated in Rome. It is no coincidence that the fullest list of the early canonical writings which we possess, the Muratorian Canon, comes from the West.

There is only one real exception to this rule of theological dominance of the East, which we must realize in order to understand the development of the early centuries. But this exception belongs to the end of the period we are considering. It is provided by Augustine. Augustine (354–430) now really furnished not only an original contribution, but also a decisive one, to Christian theology's further development. As soon as Augustine appears, we see the roles reversed. In the Pelagian and Semipelagian controversies (see pp. 206–12), the East is the observer who stands on the periphery of the events without any inner understanding, without even any inner participation, and looks on with a certain lack of understanding while the West wrestles with the problems of free will, sin, grace, and the redemption of humankind. The East took over this and that, but without really comprehending it, and thus had only a walk-on part in it, a role which for so long had been characteristic of the West. Augustine, however, as we have said, belongs to the conclusion of the period we are considering. He represents the emancipation of the West; with him we see how the two areas of the church now go ways which move farther and farther apart. The division between the church in the East and that in the West was in preparation, a division which was already a reality in the Carolingian age, even though it was centuries longer until it was proclaimed officially.

The Authors

The church's most decisive assistance in its struggle with Gnosticism, with Marcion's church, with Montanism, and the other rival churches of the second century was given by the writings of the heretic fighters. They furnished theologians and also laity with arguments they could use to counter not only the spread of the rival churches, but were also useful in strengthening those in their own ranks who were wavering. Three names should be mentioned here—or rather repeated, since we have already spoken about Tertullian (see p. 116), as well as Irenaeus (see p. 130), and Hippolytus (see p. 130). Irenaeus wrote about 180, Tertullian about 200, and Hippolytus at the beginning of the third century (died probably 235). These three are the only heretic fighters for whom we can construct even an approximate picture. It is characteristic that all three of them first became visible to us at the height of their activity; we do not know when they were born, we do not know when they died. They come out of the darkness, and they disappear into the darkness which surrounds that age. In addition, there were a great many others who attempted with their writings to assist the church in its struggle against the heretics of the time. Of them we know nothing but their names and the titles of their writings. Sometimes we possess fragments of their works, but we have no real idea of their writings. In fact, we must assume that there are a great many more whose names and whose titles of their writings have not even been passed down to us. After a writing against the heretics of the second and third centuries had performed its task, it was of no more interest to the church and was no longer preserved. After the task was accomplished, those who had done the decisive work were forgotten. At that time it was very easy for individual authors—even an entire class of writings—to be forgotten; all that had to be done was no longer to copy it. Until the invention of printing many centuries later, the fact that people no longer copied a manuscript was the equivalent of pronouncing a death sentence on the writing or writings contained in it. Naturally, a whole series of manuscripts containing a particular work or works existed at one time. But some time or another they would perish when they were no longer copied; thus the existence of the works included in them came to an end. In this way a substantial portion of early Christian writing met its doom. As far as the most significant writings and writers of the early period are concerned (for example, Justin and Clement of Alexandria), we possess only a single manuscript from each one which transmits their works to us in a more or less unsatisfactory form; and the only reason we have this single manuscript is that there was a bishop in the tenth century who was interested in history and had the old manuscripts of the Apologists—Clement, Justin, and others—copied once again.

In the early age there was not yet a Christian literature in the real sense, to which we can apply the laws pertaining to the transmission of other literature. For good reason we have previously spoken about Christian writings, not about Christian literature. Not until the second century do we find Christian literature in the complete sense of the word appearing. It is first represented in the writings of the Apologists, as well as in the writings of the heretic fighters. Now the authors of these writings also appear to us as individuals. They attempt to create a literature which exists alongside the pagan kind, is considered to be literature according to contemporary conventions, and is also distributed through contemporary means—in modern terms, we would say through bookstores. Up until then things were completely different. Naturally the church possessed a "literature" from the very beginnings.

As soon as Paul wrote his letters, from the year 50 onward, "literature" appeared surpassing the level of most of that in existence at the time. But it is not right to apply the term "literature" to it. This is seen in the fact that—except for the letters in the real sense which we possess—the authors of these writings are not accessible to us, because they do not want to be accessible to us, and this is true because they just do not want to write literature in the usual sense.

The letters of the New Testament period, insofar as they are really letters, are occasional writings, no matter how high a literary status they may have. When Paul writes letters, when Ignatius writes letters, the author clearly reveals himself in them, just as is necessary in letters at any time, that is, someone writes something quite specific to a quite specific recipient with quite specific presumptions in a quite specific situation; all of this is clearly visible. These letters were meant directly only for the recipient or recipients. That a letter of Ignatius was passed on to other churches, that a letter of Paul was read in other Pauline congregations does not alter this situation. The recipients are clearly outlined. They are clearly named, as is also the writer and everything else, in order that they may know what and who is really meant. These letters—just to repeat it—no matter how great a literary character they may have, belong outside the sphere of ordinary literature. All other writings that we possess, except for the actual letters, that is, all the writings of the New Testament, all the writings of the Apostolic Fathers, all the apocryphal writings (in other words, everything written up to the middle of the second century; here we again confront the decisive turning point around 150) are written either anonymously or pseudonymously, that is, either without the author's name or with the name of someone other than the real writer. This is continually seen as a problem when people regard the question of pseudonymity as an ethical problem and ask how it is possible that here a person can write in the name of Paul, Peter, James, John, or someone else—assuming a mantle which rightfully belongs to someone else. This way of putting the ethical question proceeds from incorrect assumptions and leads to incorrect results. To a great extent the difficulties in dealing with the problem are based on the fact that the New Testament scholars who speak about pseudonymity look only at the New Testament and do not consider the Apostolic Fathers, let alone the apocryphal writings. When we look at the early Christian writings as a whole, we see that even there where we might with certainty expect to find the writer named, he disappears totally into the background and the work does not appear under his

name. For example, 1 Clement—65 chapters long—just like all the
other writings of the Apostolic Fathers, does not name its author. The
"First Epistle of Clement" title in the manuscripts and similar comments
are additions of later writers; in the work's text itself the author is never
mentioned. Here it is simply the Roman church writing to the Corinthian church. Or let us take the Gospel of Luke. It begins in a very
literary fashion; here the recipient is named, here the purpose of the
work is given, but the name of the author is lacking. It is also missing in
the Epistle of Barnabas and everywhere else up until the middle of the
second century. Early Christian writings are anonymous. If we carefully
read through the first three Gospels looking for evidence of their writers, we shall find the writers nowhere speaking about themselves. Only
in the title or in the postscript (that is, in something added by later
copyists) do the writers' names appear. Even where it speaks about the
author, for example, in John 21 where the beloved disciple is mentioned
and people believe they can identify him with the writer, this apparently
simple identification is complicated by the fact that two other disciples
are mentioned at the same time. Wherever things are written in the early
age which are not really letters naming their writers (or in the case of an
apocalypse where a description of the circumstances of its reception is
part of the testimony to its genuineness), but rather writings which claim
a general audience and letters which are not directed to a definite
recipient (that is, circular writings to the general church), the writer
hides himself. He knows that he is only a tool, that he writes for
someone else. He is the mouthpiece of the Holy Spirit, and in this
regard his person is not only without significance, but it would be
presumptuous if he were to name his own person.

This is how the anonymity and pseudonymity of early Christian writings comes about. The writer gives his work the name of the apostle he
respects most highly, or who is most highly regarded in the church
province where he is writing or among the theological school to which he
belongs: if James is named as author, that is—remembering the historical James—part of the anti-Pauline concept represented in it, and if the
writer of Jude labels himself as the "brother of James," he does this
intentionally. We can best clarify this problem by looking at the *Didache*
which gives as its author not simply one apostle, but the Lord himself
and all twelve apostles; or at the *Epistula Apostolorum*, for which the
same is true. Without doubt, the *Didache* was first read in the worship
service, as were all early Christian writings, and in the worship service of
a church in which its writer was an officeholder. Everyone in the church

knew that the person reading this work was its author, and at the same time everyone in the church recognized that even though the work had been written by this presbyter, it still did not belong to him, but—as the beginning of the text says—to the Lord and the twelve apostles because of the spiritual authority in which it was written and because the content corresponded to what they expected of a message from the Lord and the twelve apostles. That was exactly the way it was in the early church. If the prophet—we recall the way 1 Corinthians 14 depicts it—stands and speaks in the congregation, while it may indeed be Individual X or Individual Y whom everyone knows who speaks, yet is it not that Prophet X or Y, but the Holy Ghost who is speaking through the prophet or prophetess; the message which is proclaimed confirms that. The hearer or the reader of these writings is not dealing with just any writer, but with the Lord, the Holy Spirit, or the apostles as bearers of the Holy Spirit. Only when we look at the early Christian writings in this way can we understand them correctly, and then the problem of pseudonymity and anonymity is solved by itself.

Not until the middle of the second century, at the time of the great turning point which we have mentioned again and again (see pp. 93–95)—as the blowing of the Spirit subsides, as people begin to think historically—does a real pseudonymity originate. Works are now written which intentionally bear the name of an apostle as a pseudonym. Tertullian reports such an episode. At that time a presbyter had written Acts of Paul (probably the *Acta Pauli* which is known to us); it was determined (from its contents) that it could not have been written by Paul or one of his contemporaries and he was asked why he had done it. He answered: he had done it *amore Pauli,* for the love of Paul, and therefore had issued this work under Paul's name. At the end of the second century the problem of pseudonymity originated, something which does not exist in the earlier period. It is no coincidence that it is not until the second half of the second century with the Apologists that we find the first individual authors of Christian literature and that it is then that Christian literature in the real sense originates—writings with the name of a real author who intends to perform a literary endeavor in the modern sense.

The Development of Early Christian Literature

About A.D. 150, Justin begins the writings of the Apologists (Quadratus and Aristides deserve the rank only of forerunners), who now take up the task of defending Christianity against the attacks of pagans. At that time the pagans were taking greater notice of the expanding church and consequently fighting it (see p. 5); therefore, the origination of an apologetic literature in the real sense was necessary. Naturally the apologetic task had been performed previously; in the New Testament we find sections which are clearly apologetic in nature. Naturally there were also apologists afterward; for example, Origen, Lactantius, Eusebius, and even Augustine himself wrote apologetic writings. But when we speak of the Apologists we mean a very definite group of Greek writers, brought together not only by the task they undertake but also by the ways in which they attempt to fulfill this task—by their theological standpoint and by their method of argumentation. Minucius Felix and Tertullian, for example, are not far removed in time from these Apologists. They deal with the same subjects, but still are not numbered in their ranks. There is a good reason for this. From Minucius Felix we learn about the accusations made against Christianity at that time (see pp. 72.–74). The Apologists, and also Tertullian, devote themselves to refuting these charges. Yet they do not limit themselves to this, but simultaneously undertake an attack on the pagan world view and pagan cults. This they do, as was most easy, by first using the anthropomorphic features of pagan mythology to present the low moral standards of pagan belief. As proof for the truth of Christianity, they compare this to Christianity's moral achievements, to its higher moral standards. Thus they are in agreement with Minucius Felix and Tertullian, but they go even further by using the so-called proof of antiquity. With the assistance of an extremely complicated (and questionable) chronology, they explain that Moses is older than all philosophy and all philosophers. If there is anything right and good among the philosophers and the philosophies, it can come only from Moses and the prophets. Since they are older, everything which is later—insofar as it corresponds to it—must rest upon it. Christianity is the only true philosophy, the only correct philosophy—that is the fundamental conviction of the Apologists. In addition, its truth is proved—this is the so-called prophetic proof—by the fact that everything prophesied in the Old Testament has been fulfilled in the New Testament.

When we read the writings of these Apologists—even though many of their arguments are no longer convincing for us—they are, all in all, very impressive reading material. Here the writers of antiquity are quoted profusely—the philosophers and the poets. We must not conclude, however, that the Apologists have completely read all the writings of these philosophers and poets, worked through them on their own, and inwardly mastered them. A great deal of the erudition which we meet here is not original, but comes only from the *florilegia,* the collection of quotations which were used at that time. Some of the arguments are in no way so unique as it appears when one first reads such an apologetic writing. And even the effect of the Apologists was probably different than we imagine. I believe we must largely question whether the Apologists attained their real goal, namely, reaching the educated pagan world through the "book market." At any rate, it seems certain that they never, or only very seldom, reached the people they were really addressing. Almost without exception, the Apologists dedicated their writings to the emperors reigning at the time or sent them directly to them. Yet these writings still had an extraordinary effect. It is true (as we have already said) that normally they did not get into the hands of the educated pagans whom they really wanted to address, but they definitely did come into those of theologians and educated Christians, who most probably were the real readers of these apologies and who themselves now transmitted the fruits of their reading to the simple laity. From the writings of the Apologists, they all—the theologians, the educated, the ordinary Christians—extracted arguments which they could use in their daily conflicts, with which they could defend themselves against attacks, as well as arguments which they could themselves use in attacking paganism in their surroundings. In this way the Apologists did have a great influence.

Their significance was not only limited to this, however, but went even further. These Apologists are what may be called the first systematic theologians. This they were only involuntarily and only "part-time," for the work of systematic theology could be called something only incidental to the performance of their main task. Whoever wants to defend Christianity and its doctrinal views must first be able to present it in a logical manner, or at least understand it in a systematically cohesive manner. That did not exist in previous writings. The Apologists accomplished a work of theological thought which very significantly helped the further development of Christianity and its dogmatic formation. Also, the Apologists are not simply apologists. Their apologies are preserved for us because they, above all else, were still of interest to the later ages and because a bishop in the tenth century had most of these writings copied from old manuscripts for historical reasons. Everything else was lost. We need only look at the list of Melito of Sardis's writings which we have already mentioned (see p. 130) or observe the one of Justin's writings which Eusebius transmits to us in his church history. Here we see that these Apologists engaged in a broad literary activity and wrote not only works against pagans and Jews but also sermons, practical instructions for the church, general admonitions, theological studies, and writings against heretics. Thus we do not possess a complete picture of the Apologists, but only a narrow excerpt from them. If we possessed their writings in their full variety, we would have a much more complete picture not only of the Apologists themselves but also of the theological and ecclesiastical development of the second century than we do.

But even if this lost literature were still available to us in its completeness, the total impression which we receive when we read the Apologists would certainly not change. Here they attempt a first beginning; they undertake first efforts; but the ultimate success eludes them. The Apologists accomplish a pioneering work. But they do not succeed in completely accomplishing their task. They only create the prerequisites which allowed theological thought and theological literature to make the powerful advance at the turn of the third century we have already seen in Irenaeus—indeed that allowed a high point in the entire history of both theology and the church to be reached immediately after 200. That this happens is due to the achievement of the two men who worked in Alexandria at that time, Clement around 200 and Origen in the decades after that. Clement already stood on a completely different level than the Apologists. He could take philosophy, which the Apologists still saw existing apart from Christianity, and connect it organically with Christianity, even make it a prerequisite. If we read Justin, we will see how the so-called Christian philosophy and the traditional faith of the church are different things for him, unconnected with one another, indeed opposing one another. On the contrary, Clement attempts to introduce philosophy into the Christian way of thinking, into the theological world of thought, and he even raises the demand for a Christian Gnosticism. These are things at which the second century is appalled. At that time philosophy possessed a pagan character—Tertullian, for example, fought vehemently against its influence on Christianity—and Gnosticism (see pp. 95–96), which was emphatically resisted, then appeared to be its chief opponent. With Clement, philosophy attained a significance not only for pagans (a significance which can be compared with that of the Old Testament for the Jews), but it also attained a significance for Christians, for the theological work of the Christian church. The attempt was made to lead theology and the church to a higher stage of recognizing God, to that which Clement called Christian

Gnosticism, although this Gnosticism was obviously different from that of the second century in both its starting point and its final form.

But even the theological work of Clement deserves only the character of preparatory work. Not until Origen was a real synthesis reached between the knowledge and wisdom of that time and the Christian faith. Origen stood at the summit of contemporary learning and fused it with Christianity into one unity. This occurred at only one other time in the history of Christianity—a thousand years later in scholasticism. With Origen, Christianity was led from its beginnings to the summit of the age. We need only read the tribute of Gregory Thaumaturgus who stopped at Caesarea as a tourist just to catch a glimpse of Origen's school that was so famous. But he remained there many years, bound and thoroughly captivated by what Origen taught. Here with Origen, said Gregory, one could really learn to comprehend why man was created, what heights the human spirit was capable of attaining. What was seen only in preliminary fashion in pagan philosophy here achieved its real completion. Not only Christians felt this way, but Origen enjoyed the highest reputation even among pagans. Without Origen, what we see happening in theology and in the church in the following period just cannot be understood. To overstate the case, the theological controversies of the following age can be understood as the result of Origen's theology; they occur as various groups in various ways either abbreviate or separate and expand on what Origen still viewed as a unity.

IV

History Among People

1. THE CONFLICTS OF THE EARLY PERIOD

Origen achieved a unique theological accomplishment. If we read the presentation of him, which Eusebius gives in the sixth book of his church history, we will be deeply impressed not only with Origen's theological accomplishment but also with his personality, his faith, and his moral character. Origen, among all the people of his age, has the material of sainthood. Yet, nevertheless, the church of his homeland condemned him during his lifetime; nevertheless, the church again expelled him in Justinian's time; and nevertheless, Luther confirmed the earlier age's condemnation, although with different arguments. Luther condemned Origen for theological reasons. Justinian's age damned Origen because of his students, who adopted his ideas but changed them. His own age did not condemn Origen for theological reasons, but for reasons of power politics, which we shall discuss later (see pp. 150–51).

This sort of thing happened not only around 230 in Alexandria, but in other places as well, and these kinds of deplorable activities did not first take place at the beginning of the third century, but a great deal earlier. There is a constant temptation to present the beginnings of the church in shining colors and embellish the presentation of the early period with golden colors against a golden background; and it is not only in the minds of laity and pastors where this happens but also among those who carry on scholarly work, whether in the area of church history or New Testament studies. This is understandable from the impressions of the present and even from the impressions we get from the final period of ancient church history. For example, in the fourth and fifth centuries we see many things in the history of the church which we do not like. We easily come to an interpretation about the first three centuries as programmatically announced in the title of Gottfried Arnold's early writing in 1696: *The First Love, that is, True Portrait of Early Christians and about their Living Faith and Holy Life.* This is the way Pietism saw the

143

early church, this is the way the age of the Reformation saw the early church; and this is also the way we too easily see it—even those who write scholarly literature. Therefore a chapter is necessary in which we present the other side and in which we clearly see the shadow which lies over the early church.

We cannot dispose of the evidences of decline in church history so easily by saying—as is done again and again—that it first began in the fourth century and occurred when the state began to influence the church, when the world invaded the church. It is not that simple at all. That "theory of decline," which was held by Gottfried Arnold (and which we find not only with him, but even earlier, namely, with Luther), and which is still being proclaimed in our own day, does not correspond with the reality of the early centuries. What we are now going to speak about does appear more pronounced and profoundly in recent times than in the early period. But it is not foreign to the early age. This cannot be otherwise, for the church of the earliest age also was a church made up of human beings. And human beings not only have weaknesses but also failures. This does not justify weakness and failure, and no conclusion could be more incorrect than to say that because it has always been this way, it is not really so bad that it is also this way with us. Our weaknesses and failures cannot be excused in this way. Also, we can adopt the judgment made by Martin Luther only in a very limited way and only with quite definite assumptions. In Luther we find the paradoxical statement: his favorite among the apostles is really Judas. We would hardly believe that possible, if Luther did not explain it by saying: when I look at my weakness and my failure, then I can take comfort that the Lord tolerated Judas among the disciples. If that was possible, I too with my weakness and failure can attain forgiveness. The reminder that we really cannot apply this word of Luther's to ourselves unless we have accomplished something similar, should—we hope—be sufficient to prevent any facile adoption of this approach. Therefore, we say—to put it mildly—that it is simply not possible to demand this; we can speak this way only if we have used all our available power, even to the point of self-destruction—as we see Luther did—against the weaknesses and failures of ourselves, our church, and our age. For example, those who choose the calling of a pastor or teacher should be clearly aware that they must not think of these two callings as a soft featherbed in which the chief concern is social prestige, pension benefits, many holidays, and the like. Rather, both callings should be thought of as sacrificial callings. All teachers should do their utmost to see that the children entrusted to them are formed into complete human beings and Christians. In most cases, the responsibility for the entire later lives of these youth will lie in their hands. They should constantly keep that in mind. We really do not need to mention the responsibility of a pastor; it is the most important one in existence. Certainly pastors also need relaxation, and no one can demand a twenty-four-hour day from them, but we certainly can demand that they use all their powers in the service of their congregation. And those who take their responsibility in this office seriously will find that they possess more strength than they previously believed. Those who choose one of these two callings because they think of themselves and not of the task they are undertaking are in the wrong place.

Even the writings of the New Testament show that the church of the early period was not fundamentally different from ours. When we read the Gospels from this perspective, again and again we find that they speak of the disciples' weakness and lack of understanding (this is not only a literary device, as is often the case in Mark's and John's Gospels). We can find enough tangible examples of this: it was not only Judas who betrayed the Lord, but Peter also denied him three times. The disciples fled in anticipation of Jesus' death. There can be no doubt of the historicity of these accounts. They belong to the solid deposit of the earliest tradition and would not have been included in the Gospels if everyone had not known that they were historically true. And what things of this sort we find in the Gospels continue in the conflict between Peter and Paul in Antioch, which Paul briefly reports in Galatians? As a rule, we read right past this, without thinking about what it meant for the contemporary age, what it means in general. Paul's presentation is indisputable. The most we can say is that the matter is not reported thoroughly and sharply enough. Even in Jerusalem conflicts of considerable importance had arisen, which are only briefly sketched in Gal. 2:4, 5: "But because of false brethren secretly brought in, who slipped in to spy out our freedom which we have in Christ Jesus, that they might bring us into bondage—to them we did not yield submission even for a moment, that the truth of the gospel might be preserved for you," writes Paul. According to Paul's account, in these serious arguments those who headed the church came to his side and gave him complete freedom of action. Then in Antioch it came to an argument with Peter, even in front of the assembled congregation. Galatians 2:11 reports this: "But when Cephas came to Antioch I opposed him to his face, because he stood condemned." At first Peter had maintained full table fellowship with the Gentiles; that meant that he ignored the Jewish dietary restriction, the ceremonial law. But then a delegation came from James. Peter immediately broke off table fellowship with the Gentiles and observed the Jewish regulation. Even Barnabas was caught up by his example, so that the church was plunged into great confusion. Peter, who had formerly lived with them and confessed the same gospel which had been proclaimed to them and which they believed, separated himself from them. In the congregational assembly Paul confronted Peter about it—one of the leading figures of Christianity, one of the "pillars" of the church— and this confrontation did not deal with personal accusations, but with a fundamental dispute about his conduct and the theological assumptions behind it. In all of church history there is no analogy to this event. If we could perhaps imagine two leaders rising up against one another in the general assembly of the World Council of Churches or at a synod and accusing one another of false doctrine, this sort of example could not be remotely compared with these events in Antioch (especially because something similar can take place so easily today).

Likewise the Corinthian epistles must be read with an entirely different sort of attention than is customary. To us the parties existing there easily appear to parallel modern groups and really not to have a great deal of significance. However, the parties were not formed around mere differences of theological understanding, as might be the case today in a congregation, or in the church, or even in every theological faculty; rather, they were factions which most vehemently fought one another and denied the very name of Christian to their opponents. The only comparison we can find to these party struggles is in the most vehement disputes and condemnatory judgments of the period of Orthodoxy in the sixteenth and seventeenth centuries. In addition, in Corinth there were not only these factions, but at the same time there existed serious grievances in the worship services and most serious moral deficiencies.

Naturally, these were only individual cases; not everything in the entire life of the Corinthian church looked like this. But this Corinthian congregation had lent its ear to those who slandered Paul to such an extent that it had really fallen away from Paul and could only be restored to him by a special act of providence (see p. 48). That is the way things were already at the beginning of the church. A great deal of what we can intuitively imagine in the later centuries, even those things which the theory of decline says should not have happened until those later centuries, already existed during the beginning stage. Then, when these first churches were organized into church provinces, and the church provinces were brought together into regions of the church, this also did not happen harmoniously like the growth of a flower, forming a bud which then developed into a blossom—even though we sometimes see it presented this way. In fact, the organization of church provinces with one locality at their head and the organization of church provinces into an inclusive area of the church not infrequently took place in the midst of serious arguments. We see these beginning as early as the second century and must conclude that here are characteristics which some people believe possible only in the later centuries.

2. ROME AND ASIA MINOR

The story begins with the argument between Rome and Asia Minor in the second century. In its sharpness this argument is in line with the dispute between Peter and Paul in Antioch. It did not happen by chance, but we can only correctly understand this and the subsequent arguments if we presume that in them Rome inwardly and outwardly liberated itself from the preponderance of the church in Asia Minor. In the early centuries, Asia Minor, as we have seen (see pp. 53–55), was not only numerically of greater importance, but the direct theological and ecclesiastical influences which came from Asia Minor were extraordinary and the indirect ones even greater.

Asia Minor was the heartland of the church in the early period. On the other hand, the Roman church was no less conscious of its own significance. This high self esteem was based not only on the fact that the Roman church was the church of the world capital where Peter and Paul had worked and died, but it was based also on its own accomplishments. It appears that this church had possessed influential and wealthy members from the very beginning and had made genuine use of the possibilities created thereby, so that very early Rome was accorded special recognition by other congregations. The ties which apparently had existed since very early times with Corinth, Egypt, Carthage, and other places, were also defined by these circumstances. Rome had helped these churches in their financial difficulties, as well as in other ways. We usually regard 1 Clement, written around 95 by the Roman church to Corinth, as a testimony to the highly developed self-opinion of the church. When we read the demand in 1 Clement that the Corinthians should revoke the deposition of clergy which they had undertaken (see p. 122), this self-opinion certainly plays a definite role in this. But I rather think we must emphasize another perspective as well: this demand of 1 Clement—and the letter in general—are completely understandable only if we assume that old and close ties exist between the two churches. This is the only basis on which the Roman church can speak in the way we see it doing. In any event, we know that in Corinth at the beginning of the second century they were still thankful for the support given by the Roman church. There is no documentary evidence to prove that connections must have existed between Rome and Egypt at an early date. That can be concluded only from the close connection we see existing between Alexandria and Rome during the early centuries of church history. But here it is also probable to assume that Rome had used its means to render special service to the early Egyptian church, which needed it urgently around A.D. 200 (see p. 51).

At any rate, in the argument between Rome and Asia Minor in the second century we see a church with a well-founded opinion of itself, namely Rome, opposing the center of Christianity, namely Asia Minor. The first conflict took place very early, when Polycarp visited Rome about A.D. 150. During this visit a conflict occurred over the different ways of celebrating Easter. It was the practice in Rome at that time not to hold a special Easter celebration, but, in accordance with the old practice, to commemorate every Sunday as the day of the Lord's resurrection. In Asia Minor the festival of Easter had been developing for a long time. It was celebrated on the fourteenth of Nisan, the day of the Jewish Passover, regardless of the day of the week on which the historical anniversary actually fell. When Polycarp of Smyrna came to Rome, the discrepancy became obvious and the matter was debated. But the Roman bishop Anicetus not only tolerated the practice of the church in Asia Minor, but as a sign of his esteem for Polycarp even let him celebrate the eucharist in the Roman church.

A generation later, about A.D. 190, the controversy recurred. The disputants were nominally the same, although other men now stood at the head of each group: in Rome Victor was bishop; Polycrates of Ephesus represented Asia Minor. But in reality the situation had changed. In the meantime Rome's position had grown considerably and so had its demands, and Polycrates did not possess the worldwide esteem that Polycarp had. Therefore the arguments did not proceed as peacefully as they had a generation earlier, but rather were drawn out to the ultimate consequence.

Perhaps the Romans felt themselves provoked, for we hear that a presbyter from Asia Minor is supposed to have attempted at that time to introduce, in Rome, Asia Minor's custom of celebrating Easter. In the meantime Rome had begun to celebrate Easter. But here they celebrated Easter not on the fourteenth of Nisan, as they did in Asia Minor, but they combined—another evidence of the practicality which dominated in Rome—this date with the traditional festival of Easter on Sunday and celebrated Easter in the week in which the fourteenth of Nisan fell. Thus the commemoration began on Friday and concluded on Sunday, just as today.

When the clash with Asia Minor occurred at this time, Victor inquired how the other church provinces celebrated Easter and learned that they also celebrated the festival of Easter in the same way as Rome was doing. Asia Minor stood alone with its practice, which was indeed older, in fact the oldest practice. It was historically justified, but in the meantime everywhere else this practice had been combined with the even older one of celebrating Easter on Sunday. Apparently it was demanded that Asia Minor should conform to the practice of the other provinces of the church. Asia Minor protested strongly against this, appealing to the esteemed history and tradition of its church. Consequently, Victor announced to all churches that he had broken church fellowship with Asia Minor. That was a measure which was completely unheard of, considering the cause behind it, and even more unheard of since it was the first time such a step was ever taken. Understandably enough, this action of the Roman bishop provoked serious protests from all sides, but it appears that Victor was able to have his way. At least we see that fellowship between the church in Asia Minor and the one in Rome was suspended for a long time. Rome forcibly achieved its independence from Asia Minor, from every indirect and probably every direct tutelage exercised from there. Through an act of force Rome achieved its internal independence.

3. ORIGEN AND DEMETRIUS

At the beginning of the third century a similar conflict then took place in Alexandria. Here it dealt with the person of Origen, that is, really less about Origen's person than about the claims of the Alexandrian bishop who would not tolerate another church province, even one as old and famous as Palestine, mixing into the affairs of his office, or rather what he thought were the affairs of his office. At the age of eighteen, Origen had become director of the catechetical school. When the persecution of Septimius Severus reached Alexandria, Clement withdrew to undertake other activities in more peaceful areas—as it might perhaps be officially put in academic or ecclesiastical circles—but, more plainly said, he fled from the persecution. The school was now leaderless, for there was no one among Alexandria's officeholders who could succeed Clement, who had been a famous and widely respected man of great academic achievement. Accordingly, the eighteen-year-old Origen took upon himself the task of Christian instruction, at first only temporarily. The great success he achieved soon induced the bishop to give him the task officially as well. In spite of the administration (as we would say in modern terms), through a student the catechetical school not only retained its previous position but noticeably increased its reputation in the city, in the country, and even beyond the country's borders. Origen's reputation, the basis for this, rose steeply, not only among Christians but among pagans as well. Thus, we often find Origen traveling, not only to other provinces of the church but also to the governor of Arabia and to the mother of the empress, who wanted to see and hear the famous man.

One of these journeys led Origen to Caesarea in 216. At the request of the bishops of Caesarea and Jerusalem, he delivered theological lectures in the churches there. One would suppose that there could have been no objection to this and that the bishop of Alexandria would have been happy to have the director of his catechetical school so honored in Palestine. Quite the contrary: when Demetrius learned about Origen's lectures in the churches of Palestine, he immediately summoned him to return on the grounds that Origen was not a priest and therefore was not authorized to teach in other churches. The bishops of Palestine thought they could remedy the situation. When Origen returned in the year 230, they ordained him a presbyter in Caesarea and thought that they had now done everything necessary to satisfy the requirements of the bishop of Alexandria. Now Origen was a priest, and now he could legitimately teach in the church. This was still far from the truth: Demetrius reacted even more strongly than before. First he summoned an Alexandrian synod and then an entire Egyptian synod. The Alexandrian synod did decide, following Demetrius's demand, to expel Origen from the Egyptian church, but not to remove him from his office of presbyter. Therefore Demetrius summoned a national synod in which the bishops of the dioceses Demetrius had founded followed his directions, not only once more removing Origen from his office as director of the catechetical school, but also revoking his ordination as a presbyter as well. They even seemed to be proud of their actions, for they informed the other provinces of the church and demanded that they follow this step.

The reasons Demetrius gives are insufficient to explain his action. He says Origen cannot hold the office of a priest, because he does not meet the demands of physical perfection specified in the Book of Leviticus (and which still apply in the Catholic church, even though very much revised and expanded). Previously Demetrius had praised the action of Origen to which he is referring—Origen, in following Matt. 19:12, had emasculated himself—as an act of supreme Christian virtue and a fulfillment of the gospel's demand. The real explanation for Demetrius's action can only be that he felt the action of the Palestinian bishops most deeply attacked his high opinion of himself and his position. The sensitivity of this man, who only shortly before had established his own position in the Egyptian church, here reveals the mistrust of this newly created church province toward the ancient church. This is why Demetrius so passionately fought against the activities of the Palestinian bishops. He also forcefully freed himself from the external and internal obligations, which he had had up until that time. That Demetrius's action did not meet with approval, but with sharp denunciation in Palestine, for example, is understandable. And Demetrius also had to pay dearly for this forcible action, just as every forcible action in the church, in the long run, must be paid for dearly. It is true that the catechetical school continued to exist in Alexandria, and certainly it continued to enjoy a great reputation, but without Origen, its work and its reputation lost its heart. In Caesarea a new catechetical school came into being under Origen, and the leading figures of the time were attracted there; from now on, it was the center of the church's learned theological work.

4. HIPPOLYTUS AND CALLISTUS

The arguments between Hippolytus and Callistus at first appear to deal with intra-Roman conflicts, with a dispute between two bishops over the office. But this controversy at the beginning of the third century was repeated a century later in the controversy between Novatian and Cornelius (see pp. 158–59), and comes up again every now and then throughout the later centuries whenever—either in Rome or in some other province of the church—one bishop confronts a rival bishop. Even in the fourth century these arguments took on the most unpleasant characteristics. At that time Damasus and Ursinus confronted one another in Rome. The differences between them were settled not only with words, but also with blows. We possess thorough reports about them: Ursinus's supporters had assembled in a church building; the supporters of Damasus occupied the street and prevented Ursinus's followers from leaving the church. The siege was ended when the church was stormed and numerous deaths on Ursinus's side resulted. These arguments took place in Rome, but comparable ones could also be reported from other provinces of the church.

We know about the dispute between Hippolytus and Callistus, which has been mentioned several times (see, for example, pp. 56–57), only from the description of Hippolytus himself. This description is, to say the least, influenced by passionate opposition. Again and again throughout the centuries a theologian presents the life, theology, and churchly activity of another in the way Hippolytus does here, so that with every word we must inquire what is reality and what is the product of a lively imagination, not to mention what is the writer's hateful invention. But that this sort of thing happens as early as the first half of the third century is still relatively surprising, especially since it is one bishop who is talking about another. No matter how cautiously we read it, Hippolytus's presentation definitely does show that Callistus's life had been unusual. He was a slave, and his master had placed him in charge of a bank, since he apparently was a skillful businessman. However, this bank, in which Christians had probably been the chief depositors, failed. Callistus attempted to escape the consequences by fleeing. He thought he had reached safety when he had boarded a ship which was supposed to sail to a foreign destination. When he glimpsed his master with an entourage on the waterfront, he thought he had been betrayed by the ship's crew and jumped into the sea in order to drown himself. But they fished him out and delivered him to his master. As punishment, his master put him on the treadmill. He was released from it by declaring that he could get the money back from the debtors who had caused the bank's failure. That did not work. Rather, a riot developed in a Roman synagogue (where Callistus had gone; interestingly, here he hoped to find his debtors), which resulted in an accusation of sacrilege against Callistus and his banishment to the mines, from which he was freed through the good offices of the imperial concubine Marcia (see p. 59), although, according to Hippolytus's claim, he was in no way eligible for release, and so on. At the very least, therefore, Callistus had not been leading an ordinary life when the church of Rome chose him as bishop. If we say that this was because of his practical and organizational gifts, that would describe these things just as incompletely (that is, intentionally minimizing them), as if we would praise someone like this in churchly and theological circles today.

The Roman church apparently gave serious consideration to what it was doing and selected Callistus because it thought he was the right man at the right time for the needs of the church. They chose Callistus in express opposition to Hippolytus, to whom apparently the congregation possessed no inner relation, although he was a highly educated man and an excellent theologian—or precisely because that was what he was. We spoke briefly about the Monarchian arguments above (see pp. 132–33). In them Hippolytus showed himself superior to all the other representatives of the Roman church. He could operate on the basis of Logos Christology, which at that time was the most modern and the most thoroughly developed theology. He was in complete command of the theological presumptions of his time, while his rivals Zephyrinus and Callistus could really only stammer about them (something to which Hippolytus, in his description of Callistus's life, devotes a derisive commentary). We see Callistus's significance as soon as he begins to deal with churchly affairs as bishop.

What Callistus does is bring the previous development of the church's constitution to its conclusion. We have seen (see pp. 122–23) how the office of the bishop developed: at first it had only technical functions. Then as the charismatic offices subsided, the bishop took over the leadership of the congregation, especially the administration of the eucharist. In the crises of the second century he was then given supervision of doctrine and became the one who guaranteed it. Now in the first half of the third century he obtained the full power of the office. Callistus was responsible for this. His so-called penitential edict claimed that the bishop had the authority not only—as previously—to punish sins of lesser seriousness and restore sinners to communion with the church after they performed their penance, but also the authority to punish and forgive mortal sins.

For Christians at that time there were three kinds of mortal sins: apostasy (that is, the denial of the Christian faith), murder, and immorality. The mortal sin which is continually the subject of debate and which most frequently occurs in the early church is, understandably enough, the denial of the Christian faith, that is, falling away during the persecution. The course of events is almost always the same: no later than the end of the persecution, usually while it was still going on, the ones who had lapsed regretted their denial. Under the fear of sudden outbreak of the persecution, under the threat of torture or under torture itself, they offered the required sacrifice. No sooner had that happened than great fear came over them and they attempted to revoke their denial. They sorrowfully returned to the church and begged to be taken back. But the church could not restore them to full communion; in accordance with the views which had developed in the course of generations, mortal sinners remained in a state of penance. They no longer could participate fully in the worship service; their place was in the narthex of the church. So until the end of their lives they remained uncertain if God, indeed whether God, would forgive them their denial, their apostasy. The single possibility existing at that time, to have forgiveness pronounced and thereby to regain their admission to the church, was for those who possessed the Spirit to accept the ones who had lapsed back into the church; through them it was not the church which was acting, but Christ himself. At that time the only charismatics still remaining in the early church, since there were no longer apostles, teachers, and prophets in the old understanding, were the martyrs. We do not know how the conception originated that the martyrs stood in a special relationship to Christ. Perhaps it goes back to the word of the gospel: "So everyone who acknowledges me before men, I also will acknowledge before my Father who is in heaven." At any rate, as early as the Book of Acts we see that the martyr, in the moment of his martyrdom, is close to Christ in a special way: Stephen sees the heavens opened and Christ standing beside God's throne. When Polycarp was led into the arena to be executed, a heavenly voice spoke to him. Again and again in the martyr acts we find reports of the martyr seeing a vision: Christ appears to him and comforts him. Whoever confessed Christ was accepted by Christ, and if someone from this circle accepted another, it is Christ who was doing the acting. That was the view of the time.

Understandably enough, the martyrs only very infrequently chose to restore one who had lapsed to fellowship and grant a pardon. Thus the one who had lapsed normally remained on the fringes of the church and very often could not endure this tension permanently. He could muster the strength for this continuous penance for only a short time, but then his strength failed because he knew absolutely nothing about the possible result of his actions and could learn absolutely nothing. Only too often, this is the way he finally became lost to the church. When Callistus now assumed for the bishop the right to pass judgment upon mortal sins, he did it for pastoral reasons in view of these circumstances. He certainly was not thinking of the mortal sin of apostasy in the persecutions, for Callistus's age was an age of relative quiet for Christians. Callistus did, just like his opponent Hippolytus, die as a martyr, but here it was a matter of individual cases which continually occurred, even in the so-called times of peace; we spoke of them earlier in connection with the discussion of the persecution of Christians (see pp. 69–70). As we said, in Callistus's time apostasy from the Christian faith was not in the foreground. Callistus also was not thinking about the right to forgive the act of murder, which would have happened so seldom as to be insignificant. Rather, he was essentially concerned with the right to forgive sins of immorality of all sorts, which were not now happening all that frequently in the church of a metropolis like Rome, but certainly more frequently there than in other places. Callistus really was doing nothing more than extending a right he fundamentally possessed, but he was extending that right into areas which previously were beyond the bishop's reach. In doing this, he touched off a passionate opposition—chiefly from the rigorists, the hard-liners, for whom Tertullian made himself the spokesman. In Callistus's action, and that of all the bishops who followed him, they saw a decline of the ancient Christian moral rigor, a destruction of the church from within. But Callistus was opposed not only by the rigorists but also by the traditionalists—by the African bishops, for example, with the noteworthy exception of the bishop of Carthage, who, as the bishop of a metropolis, was confronted with problems that were very similar to Callistus's. Nevertheless, Callistus had his way and thus completed the process of developing the bishop's office. In addition, when we consider that Callistus officially demanded that the bishop could not be deposed from office, it is clear how he advanced the bishop's position.

Even this demand that bishops be exempt from deposition did not signify anything fundamentally new. For all practical purposes, the bishop was already exempt from deposition. First Clement, 140 years earlier, already claimed that no one exercising his ecclesiastical office without reproach could be removed from it (see p. 122). But it was a considerable journey from the fact of nondeposition to the elevation of that fact to a basic demand. Callistus made that journey. The Roman church apparently knew what it was doing—to return to where we began—when it chose him and not Hippolytus. Callistus considerably strengthened Rome's claims to leadership. And, above all else, he significantly laid the foundation for this claim to leadership. When Bishop Victor broke off fellowship with Asia Minor (see p. 149), naturally that was also a demonstration of the claim to leadership. But that demonstration grew out of the forcible attempt to become free of inner dependence on Asia Minor, while Callistus was acting without this pressure, only because he saw the ecclesiastical necessity more clearly and earlier than other bishops did. How significant his action was, will be evident immediately.

5. CYPRIAN AND STEPHEN

When Callistus pushed through his penitential decree, there was no persecution going on. The number of mortal sinners who were then included in the bishop's sphere of power was not large. His penitential edict, and the bishop's claim associated with it, had to undergo its decisive test as soon as a persecution came, as it soon did in the great persecution by Decius in A.D. 250. For the first time, this persecution encompassed the entire empire. All citizens had to appear before specially appointed commissions and testify to their pagan faith by offering a sacrifice. If they refused to sacrifice, they would suffer the well-known penalties for Christians we have already mentioned (see p. 71). For the first time since the Christian church came into being, every last Christian was compelled to take a stand for his faith. And the number who weakened and denied their faith was accordingly large. Never before did the church have to deal so emphatically with the question of the restoration of those who had lapsed, that is, with the forgiveness of a mortal sin, as it did in the time around 250. Indeed, at that time both the Roman and Carthaginian churches were split, something we shall soon discuss (see pp. 157–59). Nevertheless, the bishop remained the only one who could solve the burning question. He was the only one who could master the difficult situation and now finally solidified his supreme position in the church, his position even superior to those who were endowed with the Spirit.

It was evident in this persecution that not only the churches as such were inwardly weakened, but also that the martyrs' status had not escaped the decline which we previously observed happening to the other charismatic offices. The corruption of the charismatic office, which we saw the *Didache* depicting with the prophets and teachers (see p. 121), is now also taking place with the martyrs. As an exception to the usual rule, we possess a more or less complete picture of the events in Carthage and in Rome, since Cyprian's letters, which have been preserved, deal relatively thoroughly with these events. In a persecution as extensive as the Decian it was impossible to execute immediately everyone who remained faithful to the Christian faith in spite of all the persuasion and threats. The confessors had to be put in prison and there tortured as much as possible in hope that they might still abjure their faith, or at least kept in prison where they would be available for future games in the circus or similar uses. These Christians in prison were martyrs in the full sense and were known as confessors, for they had confessed their faith and deserved all the privileges which accompanied such a confession.

Understandably enough, in the higher classes of the church the percentage of apostates was especially high. If someone occupied a prominent position or was wealthy, he would be caught by the persecution sooner than the anonymous majority of Christians and would also more easily weaken than someone who had nothing to lose. But the law, about which we have already spoken (see pp. 153–54), also applied to these people from the upper classes. They thought primarily about escaping by making the sacrifice and did not realize what it meant for their Christian faith. They had not anticipated how great the sorrow and inner torment would be after their denial. They searched for ways to be restored to the church and naturally first turned to the imprisoned martyrs. The prisoners were in no way completely cut off from the outside world, and it appears that they were not unmoved by the friendly persuasion, as well as the charitable gifts. Thus the martyrs first issued a small number of so-called letters of peace *(litterae pacis)* for the lapsed which granted them complete fellowship with the church. But that was just the first step. The next step was reached when they went to the members of the church especially responsible for the provisioning and care of the martyrs and requested them to intercede on their behalf. In this way it was no longer necessary for them to go directly into the prison and attempt to convince a martyr—perhaps a slave from one's own household who, in distinction to his master and his family, had remained steadfast—to issue a letter of peace. Indeed, there finally was even a black market for letters of peace which were issued with a blank in which a person could insert his own name. This was the course of events.

But that did not prevent the martyrs from emphatically claiming their old privilege in opposition to the bishop of Carthage, a bishop whose own conduct in the persecution, at least in Africa, was not above suspicion. Cyprian had escaped the outbreak of the persecution by fleeing. He went to his not insignificant estate and hid himself there. This he did without severing his connection with the church, however; he continued to exercise the complete direction of it by sending messages and letters. This conduct was possible in the church. There were examples of it from earlier times. It could even be justified, if one wished, by referring to the New Testament which said: "When they persecute you in one town, flee to the next." But that had become questionable in the third century, and Cyprian's flight gave the opponents he had in his own church the opportunity to attack him, which they had been seeking ever since his election (Cyprian had been elevated to the bishop's office only against some opposition). This opposition party therefore supported the martyrs in their claims, and thus it came to a sharper and sharper conflict, finally to a schism in the church. Cyprian had his way in these arguments, since the stance which he assumed was the legitimate one. He encouraged those who had lapsed, as well as the martyrs, to be patient. The persecution was still going on. Therefore it was too early to restore people. Before the lapsed could be restored to church fellowship, one would have to see not only their willingness to repent, but also their fruits. The martyrs, encouraged by the faction opposed to the bishop, went even further in their claims, weakening their own position. Finally they proclaimed restoration to fellowship in the church for all the lapsed, without exception—as a rule, at least in the church, the more heated a dispute becomes, that much more does a party forget its moderation and the objective of things. The martyrs revoked the excommunication of all the lapsed, regardless of who they were or the reasons why they had fallen away. And with this the martyrs finally made their privilege untenable.

This is the way things stood in Carthage. In Rome, Bishop Fabian had died as a martyr. At first no successor was chosen, for allowing that would have been to deliver the new bishop to the executioner. Rather, they let the church be administered temporarily by a presbyter named Novatian. He, in agreement with Carthage, took the same position as Cyprian in the question of what to do about the lapsed, as we see from his letters preserved in Cyprian's correspondence. This attitude was an attempt to follow a middle way between the extremes, doing what was responsible and what was ecclesiastically expedient. But in Rome they finally came to the conclusion that this undecided situation would not be responsible in the long run and proceeded to select a bishop. As once had happened in Hippolytus's time, the choice fell not on a theologian, but upon a practitioner—not on Novatian, but on Cornelius. Novatian had had justified hopes of gaining the bishop's office. There is no doubt that he was the most outstanding theologian of his time in the Roman church. He had already administered the bishop's office. That much greater was his disappointment. He could not overcome it, but had a group of friendly clergy elect him as opposing bishop. At the same time, in the question of what to do with the lapsed, he placed himself on the side of the rigorists and declared, contrary to everything he previously had said and done, that neither the church nor the bishop could forgive a mortal sin such as apostasy. With the early church's rigor emblazoned on Novatian's standard, he could count on having many rally to it from the outset, chiefly those who looked only at his stand and not at the motives behind it. Not a few of the bishops agreed with Novatian. Thus a schismatic church developed which endured for a long time and which was a not insignificant danger to the larger church—a schismatic church which arose because Novatian could not stand the insult which he felt he suffered when Cornelius was elected bishop.

Here we clearly see an event which we find occurring again and again during the later centuries, even up into our own day. Someone declares that he is acting out of purely theological motives and is taking a position purely on principle—and in reality he is acting on the basis of unexpressed nontheological and nonchurchly motives, motives which are purely or at least primarily human. That this was so in Novatian's case is shown when he, in complete contrast to his earlier attitude, proclaimed the early church's stance toward the lapsed, while at the same time he could unite with the party in Carthage which supported the most extreme moderation toward the lapsed. In Rome, as well as in Carthage, they were acting on the basis of nontheological, nonchurchly factors. All of this took place under the simultaneous and passionate declaration that everything depended on the purity of the church, upon the true gospel, and that the church had to be preserved from the destruction that would inevitably come upon it if things were done as the opposing side wished. And this has been repeated all the way down to our own day; only sometimes it is a great deal more difficult to separate the ostensible and the real motives from one another.

In spite of the size of the schismatic church, in spite of all the difficulties that confronted Cornelius in Rome and Cyprian in Carthage, the two allied bishops triumphed in their dioceses. The right of a bishop to pass judgment on mortal sins, either to condemn them or to forgive them, was finally established. But this alliance between Rome and Carthage did not last. What it developed into, under Cornelius's second successor, Stephen, was a bitter feud, the so-called dispute over the validity of baptism by heretics. What had happened over the course of years was that a number of adherents of Novatian's schismatic church had returned to the larger church. The question arose about what should be done with those who had been received into this schismatic church by baptism, either as children of those who were full members or as a result of the missionary work done by members of this schismatic church. On the basis of his presupposition that salvation was to be found only inside the church, Cyprian answered that these converts should be baptized. If the statement were true: *Extra ecclesiam nulla salus* ("Outside the church there is no salvation"), then there could be no valid sacraments outside the church. What had taken place in the baptisms of the schismatic church, therefore, could not be baptisms, but only appeared externally to be so. Therefore, the baptisms had to be repeated. That was not only logical, but followed necessarily from Cyprian's theological presuppositions. Stephen of Rome now did not—characteristically— proceed on the basis of theological considerations. He acted the way Victor had done in the Easter controversy (see p. 149) and Callistus had done in the arguments about the penitential edict (see pp. 154–55), namely, on the basis of the practical and churchly considerations and expediencies. He declared: they recognize our baptism, therefore baptism should not be repeated for those who return from the schismatic church to the larger church, but the laying on of hands should be sufficient.

Whether the consideration that it was time to bring to heel the bishop of Carthage, who had become too strong, was added to these practical and churchly considerations, is something we cannot say. That is completely possible, for in the correspondence between Cyprian and Cornelius, Cyprian had unmistakably played the leading role and on occasion significantly offended Rome's sense of its own importance. For example, he was asked by Rome how his departure from Carthage during the persecution had happened. What did Cyprian do? He returned the letter and asked the Roman church to examine whether it was genuine. In view of its contents and other marks, he had the impression that this was not a letter that could have been sent by the Roman church through the presbyter who was present there. Cyprian also formally made known to Cornelius what he, Cyprian, thought was the right thing to do and what he also would like Cornelius to do. In any case, Stephen had no theological basis for his demand. The only thing he had to say was: the others also baptize in Christ's name; therefore, they are valid baptisms. Stephen triumphed, and this understanding has remained to the present day. Without knowing what he was doing and without intending to, at that time he created with his decision a bond of unity which still encompasses all Christian churches today. Every church recognizes—at least in principle—a baptism in the name of the Trinity performed in all others. Whoever leaves one church to go to another does not need to be rebaptized (except in certain cases when someone on the Catholic side believes it essential to perform a conditional baptism, but today this stirs up considerable attention in the press, and therefore happens relatively infrequently).

Rome had triumphed, even though Cyprian was not alone in his opinion, but had at least the entire church in Africa arrayed behind him. But the theological conviction of a large, old, and important church, emphatically presented at several synods, was not able to win the day against Stephen's claims and bearing. Indeed, he was not in a position, as already mentioned, to confront Cyprian with theological arguments or to refute him at all. But, therefore, he more emphatically advanced Rome's claim to be the mother church of all other churches, the claim of the Roman episcopate to be the source of all other episcopates. It was on this that he based the demand for acceptance of the Roman decision. Cyprian countered this with his theory of the equality of bishops. Just as various rays proceed from the sun, but all have the same power, the same honor, so it also is with bishops. Among the bishops, the successor of Peter has only the rank of *primus inter pares,* first among equals. But Cyprian could not prevail against the force and passion with which Stephen pursued his claim. When Stephen demanded that all churches had to observe the practice of Rome, Cyprian could not counter this with the declaration that all churches had to adopt the theological understanding of the African church province; he could only say that this was the way they thought and acted, but wished to compel no one to see things the way they themselves did.

6. ROME AND CONSTANTINOPLE

Stephen had already raised the bishop of Rome's claim to primacy emphatically, the claim to primacy which we then see being put fully into practice under Leo I, 200 years following Stephen. In between was a period during which the center of the empire was transferred to the East, so that Rome and the West seemed to be neglected. Under Diocletian, the empire was already being ruled from the East. When Constantine established the new capital of Constantinople in the East, it very rapidly developed politically into a rival of the old capital, Rome. For this reason, some have felt that Rome's position in the church was decisively weakened during Constantine's age. Such a view is incorrect. Naturally, Constantinople achieved a decisive position for itself in the ecclesiastical hierarchy. But this first took place at the expense of the reputation and position of the Eastern episcopal sees. We need only look at how often and how fervently—and at the questionable means—the patriarchs of Alexandria initiated an attack on the patriarch of Constantinople (see p. 185), in order for us to see that Alexandria, at least, knew quite well that the development of Constantinople's position was taking place chiefly at its expense.

However, this rise of the bishop of Constantinople also had its dark side. Naturally, the bishop of the capital of the empire stood in the full splendor of the imperial court. And obviously the emperor continually did as much as was in his power in attempting to elevate the status of the bishop of his capital. But this proximity to the emperor was certainly not an advantage for the patriarch of Constantinople. He could always contact the emperor, it is true, but at the same time he continually stood under the scrutiny and direct influence of the emperor and his officials. Thus, his freedom of action was extraordinarily limited, while the West had a great deal more freedom because of its distance from the imperial court, in spite of, or even because of the decline of its political significance. It is characteristic of the Roman curia at this time that it copied the organization, vestments, and ceremonies of the imperial court, thus signalling the claims of the future. The Roman bishop is free from direct imperial supervision. And even the fact that he found himself in opposition to the civil authorities in the age after Constantine did not mean, as a first glance would indicate, a weakening of his position. Rather, what ensued in the long run was a decisive strengthening. In the East the administration of the state and the administration of the church were in agreement; in the West, they were in opposition to one another. This begins as early as the fourth century under Constantine's sons and continues to increase until finally, in the age of the Arian Germanic states on the territory of the Western Roman Empire, the state is directly, or at least indirectly, prejudiced against the Catholic church and occasionally fights against it. Nevertheless, in this state it retained an extraordinarily strong position, in fact, a position which it certainly could never have achieved in any other way. As we have said (see pp. 79–83), those who previously were outsiders, those who more or less openly sympathized with paganism, were now brought into the church. Impressed by the destruction of the Roman Empire and the simultaneous conflict between the Germanic rulers and the Roman bishop, even the outright pagans became convinced that the Roman bishop was the representative of ancient Roman splendor, and the Roman church was the continuation, or at least the body preserving the tradition, of the ancient empire. Thus they turned to Christianity, and by means of its opposition to the "occupation regime," Catholic Christianity achieved a cohesiveness and a unity which it could not have been able to reach in any other way.

The so-called Donation of Constantine *(Donatio Constantini)* is a forgery of the Middle Ages. It relates how Constantine was stricken with leprosy and how Bishop Silvester miraculously cured him. As a result, Constantine converted to Christianity and requested that Bishop Silvester baptize him. In gratitude for this, and impressed by the divine miracle of his healing attested to by the personality and the claims of Silvester, the emperor not only recognized the Roman primacy, but also placed papal power above the imperial power. He gave the Roman bishop the imperial insignia and ceded state honors to the Roman clergy. The gift of the Lateran palace to the Roman bishop symbolized his transferral of authority in the West to the pope. As an outward sign of this, the emperor moved his residence to the East. This is what the Donation of Constantine reported in the Middle Ages, and for centuries it was regarded as historical truth.

When it finally came out that the Donation of Constantine was not genuine, this shook many people deeply; for Luther, this revelation brought about a significant increase in his opposition to the claims of the curia. Although it was true that the Donation of Constantine was a medieval forgery, yet we must say that this document—even though embellished by legends—expressed the trend of this development. As early as Constantine's time, the church of the West had started on its way to dominance. It was at this time that the independent development of the Western church began. As early as the period of Constantine's sons, the church of the West freed itself from the spell which lay over the East at that time and continued for centuries, almost up to the present. Constantine was still regarded everywhere—in the West as well as the East—as a glorified figure: he was God's anointed; he carried out God's will. The East continued to regard the emperors following Constantine in the same way, even up into the Byzantine age and further on into that of the "Third Rome," that is, Moscow. After the Byzantine Empire collapsed in 1453, the Czar assumed all his claims; the Greek king (after the restoration of the Greek monarchy in the nineteenth century) acted similarly in relation to Greek Orthodoxy, almost down to our own day. As a result of the dogmatic opposition between it and the emperor, the West recognized the difference between Constantine's sons and Constantine himself, and therefore did not regard the state in the elevated way that marked the East through the centuries.

Naturally it was a long time before the church could harvest the fruits of this emancipation. Even in the West, just as in the East, the church still stood under the authoritative influence of the emperor for a long time. Even under Charlemagne, the Roman bishop was no more than the leading bishop of the Frankish kingdom. But the foundations for the development we see taking place following Charlemagne already had their beginning in the Constantinian age, the foundations for that development which reached its culmination around 1200 in Innocent III, who as a supreme master ruled not only the church, but by and large the states of Europe (see pp. 315–18).

7. THE ARIAN AND THE DONATIST CONTROVERSIES

The shadow which already lay over the history of early Christianity continued in the fourth century, even growing darker. This we have already emphasized. Something like the outbreak of the Arian controversy, which we generally like to view as a purely theological argument (see pp. 186–87), was also touched off by human, all-too-human factors. The same thing is true for the Donatist controversy. The contrasting positions which we like to deal with under the label of the Arian controversy, as well as those of the Donatist controversy, do not first originate after Constantine's conquest of the West in 312; we merely perceive them for the first time after 312. The differences of opinion in Egypt and in Africa existed for a long time before they became visible. Their origin goes back to the time of the Diocletian persecution. It was only because at that time the church was oppressed and had to fight for its existence that it endured these differences of opinion and did not have the opportunity to air them publicly.

In Egypt a schism developed over the question of how one should have acted in the Diocletian persecution. Here, as so often throughout history, the parties stood in ever-increasing opposition to one another— the prudent and cautious party against the resolute and radical Christians. Not a few people believed that the official church, represented by Bishop Peter of Alexandria, did not resist the persecution energetically enough. It did too little to heal its wounds. For example, it was not quick enough in replacing clergy who were murdered in the persecution, so that congregations remained orphaned for too long. There were more accusations of a similar sort. As a result, Bishop Melitius of Lycopolis began to take things into his own hands. Since he believed that the church administration was doing nothing or not enough, he went out and traveled on his own authority throughout the country, caring for the orphaned churches by ordaining presbyters for them. Arguments developed which continued to increase in severity, until the radicals finally separated from the official church and formed the church of the martyrs. It was to these radicals that Arius originally belonged. If we were to put it simply, we could say the Arian controversy came about only because Arius separated himself from the party of the radicals and went over to the larger church. When he belonged to Melitius's party, he held the same theological views as later. Only at that time they were not objectionable to this party of radicals, the true believers. Arius proved that he had the true faith by being one of this party's members. Only when Arius went back to the larger church did the radicals remember his theology, which in fact now did stand opposed to their inner concerns. For they belonged just as much to the conservative wing as the opponents of Bishop Dionysius once had (see p. 192). They now took such great offense at his theology that in their dilemma they could see no other way than to denounce Arius before Bishop Alexander of Alexandria for his false teaching, a bishop of a church they did not recognize and which really did not exist for them. Bishop Peter, who, as far as he was concerned, would have been happy to do nothing about Arius, was now forced by this denunciation to act. Since significant parts of the church had already taken offense at his alleged improper actions during the persecution, he had at least to give some decisive evidence that he was preserving the true faith. That is how the action against Arius came about. Since Arius was not now a private individual, and the theological views he held were not his personal opinions but those of a widespread theological school forcefully supporting Arius, the so-called Arian controversy originated, involving the widest circles and affecting the church of the East for centuries.

In the so-called Donatist controversy, nontheological factors played a very similar role. In North Africa at that time, city and country had apparently long been in opposition to one another. Here things were concerned not only with the frequently occurring opposition between the city dwellers and the rural folk, but also with the difference between ethnically different (we used to say racially different) portions of the populace. In addition, Bishop Mensurius of Carthage had enemies. A rich woman in his congregation, Lucilla, was not only especially pious, but also—as still happens today—especially liked to display her piety. Before receiving the Lord's Supper, for example, she liked to kiss the reliquary of a martyr. Unfortunately, it was not one of an officially recognized martyr, and the archdeacon Caecilian was indiscreet enough to correct her. That was an insult she did not forget during her entire life, as can easily be the case with people who are especially pious—not just then, but throughout all the centuries up to today. When there is an appearance of special piety and special humility at the same time, we should—and here we are again at one of the methodological experiences we learn from our study of church history—become especially attentive. Here the question must be asked: is this genuine piety and genuine humility which we find (no one will be more pleased to find it than the church historian), or does something completely different stand behind this piety and especially behind this humility, for example, pride which believes that it is infinitely better than the surrounding world which is not as pious and not as humble—something which must result in one's own condemnation. Attention to this methodological principle—like the one previously mentioned—has not infrequently led to surprising results in the past, as well as in the present.

As long as Mensurius was in office nothing happened, for his position was too strong. But in the moment of Mensurius's death, as his former right-hand man Caecilian was chosen as his successor, an ecclesiastical conflict broke out in which there was no longer a discussion of the differences between city and country, the differences between the noblewoman Lucilla and Mensurius, but exclusively the theological and ecclesiastical differences. The bishops of the Numidian hinterland rallied and immediately chose an opposing bishop to Caecilian (the fact that he was the court chaplain of the noblewoman Lucilla was naturally a complete coincidence), and they did this with the claim that Caecilian's consecration was invalid. Because traditors had participated in it (a traditor was a bishop who had surrendered the holy books of his church during the persecution and thus was considered to have apostatized [see p. 77]), an opposing bishop had to be consecrated. The logic involved escapes comprehension. In the first place, no examination of the facts had taken place; it had not been proved that Caecilian had really been consecrated by traditors. In the second place, there was the question (in case these facts were true) of whether that made the consecration invalid. Even if they did consider the consecration invalid, that still would say nothing about Caecilian's worthiness or unworthiness for the bishop's office. If he were worthy, his consecration could be repeated by other bishops (something which Caecilian later offered, but was rejected with ridicule by his opponents). Only if Caecilian were proved unworthy could they act to select another bishop. But no one concerned himself about these details, for the convictions at stake here were much too holy. The opposing bishop, so they said, was the legitimate bishop of the African church province simply because the consecration of Caecilian was invalid. The question about where the Numidian bishops got the authorization for their consecration of an opposing bishop was naturally not raised. Besides that, the circumstances surrounding the consecration of Caecilian were investigated several times in the subsequent period, and it was determined—this is the highpoint of the entire affair—that there was no traditor among the bishops consecrating Caecilian, while there was not just one, but several, among the Numidian bishops who consecrated the opposing bishop. Even that accomplished nothing, for they were overpowered by theological reasons; they were striving for the purity of the church and could not pay attention to such trifles, for, if they had, all the presuppositions with which they were operating would have collapsed.

At any rate, the events described are the reasons why we see the African church dividing as early as the year 312. Not only were there two rival bishops at the head of the church province, but the split extended throughout all dioceses, soon after affecting all congregations. Constantine, after he had triumphed over the West by defeating Maxentius in 312, had to decide which church he would recognize as the Catholic church in Africa. There was no doubt which one was in the right according to the prevailing ecclesiastical regulations: again and again the Donatists (so named after their leader Donatus) and their claims were rejected at conferences of bishops, at synods, and even at the imperial court of justice. But that made no impression on the Donatists. They maintained their claims and their organization unchanged; they continued their missionary activity, for it was their unshakable conviction that only they were the true church, only they had preserved the gospel purely.

Where did this purity of the church come from? From the right administration of the sacraments, answered the Donatists. And how was the right administration of the sacraments—their validity—guaranteed? By being performed by a priest, explained the Donatists, who was pure—not free of all sins, but at least free of mortal sins. And this could be only the Donatist priests. The priests of the larger church, no matter how holy their lives and actions may be, are all still decisively tainted by

having been ordained by Bishop Caecilian or his successor whose consecration was invalid because traditors participated in it. (No matter how
often the historic truth was established, it made no difference. Caecilian
had been consecrated by traditors; therefore, the other priests were
guilty of mortal sin—this was said so long that it simply must be true.) If
these priests had not been ordained properly, all the sacraments they
administered were therefore not valid, and the only real church in Africa
was the one of the Donatists. They squandered no attention on the
claim—assuming that the principle of the Donatists was legitimate—
that the church of the Donatists would be condemned at least as much as
its opposing church, since traditors had even participated in the consecration of the first Donatist bishop Maiorinus (Lucilla's court chaplain), and they also did not trouble themselves over whether the principle on which they built was valid. For if the power of the sacraments
were dependent on the purity of the administrator, then the Donatists
could not restrict this purity only to absence of mortal sin, but they
would have to go further. Even in the understanding of that time, the
absence of mortal sins was only a very incomplete standard. As soon as
one went further than absence from mortal sins, then what officeholder
was pure? If the effectiveness of the sacraments were to depend on the
absolute purity of the administrator, then there would have been a real
sacrament of the Lord's Supper only once, namely on Maundy Thursday,
and never again since then. In addition, if the effectiveness of the
sacrament were to be made dependent on one's trust in the person, or on
the moral purity of the person administering the sacrament, the sacrament would be destroyed from within.

Naturally, Constantine attempted, after he understood what was
going on in Africa, to correct the situation in the African church. He
tried using new courts of justice in his naive opinion that the opposing
side could be convinced by facts. He finally learned that this was only
partially true for theologians (by the way, not just for theologians of the
fourth century, but for theologians of every age), and that here there was
a degree of partial blindness in which one believed what one wanted to
believe. He also learned that this blindness was not decreasing, but
increasing in the course of time. Then he attempted to use force. He
sent troops to Africa in order to bring the Donatists back to the larger
church. That also made no impression on the Donatists. They resisted
mightily, and Constantine abandoned the military action surprisingly
quickly, quite in contrast to the principles which we otherwise see
motivating him (simply because it troubled his conscience to do battle

against the Christian church, even if only a sham and false church). His sons had fewer scruples, but even they could not force the Donatists back into unity with the larger church. Even in the year 411, when the religious conference of Carthage took place, the number of Donatist bishops taking part in it was almost as large as the number of Catholic bishops. The results of this conference were a foregone conclusion: the large church was declared the victor. This disputation would have had the same result, even if the Catholic side had been led not by Augustine, but by a lesser figure. Now the laws against heretics were sharply turned against the Donatists.

Now the shadow fell back over the large church—even more darkly than it had previously lain on the Donatists. But this attempt to stamp out the Donatists—we certainly cannot call it just a dispute—never did come to an end. For soon after that religious conference the first Germanic empire on Roman soil was established in Africa, the empire of the Vandals. As a result of their active Arianism, the Catholic church soon had to fight for its own existence. But the Donatists also did not escape unscathed from the attack by the large church allied with the state on them which had now been going on for over a century. Thus the power of both churches—the Donatist schismatic church as well as the Catholic large church—was decisively weakened at that time. Both did indeed resist the Germanic tribes, but more weakness was their reward for opposing the Arianism of the Vandals, so that in Africa the Christian church was already virtually destroyed by the attack of Islam before it even really began. North Africa, with what had once been its large, flourishing, and decisively important church, has been dominated by Islam from that time to the present. This is the way the consequences appear when the church and the arguments in it are dominated by nontheological factors, when the human in it wins the upper hand. Indeed, the church is always found among human beings, but it must constantly struggle against all that that implies. Human elements—in the administration of the church at all levels all the way down to the local congregation, and in officeholders as well as in congregational members—can never be completely rooted out, but all those active in it must do everything possible to repress it.

What we have reported here—in one of the briefest chapters we devote to Christianity of the early period—we have done for the sake of making the record complete. If the church keeps silent about these things, that only gives outsiders an excuse to point out these stains on its garments. But this report is also an attempt to serve as a warning. It is true that everything we have said here happened long ago, but human nature, as we have said (see p. 144), has remained the same during the centuries—as has temptation.

V

The Age of Constantine and the Close of the Early History of Christianity

1. EMPEROR CONSTANTINE AND CHRISTIANITY

Constantine's attitude in the Donatist and the Arian controversies clearly shows how the emperor participated not only outwardly, but in particular inwardly in the events within the Christian church. Even though reluctantly, he agreed to the demands of the Donatists, first for one synod of bishops, then for a second, and then for an imperial decision. In this context, he made the absolutely amazing declaration: "They appeal to my judgment, but I wait for Christ's judgment." This word should not be interpreted—as we at first instinctively do—as if Constantine were speaking about Christ's judgment upon himself. Rather he meant—this is a mild way of putting it, but it still goes far enough—that he expected Christ's judgment about the dispute to come from the meeting of the synod. Christ would speak through this synod of bishops; Constantine would judge according to its decision.

He first attempted to guide the Arian controversy by persuasion, by sending letters to those involved in it, and finally, after all that had accomplished nothing, by convening the Council of Nicaea in 325. This first imperial council was organized with the help and at the expense of the state, and took place with all the pomp accompanying such an event. The emperor participated in it personally. And not only did he appear at the council, but he also participated in its deliberations, thus putting his entire authority behind the acceptance of the council's creed. The nucleus of this creed, the often-cited *homoousios*—the declaration that the Father and the Son were identical in being—is to be found previously in none of the theologians involved in the dispute. Only the authority of the emperor could get it adopted at Nicaea. There is thus no doubt that

Constantine took a lively part, both outwardly and inwardly, in the events going on within the Christian church of his day.

However, the question about his motives has still not been answered. As recently as twenty years ago, the argument over Constantine's attitude toward Christianity and his personal faith was still exceptionally lively. Countless publications on this subject appeared at that time. Naturally the theme is still being considered today. But in comparison to the time twenty years ago, calm has returned, because most people have realized that the definite views and solutions so vociferously propounded at that time cannot be maintained. At that time some scholars said that Constantine's actions were dictated by political motives. He was favorable to the Christians because he counted on their support in his usurpation of power. This is true to the extent that Constantine was a usurper, who by the sword created an empire in the West before finally taking over the entire empire, and in both of these conquests he broke existing agreements and treaties. But the claim that he had the support of the Christian party in 312 when he attained power in the West is completely impossible (see p. 55) and without foundation even in 324 for his conquest of the East. But that is not the only political motive they ascribe to Constantine; there are several others. Perhaps he saw in Christianity the bond of unity which would replace the declining imperial cult and would hold together the disunited empire with its contrasting tensions; or finally—Constantine at least wanted peace in his empire, even though he was uninterested in religious questions and was only an irreligious power politician, just as a lack of religion is really part of the nature of those involved in power politics. Even earlier—and this explanation has been repeated up until very recent times—some claimed that Constantine was really a convinced pagan, and if he did favor Christianity—something they minimized as much as possible, although they could not ignore it completely—he did it in contradiction to his own religious conviction.

This last position is the first that must be rejected. Any objective observation of Constantine's action shows that it was and is not tenable. And an objective observation of Constantine's action also shows the impossibility of the other answers which attempt to explain Constantine's conversion to Christianity on the basis of political motives. At that time some even went so far as to characterize Eusebius's description of Constantine's life, the *Vita Constantini* ("Life of Constantine"), as a later forgery, for only if this presumption were made could this kind of position even be advanced. In the fact that even the chief participants in this controversy now no longer are maintaining their claim that the *Vita Constantini* is not genuine, we may clearly perceive the change that has taken place. As soon as at least those documents which Eusebius reproduces in this biography are regarded as genuine (something that is demanded by the contemporary state of research), a complete transformation of the picture occurs. But even completely aside from that, the claims which at that time were so firmly held should never have been advanced on the basis of methodological considerations alone: perhaps Constantine counted on the political support of the Christians in his conquest; Constantine saw in Christianity the political bond of unity for the empire; Constantine was uninterested in religious questions; he was an irreligious power politician, just as power politics is always religionless. Here we see how historians use the assumptions of their own age in dealing with the past, never even attempting to put aside their modern positions to become contemporaneous with that age of the past.

People make Constantine into a utopian, if they think he believed that Christianity at the beginning of the fourth century could have been the bond of unity for the Roman Empire. It was several generations after him, as we have seen (see pp. 82–86), before Christianity could even be thought to play such a role. Those who like to conceive of Constantine as a power politician also ascribe utopian ideas to him, because they have no real conception of the church's position in the fourth century or of the fourth century itself. Naturally it is possible, and not only possible, but very probable, that Constantine wanted peace in his empire. Every totalitarian ruler—and there is no doubt that that is what Constantine was—considers it important for his empire to be peaceful and for no major movements or arguments (whether intellectual or ecclesiastical) to be happening, because one never knows what can become of them. But this answer is not sufficient to explain Constantine's action. A so-called power politician would act differently than Constantine did. Perhaps he would go to the trouble of trying to convince the arguing parties, but not for very long; rather, he would quite quickly apply the means of force available to him: administrators, police, army. But Constantine many times attempted with great patience to move the Donatists to reason and tried everything to reach a solution to the schism within the church without using government force. Only reluctantly did Constantine finally send in the army, and just as quickly did he recall it when he noticed that this was not healing the damages. From the letters which Constantine wrote at the beginning of the Donatist controversy, we see that the schism of the church in Africa was not only a political problem for him, but also a personal one, and he offered all the means available to him in order to reestablish the unity of African Christians, since apparently there was more at stake for him than peace in this important province of Africa.

At that time, for example, he wrote to the African proconsul Anulinus: He had seen that ignoring the reverence due to God had brought great danger to the state, but when reverence was appropriately rendered, all people would participate in the good fortune of the divine benevolence. If this dispute in the church were not ended, the highest divinity, the *summa divinitas*, would not only rise up against the human race, but also against him, Constantine himself. Only when he saw all people within the Catholic religion reverencing the all-holy God in fraternal fellowship, wrote the emperor, could he be completely secure and hope for the benevolence of the almighty God of all goodness. And that was not the only statement on this subject; there are several others of the same sort (see p. 176). One cannot take refuge in the explanation that these letters were written at the court by the "ministry of church affairs" of the imperial chancellery and that Constantine had had nothing to do with them. For in a totalitarian state, which finds itself at a critical point in its history (the power had just been assumed), any statements having anything to do personally with the ruler would be examined carefully, certainly by the ruler himself. Especially in questions that were so difficult and decisive, the only thing that could appear about his personal opinion is what he himself approved. The statements we have cited were certainly read by Constantine before they went out to the proconsul, the leading man of the embattled province. Today we can no longer say that Constantine was a pagan by inner conviction, and anyone who wants to understand him as a religionless power politician can really do that only by ignoring the assumptions of that age. The religionless power politician is a modern phenomenon which is projected back into the past. And anyone who has Constantine building on the political assistance of Christians in his rise to power can do that only by ignoring the real situation and the real status of the power Christians held in the fourth century.

In 305 Constantine fled to Gaul from the imperial court in Nicomedia, where he had practically served as a hostage assuring the benevolence of his father, Constantius Chlorus, who ruled the West. Here in Gaul the number of Christians was very small in relation to the population. In comparison to the East, the West had fewer numbers, and Gaul had the least number of all. Here the Christians were numerically without any weight; a so-called power politician could base no hopes for the attainment of his political goals on them. But even in places where Christians made up half the population, namely in the East, not in the West, the Christians were politically without significance. At that time it was obvious to all that their kingdom was really not of this world. Seen through the eyes of a power politician, the Christians meant next to nothing. These Christians were incapable of political activity. They offered no resistance to government measures; the idea of joining together to resist them did not even cross their minds—although they did possess influential government posts, both in the central government and in the provinces, and although numerically they made up a not insignificant portion of the army. When the Diocletian persecution broke out in 303, it began among the civil officials and the army, without causing any unrest in this army or any resistance among the civil officials. The emperors apparently could do whatever they wished with the Christians without thereby endangering their own power. Politically seen, therefore, the Christians at the beginning of the fourth century were not only without significance, but did not even exist for a power politician acting simply from a political viewpoint marked by irreligion or even by convinced paganism.

Moreover, if Constantine had acted as a power politician who included the Christians in his calculations, he would have needed to offer them much less than he did to gain their approval, even their love. It would have been sufficient to recognize Christianity as a "licit religion," to give it status equal to other religions, occasionally to say a few friendly words to the Christians, and to give favorable treatment to this or that Christian; this would have released a wave of enthusiasm for the emperor among the Christians, whose pent-up feelings of loyalty had again and again been so cruelly repulsed. In the past, any emperor who had done nothing against the Christians, any emperor who had issued any sort of edict which Christians—regardless of how difficult it might be—could interpret as benefiting them, any emperor who had perhaps even one Christian among his close associates was lauded by the Christians as even a secret Christian and was a great and good emperor for them, no matter how successful his government was. His actual or apparent sympathy for Christianity was sufficient for them to judge him this way. If, after the Edict of Milan which went beyond the one of Nicomedia (see p. 76), Constantine had done something similar, that would have been completely sufficient to turn the Christians into his most faithful followers.

The single solution for our question about Constantine's religious activity is to assume that an inner conversion of the emperor to Christianity took place—and to put it more precisely—before that battle against Maxentius at the Milvian bridge outside the gates of Rome in October 312. In the *Vita Constantini,* Constantine's biography, Eusebius gives us a thorough account: Before the decisive battle against Maxentius, Constantine earnestly inquired which god he should adopt as his protector. The fate of the emperors, who, in contrast to his father, trusted in pagan gods, deeply impressed him because these gods brought on the collapse of their rule and their personal catastrophe. To trust in these gods, therefore, could only be foolishness (I, 27). Then comes the decisive Chapter 28 of Book I of the *Vita Constantini*: "Accordingly he called on him with earnest prayer and supplications that he would reveal to him who he was, and stretch forth his right hand to help him in his present difficulties." (That is similar to Clovis's prayer before his battle with the Alemanni. He appealed to this Jesus Christ, as we read, "of whom Clotilda [Clovis's wife] said he was the son of the true God," and declared that he would let himself be baptized if he gave him the victory over the Alemanni. Here we have a parallel prayer to the unknown God; the one praying knows little or nothing about him, but still calls upon him for help.) "And while he was thus praying with fervent entreaty, a most marvelous sign appeared to him from heaven, the account of which it might have been hard to believe had it been related by any other person. But since the victorious emperor himself long afterwards declared it to the writer of this history, when he was honored with his acquaintance and society, and confirmed his statement by an oath, who could hesitate to accredit the relation, especially since the testimony of after-time has established its truth?" Around the hour of noon, so the emperor said, with his own eyes he saw in the heavens above the sun the victorious sign of a cross formed of light and bearing the words, *touto nika* (Greek for "By this sign, conquer"). He and the entire army which beheld this miracle were amazed at the sight.

It is impossible to fail to note the reserve with which Eusebius makes this report. He even declares—something that in the fourth century was amazing (for Eusebius's *Vita Constantini* plainly follows the rules for writing official laudatory addresses)—that no one would believe this if the emperor himself had not told it and underscored it with the greatest emphasis. This reserve does honor to Eusebius the historian. He limits himself to transmitting simply the official version, that which Constantine himself reported ("long afterwards," as Eusebius emphasizes), that is, that which he wanted to have reported. Nevertheless—and this is the significant matter—after 312 we see Constantine acting as if what is reported here really had taken place. Fortunately, the correspondence already mentioned (see p. 174), which Constantine immediately after 312 addressed to the matter of the Donatist controversy, has been preserved for us. No other conclusion can be drawn from these very personal and private letters of the emperor than that a great change had already taken place in him. Besides these letters already mentioned, there are still more of them which can just as little—even less—be labeled products of the imperial chancellery, not even a product of Bishop Hosius (who, remarkably, was already accompanying the emperor; what would a Christian bishop be doing at the court of an emperor who was allegedly devoted to paganism?). What is in these letters could have come only from the emperor. When he writes in them to a governor: "I see that you are one who also reveres the highest god (that is, you are also a Christian)," this may perhaps be ascribed to the court chancellery or to Hosius. But the letter continues: "God always opens for the human race a pathway to salvation; I myself have noticed this. At the beginning of my life there was wickedness in me, and I did not believe that anyone, not even a god, could even see it, and the consequences of that could have been nothing but ruin. But the almighty God, enthroned in heaven, had mercy upon me and gave me, his unworthy servant, countless and endless blessings, which I cannot number here." If this is the emperor's letter, it goes back to Constantine himself; no one at that time would have dared to write something like that in his name without his express approval. Thus there is no other conclusion possible than one that actually places Constantine's turning to Christianity—his "conversion," if one chooses—in the year 312.

Obviously this Christianity is still incomplete in many respects. When Burckhardt in his famous *Leben Konstantins* ("Life of Constantine"), which has been reprinted many times during the last 120 years, so passionately rejected the idea that Constantine was a Christian, he did so on the basis of his conviction that anyone who acted the way Constantine did could not have been a Christian. The ethical standards of his Christianity were, in fact, extremely insufficient, for even as a Christian he stained his life with some bloody deeds, even by an irresponsible murder in his own family; there can be no doubt of this. And certainly Constantine would have failed an examination in Christian dogmatics miserably. But if we proceed the way Burckhardt did, if we form our opinions in the way people have done many times since Burckhardt, then I believe we are thinking unhistorically in the name of history. The main thing is not whether someone from the past measures up to our standards, not that *we* determine what he was or was not, but the main thing is what the person concerned wanted to be in his own heart.

Even when we turn to later times and look at the emperors who wanted to be professed Christians and who were recognized as such in their own time as well as in ours, we find there the same ethical or unethical actions as we do in Constantine. We have already mentioned that Constantine's sons began their rule with a bloodbath in the family (see pp. 80–81). And even the way Constantius led his life is questionable in various aspects. Even the truly Christian emperor, Theodosius, was able in his rage to order the populace of the city of Thessalonica to assemble in the amphitheater, and then to have his troops surround the circus and slay those gathered there, simply because a riot had occurred there in which the commanding general had been killed. No one contests the fact that Constantine's sons and Theodosius were Christians; with this reasoning, we should not argue on the basis of Constantine's action that he *wanted* to be a Christian. It is certainly impressive to view history in a moral way. This was especially characteristic of the nineteenth century. But if we want to understand times past, we must liberate ourselves from that way of looking at things. We must, I repeat, free ourselves from all of our own standards of measurement. Let us not even mention that these moral standards—or really moralistic ones—of the nineteenth century are themselves justified only in very questionable ways, just as we ourselves and those of our own time are. We should not ask, for example, how much blood stains the hands of some "Christian" statesman of modern history, and need only mention that the "most Christian kings"—that was the official title of the kings of France from the Middle Ages onward—could successfully compete with Constantine in regard to bloodletting, murder, and cruelty.

Constantine did consciously have his sons raised as Christians, and he married the female members of his family to Christians. Finally, his mother Helena is a demonstration of Christianity in Constantine's family which could not be more impressive, a demonstration which is almost offensive. There can be no doubt that Helena was originally a pagan. If she had shown any signs in the time before 312 of leanings toward Christianity, Eusebius would not have failed to praise Helena's Christianity even in those early times. Yet we later find her as a pilgrim to the holy places of Palestine, seeking relics (and when an emperor's mother seeks relics, she also finds them), building churches, and giving the entire world a model of an exemplary Christian. I would believe that the Christianity of the mother grew out of the Christianity of the son. Would a power politician who was indifferent to Christianity, who was without religion himself, find it necessary to have his mother travel through Palestine with great expense as a Christian pilgrim and thus make himself the laughingstock of all educated pagans? I believe that even asking the question calls for an answer of No.

It is true that Constantine was not baptized until he was on his deathbed, but that does not support the theory that he was a pagan or merely a formal Christian. Rather, that was the sign of a definite type of piety which we find at that time and even later—Constantius was also not baptized until on his deathbed. This is a piety of scrupulousness, virtually a sort of countinghouse piety. One waits until the last moment so that one will be assured of salvation. If one lets himself be baptized today, one does not know what may happen tomorrow, and it might be that tomorrow's action may irreparably destroy today's baptism. Especially might this be the case if one were a fourth-century emperor. If one is baptized immediately before death, then there will be no sins on the record read in the judgment, and salvation will therefore be assured. Constantine had himself buried in the Church of the Twelve Apostles in Constantinople which he had ordered built during his lifetime. In it were twelve sarcophagi for the apostles and a thirteenth one in the center for himself. This is proof, even a demonstration, of Constantine's Christianity and one that not only shows a Christian faith, but—I would almost believe—one that also shows the emperor's consciousness of a Christian mission.

Constantine advanced Christianity a decisive step along its way. Yet the same is true for Constantine as applied to Julian (see pp. 80–81): even without his intervention the same development we have observed would have happened. Even if he had reigned longer, Julian would not have been able to check the course of Christianity, and Christianity would also have triumphed without Constantine—perhaps later, perhaps in another manner, but of that fact itself there can be no doubt. That does not minimize Constantine's significance. The church rewarded him with overflowing gratitude and honor not only during his lifetime, but also afterward. After his death it preserved his memory: even today the name of Constantine echoes in the liturgy of the Orthodox church. As virtually the single ruler of ancient history, he still plays a role today in the general consciousness of humankind.

It is methodologically interesting and important for checking the interpretation given here, that later in history we find rulers—Clovis in the fifth century and Frederick the Wise in the sixteenth century—who attained a similar significance for the history of Christianity, and the genuineness of their motives is just as questionable for many historians as is that of Constantine's. Clovis has decisive significance as the one who turned the Germanic Middle Ages into the Catholic Middle Ages. As the Catholic church emerged from the defensive position into which it had been forced by the Arianism of the Germanic tribes, and now undertook a counterattack, this counterattack was assisted decisively by the Frankish prince, Clovis, who accepted for himself, and thus in effect for his tribe, the Catholic form of the Christian faith, not the Arian. This happened in opposition to everything that was likely and contrary to all that was politically necessary. One thousand years later, Frederick the Wise protected Luther and the Reformation, thus determining the course of events. If the curia and the emperor had not needed to be concerned about Frederick the Wise, human judgment would have predicted that Luther would not have had a long period of activity, not even a very long life. One can certainly say (as in Constantine's case in the fourth century), that in both cases—in the Middle Ages as well as in the Reformation period—the development would probably have differed in detail, but the end effect would have been exactly the same as it actually was. But this does not minimize the decisive significance which belongs to the two princes in the context of these events. Both acted in opposition to the political constellation; both took a considerable risk on themselves. Clovis (see pp. 230–33) can be compared to Constantine in many respects (just as Gregory of Tours already did in the Middle Ages). His life and actions were controlled by the same laws as Constantine's were: he had to be victorious if he were to retain his rule, even his life. And the risk taken by Frederick the Wise (see vol. 2) was an extreme one. It is true that the Schmalkaldic War, which brought the loss of a great part of the territory previously ruled by his house, broke out after the death of Frederick the Wise, but this danger was already present during his entire activity. He was well aware of everything that was involved in what he was doing for the Reformation. Why did these princes take this risk, why did they act contrary to everything suggested by wisdom, prudence, or whatever we might like to call it?

Each time, the answer that many historians have to give is the same as with Constantine: behind the action of the princes, Clovis as well as Frederick the Wise, stand political considerations. When we get the answer three times—for Constantine, for Clovis, and for Frederick the Wise—that here things are being done for political considerations, this answer does not become more probable by repeating it (at least as far as I am concerned) but only more doubtful. I would believe that the modern writers of history only prove with this that they cannot extricate themselves from the circle of contemporary thinking, that in the last analysis they think unhistorically because they are able to measure the preceding centuries only with standards that apply to our own time. Only too frequently, the modern historian finds nothing in history except himself, his own skepticism, his own insecurity, his own estrangement from the phenomenon of religion, and therefore comes up with this conclusion. It should have become clear in the course of our treatment that adopting political reasons to explain Constantine's religious politics is not justified by the historical record; that this explanation also does not suffice to explain the actions of Clovis and Frederick the Wise will be dealt with later (see pp. 231–33 and vol. 2).

At any rate—to return to our original presentation—the church finally pushes into the world during Constantine's age, something that was tangibly demonstrated to all its contemporaries by the great church buildings which now were begun everywhere. Until the end of the third century, the exterior appearance of church buildings was quite undistinguished. Christians gathered in private houses for worship. If they met in larger buildings, these were located in garden areas which hid them from the public. The Christians buried their dead in the public cemeteries. They did also have their own cemeteries, but these were located underground. The catacombs extended under land which was either owned directly by the church or indirectly through the good offices of someone who held title for it. Under Constantine that changed. Now the church buildings demonstrated, to everyone who could see them, how things had changed. For even the churches not located in the seclusion of a park and those not identical with a private residence had very modest dimensions in the time before Constantine. The so-called "Great Church" in the capital of Nicomedia was celebrated in its time as a wonderful structure. But this wonderful building, when the Diocletian persecution broke out, could be torn down within a few hours by a company of soldiers. We know this from Lactantius's description: The emperor stood on the palace roof and watched as the church across the street was razed to the ground in the shortest time (see p. 77). Now, in Constantine's age, churches of extraordinary size and splendor were constructed, and in connection with their construction and furnishing neither the funds needed nor the difficulties involved had to be considered. For example, let us take St. Peter's Church at the Vatican. It was constructed in such a way that the altar stood precisely above the memorial where Peter's grave was believed to be located, as excavations under the church in recent decades have shown. This spot lay within a cemetery in which burials were still taking place. In opposition to current law, in opposition to the extraordinarily strong feeling of piety toward the dead at that time, the cemetery was closed and the graves were filled or leveled. Besides this, because of the location of the grave, the church had to be constructed on the slope of a hill in such a way that half of it would have stood in the air, and therefore extraordinary excavations and massive foundations were necessary. All of these technical difficulties were mastered by the local governmental authorities, because the center of the church had to be constructed precisely over the location of this memorial. An undertaking of that sort was possible only with the express permission of the imperial administration and, I would imagine, only at the initiative of the emperor himself. This sort of thing happened not only in Rome, but also in Palestine in a similar fashion, and all through the area of the empire.

And it was not just these church buildings which could not be overlooked, but also the property which the church was starting to amass right at the beginning of the fourth century. The bishops of the fourth century were not only influential, but also prominent men, who were indistinguishable from the higher government officials when they appeared in public; we know this from the pagan Ammianus Marcellinus, who made a spirited, if also hypocritical, complaint about this.

It was apparent to all that the church was gaining ground in the world. But this advancement of the church in the world did not happen without a reaction. Now the world was also coming into the church to an extent that exceeded anything possible in the third century. Previously, anyone who became a Christian had to be clear that he was taking a considerable, possibly a fatal risk upon himself. His faith—even if he did not aspire to a career in government service (if he did, the difficulties multiplied)—was no advantage to him, but a severe impediment. But no later than the middle of the fourth century it was clear to those who wanted to advance their careers that things had changed; probably this was the case even earlier. Now it was an advantage to be a Christian, and so some let themselves be baptized who would not even have thought of doing so under other circumstances, with the result that the spiritual as well as the moral level of the church declined. A reaction to this was unavoidable.

2. MONASTICISM

Even in the early period an actual or imagined relaxation in standards of morality always produced a sensitive reaction in the church, as shown, for example, by the reaction to Callistus's penitential edict (see pp. 154–55) and similar things. If the world were now to penetrate the church to such an extent, the reaction would have to be of a corresponding magnitude. Thus at the end of the third century, as the church enjoyed a forty-year respite before greater persecutions, we see in Egypt the first emigrants beginning to withdraw from human society and going out into lonely places because they believed that only there could they remain free from the temptations of the world and live in a way that would bring salvation to their souls.

If we read the *Vita Antonii* ("Life of Anthony"), the depiction of Anthony's life from Athanasius's pen, we get a very clear and impressive picture of this. First, these eremites lived near the small villages. But for Anthony that was not enough; he went farther and farther away from human beings because he preferred to have nothing at all to do with them. The hermit believed that he could live a correct life only if he were independent of everyone and everything. He chose a site by a spring where date palms grew and there cultivated his own grain for bread so that he could sustain himself and not have to depend on the help of friends. Then, we might say, the hermit was happy over all who did not visit him, no matter how honorable their intentions—whether to learn how to live the life of an eremite, to obtain help in trials, or to be healed of an illness. That only thrust the hermit into the world and kept him away from his real, spiritual life (naturally, as he conceived it). Deeper and deeper into the desert fled the emigrants, therefore, and greater and greater became their ascetic practices, until we see the final consequences in the pillar saints of the fifth century. After they first lived in an enclosed area, they erected pillars that they gradually built up from modest beginnings to great heights. On this pillar was located a platform only a few square yards in size. Here the ascetics spent their lives in continual adoration of God, exposed to summer heat and inclement winter weather. Through the most extreme self-torture they intended to serve God and win salvation for themselves.

The surprising thing is that this phenomenon did not appear to Christians of that age for what it really was, an attack on their lifestyle, an attack on the reduced demands made on them, the sharpest protest against the current conditions of the church. Rather, these ascetics, from the eremites to the pillar saints, were nothing but objects of edification for Christians living in the world at that time. Christians and the church viewed the eremitic life as a vicarious performance at which they marvelled, but which also allowed them to be satisfied with themselves and then resume their normal lives. The number of those caught up in the ascetic movement continually grew. At first it was only a few who went out into the desert, which they believed was ruled by demons, in order to bring even the desert under the lordship of Christ. But gradually we find the caves of the eremites throughout the desert and everywhere monasteries appearing after the model of the community founded by Pachomius in which people lived communally in isolation from the world until finally—as we read in *Vita Antonii*—the desert appeared to be inhabited. Monasticism's strength at that time is an expression of the power of the forces which were taking offense at the church which was gradually beginning to lose its original strictness. If we want to have a complete picture of the church at the close of the early period, we should not look only at the patriarchs of the metropolitan churches and the pope in Rome, or at the bishops who were becoming secular rulers whose outward trappings of power came more and more to resemble those of the high state officials. We must also not look merely at the theological controversies. Rather, we must observe the ascetics and the monks who in their radical withdrawal from the world accomplished—for themselves at least—a return to the early period, even though they were in no position to take the entire church back there. Without a doubt, many critical questions must be addressed to this monasticism: these ascetics separated themselves from the world; they thought only of themselves, of their salvation, of their escape, not of the task which the neighbor imposed on them. Yet we will be greatly impressed with what earnestness they here strove for salvation, in contrast to a church which more and more was uniting itself with the world.

3. THE ARIAN AND THE CHRISTOLOGICAL CONTROVERSIES

Introductory Remarks

As we now turn to a consideration of the Arian and the Christological controversies, a few introductory remarks are necessary. The first is directed to those for whom these controversies frequently become the actual content of church life in the fourth and fifth centuries. The Arian and Christological controversies are often discussed in a way that makes it appear that nothing else was happening then, while the truth is that alongside these arguments the life of the church continued in its entirety—worship, prayer, interpretation of Scripture, and preaching— and the theological writings of the time in no way devote themselves exclusively to this theme, even when addressing the Arian or the Christological controversy. If we were to think only of the Arian or the Christological controversy when we speak of the fourth and fifth centuries, things would be skewed in an inappropriate manner.

Second: There is always the danger of viewing these controversies in the wrong light when the human, the all-too-human element is placed too much in the foreground. We have spoken thoroughly—really enough, I hope—about the roles played by the human element in the Donatist controversy (see pp. 164–69), and what significance all-too-human considerations had for the outbreak of the Arian controversy. This keeps on occurring. When we look back at the Christological controversy it is unmistakable that this human, all-too-human element had a significant share in it, that the power struggle of the patriarchates significantly determined, if not the origin, at least the severity of the Christological controversy. Again and again the Alexandrian patriarchs attempted to limit or completely eliminate the constantly ascending position of Constantinople. The Christological controversy draws its extreme harshness from the efforts of Cyril, bishop of Alexandria, to strike a fatal blow at his rival Nestorius in Constantinople. His predecessor, Theophilus, had been able to bring about the removal of the Constantinopolitan patriarch, Chrysostom, truly a shining light of this fourth century which otherwise displays so many things which we can view only with reservation. Chrysostom had to go into exile. He died miserably during his deportation—this is certainly what we can call it— because such an *anima candida* ("sincere soul") was no match for the intrigues of the cunning patriarch of Alexandria. Theophilus had managed to topple Chrysostom, but his office as such and the position of the patriarch of Constantinople were not affected. That was now Cyril's intention. He wanted not merely to defeat Nestorius, but also desired to tar him with the brush of heresy and thus discredit the patriarchate of Constantinople as an institution and along with it those associates of Nestorius who shared his theological views. In that he succeeded. Not only was Nestorius destroyed, but in his demise the entire Antiochene school was pulled down with him within a few generations.

Here there is certainly enough of the human, the all-too-human element. But the fourth and fifth centuries would not understand the sort of interpretation we find in someone like Goethe who called church history a "mishmash of error and of force" and proclaimed in *Zahme Xenien*: "Two opponents there are who box, the Arians and the Orthodox. Through many ages it's been this way; and it'll last until the Final Day." We must look at the nontheological factors connected with these struggles, in which not only does church politics play a role, but to an extraordinarily strong extent, imperial politics as well. Yet at the same time we must be aware that if we limit ourselves to such a view of things, we will fail even to establish the facts of the events, let alone attempt to understand these events. If these arguments were only concerned with power struggles—power struggles between bearers of high ecclesiastical offices or power struggles between areas of the church—these struggles would never have had such an extent, never such an intensity, and never such a duration.

There can be no doubt, as we have said, that the Donatist controversy (see pp. 165–67) was measurably conditioned, initiated, and nourished by nontheological factors. But the schismatic Donatist church did not derive its power for the rapid expansion it enjoyed or its power to withstand and outlast the persecutions it had to endure from these nontheological factors—from its nationalistic opposition, its social opposition, and everything else connected with this—but rather from the fact that here a very definite interpretation of Christianity was alive. The same is true for the Arian and for the Christological controversies.

Third: The person who views the Arian and the Christological controversies as if they dealt merely with theological definitions—as has again and again been done—will also fail to understand these disputes. It is true that such an interpretation has a great deal of validity, for this is indeed an argument among theologians that is primarily concerned with very difficult concepts. Whoever holds this opinion will be in a position, with appropriate effort, to enumerate the various definitions, list the synods at which these definitions were worked out, and give information about the writings of the theologians which explain these definitions. But the whole will be dead and lifeless. For if it had had to do only with such theological definitions and only with an argument among theologians, the Arian and the Christological controversies—just to repeat it once again—would never have attained the significance, the duration, and the intensity that in fact they did. This was not only a dispute among theologians or at most among monks, but these arguments deeply gripped and passionately moved the populace of the East, and to a certain extent also the West, so that often enough civil intervention was necessary when a theological definition was officially altered. The churches were in no way disposed to adopt changes in the official theological formulation automatically. When it happened in the course of the Christological controversy that entire ecclesiastical provinces separated from the church and formed national churches it was because the Christians there believed that only in this way was it possible for them to be true Christians. Behind the abstract formulas and the apparently theoretical arguments stand diametrically opposed concepts of the nature of Christianity. In the Arian and the Christological controversies the struggle was about the ultimate assurance for humankind's longing for redemption. Whether Christ was of the same nature or of similar nature with the Father and how the relation between the divine and the human in him should be described was no theoretical question for people in the third to the seventh centuries, but for them it was of direct, decisive significance for their existence as Christians. From this comes the length, from this comes the vehemence, and from this comes the extent of these struggles.

Fourth: In the church history textbooks, the Arian controversy usually begins in the fourth century. But that is not quite correct. These conflicts begin rather in the second century, at that moment when people were no longer able to make do with the New Testament statements about the Trinity, when the age of the unreflecting statements of the Apostolic Fathers is over. Ignatius could still say without difficulty that "our God" suffered on the cross. In his day that was a completely valid statement; only two generations later this formulation was being severely criticized.

Fifth: The Arian controversy brings the definition of the Trinity to completion. But in the moment when, after long effort, unity is attained in a theological statement which defines the relation between the three persons of the Godhead, theological thought has already taken the next step and turned to the question of the relation between the divine and the human in the second person of the Trinity, Jesus Christ. Here we observe how the leading theologians of that time, after just bringing the Arian controversy to a conclusion, stand helpless before the new question that is posed, not indeed because they are unable to think sufficiently theologically about it, but because for them this problem of

Christology just does not yet really exist. For them the essence of Christianity was described with the right answer to the question about the Trinity. The next generation had quite a different opinion; for it the question of Christology was the central question and everything depended on its answer. From then until the present day things have gone this way: The concentration on one question occurs again and again, and for a generation everything is wrapped up in it so that not only does theological orthodoxy depend on the correct answer to that question, but the very existence of the church and the salvation of each individual Christian as well. The next generation clearly sees the incompleteness of the question as well as the answer given by the previous one, but it falls into the same error in respect to the problem troubling it. That can happen even when the question of the next generation in a certain sense unavoidably grows out of the previous one. For example, the Christological controversy was only a wider development of the Arian controversy. However, it can also be that the question of the next generation stands in direct opposition to the question of the previous one. Things do not always go as smoothly and as consistently as in the Arian and Christological controversies; frequently they zigzag, even to the present day.

If we look sharply enough we shall observe this same general law prevailing today in the twentieth century as it did in the third or fourth and in the following centuries. Each generation believes it has finally broken through and attained clarity about the significance of Christianity, theology, and the practical consequences derived from them. And each generation has the experience that a new one comes along which it no longer understands. Let us think only of Harnack's age. Harnack was the embodiment of academic theology at the turn of the century. He stood on the pinnacle of contemporary theological thought and not only summarized all possibilities of the time in his theological work, but also achieved a prominent reputation for academic theology among all other disciplines. This same Harnack had to watch as Karl Barth, who had participated in his seminars and could be called his student, taught a theology which to him, although he could master the most complicated things (and not just in theology), appeared incomprehensible both in its totality and in its details. And since then it has continued: Karl Barth and dialectical theology, the theology of the *Kirchenkampf*, the demythologization of Rudolf Bultmann, hermeneutics, and other problems demonstrate how rapidly and fundamentally the questions can change and how a new generation discards without understanding what to the previous one was the key which unlocked all problems; then it propounds new problems with new solutions for which it claims the same absolute value. If we see how the same principle has been at work from the beginning until the present day, we will then view some things in the modern age with reserve. We will not be able to share the certainty, the self-confidence claimed by some contemporary theological schools. This certainty and self-confidence indeed seem to be apparently necessary concomitant manifestations of every new theological declaration. Nevertheless, we will not be able to adopt the intolerance with which, as a rule, a new theological statement excludes or condemns an old one. This does not mean relativizing things. It is precisely the historical view that is evidenced in the waves' crests and troughs, the logical and compelling movement which permeates the history of theology, that leads us most emphatically to demand that every era must work out its own problems as best it can. It has been proved again and again that bitter vengeance is in store if a generation ignores or hides its problems before introducing whatever solution is possible at that time. It is self-evident that in numerous respects our age suffers from the omissions of the nineteenth century and that many of the problems we confront today are our problems only because our grandparents and great-grandparents did not discuss them to a conclusion. Even in the twentieth century many things have not been brought to their end. The Luther renaissance which we experienced after World War I was not fully productive, for other questions were pushed aside before they could be discussed completely. By this I mean not only the question of demythologization, but also the question of the history of tradition along with everything which belongs to it, the questions of hermeneutics, and so forth. If we avoid such things in our path instead of dealing with them, we are only creating problems which in all likelihood the succeeding age will have difficulty in bearing. It is unmistakable that not just in the nineteenth, but also thus far in the twentieth century we have been too disposed to circumvent our problems and not meet them head-on. That is more comfortable for the individual theologian and more comfortable for the church, but this brief and transitory comfort will be very uncomfortable for the next generation and can lead to much greater difficulties than would have been faced by the previous generation if it had really dealt with the problems.

As a rule, unfortunately, it is not the case that the mistake once made and its results in the next generation or the following ones are recognizable as directly related to each other. Not always is it clear at first glance that the needs with which a generation is concerned result from the deficiencies of its forebears. Rather, as a rule the new need comes in disguise, in a mask which is sometimes very difficult and often impossible to see through. If it were not so, everything would be much easier. In summary: Inertia, comfort, and—said plainly—cowardice of the theologians and sometimes also church leaders has always wrought the most painful vengeance. We may not avoid the problems posed for theology and the church. We must not only struggle with them in all earnestness, but must also take care to determine their cause and their previous history in order to master both the actual problem and also its past, inasmuch as that is possible. Enough for the introductory remarks.

The Controversy About the Divinity of Christ (Arian Controversy)

Let us return to the second century, when it was first sensed that the formulations of the New Testament and the Apostolic Fathers were not sufficient to describe the nature of the divinity. A new way of doing this was attempted. Thus the so-called Monarchian controversy occurred, about which we have already spoken (see pp. 132–33). These Monarchians were not unified, but are only identified with this title. In addition to the Modalists (prominent names: Noetus of Smyrna, Praxeas, and Sabellius), for whom Christ and the Holy Spirit were modes in which the one Godhead appeared, there were the Dynamists or Adoptionists (Theodotus the Cobbler, Theodotus the Money-changer), who conceived of Christ either as a man who was raised up by being adopted by God, or as a man filled with God's power.

These Monarchianistic statements grew out of the attempt to preserve monotheism. God was *one*—that was the fundamental principle that could not be compromised. The problems originated when this fundamental article of monotheism had to be harmonized with the fact of the independent existence and the divine activity of Jesus to which the Gospels bear witness. This was the problem the Monarchians attempted to solve; this was the problem in the Arian controversy which then followed it; this was the problem in the Christological controversies. The monotheism of the deity, something that was not open to discussion, had to be reconciled with the facticity of the statements of the Gospels.

At the conclusion of the second century, a way out of these difficulties was found in the Logos Christology, in which Christ was described as the Logos who proceeded from God. This Logos Christology, held by Irenaeus, Hippolytus, Tertullian, and others, was indeed the most advanced sort of theological thinking at that time, but was still no solution to the problem. Logos Christology, in the final analysis, was only a way of speaking, quite apart from the fact that this Logos ("Logos" has been translated variously as word, reason, *sermo, ratio,* and the like) identified something that was constantly changing. Logos Christology overcame Monarchianism among the theologians and in the official church, but not among the laity. For ordinary people things were quite clear: Christ equals God, Christ is God, Christ must indeed equal God, Christ must be God, because this is the presupposition for the redemption of humankind. In baptism and in the Lord's Supper a Christian participates in Christ, so that we who want to be redeemed must fight against whatever threatens Christ's complete divinity. Thus it happened, in spite of all the advances made in theological expression, that until the conclusion of ancient church history, the attitude of the laity was characterized by a tacit Monarchianism, even though Monarchianism had been numbered among the archheresies for centuries. This was true not only for the ancient church, but the same—at least in the practical understanding of the laity—is still true in our own day.

We can study the difficulties of the fourth century in the example of Athanasius. Athanasius was *the* theologian of the Arian disputes, the defender of orthodoxy, the revered master of the West and also for a large portion of the East. He expressed himself on this matter in numerous writings. But when we read these writings we quickly see that Athanasius had a real interest only in guaranteeing that Christ had the same nature, the same power, as the Father. Athanasius is considered the chief advocate of the *homoousios,* which he raised as the banner of orthodoxy. That is correct in substance, but applies literally only to a later time. Seen at close range, things look much different. Almost thirty years after the Council of Nicaea, Athanasius still did not say, in speaking about the second person of the Trinity, that the Son was *homoousios* with the Father, but rather that he was *homoios kata panta,* "like him in all things," *homoios kata tēn graphēn,* "like him in accordance with the Scripture." Only after 352 did he adopt the *homoousios* because he thought it best expressed what was at stake. For Athanasius, just as for the laity, the important thing was to preserve the divinity of Christ, for if we participate in Christ, we must then participate in God, if our redemption is to be assured. Again and again this is found in Athanasius; everything else is of less significance for him, so that he indeed holds fast to monotheism and preserves the redemption of humankind, but he constantly stands in danger of coming up with something that is opposed to the plain statements of the New Testament.

The other side did not begin from what we would call religious necessity, but rather from academic and theological considerations. It began with statements from Scripture and then tried to present and interpret what was said by the Gospels about Christ's existence and activity. Thus it emphasized the ways in which Christ was different from God. The one side drew Father and Son together in such a way that no difference could be seen any longer, and the other side—because it wanted to present things clearly—pulled the two apart. This academic thought and congregational piety did not first come into conflict in the fourth century, but when we look at the argument in the middle of the third century between Dionysius of Alexandria and Dionysius of Rome, both of them bishops of their cities, we find the same things already being debated here. Dionysius of Alexandria was severely attacked by churches of his diocese over his statements about Christ. Some of the details are obscure, but it is certain that Dionysius of Alexandria paraphrased the relationship of the Father and the Son with the image of boatbuilder and boat, gardener and vine, and similar analogies, that is, of a creator and his creation. This was a severe offense to parts of his church, and they sought assistance from Dionysius of Rome. The latter apparently did not understand the theological question in all its depth, but nevertheless sent a letter to Dionysius of Alexandria which repeated the traditional statements. Dionysius of Alexandria admitted that perhaps he had gone too far in his statements, but that he would not retreat in this matter since he had acted out of theological conviction and could not do what the churches and Dionysius of Rome demanded. The *homoousios* was an insurmountable stumbling block to every person who thought in theological terms at that time. *Homoousios* did not mean "of the same being," as it was continually translated, but, translated more precisely, it meant "of an identical being." The offense which every theologian worthy of the name took at this statement about the identity of the natures of the Father and the Son is only too understandable. Christ cannot have the identical nature of God; he is God, but he is distinct from God and can be described only in a distinctive way.

At the Council of Nicaea in 325 this *homoousios* was now given official status. In the most remarkable way a creedal formula was proclaimed here, one which was held by no theologian at that time, and one which met a demand no one was making. Some scholars have claimed that the *homoousios* at Nicaea was attributable to Hosius of Cordova, that is, to the influence of the West. It is true that Hosius of Cordova spent time at the emperor's court, and it is also true that he advised Constantine in ecclesiastical and theological questions. But the events at Nicaea cannot be explained merely on the basis of the influence of Hosius of Cordova; even if the idea had stemmed from him, he would never have been able to force it through the council. Only Constantine was in the position to get the synod to decide something about which it knew nothing in advance, and which had already become a great vexation at its adjournment. The introduction of the *homoousios* into the creed adopted by the synod also precisely corresponds to what we could presume was in Constantine's mind. At the middle of the third century we met the *homoousios* as the standard of piety in the congregations, the standard of lay Christianity in Egypt (see p. 192). If Constantine adopted it for himself, he did it because it agreed with his piety and his concern—and his ability to comprehend things. Constantine, the lay Christian, did not understand that difficult theological problems were associated with it; that was beyond his comprehension. He adopted the *homoousios* for himself because it also expressed exactly that which concerned him. The powerful impression of his personality, the splendor of the event, the uniqueness of the situation—only a year before Nicaea, the hour of freedom from persecution had finally come for Christians in the East—all of this combined to bring the bishops to agree to the *homoousios,* the same statement which appalled them as soon as they got a little away from Nicaea. To the overwhelming majority of them, standing under the theological influence of Origen, this *homoousios,* this "identical nature," could have appeared just as bad as the old heresy of Monarchianism. Thus, immediately after Nicaea every academically educated theologian attempted to repudiate this *homoousios* which he, overwhelmed by the special situation, had adopted without thinking much about it. We can study this in the person of Eusebius of Caesarea who, returning to his church, had the utmost difficulties in explaining why he had approved this *homoousios.* We may well say that with Nicaea the opposition within the church has its beginning.

Constantine, who was very proud of this council, probably because of his special participation in it, at first energetically resisted its opposition, but then finally succumbed to the theologians with the understanding that nothing would be done to disturb the Nicene decision and the synod as such. Various ways had been attempted after Nicaea to describe the relationship of the Father to the Son. For a time this was the only thing that was considered; the third person of the Trinity, the Holy Spirit, was excluded from the discussion until almost the end of the controversies (see pp. 196–97). The formulations which were produced in the decades after Nicaea—regardless of who the theologians were, regardless of where and when the synods took place—continually represented the same two groups: one coming from Origen that was marked by scholarly thought, and one whose theology was based on soteriological thought and the needs of the church. The one attempted not to identify Christ with the Father in such a way that he completely disappeared in him, but to distinguish him discernibly from the Father. According to the testimony of Scripture, the Father was greater than the Son, so this group of theologians very clearly spoke of the distinction between them, but ran into difficulty in defining the relationship between the Father and the Son. The opposing side, which knew it had to speak about the relationship between the two in order to guarantee humankind's redemption, had the opposite difficulty of distinguishing Christ from God to any extent. This latter group, led by Athanasius, had the greater strength, supported as it was by the piety of the laity, who from the very beginning mistrusted academic and theological thinking, a phenomenon which has continued from that time until our own day. The greater churchly and religious force was on Athanasius's side, therefore, while the other side had the stronger theological arguments and thus a larger number of adherents among the bishops and theologians.

After Constantine's death the nimbus surrounding Nicaea and its symbol disappeared, so that under Constantius the anti-Nicene opposition could finally triumph and force the offensive symbol aside. But now something took place which we see happening again and again in the course of church history: as soon as an opposing movement triumphs, it falls apart. The anti-Nicene opposition had previously been held together by its opposition to the *homoousios.* Now the stumbling block was removed, but at the same time the unifying bond of negation had been lost. Now when it was asked what could be said positively, the fundamental differences existing among those who had been fighting on the same side with great energy and passionate effort were clearly revealed: the opposition (as again and again in church history) was composed of the most disparate groups. Here we find theologians who knew that they were thoroughly at one with Athanasius in this matter, but could not bring themselves to accept his *homoousios.* But, just as before, there were also the radical Arians whose unaltered slogan said that the Son was *anhomoios,* "dissimilar to," the Father. In the middle were those theologians who wished to limit themselves to the apparently neutral formula of *homoios* ("similar"). For example, they played a decisive role at the court of Constantius, and with the help of the elastic formula of *homoios* they were able to accommodate themselves to everyone and everything. In fact, however, the *homoios* only very thinly veiled their Arian sympathies.

Thus the controversy did not come to an end with the victory of the anti-Nicene opposition, but really just began then. This controversy lasted until a way was found to make a clear theological expression of what was at stake, or, to put it another way, until *"ousia"* and *"hypostasis"* could finally be distinguished from one another. At the beginning of the controversy, *ousia* and *hypostasis* were the same thing: both of them were conceived of as "essence," "essentiality." There were only very few then who distinguished between *ousia,* the essence of divinity, and *hypostasis,* the form in which it appeared, as Tertullian had already done a century and a half earlier in speaking about *"substantia"* and *"persona,"* about the substance, the essence of divinity, and the form in which it appeared. When Greek theologians spoke about one *ousia* and three *hypostases* (that is, about the one essence of God which expressed itself in three forms of appearing), it was not just the church but also the majority of theologians at that time which was not prepared to accept that; they thought that speaking about three *hypostases* was speaking about three divinities. A good part of the discussion and a good part of the heat and sharpness of the condemnations on both sides can be explained by the way the different sides misunderstood the different ways of expressing this. It took some time until the distinction between *ousia,* the one essence of God, and the three *hypostases,* the forms in which it appeared, won the day. The so-called Cappadocian theologians, Basil the Great, Gregory of Nyssa, and Gregory of Nazianzus, were able to accomplish this. They could speak about the *ousia,* about the one essence, which is exhibited in three forms of appearance, in the three *hypostases,* in three persons. And this statement was then adopted by the majority of the theologians. The *homoousios* was also unacceptable to the Cappadocians. They replaced it with the *homoiousios,* which now meant, "of like essence," "of one essence." Because of this, the Arian controversy has somewhat cynically produced the *bon mot* that it dealt only with an iota. The two words are, in fact, distinguished only by an iota, an i, but in this one iota, in this one i, the entire contrast lies; *homoousios* expresses the "identical essence" *(Wesensidentität), homoiousios,* the "of one essence" *(eines Wesens).*

With the greatest mistrust, Athanasius watched the path taken by theological thought of his day, the same Athanasius who from 352 onward, as we mentioned (see p. 191), demanded that *homoousios* be the single possible expression—something that was quite characteristic of Athanasius and his involvement in the entire movement. Athanasius fought with reckless disregard for his own person for the view he held (for example, he repeatedly suffered exile for his views), but he was never able to think beyond it. He did not comprehend that one could properly use *homoiousios,* and that this other manner of expression simply came from the advancement of theological thought. Not until 362, after many bitter personal experiences, could Athanasius bring himself to declare that, even though *homoousios* was the only valid expression, if someone were insistent and really concerned only about a word, then he might also be free to use *homoiousios.* Thus, the controversies gradually reached their conclusion that was marked by the Council of Constantinople in 381. In the symbol adopted by this council, the word used was *homoousios,* but the interpretation immediately showed that this *homoousios* was no longer understood as "of identical essence" *(wesenidentisch)* or "of the same essence," *(weseneins)* but as "of one essence" *(eines Wesens).* The first two persons of the Trinity are of one nature *(eines Wesens)*—that is now established.

But at the same time, the creed adopted by this council said the same thing about the third person of the Trinity, the Holy Spirit who proceeds from the Father. This statement of the Council of Constantinople in 381—let us note in passing—is still used by the Greek church to the present day, in contrast to the Western church, which during the course of the controversy in the Middle Ages over the *filioque* (see pp. 267–68) generally adopted the doctrinal position that the Holy Spirit proceeds from the Father *and* the Son. And this difference from the Orthodox church, which is not merely a dispute about words but one about an essential difference in the fundamental conception of the divinity, has not been resolved to the present day.

The third person of the Trinity was—as we have mentioned (see pp. 193–94)—not discussed at all until the final period of the Arian controversy. The Trinity was always mentioned, of course, but what was meant by this was only Father and Son. Not until the end of the controversy, as an agreement about the relationship of these two to each other appeared to be in sight, did the theologians discover, really to their own amazement, that the previously ignored question of the Holy Spirit's relationship to the Father and the Son still had to be answered. We see this happening with great rapidity, almost with violence, and it also follows the laws which we continually observe in theological and ecclesiastical controversies: A question has been discussed for a long time. It appears to be virtually solved. Both theology and the church are tired of the argument, so they rapidly move toward the certain goal and no longer take the time and trouble to discuss the problems still remaining with the same intensity as before, that is, in our case, the question of the Holy Spirit. So we find theologians who until then were on the same side and made the same theological statements now suddenly split by deep differences of opinion, for not all of them would also attribute the *homoiousios* to the Holy Spirit. Old friendships were dissolved, those who had reservations about also saying *homoiousios* of the Holy Spirit were cast aside, and with the label of "Pneumatomachi" they were, so to speak, cast onto the trash heap of the history of dogma.

Put bluntly, we could say that when we look at the results of the Council of Constantinople in 381 we see only a repetition of what had already been formulated almost two hundred years earlier by Tertullian, who spoke about the *tres personae,* the three persons, and the *una substantia,* the one substance. The Council of Nicaea does still retain its great reputation, but to a certain extent it has been absorbed by the Council of Constantinople. Nicaea disappears completely behind Constantinople. It is characteristic that we no longer possess the records of the Council of Nicaea, and also that when the church, from that time until our own, speaks about the "Nicene Creed," it is not referring to the creed adopted at the Council of Nicaea in 325, but to the one adopted by the Council of Constantinople in 381. That is why this creed is also known as the Nicaeno-Constantinopolitanum.

In the year 451 at Chalcedon, after the Christological controversy had reached a definite conclusion, this Council of Constantinople was once more ceremoniously confirmed. It has attained the highest reputation within all of Christendom, in fact among all the churches of Christendom (something that cannot be said about the creed of Chalcedon, for example). The number of confessional branches in the church is a great deal larger than we usually think, for understandably enough we tend to overlook the churches of the Orient—for example, those Nestorian churches which today still number twenty million Christians and have been of significant importance for Christendom. For example, during the Middle Ages Christianity was represented in all of Asia, from Persia as far as China, by the Nestorians, who are virtually nonexistent for our awareness today.

When we examine this creed of the Council of Constantinople, which has really been adopted by all confessional bodies, the question arises which had to be asked over again in the Christological controversy as a result of the Council of Chalcedon: has the problem which has been at the center of this controversy for generations really been solved here? This question we can only answer with a No. The problem is still unsolved; the questions which are really involved remain unanswered—after Constantinople, the Trinitarian question; just as the Christological question after Chalcedon. Both times the theologians as well as the church were only given a formula. With it we can summarize the results of the theological work, with it we can describe the facts of the case, but with it we cannot explain the thing about which we are talking. The theologians and the church should not be blamed because the thing under debate cannot be explained and cannot be formulated. For in both cases, in the Trinitarian as in the Christological controversy, the arguments are about facts which are closed to all arts of formulations and to all theological acumen. Both times, in the Trinitarian as in the Christological controversy, the theologians are attempting to go beyond certain limits—something which is indeed necessary, but also something which cannot succeed, for not even theology can penetrate into the mystery of God. It can only stammer about it, just as Paul declares in 1 Cor. 13:12: "For now we see in a mirror dimly, but then face to face. Now I know in part; then I shall understand fully, even as I have been fully understood."

The Controversy About the Humanity of Christ (Christological Controversy)

As early as the conclusion of the Trinitarian controversy in Constantinople in 381, it must have been clear to at least the most farsighted theologians that, in the first place, they had produced nothing but a formula, and, in the second place, that this formula dealt only with a part of the problem. The divinity of Christ was secured and, as well as possible, defined. Now what about his humanity? They had contended for the divinity of Christ in order to secure the redemption of humankind. But when that was examined closely, it was not sufficient. If Christ had not become human, a human being like us, this divinity would have been of no use to the Christian, because it would have had nothing to do with human flesh and blood. Anyone who, for the sake of soteriology and the certainty of redemption, had contended for the divinity of Christ during the Trinitarian controversy, now had to take up the strug-

198

gle for his humanity for the same reason, or, more precisely, *should* really have fought for his humanity.

In the Christological controversy, seen as a whole, the same positions were struggling with one another as in the Arian controversy. The schools had different names, different theologians appeared, but they dealt with the same contrasts. The one side was chiefly concerned with the guarantee for the redemption of humankind. In this connection, since redemption depended more on the divinity than on the humanity, the man Jesus was encompassed in the God Christ. So this side spoke exclusively or overwhelmingly about the one divine nature (*mia physis* = one nature, from which later came the designation of Monophysites, those holding a doctrine of one nature). This theological position and the groups that emerged from it were supported by the laity, because this theology corresponded to their needs. We find this Monophysitism or the tendency toward it not only among the theologians of the ancient church, but chiefly in the popular piety of the church of that time, as we really do in all centuries down to the present. Just as there is a secret Monarchianism in the church, so there also is a secret Monophysitism in it. It gets its strength and endurance from the piety in the congregation. The other side was still concerned about a precise theological definition. They proceeded from the statements of Scripture, from the facts presented in the Gospels, and therefore spoke about the humanity of Christ to which God had joined himself.

The dilemma of the Arian controversy was repeated. One group had a definite understanding only about the unity between God and man, which they wanted to emphasize for the sake of redemption. But they had difficulties when they had to describe in a distinguishing way the two natures which were joined in a unity in one person. The others always spoke concretely about man *and* God and had difficulties in describing how the two were joined together in a unity and how the redeeming activity of this one Christ was now to be conceived and presented. Both sides were concentrating so much on their own concerns that they could look at the other side of the problem only incidentally and under duress. But the dangers are quite clear: with the one group there is the danger of a Docetism of humanity, that is, a pretense of humanity. Since only the divine nature is mentioned, at the very least the humanity is in danger of evaporating. On the other side there is a danger of a Docetism of divinity. Where only the humanity is mentioned, there is a danger that the divinity will evaporate.

That is the situation in which the East found itself. For the West the entire controversy was really superfluous. Tertullian had already spoken not only about the *una substantia,* the one substance, and the *tres personae,* the three persons, but also about the *unitas substantiae,* the unity of substance, and about the *coniunctio duarum personarum,* the union of the two persons together in the unity of substance. Tertullian had expressed the problem in the formula which we finally find resulting from the protracted controversy in the decision of the Council of Chalcedon in 451, and even used the special vocabulary which there described it: *Videmus duplicem statum, non confusum, sed coniunctum* ("We see the twofold status, not confused, but joined.") (That is the significant portion of the creed of Chalcedon: here in a solemn fourfold statement it repeated that the two natures were united with one another, were not confused with one another, and could also not be separated from one another.) When we find this as early as Tertullian, the question which we have already asked arises once again, about whether Tertullian's dogmatic statements are guided only by a fortunate coincidence which led him to these formulations. At that time we determined that this explanation is certainly to be excluded (see p. 131). The phenomenon also cannot be explained by saying that what we see here is the result of the gifts of Tertullian the jurist at producing formulas. Tertullian apparently thought through these theological questions. It is true that he probably did not fathom all their depths, but not only did he see the problems, he also gave an answer to them which proved a decisive help to the Western church and through Leo I's *Epistula dogmatica* came to the aid of the entire church.

The controversy began with the battle cry of Apollinaris of Laodicea: it was impossible for Christ to be completely human, for to humanity belongs sin, and in Christ there was no sin; therefore, it was impossible for him to be fully human. With this the Christological controversy began, and at a time when the Arian controversy had really not yet ended. All the theologians attacked Apollinaris, for they were all in agreement that this understanding destroyed the redemption of humankind just as much as that—and here is where they continued in different ways: those who were Arians said, "just as much as the attitude of Athanasius," and those who followed Athanasius or the Cappadocians said, "just as much as the ideas of the Arians." So they attempted, from different sides, to refute Apollinaris. These attempts, however, were often very clumsy, for we are still in the stage in which the problem of

Christology is really not yet acute, and all the thoughts of the theologians were centered on the Trinitarian question.

Then in the second stage of the controversy a statement that was correct in itself was declared heretical. In 428 Nestorius became patriarch of Constantinople and found here a lively argument about the position of Mary (which even in earlier times, as we mentioned [see pp. 64–65], was extraordinarily elevated). This controversy in Constantinople, which involved wide circles of the church, dealt with whether Mary should be labeled "anthropotokos" or "theotokos," that is, "the one who gave birth to a human" or "the one who gave birth to God." The "theotokos" expression was extremely offensive to Nestorius, who belonged to the Antiochene school: how could a human give birth to God? A human could give birth only to a human. But the "anthropotokos" expression also had to be incorrect, since that which was born of Mary was not a mere human, but was Christ. Therefore, after some hesitation, the answer that appeared correct to him was to say "Christotokos," or "bearer of Christ." This would not solve the mystery, but express it. That was Nestorius's eventual answer in the controversy, one that was certainly the theologically correct one. But Nestorius was attacked by Cyril of Alexandria (d. 444), who, although with very questionable methods, triumphed over Nestorius at the synod of Ephesus in 431. It did not go quite the same way in Ephesus at the "Robber Synod" of 449, but the bending and violation of the laws in 431 were more than enough. Cyril did not follow the agenda of the council, nor did he comply with the council's decision, or anything else. The end effect was the deposition first of Nestorius—illegally—and then of Cyril—legally. With the assistance of the populace mobilized by the local bishop, the monks, and—we have to say—a very flexible conscience, Cyril remained in office while Nestorius, to his credit, bowed to the decision of the council. Besides this, he was left in the lurch by his theological comrades. They thought they could save the issue at stake if they sacrificed Nestorius. Later they learned the hard way that even in the church, decency, character, and courage cannot be neglected with impunity. All of them—unfortunately, but we must add, deservedly—were eventually sucked into the whirlpool that had swallowed Nestorius, even though in some cases it took several generations.

But the victorious party of Cyril now exaggerated and generalized the statements. Among their exponents was the Constantinopolitan archimandrite Eutyches, who declared: "Before the union of the two natures

I recognize two natures, but after the union only one. The flesh of the Lord is not like ours." With this we come to the third stage of the controversy. Eutyches was deposed; Dioscorus (444–51), the successor of Cyril, at the "Robber Synod" of Ephesus in 449 could justify the position taken by Eutyches and triumph, but when confronted with the unified opposition of the West and the theological conviction of the East he could not endure. In 451 the counterattack took place at Chalcedon. Even though taking considerable notice of Cyril, this fourth ecumenical council held fast to the statement of the two natures, establishing that even after the union of the two natures into one Christ, each of the natures retained its own properties, and the two natures thus joined together in one person, in one *hypostasis,* only in such a way that they were not fused together, but also could not be separated from one another. Thus they believed they had solved the problem. In fact, as in the Arian controversy, they had only created a formula. With it they described the unity of God and man in Christ, but the *how* still remained unexplained, just as before, simply because it is inexplicable. The only thing they accomplished was to produce the statement: Christ is true man; when we speak about his humanity, we do not mean a semi-divine human nature, but Christ is also totally God, just as Nicaea had defined it.

In Chalcedon, thought some, the controversy was now at an end. But even the conduct of the Egyptian representatives who refused to sign the creed of the council (the reason they gave was that they might as well be struck dead in Chalcedon, because that would be what would happen to them at home) should have shown them that there could be no mention of that. Instead, the controversy about Christology really began to take on its full force after Chalcedon, after the argument had theoretically come to a conclusion. The Monophysites immediately initiated passionate opposition, and this opposition was generally crowned with results. Theologians and bishops who adhered to the Council of Chalcedon could keep their positions in vast areas of the church, especially in the East, only if standing behind them was not merely a garrison of troops, but an especially strong garrison. The last phase of these arguments, which now not only brought serious disorders to the church, but also involved great political difficulties, lasted into the seventh century. For a long time it appeared that the Eastern empire would not survive the arguments but would go down to defeat along with the church. The Western empire had long since been eliminated by the Germanic peoples. It was Justin I (518–27) who first brought the empire out of this danger. He was also the first to abandon the indecisive stance toward the Monophysites. But even his action against them did not produce a final result. His nephew Justinian (527–65) was the first one who could continue the development. It is true that he was seriously threatened by a revolt in Constantinople, but in his thirty-eight-year reign he was able not only to rebuild the empire in the East, but chiefly to regain territories in the West which had long since been lost to the Germanic tribes. The Vandal kingdom in Africa collapsed under the attacks of his army, as did the Ostrogoth kingdom in Italy.

Incidentally, the result of this liberation was not especially pleasant for the Catholic church. Previously the popes had stood under German tutelage. That was already uncomfortable enough. But now as they came under Byzantine rule, it actually proved more oppressive and even extended to theological questions. For the East compelled—there is no other way to put it—the West, which unambiguously held the doctrine of the two natures, to make stringent concessions. Even Justinian, who unambiguously held more strictly to Chalcedon than almost anyone previously, interpreted its creedal formula in a way that was extraordinarily favorable to the Monophysites, and therefore one that was extremely distasteful to the West. So the fifth ecumenical Council of Constantinople in 553 interpreted the decision of Chalcedon in such a way that it closely resembled the position of the Monophysites. Not until the sixth ecumenical council of 680–81, again in Constantinople, were statements adopted which led back to the intention of Chalcedon. They resulted from a further specialization in the question under consideration. At Chalcedon the two natures had been discussed; here at the sixth ecumenical council the topic was Christ's energies or wills which proceeded from the two natures—whether Christ acted with one energy and one will or with two energies and two wills. Thus the same problem was discussed as at Chalcedon, only on a different level. Paralleling the experience at Chalcedon, the result of the argument was the decision that there were two energies, two wills of Christ, united with one another in the same way as Chalcedon had said the two natures were united. As a result, it is not until the seventh century that we see the doctrine of the two natures coming into the foreground once more.

After many generations of trying to win the Monophysites, it was finally recognized that they could no longer be retained in the church. For all practical purposes, under the influence of an increasing radicalization, they had long ago withdrawn from it. This radicalization resulted not only because of the effect of nontheological factors, that is, the banner of political and national feeling (the Monophysite churches grew in the Orient in opposition to the Greek-speaking church and to the "occupation force" which stood behind it), but it was also the theological position that became more and more radical. One could no longer keep the Monophysites in the church, even if one were willing to repeat Cyril's statement of the fifth century without alteration—the Cyril who played the same sort of role, even a more prominent one, in the Christological controversy as Athanasius had done in the Arian controversy. The demands of the Monophysites could have been satisfied only if the church had been in a position to adopt in its most extreme form the entire doctrine of one nature with all of its ramifications. There could be no discussion of this in the theologically educated East, not to speak of the West.

4. THE ORGANIZATION OF SEPARATED CHURCHES; AUGUSTINE AND THE PELAGIAN CONTROVERSY

The Monophysites separated from the church and formed their own church bodies. But even in the church of the East itself, decisive changes occurred during the course of the controversies. Under Justinian, church and state assumed the characteristic relationship to one another in which state and church were joined so closely that sometimes it even seemed they were fused into one. In addition, practices within the church were also developed in independent ways that led them farther and farther away from the West. Something like the Iconoclastic controversy in the eighth century was something that did not really pertain to the entire church, but was an intra-Byzantine concern. The West did indeed participate in it officially; representatives of the Roman pope were present at the seventh ecumenical council in 787 in Nicaea, and they also participated in its deliberations. But the results, just as the question under consideration, were nevertheless specifically Byzantine. The veneration of icons could become a decisive problem only for a piety which had already diverged greatly from that of the West—in the West the question never existed in this form.

We are accustomed to speaking about the "second-class Christianity" which finally triumphed at that time in the church of the East (a formulation which is generations old, but in certain contexts still appears extremely up-to-date; it is virtually the fashion in the West to view Christianity in the East condescendingly). In the first place, the expression "second-class Christianity" definitely goes too far, and in the second place, it is not only in the East where we find this so-called "second-class Christianity" triumphing; things are no different in the West. Here popular piety also invades the church, a certain paganization takes place here too—and this is not only a result of the attempt to win over the pagan rural populace, whose remnants were increasingly attaching themselves to the church in the fifth century. The church in the West, which by now has become an actual *Volkskirche* ("people's church"), considered itself forced to undertake a massive development of certain views which up to then existed only in preliminary form, so that the needs of the populace might be accommodated. Therefore, we will not be able to accuse the East of a special degree of "second-class Christianity." Naturally it is correct that the East undertook its own development because of the needs of the Greek-speaking populace which for centuries had had no contact with the West because of the language barrier which had gradually become almost insurmountable. East and West continued to develop in isolation from one another. Under Justinian the unity of the empire was restored, but this lasted only for a brief time and could not compensate for the intervening time of separation during the period of Germanic rule. In addition, there is the fact that the populace of the West welcomed the destruction of the Germanic rule, but not in every case—especially not in the long run—did it welcome the Byzantine rule. This was only an interval, for in the seventh century the Lombards pushed into Italy, the Franks followed them, and under Charlemagne (at the time of the second Council of Nicaea) we once again see a unified empire arising in the West, but now one that was not marked by Roman or Byzantine, but by Germanic characteristics. And the longer time went on, the more this empire was marked by an attitude of political independence and individuality.

In the fifth century and even later, the West was still participating actively in the theological arguments of the East. From the fifth century onward, this Western participation takes a different character than in the previous age. Also, at that time the problems of the East are really no longer those of the West; in this respect the early period and the later period are similar to one another. But where the West in the early period had always trailed the East, now it begins to take its own independent position. This we can make clear with two episodes of the Christological controversy. Under Cyril, the Roman pope Celestine (422–32) accepted the condemnation of Nestorius without any trouble. He gave Cyril what might be called a blank check for his action in Ephesus in 431 without taking the trouble to examine the theological positions of the combatants. If he had done so, it would have become clear to him that Nestorius's position, which he had just condemned sight unseen, was really the same as his own. A few years later, under Leo I (440–61), the situation had already changed completely. Here, contrary to all of its tradition, contrary to all of the history of the preceding centuries, the West allied itself with Constantinople against Alexandria, simply because of common theological concerns. In this respect Leo I's *Epistula dogmatica* signified a decisive advance. The West had now become theologically independent of the East; it stood on its own feet. In the so-called Monenergistic and Monothelitic controversy, the controversy about the one or two energies or Christ's two wills, (see p. 203), this is seen even more clearly.

From the fifth century onward the West also developed its own theological concerns. For the first time since the period around 200 (that is, for the first time since Tertullian), the West had a theologian in Augustine (354–430), who in his own peculiar way asked questions and gave answers which opened completely new dimensions on the basis of Paul. Here we see the relationship between the West and East reversing itself. Previously the West had looked at the East without any real comprehension, while now the East did the same thing with the theological endeavors of the West. The East did take part in them, however. For example, at the Council of Ephesus in 431 it approved the condemnation of Pelagianism, but to a certain extent only as an oversight and without knowing what it really was doing. At that time the Pelagians had sought refuge with Nestorius. Although he had not received the Pelagians, that was enough for them to be condemned along with him. In reality, those in the East took a completely different stance in the question about free will and the cooperation of man in justification than this condemnation expressed; in condemning the Pelagians they really condemned their own theological position. Just as the East was affected by the controversy over Monophysitism up into the seventh century, so the West was involved in the controversy over Augustine's position up until the beginning of the seventh century. In this the East had no access to the questions being asked in the West, and the West worked with assumptions which were completely different from those of the East. In summary we can definitely say that the unity of the Eastern and Western churches at that time was something that existed only nominally and purely in theory. Each church had already gone so far along its own way that it had taken on its own peculiar form and had already separated from the other. It was many more centuries until this division was officially proclaimed (see p. 291); in reality it had already been achieved by the time the second great period of church history, the Middle Ages, began.

The questions asked by Augustine were foreign to the East, we said. How foreign, we can see in Jerome (ca. 347–420?), who was really from the West. But he lived in the East and in interest and attitude is numbered among the Eastern theologians. He jumped into the Pelagian controversy with great enthusiasm, radically supporting what he thought was Augustine's side. But when we look at what Jerome said in this context, it must be called at least Semipelagian, if not Pelagian (see pp. 210–12). While sharply condemning the Pelagians, Jerome, who must really be labeled a highly educated theologian, at the same time held to things which really corresponded to the position of the people he wanted to attack. For the East, the freedom of the will is one of the essential elements of a human being. It was given in creation and not lost in the fall. As Chrysostom, for example, said, God does not want to forestall human decisions. Grace needs the human will, just as the stylus needs the hand which writes with it, declared Cyril of Jerusalem, and this or something like it is found over and over again in the fathers of the Greek church. This accords with the fundamental conception of the Greek church.

It goes without saying that this conception was also not infrequently held in the West as well. Pelagius and Celestius were not isolated individuals, but exponents of an attitude that was widespread. On the other hand, the questions asked by Augustine corresponded to the concern, the attitude, and the development of the West. If we want to summarize the difference between the church of the East and the church of the West in the early centuries, perhaps we can say: In the East we find the *theologia speculativa* ("speculative theology"), and in the West the *theologia practica* ("practical theology"). This is no coincidence: while the church of the East was consumed in theological controversies, the West almost exclusively, insofar as it was not compelled to take part in the controversies in the East, directed its attention to the organic establishment and organization of the church. This began very early; it is very typical that the first written evidence we possess of the church in the West, I Clement (see pp. 97–98), is concerned with these questions. And similar attention to the praxis of the church is continued by Tertullian (see pp. 130–31) and Cyprian (see p. 131). Of course the West also had a theology, but I believe that prior to Augustine it was a theology of results, and not a theology of asking questions. It was concerned, whenever it did deal with theological questions, not with the question of the nature of God, for example, but with the relationship of God to man or of man to God, a question that Tertullian, because of his background, had considered as a legal transaction and accordingly dealt with it as a concept of a requirement man must fulfill. It is very characteristic that we begin to find hints of a doctrine of original sin with Tertullian, hints which then crop up again and again with his successors down to Ambrose, until Augustine then develops the doctrine of original sin as a substance that really comes upon man after the fall. Humanity is a *massa perditionis* ("mass of perdition"), and nothing can be rescued from this corruption except through God's *gratia preveniens* ("prevenient grace"), the gracious activity of God which precedes everything, which seizes man and irresistibly *(gratia irrestibilis)* leads the one elected to salvation, to the goal of his salvation, while the one not elected by God at the beginning *(praescientia Dei* ["God's foreknowledge"], for Augustine, is not God's advance knowledge of what man, but what God himself is going to do!) falls into destruction, regardless of whatever he may do. Beyond discussion, beyond change, God's decree about man stands at the very beginning; one is led to salvation, another to condemnation *(gemina praedestinatio* ["double predestination"]; the moment one speaks only about election to salvation and not simultaneously about election to condemnation—which soon happened—one departs from Augustine).

The development of Augustine's theology took place step by step—similar to the way it happened in Luther's case—and occurred in arguments with his opponents. They both advanced from problem to problem, from result to result. The more Augustine worked theologically, the more questions were raised for him, and the farther he went with his answers. In this connection we should not forget that Augustine was not a theoretical theologian who gained his knowledge in an ivory tower, but that he himself had inwardly lived through all the problems of his theology and that the results of his theology were really the results of his inner struggles. In this he is also related to Luther to a great extent. In his conversion, which Augustine describes so impressively in Book 8 of his *Confessions,* he did not attain clarity about the fundamental truth of Christianity, as we often suppose. He did not have to be converted to a Christianity that was previously foreign to him. Rather, Augustine had been under Christian influence from the very beginning, and this influence was much stronger than previously believed. Long before his conversion, Augustine had also recognized the emptiness of the teachings in which he had sought refuge before his conversion: Manichaeism, Skepticism, and so on. For him the conversion experience had a different content: for him it meant freedom from the bondage in which he previously lived, from slavery to the flesh and, above all, freedom to submit himself to the will of God. He had experienced where his own will had led, namely, into a deeper and deeper entanglement in sin. Again and again he had attempted to free himself, again and again without success—now he experienced this freedom. The bonds had fallen away from him, God had set him free—the God to whom he now totally committed himself and before whose will he bowed without resistance.

That was the real content of Augustine's conversion. After it, he did not immediately seek an ecclesiastical office, but rather sought solitude, which provided him the opportunity for academic endeavor and gave him the chance to think more deeply about what he had experienced. Against his resistance, he now followed the call of the church away from this solitude into the bishop's office. But this entrance into ecclesiastical office nevertheless signified a very essential advance for him. It was precisely the needs of this ecclesiastical office, as well as his increasing occupation with Paul, which led him far beyond the level of thought which he, under the influence of Neoplatonism, had then attained. Augustine's concepts of God, such as the doctrine of the Trinity, continued to be strongly influenced by this first period, the influence of Neoplatonism, and we can also see this in Augustine's arguments with Skepticism and Manichaeism.

But now the ecclesiastical concerns entered, but now above all else the influence of Paul arose, and thus the Neoplatonic component is reduced. In the struggle against Donatism, Augustine developed his doctrine of the church, and then in the third period, the struggle against Pelagius, the details of his doctrine of justification. Naturally it was not the case that Augustine developed his doctrine of the church and the doctrine of sin and grace for the first time in these controversies. Their outlines were there from the very beginning, but they were first filled out and thought through in these controversies, which Augustine did not seek out but into which he was forced. With the Donatist controversy this is clear from the outset, but it is also clear in the Pelagian controversy. Perhaps Augustine would have preferred to avoid a direct confrontation with Pelagius, a man highly regarded for his piety and erudition. But Pelagius and Celestius, fleeing from the Visigoths who had conquered Rome, came to Africa from Rome in the year 410. It was not just their appearance, but in Carthage, Celestius even applied for the office of a presbyter. In view of this, Augustine had no choice. Initially this struggle was carried on only to a certain point, until both of them were forced out of the African church province. But when the East in 415 solemnly recognized Pelagius as orthodox at a synod, Africa could not remain silent, but had to bring its synodical authority into the fray as well—at two synods Pelagius and Celestius were condemned. The way things went was typical: the Roman bishop was informed of these synodical decisions by an official communication. But this was accompanied by a personal letter from Augustine and other bishops. Thus, there was no possibility left to the Roman bishop of reaching his own decision. He could do nothing but officially adopt as his own the standpoint announced by Africa, even though no one less than Innocent I (402–17) was involved. The theological decision was made in Africa; then the pope adopted it. It is not completely clear what Innocent I personally thought about the argument. But there can be no doubt that his successor Zosimus (417–18), at least, would have been happy to take the side of the Pelagians. He attempted to enforce such an attitude officially. .As a result, blunt letters came from Africa. In addition, the Africans (that is, Augustine) made use of their connections with the government. Thus Zosimus declared that he had merely been misunderstood (that is the way defeats have regularly been covered up over the centuries). With some coaching, therefore, Zosimus was brought to think and teach theologically according to the rules (that is, according to the African understanding).

Zosimus's actions show, if there is a need for proof, that the fundamental attitude of Pelagius also corresponded to that of many theologians in the West. We certainly should not deceive ourselves into thinking that the successful struggle against Pelagius and his adherents, as well as the one against the subsequent development of Pelagian doctrine by Julian of Eclanum, resulted in more than the condemnation of Pelagianism. In no way did it mean the acceptance by the church in the West of Augustine's doctrine of sin and grace. What had triumphed was only Augustine's negation, in no way his position. Rather, even during Augustine's lifetime, a powerful opposition to his doctrine of sin and grace arose in southern Gaul—the so-called Semipelagian controversy—which was fed from two sources: the ascetic and the traditionalist. The famous and continually cited word of Vincent of Lérins, that "catholic" is that which is taught always and everywhere, came out of this controversy and was intended to be an attack on Augustine. It was directed against the new things Augustine had introduced, because that which Augustine proclaimed had not been taught always and everywhere. That the monks opposed the Augustinian doctrine is quite obvious. They felt that it would destroy the meritorious nature of works and everything connected with them, that is, the destruction of the presuppositions of the monastic existence. The struggles with the so-called Semipelagians had a very checkered course; for longer periods of time it appeared as if this abridged Pelagianism would triumph.

The most astonishing and really most frightening thing of all was this: even the exponents of Augustinianism in these arguments did not hold to Augustine's complete theology, but only to a very pronounced abridgment, one which simply ignored all those of its extremes which were offensive at that time. In subsequent ages we meet the total Augustine again only very infrequently: surprisingly enough, in the Carolingian age in the so-called Gottschalk controversy (see p. 270), and then with Luther in his early lectures (only here the scholars do not sufficiently recognize Augustine, but incorrectly attribute to Luther's own understanding what was taken over from him [see vol. 2]).

In the sixth century these disputes recurred; once again Semipelagianism appeared. Finally under Gregory the Great (590–604) these disputes come to a conclusion. It was one that was completely characteristic of that time, as well as for the Catholic church in general. Gregory's doctrine, as well as that of subsequent Catholicism, stood under the name and aegis of Augustine. Thus Augustine had triumphed in his struggle against his opponents. But it was only Augustine's name, only a portion of his theology, not the complete theology he held which we find here. The Augustine who triumphed here, who is so frequently cited, is abridged in decisive points of doctrine. We must make this observation at the very outset. The church of that time accepted Augustine's statements—but not in their entirety, only what accorded with the Catholic church and the internal laws it had already developed, that which fitted in with the foundations which had been laid from the very beginning. With great sensitivity Catholicism in the early centuries (this is true from the beginning onward) removed all hints of elements in its theological expression which were foreign to its nature and adopted only that which was related inwardly to it. Here we can easily let ourselves be deceived. For example, when Gregory the Great repeats numerous sentences from Augustine, when he appeals over and over again to Augustine, it appears as if Augustine's influence were continuing. But in fact Augustine was abandoned at the decisive point. According to Greg-

211

ory, grace did not work alone, and it did not work irresistibly, but rather—and this we can best express with a quotation from Gregory's *Moralia*: "The good that we do belongs to God"—that much is Augustinian—but then he continues, "*and* us." Here he departs from Augustine and joins the camp of the Semipelagians. "And us": "to God by means of prevenient grace; to us by means of free will." That is a statement which abbreviates Augustine in a decisive way, one that appears to adopt his doctrine, but one that in reality demonstrates something quite different.

A second decisive departure was also undertaken by Gregory, one that followed quite logically and one that was also justified on the basis of his presuppositions: this grace that we have described works within the saving institution of the church and is coupled with its ministrations. According to Gregory, the ecclesiastical institution of salvation is identical with the *civitas Dei* ("city of God"), a statement that would have been impossible for Augustine. Here Augustine is precisely abridged or reinterpreted in a genuine Catholic sense, just as was the case with his entire theology. This was the way the church entered the second period of its history, the Middle Ages. With Gregory the Great, the Catholic church of the West had reached a decisive point in its development, just as had the Orthodox church of the East under Justinian and his immediate successors. Both of them completed the first stage of their development in the seventh century.

CHRISTIANITY IN THE
MIDDLE AGES

1

The Germanic Middle Ages

By the seventh century, western Europe had already been under the influence of the Germanic tribes for centuries. The Visigoths under Alaric drove into Italy for the first time in the year 401. In 405 the Germanic tribes repeated their invasion, this time led principally by the Ostrogoths. In 406 the Vandals, Quadi, and Alani crossed the Rhine and inundated Gaul, extending their advance to Spain in 409. In 407 the Burgundians and Alemanni also crossed the Rhine, and in 408 Alaric and the Visigoths invaded Italy for the second time. Three times he stood outside Rome before finally conquering it in 410. Abducting Galla Placidia, the emperor's half-sister, Alaric pressed on with his great plunder into southern Italy.

In 418 the kingdom of the Visigoths was established in Gaul with its center at Toulouse; in 429, the Vandal kingdom was established in Africa. Some of the Germanic kingdoms were destroyed, but others took their place. In 455 a Vandal fleet appeared at the mouth of the Tiber, and the Vandals spent two weeks plundering Rome. The Germanic reign continued to spread, until the German Odoacer was proclaimed king of the army in 476 and all of western and central Europe stood under Germanic rule.

Not until 534 under Justinian did the East begin its counterattack. Justinian's commander Belisarius first destroyed the kingdom of the Vandals in 534–35, but it took almost twenty years more of bitter fighting (from 535 until 553) until he and his successor Narses had destroyed the Ostrogoth kingdom as well. At that time the kingdom of the Franks had already taken over great amounts of territory and had incorporated the old areas of the Alemanni, the Thuringians, and the Bavarians. By 539 it had already—even though temporarily—conquered portions of northern Italy. In 568 the Lombards invaded Italy, extending their reign farther and farther toward the south. All of this was happening at the same time as the things we have already discussed, but had to be excluded from our presentation then so that we could deal logically with the material under consideration. All these occurrences are not just political events; they also have a direct relationship to the history of Christianity.

1. CHRISTIANITY AMONG THE GERMANS AT THE TIME OF THE MIGRATIONS

The Conversion of the Germans to Christianity

All of these Germanic people were Christians, except for the Lombards, who represented a rather militant paganism until the beginning of the seventh century. How did Christianity come to the Germanic tribes, and what motives led them to accept Christianity?

During the "Thousand-year Reich"—that is, from 1933 until 1945— the answer loudly given to this question was: Raw power extinguished the bright religion of the Germans and forced the dark Christian faith upon them. At first glance it is obvious that this claim has a certain amount of justification—if at all—only for the period after the eighth century, that is, after the Saxons were Christianized by the Franks (here those who hold this hypothesis of the Germans' forcible conversion to Christianity deliberately prefer to ignore the fact that in this it was Germans who were proceeding against Germans). For the preceding four centuries no scrap of proof for this claim can be advanced—either for the period of the migrations, in which Christianity dominated all the Germanic tribes, or for the turning of the Franks to Christianity, that is, from the time of Clovis's conversion until Boniface's missionary work which brought significant portions of the Frisians, Hessians, Thuringians, and Bavarians to the Christian faith. In the former period, Christianity took hold in all the large Germanic tribes, except the Lombards; in the latter period, the Frankish church grew to a magnitude that spanned central Europe. Moreover, until the coming of Islam, Spain, which was under the rule of the Visigoths, held the Christian faith.

Who would have been able, even if he had wished, to force Christianity upon the Germans when they came into contact with it? During the entire period of the end of the ancient world and the beginning of the Middle Ages the Germans were constantly on the attack. From the second half of the second century onward, the *Imperium Romanum* ("Roman Empire") had more and more difficulty in defending itself against these attacks, until the sack of Rome by Alaric's Visigoths in the year 410 made the signs of the new age gruesomely clear to everyone. Of course, in the campaigns of the preceding centuries Germans were often captured by the Romans, and not a few Germanic contingents were taken into the Roman army as soldiers or into the Roman Empire as settlers to strengthen its boundaries. At best, forcible conversion was possible only for the Germanic prisoners; for the settlers and certainly for the soldiers this sort of influence did not enter the picture—here the only way was that of peaceful missionary work. Strangely enough, the Roman populace apparently did not attempt this. In the boundary area along the Rhine, where for a long while Germans and Romans had not only not been fighting, but (for not brief periods of time) had even been living alongside one another in peace, Christianity just did not go out to the Germans. The Christian churches in the Roman cities in this border area apparently lived in isolation and never came to the idea of carrying on mission to the populace at their gates. It may also be true that the Germans kept their distance. At any rate, as far as we know, these Christian churches had a purely Roman character; they had members from the various tribes of the racially mixed Roman Empire, but none from the German tribes. Thus, at least for the Germanic tribes on the soil of present-day Germany and France, we must also keep in mind a second possibility alongside that of forcible conversion: that the change of culture in accepting Christianity was important to the Germans, so that when they adopted the higher culture of the Roman Empire they would also have adopted its faith.

Actually, the history of Christianity among the Germans begins rather in the Danube area with Ulfilas. His biography is typical: his grandparents were war prisoners who had been captured as slaves by the Goths on one of their campaigns in Cappadocia. The grandparents were Christians. Their daughter married a Goth; she at least was a Christian, for Ulfilas was baptized as a child. Things were just the opposite of what we might expect. It is not captured Germans who are turned into Christians in the Roman Empire, but captured members of the Roman populace who bring Christianity into the Germanic area. Ulfilas's grandparents could not have been the only representatives of this type. In addition, the Goths pushing beyond their previous boundaries into the Roman Empire would probably have met Christians in not insignificant numbers. But they too were subjugated; their legal status was the same or not much different than that of Ulfilas's grandparents.

There can, therefore, be no doubt about the voluntary acceptance of Christianity, at least by the first Goths. But after the initial stages, the conversion of the Visigoths to the new faith had the same character: for as soon as the number of Christians increased somewhat—and that apparently took place in a very brief time—the first wave of persecution in 348 hit them as well. This time it was the protest of Germanic paganism; what we learn about it is the same as we know about the persecutions in the Roman Empire. Ulfilas and the Gothic Christians had to leave the area of the Germanic tribes and find refuge in the Roman territory where Christianity held sway (Constantius was ruling at the time). But this did not end the history of Christianity among the Visigoths. Rather, it continued to grow, apparently nourished by Christians who remained behind, and once again built up a not insignificant number of adherents. This is the only thing that can explain the second persecution which broke out in 369 under Athanaric. In their severity the methods of persecution undertaken against the Christians, who obviously were now regarded not only as having rejected the traditions of their ancestors, but also as having broken the tribal bond of fellowship, left nothing more to be desired. Nevertheless, within a few years the religious controversy was decided in favor of Christianity: the majority of the tribe turned to Christianity and crossed the Danube in 376 with Fritigern in order to settle in the territory of the Roman Empire. Only a few, the convinced pagans among them, remained behind with Athanaric, but even they followed their compatriots a few years later.

Not long afterwards, as the Visigoths started their migration under Alaric's leadership, they were almost exclusively Christians, or at least the pagan element—if there even was still one at the time (which was certainly the case in 376 when they crossed the Danube [see p. 224])— was not in evidence. They were even convinced Christians and of the Arian persuasion. Their way, which finally took them as far as Spain, led through four countries with Catholic populations, but none of them had any influence at all on the ecclesiastical attitude of the Visigoths. They continually emphasized the Arian character of their Christianity. They offered protection and refuge to previously persecuted Arian bishops. When Alaric felt himself compelled to set up an opposing emperor, Attalus, against the Western Roman emperor, Attalus first had to leave the Catholic church and become an Arian. Not until the end of the sixth century, almost two hundred years after their departure from the Danube area, did they convert to Catholicism.

The Christian faith in its Arian form began its victory march through the Germanic tribes with the Visigoths. As we mentioned above (see pp.

216–17), exceptions on the one side were the Lombards, among whom paganism held sway even longer and was not overcome until a later period, and on the other side the Suabi, whose several religious changes present not just a singular situation but also a great number of un-answered questions, and finally the Franks, whom we shall discuss later (see pp. 230–37). It is not surprising that the Christianity of the Visigoths enjoys this sort of echo. Ulfilas had not only given them the Bible in the Gothic language, but also a liturgy. Moreover, he made it possible for Gothic to express the concepts of Christian theology and enabled the missionaries to preach to their hearers in a language they understood. Just as in the ancient church, when Latin triumphed over Greek in the West because Tertullian had equipped it to express Christian concepts, so Christianity was prepared for its victory over the Germans as soon as it could express itself in their language.

The Faith of the Pagan Germans

It is self-evident that the Visigoths did not use forcible means in their missionary endeavors among other Germanic tribes, but followed the course of peaceful persuasion; after what we have said above (see pp. 216–17), this needs no proof. But how did it happen that this missionary work brought results so rapidly? From Augustine's testimony we know that the Ostrogoths were still pagans when they invaded Italy for the first time in 405 under Radagaisus. In 488, when they again entered Italy under Theodoric, they were Arian Christians. Theodoric had even been baptized as a child. Therefore, no later than the middle of the fifth century this change in the Ostrogoths' faith must have taken place, and it happened for the whole tribe in no more than a generation. Just as rapidly must Christianity have taken hold among the Visigoths. Around 341 Ulfilas was consecrated a bishop, and by 376 the majority of the Visigoths were already adherents of Christianity. In spite of all opposi-tion, it also took only a generation for Christianity to triumph here. What are the reasons for this very unusual episode in the history of Christianity?

It is very difficult to answer this question, because the documentary sources are very sparse and only with great difficulty can a picture of the Germanic religion be assembled from the tiny pieces of the mosaic. It was easier in the nineteenth century. Then the *Edda* was studied, and people deduced from it that there was a close relationship between the Germanic and Christian faiths, so it appeared that the path of the Germans to the new faith was short and easy. This beautiful picture of the inner unity of Germanic and Christian faith has collapsed, now that the Christian infiltration of the *Edda,* which was not written down until the turn of the millennium, has been recognized, and scholars have correctly concluded that what is needed is a very meticulous differentiation between the Germanic nucleus and Christian additions in the *Edda* before any statements about the religiosity of the Germans can be deduced from it. A more recent age had an even easier time, or made it easier for itself: it considered only those sources genuine which presented the faith of the Germans as well as the Germans themselves in a favorable light and regarded all other reports simply as slander or as proof of the Christian influences which falsified the original faith of the Germans.

When we inquire today about the faith of the Germans, we cannot fail to recognize the bright features in it which are supplied, for example, by its "Friendly God" character. But, on the other hand, we also cannot overlook the gloomy features which are connected with the Germanic religion from its very beginning. These sort of features may be typified by Tacitus's description of the Semnones who entered the sacred grove only while bound; human sacrifice is a fact that cannot be denied, as is also the faith in omens and oracles, at least in the later period. The relation of the Germans to their divinities had to have been based principally on the concept of power. Thus, when it was possible to destroy the image of a god or his immediate activity, as Boniface did with the Oak of Thor near Geismar and Charlemagne did with the Irminsul, far-reaching effects were the result. The god whose impotence or inability to act was thus demonstrated lost the trust of his followers. This indicates that the faith of the Germans, even before Christianity encountered it, must have been having an inner crisis. For a long while the gods apparently no longer held the supreme power, but above them stood fate, to which even the gods were subordinate. This belief in a fate which was inscrutable, obscure, and threatened to work evil also changed the way of looking at both the gods and the world by introducing gloomy elements. No one could have a personal relationship to such a fate; he could only accept it and bear it like a man. It appears, at least as far as we can obtain a picture of it, that the Germanic religion had lost its inner power when it confronted Christianity. It still lived from the power of the preceding age but was no longer able to produce anything new. When a religion reaches this state it is doomed to destruction as soon as it comes into competition with one that is more vital.

What happened to the faith of the Germans when confronted by

Christianity was the same thing—just to inject this here—that happened to Christianity in Egypt and North Africa in the seventh century when Islam arose as its competitor (see p. 42). This is something that happens again and again: a faith which has become powerless or has declined from its original height into something like superstition, or has become a petrified ceremonial, will be overcome by other forces without resistance, or at least without a great deal of resistance. Islam taught us this not only in Egypt and North Africa, but it also achieved the same results in other places in later times. It is true that the use of force played a great role in this; Islam missionized not only with the Koran but also with the sword. But its successes cannot be explained merely by its use of force; it would be shortsighted to fall back on this excuse. We need only look at modern Islam's power, which today has attained strength which is often astonishing (Africa and Iran are impressive examples), so that the advance of Christian missionary endeavor is made so difficult that it is often even impossible. By no means is it the case, as the Christian in Europe often too easily and self-evidently believes, that Christianity automatically possesses the greater power. Luther compared the Word of God to a downpour which ends as quickly as it begins, and if a people do not know how to make use of it, its blessing will go to another. A great deal depends on what each generation, and also each nation, does with the capital entrusted to it. And who can deny that our Christianity, at least in the territories where it has been in existence for many centuries, is showing signs of fatigue and a decline in power, so that it cannot stand up when put to the test, or performs only unsatisfactorily? It is not sufficient to be aware that the spring from which this power flows is still there, only filled up, if we do not make serious arrangements to open up this spring of power again and let it flow freely.

The Motives for the Conversion of the Germans to Christianity

accordingly, if we now inquire why the Visigoths accepted Christianity in the Arian and not the Catholic form, a relatively unambiguous answer is possible. Without doubt, a historic constellation of events played a decisive role here. When Ulfilas was sent as a member of a political delegation to the Roman imperial court in 341, Constantius was then on the throne, and what we are accustomed to call "Arianism" (although the name is only loosely related to the subject itself) was in full bloom. It was Eusebius of Nicomedia who apparently inspired Ulfilas for his task;

at any rate, he was the one who consecrated Ulfilas as "bishop of the Christians in the land of the Goths." Eusebius of Nicomedia, the leader of the anti-Nicene opposition (see pp. 194–95)—as it should be called (we can speak here about Arianism in the real sense only conditionally)—was a powerful personality. What confronted Ulfilas most impressively and what marked him from that time on, was this sort of theological and ecclesiastical attitude. Ulfilas preached the "Arian" faith in his homeland; his tongue and gift of persuasion gave it power. In this way "Arianism" took root among the Visigoths, and it continued to flourish among them after Ulfilas's departure. And as the second great wave of migration began, or in the time when preparations for it were underway, "Arianism" was enjoying a period of renewed strength in the Roman Empire under Emperor Valens (364–78). Although the Visigoths who settled in the Roman Empire came into conflict with the form of Christianity they found there, this served only to strengthen their predisposition. By the time the theology of the neo-Nicenes triumphed in the Roman Empire, by the time the "Catholic" party won out in 381 at the Council of Constantinople (see pp. 195–96), Christianity was already so strong among the Visigoths that its fundamental disposition could no longer be changed, and this Christianity had probably already become a constituent part of the national identity of the Visigoths. That the other German tribes accepted this form of the faith and not the Catholic form, can be clearly explained by the fact that they confronted it chiefly, if not exclusively, in the form minted by Ulfilas and the Visigoths. The missionaries who went out from them had the advantage over all others because they had the ability to make themselves understood directly in the language, as well as a similar culture and history, a knowledge of the mentality of those they were trying to convert, and many similar advantages; thus, they were invincible in their endeavor, if any opposition to them even appeared.

In speaking about the "Arian" Christianity of the Germans, we must establish, in order to avoid the instinctive and virtually unavoidable connotations of this word, that this label has only a very limited application. This "Arian" Christianity of the Germans is unrelated to the characteristics distinguishing the theology held by Arius and the real Arians, who appeared as its left wing after the collapse of the anti-Nicene opposition (see pp. 194–95). At least, an examination of the extant fragments of the writings of Ulfilas reveals nothing of the sort. The doctrine of the Catholic church about the Trinity which went back to Nicaea was rejected as unbiblical—this was the essential difference between it and the faith of the Roman populace. In their arguments with the African Catholics, the Vandal bishops emphatically emphasized that their church alone stood on the foundation of Scripture, while the Catholic church with its unbiblical doctrine of the Trinity was the synagogue of Satan—but was it either the Nicene or the anti-Nicene view of the Trinity that was really the decisive influence in the original conversion of the Germans to Christianity? The real conclusion is that it was the historical constellation of events that was decisive in first bringing the Germans to accept Christianity in its semi-Arian form. To this extent we can speak about a contribution of nontheological factors to the conversion of the Germans to Christianity.

However, these nontheological factors are limited to the Visigoths' acceptance of Christianity and cannot be extended to the acceptance of Christianity by the other German tribes. If the latter adopted the "Arian" faith of the Visigoths, this factor was excluded from the outset. For at the time the other German tribes became "Arians," Arianism had long since been declared heretical in the Roman Empire. The Arian Germans were tolerated only when they were so strong that they could not be treated in accordance with the laws against heresy as the Arians were dealt with in the entire Roman Empire. How the populace would have preferred to deal with the Germanic Arians—if they ever had the opportunity—is revealed by the episode of the Gothic troops in Constantinople. Gainas was their leader. He demanded a church for his troops in which they could worship God according to their Arian faith. That took place in the year 400 while Chrysostom was in office. Their demand became known, and the populace of Constantinople rose up and slaughtered the Gothic troops, down to the very last man.

This brings us to the question that is frequently—much too frequently—asked, of whether political motives played a role in the Germanic tribes' change of faith. That seems possible when we first look at the history of Christianity among the Visigoths. Here Athanaric and Fritigern stood in opposition to one another—Athanaric determinedly adhered to the ancient faith, while Fritigern took a friendly attitude toward Christianity. It might have been possible—just to exhaust all the possibilities—that Fritigern was friendly toward Christianity because he wanted to attract followers among those who adhered to Christianity or those among the Visigoths who sympathized with it, and that with this favorable attitude toward Christianity he also had an eye on the Roman Empire on which he was becoming more dependent as time went on. Thus, there is a certain possibility that political motives may have played a role in the attitude of Fritigern himself. But for the Visigoths in general we can say with virtual certainty that this was not the case. It is extremely improbable that the Visigoths as a people would have adopted Christianity or drawn close to it as a precaution because they were convinced of the advisability of turning to the Roman Empire. By no means were the Visigoths all Christians when they crossed the Danube to settle in the Roman Empire; rather, the report which tells us of the crossing of the Danube in 376 speaks not only of bishops and monks, but also of pagan tribal sanctuaries. And, above all, this tribe which crossed the Danube was not internally demoralized. It was not seeking protection at any price, but was conscious of its powers. Soon afterward conflict did arise; when Rome did not live up to the conditions agreed upon, the battle of Adrianople in 378 led to the defeat of the Romans and the death of Emperor Valens.

The single possible way of explaining the turning of the Germans to Christianity is to assume that the German faith was inwardly overcome by the power of Christianity. Perhaps the fact that the Germans had abandoned their old homeland, had lost the inner moorings they once had, and had experienced an increasing number of crises during the migration may have played a part in this. But all of this is secondary in comparison to the religious motive which, taken by itself, is sufficient to explain the events we observe in the centuries we are discussing. The Germans did not lean toward abandoning their special form of faith because they were in a hopeless situation. When the kingdom of the Vandals was destroyed, Gelimer, the last king, was brought as a captive to Byzantium. Again and again they attempted to persuade him to adopt Christianity, and again and again he refused. Not only did he refuse to convert, but he also rejected the secular post of honor offered him simply because he would not have been able to take it without changing his faith. At the time, Belisarius, as a matter of course, closed the Arian churches or returned them to the Catholics. Under the Vandals, and under the Germans in general, Arianism found itself in a hopeless situation. Yet those Germans who survived the slaughter continued to hold fast to Arianism. A revolt in Belisarius's army even occurred. Led by their Arian priests, the Germanic mercenaries who had helped destroy the Vandal kingdom and the Ostrogoth kingdom rose up because they no longer had churches available to them and thus could not have their children baptized at Easter in the Arian church. In the face of these facts, the attempt to use political motives as an explanation for this change of faith finally collapses, even if it may at first have had some appearance of probability.

The Internal Structure of the Germanic Churches

If we then ask how this close alliance between the Germanic people and "Arianism" could have come into existence, various answers are available to us. Once again some people have attempted to explain this from outside and have said that the Germans' confession of Arianism, their identification with the Arian form of faith, had external causes. We need to think of the situation of the Germans in the territories subject to Rome. They always found themselves in the position of a minority over against the Roman populace. In addition, there was the fact that the culture of the Romans was far superior to that of the Germans, so that the Germans in the conquered territories were constantly in danger of being absorbed and losing their national existence. In fact, in structure and in life style the Germanic tribes were completely different from the Roman populace. In the Roman Empire the peasantry had continually been on the decline and had been swallowed up by the large landholders. In this regard, Italy had changed from a land which exported agricultural produce into an importing country, something which was extremely significant for the import of African grain. The populace was squeezed into the cities; the warlike attitude of the populace had relaxed. On the other hand, the Germans were an agricultural and warlike people, and this distinction would have led them from the outset into a virtually castelike separation. Here the Arianism they already held soon became especially important to them, for their Arian Christianity strengthened the barrier separating them from the native populace. Thus they consciously soon came to nourish this Arian Christianity in order to preserve their "ethnic identity"—this is the way some have argued and some continue to argue today.

It is certainly possible that this explanation has some merit to it. But it breaks down in the face of the circumstances surrounding the beginning of Christianity among the Germans, and it breaks down in the face of the circumstances following the defeat of the Germans and the destruction of their rule. And it also breaks down in the face of the circumstances during the Germanic rule. To be sure, only occasionally do we have an insight into the events of that time; but whenever we do catch a glimpse of them they show that the Germans were convinced that their form of Christianity was far superior to the Catholic church in the

Roman Empire. It was their faith alone which agreed with Scripture. In numerous discussions that was expressed over and over. Even Ulfilas plainly declared: whoever teaches something else is not in the church of God, but in the synagogue of Satan; he is not a worshiper of God, but of the antichrist. This attitude of superiority held by the Arian Germans was based precisely upon a serious appeal to the testimony of Scripture. While a number of traditions and theological opinions had grown up in the Catholic church alongside Scripture, the Germans were beginning their ecclesiastical and theological existence with an unimpeded and unprejudiced encounter with Scripture, which for them was not limited by any sort of preconceived notions. The theological literature of the preceding centuries was completely, or at least for the most part, inaccessible or unknown to them. Even the Vandal king Thrasamund used this concept of the direct approach to Scripture in his theological discussions with Fulgentius of Ruspe (467–533).

That the Arian Germans held their worship services in the vernacular is not as important in our context as some have often believed. For it was not only the Arian Germans who read the Bible in the Gothic language. They were not the only ones who held their services in the Gothic language, but the Catholic Germans also did. The matter of holding services in the vernacular appears significant to us, because we cannot help looking at things from the perspective of later developments. At that time the Catholic church of the Western empire naturally held its services in the Latin language. But there was no claim raised then that this was the only proper approach; rather, we also have considerable numbers of services in the West being held in the Greek language (just as in the East, in addition to the services in the Greek language, there were ones in Syrian, Coptic, etc.). Not until later was the Latin language declared to be the sole cultic language of the Catholic church, so the fact that services were held in the Gothic language is less significant than we would like to believe.

That monasticism played hardly any role among the Germans, or that the clergy were generally married, also does not have the divisive significance we would like to believe, looking at it from our perspective. For monasticism (see pp. 183–84) had played a very insignificant role in certain parts of the West; its introduction here (in distinction to the East) met with considerable difficulties. In no way was the demand of celibacy for priests generally enforced in the Catholic church at that time.

Noteworthy, however, is the organization of the Germanic churches, which we can properly call national churches. Even in the time when the Arian Christianity of the Germans extended throughout the entire empire, we see the Germans making no attempt to unite or even to bring the churches of the various tribes closer together. They limited themselves to the area of a tribe, although the churches of the various tribes, as far as we know, were not just related in organization and doctrine, but were really the same. The clergy were always members of the tribal organization; the king named the bishops and also summoned the councils. It has even been called a military clergy under the command of the king. That is definitely an exaggeration. Just as the king had influence over the clergy, the clergy had influence over the king. Only in connection with the appointment of presbyters do we find the congregation taking part, and to a higher degree here than in the Catholic church.

It is obvious that all of this can be explained by the history of the Germanic people. These state or national churches, this "state religion," is explained by the fact that Christianity replaced a Germanic faith to which the tribe had also given a special character. According to everything we know, the Germanic faith did not differ from one tribe to another in its basic substance, but still it did to a significant degree. Christianity assumed the same role of a "state faith" which had characterized the pagan period of the Germanic people. The division of the Germanic churches is explained by the necessities of the migration. Here every group of a thousand had a bishop and every group of a hundred had its priest. During the migration there was no other possible way to organize the church. And then when the tribes ceased their wandering, they also settled according to the thousands and the hundreds, so that the organization of the church created in the time of the migrations was preserved later.

We have already mentioned (see pp. 225–26) that the Arian Germans considered themselves equal, in fact superior, to the Catholic Romans. Whenever Arian bishops confront Catholics we always find this attitude of absolute confidence, this superior attitude on the part of the Germans. It was based not only on the fact that the Germanic bishops were part of the ruling power, but principally on their consciousness of the superiority of their own form of faith, one which was closer to the original because it was better founded on Scripture, while in the Catholic church unbiblical speculations had been added to the original Scriptural basis (see p. 226). In spite of this attitude of superiority of the Germans, we still see them maintaining an attitude of tolerance toward the Catholics. Some people have felt that even here there were essentially political reasons for this. Missionary work could not be carried out among the populace if barriers were erected. If they had demanded rebaptism of those who converted that would consciously have served to raise this barrier. If they did not want to arouse the passions of the populace, if they did not want to provoke unnecessary rebellions, there was nothing else for the Germans to do but maintain an attitude of tolerance. This attempt at explanation can be correct only under certain conditions. The example of the Vandals shows us how the German tribes could act without considering the religious convictions of the populace. Not only here, but in every case they had the ability to destroy any resistance to their authority as well as to their religious policies. When they nevertheless practiced tolerance within the limits we shall discuss later, there must have been a deeper reason than this.

Gregory of Tours (538–94) tells us of two ambassadors sent by the Visigoth king Loewigild into the Roman Empire. Naturally, both of them were Arians. One took part in the Catholic worship service up until the kiss of peace and the eucharist, thus practicing a tolerance, which, however, stops at the decisive point and does not identify itself with the Catholic church. The latter, in a dispute with Gregory of Tours, declared about Arianism: "Do not slander the faith which you do not share; we do not slander yours, and we would not regard two kinds of faith as a crime. As our proverb says: It does no harm if, when walking between a pagan altar and a church, one reverences both." The tolerance we observe here seems to have a syncretistic background. However, when Theodoric declares: "We cannot command religion, because we can compel no one to believe against his will," then this tolerance has a different background. Naturally we cannot ignore the fact that this statement was not proposed as a general principle, but was made in a very limited context. This word was directed toward Jews who were attempting to have a synagogue repaired. The ruler's permission was required. Theodoric allowed the renovation within the limits of applicable law, but the synagogue could not be enlarged or embellished. He would have severely punished that. Then at the conclusion of the decree he said: "Why do you strive for that which you should eschew? We are indeed giving you permission, but we believe it is commendable to disapprove the petition of those who are in error. Yet religion is something that we cannot command. . . ."

This tolerance is not that of the present day, which in the last analysis arises from skepticism or indifference, but this was tolerance that was practiced even though they were convinced that their own form of faith was not simply correct, but the only possible one. Thus the tolerance expressed by the Germans at that time had definite limits. It was self-evident that the ruler claimed legal supremacy over the Arian church. That accorded with his legal position in this Arian church. But he claimed it not only over the Arian, but over the Catholic church as well. The freedom which the Catholic church possessed in the empire of Theodoric the Great, who went farther than anyone else in showing tolerance, met its limits when it encountered the power of the ruler. This is evidenced by the way laws also affecting the church were proclaimed, administered, and judged. Within the framework of their lawgiving, we see the Germans also regulating ecclesiastical questions, both for the Arian and the Catholic church. Theodoric and the other Germanic tribal princes not only took part in affairs within the Catholic church, but also had direct influence on them. Theodoric established his position as supreme judge over the Catholic church as well, as we see from a whole series of judgments he rendered.

Theodoric was a convinced Christian of the Arian persuasion and sought to preserve the position of "Arianism" wherever he could. For example, when Emperor Justin I extended the heresy laws to the Goths in 524, Theodoric stepped in. At that time in the Eastern empire the heresy laws naturally applied to all the Arians and forbade them not only to possess their own church buildings but prohibited their very existence. Previously the Goths in the Eastern empire were excluded from these heresy laws. Now they were expanded to them as well. When Theodoric heard of this, he immediately initiated negotiations and even went so far as to dispatch Pope John I (died in prison in 526) to Constantinople in order to obtain the repeal of these regulations. This Theodoric achieved. The confiscated churches were returned to the Goths. However, the Goths who already had been converted (by force), had to remain Catholics. Theodoric's mistrust of the Roman bishop dates from this episode. Apparently he was not satisfied with what Byzantium approved at that time, and partially blamed the Roman bishop for not achieving more and winning the complete freedom which Theodoric had demanded for the Goths.

This shows the second limit of the toleration of the Arian national churches. Wherever the Catholic church was suspected of being the source of opposition, wherever it was believed to be the rallying point of national resistance to the Germanic rule, more or less severe measures were undertaken. Likewise, measures were employed against the Catholics when they attempted to missionize among the Arian Germans or when they resisted the missionary endeavors of the Arian Germans. For by no means it is true, as those claim who postulate a political motivation, that these Arian churches did not engage in missionary endeavors. Naturally the Arians missionized among the Catholics; no Christian faith which considers itself right and true can exist without attempting to bring those whom it regards as false believers to this right and true faith.

This is how the attitude of the Germanic national churches toward the Catholic church appeared at that time. The Vandals seem to be an exception. Not only were they extraordinarily active in their missionary work among the Catholics, but they also attempted to suppress the Catholic church, even to limit its basis for existence by employing the heresy laws against Catholics, thus evoking their extreme anger that the methods they had liberally used against other Christian groups were now being turned against them. It is difficult to say what the motives behind this were, for we possess only the account from the Catholic side. Probably the motives already mentioned played a part; but, in addition, there was a predisposition of some of the leaders—not of the Vandals themselves—to use force. These Vandal rulers used force not only against the Catholic church, but against their own church too. For example, it made no difference to King Geiseric that he not only sent Catholic bishops to their deaths by deporting them in an absolutely unseaworthy vessel, but he publicly burned his own Arian patriarch at the stake as well. But this was a special situation, and we can draw no general conclusions from it.

2. CHRISTIANITY AMONG THE FRANKS

Around 500, when the Western portion of the Roman Empire was ruled by Germans who were all Arians, we suddenly see among the Franks a Catholic island arising in the midst of this Arian ocean. Here what gradually develops is a kingdom which—insofar as it is Christian at all— adheres to the Catholic form of the Christian faith. At the outset we must mention something that often is not given sufficient attention—the Franks were at first not a unified tribe and a correspondingly strong force. Not until the middle of the fifth century did the different tribal communities, which until then had usually lived together peacefully— but sometimes also very unpeacefully—begin to take the form of a larger unity.

Childeric, the first Merovingian—not prince of the Franks, but only prince of a portion of a tribe—begins to play a leading part in this development. His son Clovis (Chlodowech), who succeeded him in 482 at the age of sixteen, assumed this heritage. At the end of his life he had united the various Frankish tribes. Most of the means he employed to accomplish this were questionable, but they corresponded with what was typical during the Merovingian age and the one following it. Around 496 Clovis converted to Catholic Christianity. Before the battle against the Alemanni—so Gregory of Tours informs us—he called upon Christ, "who Clotilda said was the Son of the living God," and promised to become a Christian if he won the battle. At the time he uttered this prayer the victory still appeared doubtful, but shortly afterward he had triumphed. Clovis had himself baptized, and it was a Catholic bishop who performed the ceremony.

Clovis's Conversion to Catholic Christianity

The question about motives must now be asked with the same intensity as it was with Constantine and Frederick the Wise, which we discussed briefly above (see pp. 180–81). The usual answer that it was political motives which induced Clovis to accept Catholicism is one we find given not only by historians, but also by church historians. That is really amazing, for a glance at the map of that time would be sufficient to determine that conversion to Catholicism could not promise political advantages to Clovis, for all the kingdoms surrounding and virtually crushing his modest domain, which was by no means stable yet, adhered to the Arian faith. What advantages could Clovis have really gained by joining a faith that was antithetical to all the other Germanic tribes? Besides this, the Arian faith had already gained a foothold in his family. Two of his sisters adhered to it, and one of them was married to Theodoric, the most powerful Germanic prince of that time. If his actions had been motivated by political considerations, then we would have expected Clovis to attempt to strengthen the bonds to Theodoric as much as possible. That would have required the adoption of the Arian faith, however, for Theodoric, as we have seen several times (see p. 229), was a convinced Arian. Characteristically, Theodoric, after Clovis became a Catholic, again and again stood in the way of his expansion. Each time Clovis set out on a campaign of conquest, Theodoric opposed him directly or indirectly. When Clovis was successful over the Alemanni and Burgundians, Theodoric blocked further gains. And when Clovis began the struggle against the Visigoths, Theodoric even sent an army that fought the united Franks and Burgundians and, as we might expect, defeated them. Whenever Clovis wanted to extend his rule, he always ran into the opposition of his brother-in-law; if he had wanted to act politically in changing his faith, the only thing he would have considered would have been a conversion to Arianism.

If anyone claims that he did this for political reasons, and these political actions only brought him disadvantages, then the only explanation that remains is that either he was completely mistaken in his political evaluation, or that political motivations just could not have entered into the matter. Yes, the retort is made, this conversion of Clovis to Catholicism instead of to Arianism shows precisely how farsighted he was in his political considerations. Not only was he making natural allies of the Roman inhabitants of his empire, but he was also building a relationship with Byzantium and Italy. That is right if we consider the time some hundred years later. But here, as so frequently, this is making use of a modern reflection which comes from a later period and has no relevance to the actual circumstances of the time under consideration. An action that takes into account a time several hundred years later, and thus creates considerable difficulties in the present, is something that cannot be ascribed even to today's statesmen and absolutely cannot be expected of them either. Demanding this of the fifth century is something that can happen only in an ivory tower. If Clovis, then about thirty years old, really was looking into the distant future when he converted to Catholicism, then at least we would expect, for example, that he would treat the Roman inhabitants of his domain (who, according to this theory, would have become his allies) differently than they were normally treated by the Arian Germanic rulers. There can be no doubt that the Romans subject to the Franks were treated no differently, not even in the slightest, than they were anywhere else by the Germanic conquerors; Clovis treated them just the way they were treated by the Ostrogoths in Italy and the Vandals in Africa. No matter from which perspective we observe these things, we can reach a complete explanation, as well as a clear and realistic evaluation, of Clovis's conversion to Christianity only if we regard it as happening from personal conviction. This Christian conviction would stand up to the scrutiny of a contemporary theologian no more than would Constantine's; both of them would have failed a dogmatic examination given by one of today's theologians. Here it is a Merovingian of the fifth century who is acting, one who has been mostly, but not completely, won over to Christianity, a peculiar version of Christianity, just as was Constantine's.

If we inquire about the preceding history, we discover a relationship between Clovis and the Christian church going back into his youth. And for him this relationship to the Christian church was a relationship to the Catholic church. Clovis's father, Childeric, had good relations with the Roman Empire and was also influenced by Roman culture. Ever since the beginning of his reign—we should not forget that he was only sixteen years old at its beginning in 482—Clovis seems to have maintained friendly relations with the bishops of his domain. Since he had at least no negative relationship toward Catholicism, he was able to marry a Catholic. The influence of his wife, Clotilda doubtless had a significant importance for his conversion. If Clovis addressed to Christ the prayer about which we are told, perhaps he may have been doing so because of inner insecurity in the moment of need, and perhaps also in an attempt to secure a powerful helper—the concept of power played a significant part in the faith of the Germans, whether pagan or Christian. When Clovis received baptism after the battle as a fulfillment of his vow, he was at that time certainly not a convinced Christian according to the standards of later ages, but he was at least as much a Christian as many in that age in that territory were Christian. He adopted Catholicism as that form of Christianity with which he was familiar, but not because of political calculations. Baptism was a considerable risk for Clovis. That he recognized this is shown by the fact that he made sure before the baptism that at least a substantial portion of the warriors of his tribe converted to Christianity at the same time he did. The rest of the tribe remained pagan. It still took considerable time until the Franks were more or less completely won over to Christianity. Even in 538 the third Synod of Orleans speaks as if the conversion of the Franks had just been initiated.

The Development of Frankish Rule After Clovis

The expansion of the Frankish kingdom after Clovis's death did not take place toward the south or west, as the hypothesis of the politically conditioned conversion presumes, but toward the east. Clovis's sons subdued the remnants of the Burgundians, the Thuringians, and the Alemanni, that is, they persevered in the territory where their father could not accomplish anything more because of his concern for Theodoric. A grandson was the first one to act differently: Theodebert undertook an advance into Italy, even planning a campaign against Byzantium. Here the defenders of the political motivation of Clovis's conversion could find confirmation for their hypothesis by pointing to Theodebert's action as documenting the far-reaching plans of Clovis. However, the reality is something different. Theodebert moved into

Italy because he hoped to gain advantages for himself from the struggles going on there between the Ostrogoths and Byzantium (we too easily forget the contemporaneity of events). This was not a great undertaking, and its results were just as modest. Theodebert could not maintain his position in northern Italy, but he did win Provence and took Raetia, a territory along the upper Rhine, from the Alemanni. And the plan of attacking the Eastern empire was just not a realistic expectation. It is only evidence of a phenomenon which was characteristic of the ruling class of the Merovingians, and for the Franks of the early period in general, namely, surplus energy seeking an outlet and surplus power seeking activity. The internal history of the Merovingian kingdom is the most turbulent of all the Germanic kingdoms, and not only the most turbulent but also the most unpleasant. We need only read what Gregory of Tours wrote about them in his history of the Franks. There virtually everyone was fighting against everyone else—the king against the nobility, the nobility against the king, the nobility against the bishops, the bishops against the nobility—and with every means available, not just with open battles, but also with dagger and poison, with treachery and force, and this was the case not just for the men, but also for the women who with these means were competing rather successfully with the men.

The power of the Franks, displayed in its expansion in all directions, and which originally appeared invincible, then began to wane. The Merovingians as rulers and the Franks of that time mutually paralyzed one another until the unavoidable finally took place, the displacement of the now powerless line of the Merovingians by the Pepins, that is, the members of the family which the Merovingian kings, since they were constantly occupied with other matters, had installed as mayors of the palace. They were supposed to assist them in maintaining the rights of the crown against the nobility. But very soon things were reversed, and the mayors of the palace became the leaders of the opposition of the nobility against the kings. When they then felt strong enough, they fought against the king as well as the nobility and simultaneously attempted to obtain the monarchy and subjugate the nobility.

The first attempt was undertaken in 656 by Grimoald, who proclaimed his son king. He failed, and the result was that Grimoald, as well as his son, vanish from our view. It was his grandson, Pepin of Herstal, who first regained for his family the position of power that it enjoyed two generations earlier, that is, the real power in the kingdom, but without the royal title. But as soon as he died, the old struggles of everyone against everyone else began all over again. His son, Charles Martel, during his reign (714–41) could then defeat one opponent after another and also remove the centrifugal forces in the neighboring principalities. They were closely joined to the central authority: Burgundy, Alsace, Thuringia, and Alemannia once again become firm components of the Frankish kingdom. It was not possible to include Bavaria at that time, but the foundations were laid for later. Charles Martel conquered northern Frisia, and he began the first campaign against the Saxons; thus we see the expansionary force of the Franks, which they possessed during the time of Clovis and his first successor, restored in its full dimension. Charles Martel was also able to overcome the danger of invasion from the West—we are living in the age of the expansion of Islam. In 732 at the battle of Tours near Poitiers, Charles Martel was victorious. Thus, the danger that the West would be overrun by Islam, just as Egypt, Africa, and Spain already had been, was averted. Charles Martel assumed the heritage of his ancestors anew but always as mayor of the palace without the title of king, even though acting like a king. In this he correctly read the signs of the time. His position was incomparably stronger than that of all of his predecessors, but it still could not be inherited. When he died and his kingdom was divided between his sons Carloman and Pepin the Short, both of them had to fight the same destructive forces which Charles Martel had at the beginning of his reign.

Several years were thus occupied with recurring struggles against lesser princes and members of their own family, until the authority of the brothers was finally secured. In addition, Pepin the Short had the good fortune of his brother Carloman voluntarily abdicating his share of the rule and entering a monastery. Thus, in 751 Pepin the Short could be chosen as king, something about which we shall speak more thoroughly later (see pp. 252–53). The kingdom was in his hand; finally the position has been reached which, as a rule, is ascribed to Clovis in the discussion of his conversion to Christianity (see p. 231). It is not until the middle of the eighth century, not at the beginning of the sixth century, that we can begin to speak either about a consolidation of the Frankish kingdom or about a Frankish church. Both of these parallel each other in a surprising fashion.

Perhaps a brief explanation is necessary for why—in contrast to the usual presentations of church history—we have spoken relatively thoroughly about the history of the Franks and why we will say even more. It is really obvious. When we talk about Christianity among the Germans, it is not sufficient to speak only about Ulfilas, Clovis, the Scotch-Irish, and subsequently about the Anglo-Saxons—that is talking in a vacuum. If we are to get any kind of complete picture, we must also speak about the external circumstances, about the political history which is intertwined most closely with the history of Christianity from the beginning of the Middle Ages until their very end.

The Church in the Kingdom of the Franks After Clovis

In order to understand and evaluate the ecclesiastical development, it is advisable to return once again to the sixth and seventh centuries, where we began this presentation (see p. 215). The situation at that time was anything but encouraging for the Catholic church. In the sixth century, Byzantine armies had destroyed the domination of the Arians in Africa and Italy. These battles had indeed brought freedom from the Germans, but actually it was not freedom as such but really a yoke which in many cases was more oppressive than that of the previous masters. We cannot claim that under Germanic rule the popes always were in a favorable situation, but under Byzantine domination the popes not infrequently were in one that was even less favorable. We are in the age of the final stages of the Christological controversy, in which Byzantium was attempting to come to an arrangement with the Monophysites or at least with their intentions. The council of 553 had made statements that were really opposed to the internal attitude of the West (see p. 203). In the controversy about the so-called Three Chapters, the West was compelled to condemn views which it cherished; again and again it had to deny not only its fundamental principles, but also the presuppositions on which they were based. Thus the church of the West suffered greatly under Byzantine domination. In addition, this liberation from foreign domination was only temporary, for in the year 568 the Lombards appeared south of the Alps and step by step took over all of northern Italy. At first only a few units continued marching farther southward, but the number and strength of these units grew, so that Rome was threatened several times. Until the eighth century the Lombards continued their attempt to bring all of Italy and especially Rome under their domination, so that the popes were continually insecure and not infrequently thought they were standing on the precipice of personal catastrophe and the catastrophe of their church. For these Lombards were pagans, and those among them who were Christians were Arians. In both cases their faith had a rather militant form. Only gradually could Catholicism gain a foothold among the Lombards. In addition, the direct land route to Byzantium had been cut, for in the course of the struggles between the Lombards and Byzantium, the Balkans were occupied by Slavic tribes.

Meanwhile, in Spain the Arian form of Christianity was replaced by the Catholic. The Visigoths had also gradually turned to Catholicism. In 589 a council at Toledo solemnly issued the sharpest statements condemning Arianism. This decision was supported not only by the clergy, but also by the nobility. But this meant next to nothing for Rome. It is true that a close friend of Gregory the Great played a significant part in what went on in Spain at that time, but no improvement in the situation of the Roman bishops resulted from it. And even though the proportion of Catholics among the Franks continually increased, nothing more than an increase in the status of the pope was the result, for this Catholic church in the Frankish kingdom developed into the form of a national church, just as happened among the Arian Germanic tribes. The king named the bishops, they were directly subject to him, and he had decisive influence over them, just as the bishops in their turn had over him and his government, so that from the very beginning they were constantly in danger of becoming more secular than spiritual lords. The more time went by, the more they as members of the upper class became enmeshed in the struggles of everyone against everyone else, and became correspondingly corrupted. As can be imagined, the moral level of this upper class in the Frankish kingdom was low. Here passions dominated, very tangible passions. We can certainly not absolutize what Gregory of Tours describes for us; he was talking about life among the ruling class. It is possible that things looked quite different among the ordinary people, but it is certain that there paganism played a decisive role and that Christianity among the ordinary people was strongly influenced by this paganism. Church property was regarded completely from a secular viewpoint. It could come into the hands of a layman who, without demonstrating any sort of qualification for the office, could be promoted to a bishop by the king. This does not go too far afield, for even the bishops who obtained their office in the normal way were often more interested in all sorts of other things than executing the duties of their offices. This church did nothing but exist—vegetate is a better word; no sort of activity was carried on by it beyond the borders of the Frankish territory, for example. Christianity in the bordering territories was left completely on its own, and there was no concern at all that considerable stretches of territory within the kingdom itself were completely untouched by Christianity.

3. THE SCOTCH-IRISH AND
THE ANGLO-SAXONS

Thus, the situation at the beginning of our period, seen from Rome's perspective, is something other than a cause for rejoicing. The number of Catholic Christians had grown in the preceding generations, and the territory covered by Christianity had significantly increased. But at that time, humanly speaking, no one could foresee who or what power would be able to turn these varied elements in western Europe into a church worthy of the name, that is, a united organization and at the same time an institution which could even try to meet the demands placed upon it. The way toward this goal was paved by men from a territory which at that time was surely beyond the horizon of all those involved. The help came from the far North, from Ireland and Scotland, from Christian communities for whom the continent, even Italy, had done nothing for many centuries.

The Scotch-Irish Church

As the Romans withdrew from Britain about the beginning of the fifth century, there were already Christian churches there, as everywhere else in the Roman Empire. The same thing is true for Ireland. The details of the early history of Christianity in Ireland are obscured by legend, but decisive significance must certainly be ascribed to St. Patrick who lived in the first half of the fifth century. The churches in Ireland were isolated from all others because of the sea. That meant that they had to fend completely for themselves, but it also meant that they were not threatened from outside, either by the vicissitudes of the great migrations or by an invasion such as England experienced. This isolation led to a very peculiar form of Christianity and church life. The feature externally distinguishing this church was not the office of the bishop or an episcopal organization, but the monastery. A network of monasteries, normally not connected to each other, gradually spread throughout the entire country. It was individual clans or families who founded and supported these monasteries, and the office of abbot was thus controlled and passed on by the clan or family who provided the land for a monastery. Thus, the area in which a monastery functioned came to be identical with the territory ruled by the corresponding family or clan. The diocese was administered by the abbot, not by the bishop. There were bishops, of course, but their function was only to ordain, and they played a completely subordinate role, unless the position of the bishop chanced to be identical with that of the abbot.

For this monastic organization, inasmuch as we can call it that—it would be better to speak only of monasteries—the church of Italy, for all practical purposes, did not exist. This Irish church led a completely isolated existence. But the life it led was one that was amazing in every respect. It was dominated by the ascetic principle, but by an ascetic principle that was not concerned with the salvation of one's own soul, as the Egyptian ascetics, for example, were, but one that was accompanied by a concern for the other person—in other words, by missionary impulse. Here it was not only the monks who lived an ascetic life, but also the laity, so that the danger of secularization, which at that time had almost devoured the Frankish church, just did not exist for the church in Ireland. Here everything was focused on the sanctification of the individual, as well as of society. It is no coincidence that the penitential books which impose a strict discipline upon the life of a Christian come from Ireland. But in amazing combination with this asceticism stood an extraordinarily high educational level. In these Irish monasteries the ancient world lived and survived, not only Latin antiquity but Greek as well. Here there was no break in the development. The Irish church preserved an unbroken connection with the beginning, developing it in the way we have described. Thus, what came into being in Ireland was a monks' church, a monastery church, dominated by the idea of asceticism and education, something totally inconceivable, for example, for the Frankish kingdom.

As a result of the missionary impulse animating these ascetics, the work of Christianizing all Ireland was completed at an early time. Thus, Ireland's church soon reached out beyond its natural boundaries, at first toward Scotland. Here Columba founded a new monastery on the island of Iona, which soon became the mother of many daughter monasteries. Soon even Scotland became too confining for the monks, and they went to the Orkney Islands, the Shetland Islands, to Iceland, and finally to the European continent. As this happened, an essential change in the nature of monasticism occurred. In Ireland the monasteries were still independent of one another. Now the new monasteries were centralized, that is, the original monastery linked the daughter monasteries closely to itself; the latter regarded the mother monastery as the center to which they felt themselves closely attached. Thus the monastery on the island of Iona not only became the nucleus for founding other monasteries, but also the center to which they were closely related. The same thing was true of the monastery at Luxeuil in the Vosges Mountains, which originated as the first Scotch-Irish establishment on the continent. It became the center of numerous monasteries founded by the Scotch-Irish in the territory of the Franks.

This thrust toward the continent around 600 was led by Columbanus, who, against his abbot's opposition, entered the new mission field along with twelve of his comrades. As soon as the Scotch-Irish appeared in the Frankish kingdom, something new began for the Frankish church. Its church appeared to its faithful to be in a state of worldliness. Its bishops were more warriors than shepherds, and they believed their real task lay in participating in campaigns against real and imagined internal enemies, in going hunting and doing everything else that characterized the life of the upper classes at that time, not in administering their dioceses. For the first time the Franks now became acquainted with a Christianity which made extraordinarily high demands—but not on others, rather on itself. They saw clerics offering themselves in service to others. And these were not blind zealots, but in their learning surpassed anything that could be found in the Frankish kingdom. Thus, Columbanus and his brothers soon achieved extraordinary influence. The faithful streamed to them from all sides, not exactly something that was received with enthusiasm by the existing Frankish church, for each of these monks was a walking reproach for almost every one of their dignitaries. Besides this, the foreigners were not interested in conforming to the existing ecclesiastical organization, but they energetically, virtually stubbornly, maintained their independence. To a certain extent they formed a new church within the existing Frankish church. Thus a conflict with the episcopacy could not be avoided. The Scotch-Irish not only would not cooperate with them, but also refused to subjugate themselves to papal authority. We hear about a conflict between the Scotch-Irish Columbanus and a papal legate who confronted him with the old tradition of the continental church, to which Columbanus retorted: The truth which drives out error is older than every tradition. Columbanus knew that this truth was on the side of his church, not only in its message, but also in its organization.

By themselves the bishops would probably not have undertaken anything against the Scotch-Irish. They were satisfied with the assurance that there was no intention of forcing the Frankish church to adopt an organization similar to that of the Scotch-Irish. But, combined with the overt hostility of the monarchy, the latent opposition of the bishops became a serious threat to Columbanus and his comrades. Columbanus and his brothers did not restrict themselves to calling the laity to change their lives, but their call to repentance, their criticism, extended to everyone, no matter what his status—including the court. Thus conflict came about. Columbanus was imprisoned and the Luxeuil monastery dissolved. They wanted to deport him to Ireland, but Columbanus was able to escape. He left the Frankish kingdom, going first to Bregenz on Lake Constance and on from there to the territory of the Lombards in Italy, where he founded the monastery at Bobbio, which for centuries was a center of asceticism and intellectual pursuits. Here he died in 615, having continued his activity unbroken until his last moment.

They had now been able to force Columbanus from his area of activity, but they could not get rid of the forces he had unleashed. As soon as the crisis passed, the brothers who had been driven from Luxeuil reassembled and finally turned Luxeuil into a central monastery in accordance with the Scotch-Irish tradition. Numerous new monasteries were founded, all of them looking toward Luxeuil as their head and following the instructions emanating from it. In this way monastic life in the Frankish kingdom was raised to a new level by the activity of the Scotch-Irish. Since extraordinary forces flowed from all these monasteries, they had direct results on education and morality, as well as on church life. This church now also began to develop missionary strength. Not only was the kingdom of the Franks permeated with it, but Christianity also spread more and more strongly through the territories bordering the Frankish domain. Columbanus himself had already worked in the territory of the Alemanni, Gall missionized in the area around Lake Constance, and itinerant bishops also traversed the land, as Killian did in the area along the Main River. The stagnant Christianity of the Frankish kingdom was set in motion anew; the church on the continent had taken a significant step forward. But it is obvious that this advance, seen from Rome's perspective, was only a very conditional one. The result of the work of the Scotch-Irish monks was nothing else but an organization of a church within the church, a monastic organization which kept to itself, observed its own law, was insulated from the influence of the larger church, and maintained its own practices in distinction to it.

In this isolation lay the strength, but also the limits of the Scotch-Irish activity. In addition, the longer time went by the more the danger of internal dissolution threatened it. The more extended the Scotch-Irish mission became, the more difficult it became to maintain its cohesiveness. An essential part of the Scotch-Irish system was its restriction to a limited area. It was possible to permeate Ireland, and it was possible in certain Scottish territories to build a monastic organization involving the entire populace. But it was impossible to achieve the same thing in the Frankish provinces. The farther away monasteries were established, the looser became their connection with the central one, and that much more was the system fundamental to the Scotch-Irish church weakened. Thus, the mission of the Scotch-Irish was of extraordinary significance for the history of Christianity on the European continent, but it was only a preliminary stage for the actual Christianization of the Germans. Not until the thrust of the Anglo-Saxons in the seventh and eighth centuries was the Christianization of the Frankish kingdom completed.

The Conversion of the Anglo-Saxons

At the beginning of our age the Anglo-Saxons were pagans. They had just embarked on the conquest of England, thus contributing to the threat to Christianity there. There were still remnants of Christianity from the Roman occupation remaining in central and southern England, but in the face of the invasion by the Angles, Jutes, and Saxons who were now taking over England, the Celtic tribes in the south of England, Christianized at least to some extent, moved northward, so that Christianity in England was not only reduced in numbers but also weakened in strength.

In the year 596 a change took place: a group of Roman monks landed on southern English soil. After only a year, their leader Augustine could report to Rome the first mass conversion of the Anglo-Saxons in Kent. This mission to the Anglo-Saxons goes back to a personal decision of Pope Gregory the Great (590–604). The legend relates that he—even before being chosen pope—had gone through the slave market in Rome and noticed a number of tall, strong, handsome youths. When he asked them their tribe, they answered that they were Anglo-Saxons. These slaves impressed him deeply, and at that time he planned to go to England himself in order to bring Christianity to the people there, but the Romans, out of love and respect, would not permit him to go.

This is certainly not the way things happened, yet the legend does have a kernel of truth in it. We know that in 595 Gregory devised a plan of buying Anglo-Saxon slaves in the Frankish kingdom and educating them in Italian monasteries, so that they could be prepared there to carry on missionary work in their homeland. This was never implemented. He then sent a first group of monks under the leadership of the provost Augustine in the year 596. Even the selection of the leader, as well as the members of this enterprise, indicates how closely Gregory was associated with this undertaking, for Augustine was the provost of a monastery which had been founded by Gregory himself. Gregory also attempted to direct the mission in England in detail by means of numerous letters to Augustine. The question is: why did he do this? What were the motives behind this astonishing dispatch of a missionary delegation to Kent?

On the surface the situation appears clear. If they were to missionize in England, they had to begin in Kent. It lay directly opposite the kingdom of the Franks and was connected with it in various ways. The king of Kent was married to a Christian, a Frankish princess, so that missionaries coming to Kent would find several points of contact. But this does not answer the decisive question of why Gregory decided to missionize in England at all. He jumped over the entire continent; he made no attempt to build on the base existing on the continent and reform the Frankish church. It is true that he did occasionally undertake relations with Bavaria, but nothing resulted from them. At that time he did nothing more than consider the idea. Instead, Gregory struck out into absolutely virgin territory. Perhaps the reports he had received about the Scotch-Irish gave him hope that there would be great opportunities for a Christian mission in England; perhaps what motivated him was the wish to extend the boundaries of Christianity, since the Franks were not responding to the task confronting them. We do not know.

It is certain, however, that Gregory's decision to carry out missionary work in England was decisive for the following centuries. The sending of that modest delegation in the year 596 created the basis for the later union of all the churches of Europe under Rome's domination. The Anglo-Saxons received Christianity directly from Rome; they became acquainted with it in the form which prevailed in the city of Rome. Thus, for them Rome was the center of the church. They felt themselves connected so closely to Rome that they could do nothing—then or in the future—without obtaining approval or advice from Rome for it, especially when they initiated missionary work on the European continent. Wilfrid, Willibrord, and Boniface—these three names are synonymous with the three stages of this Anglo-Saxon mission which introduced the spirit of Anglo-Saxon Christianity to western Europe. Once again, the history of Christianity among the Germans had a new beginning. The first epoch of Christianity among the Germans was characterized by

Ulfilas (see pp. 217–18). At the time of the migrations, Arian national churches were established everywhere in Europe (see p. 227). They perishcd. The second time, Christianity began with Clovis's conversion to Catholicism (see pp. 231–33). What resulted was what we must call a sterile Frankish national church. The next stage was marked by the activity of the Scotch-Irish (see pp. 238–42), but their monastic organization was not in a position to mold anew the church of an entire continent. Now, under the Anglo-Saxons, what comes into being here is a Catholic church which is oriented toward Rome. It still took centuries until the fruits were fully ripe, but there can be no doubt that the development which created the Catholic Middle Ages began when Gregory the Great decided to send the provost Augustine to England.

The beginnings of the mission among the Anglo-Saxons were very promising; after only a year, as we mentioned above (see p. 242), a mass baptism could take place. But apparently Augustine was not in a position to recognize the special situation in which he found himself, let alone master it. Although Gregory had given him very detailed instructions, Augustine committed very serious errors, retarding the development of the English church for about seventy years. He gained a foothold in Canterbury, he consecrated bishops, and something previously unheard of happened—an English bishop appeared at a synod in Rome. But this church, which offered such an externally attractive picture, was not on a very firm foundation. Augustine had won Ethelbert, the king of Kent, but he missed giving Ethelbert's sons a sufficient grounding in Christianity. After Ethelbert's death a pagan reaction took place, leaving only remnants of what at one time had been such a glorious church. Augustine also failed to create a bridge to the Christians in the northwest of the country. An encounter with the Scotch-Irish church even took place. Emissaries of that church came to Augustine, but he was apparently deluded with his initial successes and approached the Scotch-Irish church as a conqueror. He could not distinguish between the pagans of the province of Kent, who were on a lower level of civilization, and the Scotch-Irish monks who enjoyed a completely different sort of life and education, and Augustine thought he would most impress them if he demonstrated Rome's power. For this purpose he also performed a miracle, as he apparently had frequently done before; a blind Anglo-Saxon was healed. But all of this only served to frighten the Scotch-Irish away. They discussed outward differences, such as the different celebrations of Easter and so forth. But to a certain extent they did this only to have something to do at all. The fact was that the Scotch-

Irish, when they met with Augustine, were convinced from the very beginning that they could not affiliate with the church he represented. If this is the way he acts with us now, they asked themselves, how will he act after we subject ourselves to him?

Thus, the contact produced no results. Christianity in the north of England continued in the fashion of the Scotch-Irish church, extending its mission farther and farther toward the south, until things changed with Wilfrid. Wilfrid was born in 634. At the age of eighteen he went to Canterbury and from there to Rome, where he lived for some time. Deeply impressed by Roman Christianity, he returned to England in 660 and appeared as an emissary of the demands of the apostle Peter, as a representative of the Roman claims. In Northumbria he gained influence over the kings, and at the Synod of Whitby in 664 succeeded in settling the dissension between the Scotch-Irish and the Roman church. Wilfrid rejected the claims of the Scotch-Irish church by appealing to Peter. Peter and the Roman church not only had an older, but also a higher tradition and authority than anything the Scotch-Irish could claim. What was done in Rome agreed with what Peter wished, and if they did not follow what Rome demanded, they would be excluded from heaven. Peter was the doorkeeper of heaven, and he would admit only those who belonged to the church he had established. Today this sort of argument seems extremely crude, but it accorded with the mentality of the time. The king and the nobility decided in favor of Wilfrid and the form of the church he represented; the Scotch-Irish left the country. England had now finally decided in favor of Rome.

The Beginning of the Anglo-Saxon Mission on the Continent Under Wilfrid and Willibrord

Wilfrid's activity, as well as his personality, is decidedly important for the English church. But despite all the missionary success he achieved in his tireless activity throughout the country, he was not fully recognized by the church which owed so much to him. It is true that he became bishop of York. But the highest honor was denied him. It was not he who was named archbishop of Canterbury and thus primate of the English church in 669, but the Greek monk Theodore. At that time they were not yet ready to trust an Anglo-Saxon with that office. Wilfrid could not even hold his diocese of York without opposition. When it was partitioned, he went to Rome to oppose the measure. He was vindicated, but when he returned to England with a bull stating that fact, they did not recognize it and claimed it had been forged.

Wilfrid was given little credit, therefore, although he performed pioneering service not only for the English church, but also for that on the continent. One of his trips to Rome led him through Frisia. He recognized the special situation of Christianity there and undertook the initial steps toward strengthening the congregations in existence and further expanding Christianity, thus preparing for the future. The future belonged to Willibrord. Willibrord was Wilfrid's pupil. He had grown up in a monastery that Wilfrid headed and was educated more or less under his supervision. But then he left England, probably in connection with the difficulties Wilfrid experienced. While in Ireland, he heard of Wilfrid's visit to Frisia and of the successes and needs there, and this awakened in him the desire to continue building on what Wilfrid had begun. At the time the prerequisites for this were favorable, for Pepin had managed to conquer the Frisian prince Radbod. Willibrord first obtained permission from Pepin to undertake missionary work among the Frisians. Pepin gladly gave his permission, for this Frisian area was of special interest to the Franks; not only did the Frisians hold the territory around the Rhine estuary, but the islands lying off the continent as well (that is, the area of the present-day Netherlands; here Utrecht became the center of missionary activity). If he could win them for Christianity, the Franks hoped for themselves that at least their influence, if not their rule, could be extended.

Willibrord first obtained the permission from the state. But then he went immediately to Rome and there requested an ecclesiastical appointment for his work among the Frisians. This shows that fruits were already beginning to result from Gregory's decision to carry on missionary work among the Anglo-Saxons; certainly the missionaries attempted to avoid all possible difficulties from the side of the state, but much more important to them was the connection with the Roman church. They could conceive of themselves performing a missionary task only with the pope's permission. Something else also motivated Willibrord when he went to Rome. He wanted to obtain relics there, something which apparently had great significance for the work among the Germans. If their cultic deities were taken away, if their sacred trees were felled, if everything which previously served the Germans as an outward symbol of their faith were removed, then a tangible replacement would have to be offered them. This was the reason for the relics which play a role in the Germanic church from early on, obviously because they met the needs of the Germans in a special way. The piety of the Germans had many strains which appear foreign to us. We have already spoken about the human sacrifices of the pagan Germans (see p. 220). In no way was this something that took place only in the early period, but the laws given by Charlemagne still tell us about human sacrifices among the pagan Saxons, and at the same time we hear about the Germans' belief in witches—all things which surprise us when we recall what not long ago was told us about the high moral and religious level of the Germans.

When Willibrord returned from Rome, he learned that his companions had been industriously at work during his absence. They had undertaken missionary expeditions into the Saxon territory, they had founded monasteries such as the monastery of Kaiserswerth on Wörth, an island in the Rhine, and they had also taken the first steps at creating an ecclesiastical organization by having one of their number consecrated as bishop. Thus Willibrord was confronted with many unresolved questions. A few years later, therefore, he journeyed to Rome a second time—this time not on his own, but at the direction of Pepin. Pepin wanted Willibrord to be named an archbishop, so that the prerequisites would be in place not only for a mission on a grander scale, but also for an organizational development of the Frankish church, something that was characteristic of the future development of things. Willibrord returned as Archbishop Clement. Then in forty years of work in the Dutch portion of Frisia (that is probably the best way to identify it) he built a new church province. To be sure, this work was not accomplished without difficulties. Radbod returned and waged war against the territory now ruled by the Franks, until Charles Martel was finally able to defeat him in several campaigns in 715–19. Then Willibrord could rebuild what was destroyed and create the basis for something new. Yet it was not possible for him or his comrades to extend their mission beyond the border that marked the boundary of Frankish domination. Attempts to carry out missionary work in the Saxon area were temporarily without results. But because one of the monasteries (Echternach) founded by Willibrord was given territory outside the Frankish dominions, the basis for Christianity's expansion there in the future was established. The monastery was given possessions in Thuringia in the vicinity of Gotha, in the vicinity of Weimar, and the fortress of Hammelburg on the Saale. All of these locations became key points for the expansion of Christianity in the next generation.

4. BONIFACE AND THE RENEWAL OF
THE FRANKISH CHURCH

The success which Willibrord could report to England continuously brought him new coworkers. Among them was Wynfrith (Boniface). A member of the third generation, so to speak, he took over the work of the Anglo-Saxon mission among the pagan Germans, as well as the task of reviving and renewing the Christianity that already existed and finally subjecting the whole to Rome.

Life and Work

We do not know much about Wynfrith's life. He was born about 675. He was of Saxon descent. While still a child he was entrusted to a monastery. Here it very early appeared certain that Wynfrith had a brilliant career ahead of him. He became a teacher at the monastery school, he was ordained to the priesthood, he was given special responsibilities within the church. But despite the brilliant prospects for him in the church of his homeland, Wynfrith decided to leave England to become a missionary and work on the continent. He had the choice between an academic and an ecclesiastical career, but both of these were less important to him than the obligation of spreading Christianity among the pagans. In the year 716 he journeyed to Frisia for the first time. But this trip was brief and fruitless, because paganism in Frisia had regained the upper hand in the confusion after Pepin's death. So Wynfrith returned to his home monastery. But the failure could not deter him from his original intention. When he was chosen abbot of his monastery, he refused and in 718 again set off with several brothers for the continent. From the outset his attention was not directed exclusively toward Frisia, but also to the Germanic territories to the east of it. Just as Willibrord had done, he naturally went first to Rome. From Pope Gregory II he obtained a commission for mission among the Germans.

At that time he received the name of Boniface. All kinds of speculations have been associated with this name (Boniface = well-doer), but these speculations are unjustified. Boniface was the saint of the day preceding the appointment. It was therefore a purely external reason that determined that Wynfrith received the name of Boniface, just as took place with Willibrord who was named Clement when consecrated archbishop, since Clement was the saint of the day preceding the consecration. Boniface first went to Thuringia, then to Frisia in 719 after Radbod's death, where he initially worked alongside Willibrord. Willibrord recognized his importance, wanted him to settle in Frisia, and at the same time to consecrate him bishop. But Boniface refused, going into the area of the Lahn River and Hesse, where his missionary work achieved extraordinary results. When he reported this to Rome, the pope ordered him again to Rome and in 722 consecrated him a bishop. At that time Boniface did not take the general vow of a bishop, but the vow of the bishops of the city of Rome.

This shows the special significance ascribed to the activity in the North by the popes following Gregory as well. They wanted to link Boniface, the representative of that mission, as closely as possible not only to their own persons, but to Rome as well. Boniface, consecrated a bishop and furnished with a letter of recommendation to Charles Martel (to whom he initially had only a loose relationship), first continued his activity in Hesse, achieving very great results. He was able to fell the Oak of Thor near Geismar. This event had an extraordinary significance for the spread of Christianity. The Oak of Thor was an image of the dominion of the gods visible from afar—as the Irminsul later was for the Saxons (see p. 257), and the statue of Serapis in Alexandria was for the ancient world (see p. 84)—a sign the gods had planted on earth. When this sign was cut down without the punishment of the gods immediately striking the one who destroyed it, its powerlessness was most emphatically proved. With the felling of the Oak of Thor, therefore, a new prerequisite for the mission among the Germans was fulfilled.

Boniface also had no reason to complain about a lack of helpers. The news of his successes spread quickly, and numbers rushed to assist him. Thus, he could begin to organize the church in Bavaria, as well as in Thuringia and Hesse. Christianity now took permanent root in these territories; it was no longer limited to isolated monasteries as it had been among the Scotch-Irish, but was held together with a strong organization which temporarily existed alongside the official Frankish church. This new ecclesiastical organization, in distinction to the Frankish church, was oriented toward Rome. External honors were not denied Boniface. In 732 he became an archbishop, and in 738 during his third visit to Rome he was made a legate for all Germany and a papal vicar. The first phase of his activity—expanding and strengthening the young church among the Germans—was concluded.

Alongside this young church which was oriented toward Rome stood the Frankish church, and its condition we have already depicted (see p. 237). Even under Charles Martel nothing of its worldliness, and thus the increasing internal disintegration, of the Frankish church had changed. Charles Martel dealt with church offices entirely according to political points of view and granted ecclesiastical honors, for example, as rewards for valor in battle or even for support of his political maneuvers, without regard to the ecclesiastical regulations pertaining to them. For example, his nephew Hugo, who already possessed the archbishopric of Rouen, received two more bishoprics and two rich abbeys. The bishopric of Mainz was filled with the son of the previous bishop. This is something which offends our age, but not that one; at that time the bishoprics were what might be called inheritances of families, just as it was a normal occurrence that clergy have sons. None of this, however, should be thought of—as some wish to believe (when they judge things according to contemporary standards)—as an intentional secularization of church property by Charles Martel; nor did it result from a disinterest or even animosity on his part toward Christianity or the church. Instead, Charles Martel was friendly toward the church, supporting Boniface and encouraging missionary activity wherever he could. But he was following in the path of the sort of piety which for generations had been usual in the upper classes of the Frankish kingdom. If he dealt with the possessions of the church as his own, he thus was remaining within the framework of an old tradition.

Not until the sons of Charles Martel did a change take place. This change occurred as a result of the work of the Scotch-Irish; here we see the first fruits of the Anglo-Saxon missionaries. Now Christianity in the Frankish kingdom was gradually renewed from within, and the longer time went on the more it changed from a formal to a real Christianity. And its effects also did not leave the ruling family untouched. For example, when Charles Martel's son Carloman chose to enter a monastery (see p. 235), he was not motivated by resignation, but abdicated his authority because he wanted to save his soul. Under Carloman in the year 742, a synod took place, the first synod in Frankish territory, something that previously would have been inconceivable. It is self-evident that this synod was called and led by Carloman himself; it is self-evident that the nobility took part in it and influenced its decisions. But nevertheless this synod had an extraordinary significance. Here the work of reforming the Frankish church was undertaken. First it confirmed the bishops in their offices, then began to limit their dioceses, both of these an improvement. In addition, it resolved that regular synods should be held. The reform of the monasteries, instigated by the Scotch-Irish, was legitimatized. The monasteries were bound to the Benedictine rule, thus encouraging their expansion. And finally it made the decisive ruling for the Frankish church that property which had been alienated from the church in the past had to be returned.

All in all, we can certainly say that this synod, if its decisions had been carried out, would have put the ax to the root of the previous state church system of the Frankish kingdom. For the most part, however, they remained only theories. Primarily those affected by the decision to return property—but not only they—united in bitter opposition. Thus, it did not happen that all the territories which the church had lost to the nobility or the state were returned; instead, it remained true in the future that the state treated the church's property just as it did its own. Charlemagne acted the same way with the possessions of the church as Charles Martel and his predecessors had done. But this now took place under altered circumstances. Now the church's right of ownership, as such, was expressly acknowledged, and those who took over church property were required to compensate the church by paying interest. Most importantly, the regular tithe was now instituted for everyone. At first this took place only in theory, but the longer time went on the more this payment of the tithe became common, so that the existence of the Frankish church was given a new foundation. Its income from the property it owned was either discontinued or limited; not until the church gained the income of the tithe did it have the ability to carry on its increasingly widespread work.

This first synod in the year 742, which was limited to Carloman's territory, was followed in 745 by a synod for the entire kingdom, which made parallel decisions. The real work of Boniface was completed: Christianity's area of influence had been decisively expanded, new territories had been won for the church, what already existed had been strengthened, and the reform from within had begun. The newly won territories, along with the old Frankish organization, were subjected to Rome, so that the requirements for the growth of a unified area of the church were created.

Boniface ended his life among the Frisians where he had begun his work. On June 5, 754, pagans who had been embittered because of his missionary success fell upon him and murdered him along with his companions. His last words were characteristic of him: Be strong in the Spirit and fear not.

The Beginnings of Relations Between the Papacy and the Frankish Kingdom

The age of Boniface was the third stage of the activity originating in the Anglo-Saxon church. He brought it to a peak and then stepped back. The Frankish state itself now assumed the task of strengthening its relations to Rome. The initial contacts between the monarchy and papacy had taken place very early. Hesitant at first, the Frankish princes began to develop relationships more and more frequently with Rome:

Willibrord was sent to Rome by Pepin in order to be consecrated archbishop. On their part, the popes entered into correspondence with the Frankish rulers by first supplying missionaries with letters requesting the rulers to support the missionary work. Soon more came of this. For example, Pope Gregory III offered Rome to Charles Martel as a protectorate. He regarded the papal offer with hesitation, for his position in the Frankish kingdom was not yet strong enough to allow him to engage in an adventure in Italy. This protectorate over Rome would have meant a military confrontation with the Lombards. At that time the Franks felt they were not yet up to that task.

Things changed as soon as Pepin the Short had become the sole ruler over the Franks. Now he could proceed to realize the dream of his predecessors. Once Grimoald had attempted to make his son king of the Franks (see p. 234). He had failed, but Pepin now renewed the attempt to gain the monarchy for himself and thus for his family. The prospects for this were somewhat unfavorable, for in 743 he himself had placed the Merovingian Childeric III on the royal throne which had previously been vacant. This Merovingian on the throne was nothing but a puppet; nevertheless he existed, and Pepin had to proceed extremely carefully if he wanted to avoid a collapse of his own rule. Therefore, he sent an embassy in 749 to Pope Zacharias (741–52), reigning at the time, to ask the remarkable question: Was the present situation in the kingdom of the Franks good, one in which there were kings who did not have kingly power? This question, remarkable in itself, nevertheless received the anticipated answer: It was better for the person who possesses the authority accompanying the office to be called king, so that order not be destroyed. The situation is clear: by his answer the pope is legitimatizing what we would call Pepin's coup d'état. The pretender to the throne who asked this and the pope who replied are acting on the basis of what we would today call *Realpolitik;* they were doing what might be expected of them. After the pope had encouraged him in this way, Pepin had parliament elect him king in 751. Boniface, the papal legate, confirmed his election by anointing him king.

A few years later, Pope Stephen II (752–57) personally repeated this rite. He came to the kingdom of the Franks and there used all the means of the church to support Pepin's rule. There are reasons for this. Stephen II appeared in order to request assistance from the Frankish rulers against the Lombards. The situation during Charles Martel's time was repeating itself. The Lombards were threatening the States of the Church which the popes had been endeavoring to build up for generations. Not only were they endangering the States of the Church, but also the authority and existence of the pope himself. Thus, Stephen II asked for an invitation to come to the Frankish kingdom. He received it. He had to pass through Lombard territory to get to the Franks. It would have been simple for the Lombards to put an end to all their problems by capturing the pope. But this they did not attempt. Superstitious fear prevented them—Arians or pagans—from laying hands on the person of Peter's successor. Thus he could come into the kingdom of the Franks and personally appeal to Pepin for help. Pepin granted the pope's request, even though his brother Carloman hurried from the monastery at Monte Cassino where he had been staying in order to prevent Pepin from promising assistance to the pope. Naturally, Carloman's intervention had no effect. The only result was that he was not permitted to return to Monte Cassino, but placed in a Frankish monastery where he could better be kept under supervision. At the same time, his sons were also excluded as possible competitors for Pepin's throne by having their hair cut and being placed in a monastery.

At that time the symbol of the royal office was long, unshorn hair. As soon as one's was shorn, he not only forfeited his claim to the royal office, but also the mysterious power which at that time was apparently seen residing in the long hair worn by a descendant of the royal family. And, in addition, in the monastery the necessary supervision could be exercised over him.

The papacy and the Frankish monarchy allied themselves closely. The question is: What were the motives of the pope and the king? The pope's motive is unambiguous: he needed help if he and his rule were not to be threatened or even completely destroyed. Thus he appealed to the strongest power in existence at that time, the Frankish king. To obtain this anticipated help, he had performed some services in advance: his answer to the Frankish delegation in 749 (see p. 252), the anointing of the king by Boniface, his own anointing of Pepin again, and forbidding election of a king—this is how far the pope went—from another line than the Pepins under penalty of the ban of the church. In this way he not only compensated for the lack of royal birth which clearly existed in Pepin's case by giving him the church's blessing, but also furnished the strongest means of supporting the Carolingian dynasty.

In this meeting with Stephen II we see the king displaying an attitude of absolute devotion toward the pope. He went out to meet him, led his horse by its bridle, and presented a deed of gift conveying numerous Italian territories to the pope. It is true that the territories did not belong to the king and he had no power to dispose of them. But it is always this way in history: one most easily gives away something one does not own (this is repeated over and over right down to the present). However, Pepin did not simply promise the gift, but in accordance with the promised donation, he fulfilled the resulting claims of the pope by conducting two campaigns against the Lombards, even though this created external political difficulties for himself (the legates of the Eastern Roman Empire raised vehement objection against this intrusion of the Franks into Italy which they regarded as territory under their rule). The deed of gift issued by Pepin was ceremoniously placed on Peter's tomb in Rome. At first these not insignificant promises were undoubtedly a way of reciprocating for what he had received from the pope. Pepin was also certainly filled with a superstitious veneration for the successor of the apostle Peter—we find this, as we mentioned (see p. 253), even among the pagan or Arian Lombards. Thus there is certainly some truth to Pepin's response to the Eastern Roman Empire's protest that he moved into Italy out of love for the apostle Peter and for the forgiveness of his sins. But the question is whether that completely sums up Pepin's motives. There is no doubt about his devotion, and the consciousness of duty is just as plain. But in addition to all of this, there was probably a plan for the future, that is, the preparation for an expansion of the power and authority of the Franks beyond their previous territory into Italy as well.

Both as a whole and in its details, this alliance between the Frankish monarchy and the papacy definitely had its ups and downs, but it had the greatest effect on the future. This agreement between Pepin and Stephen II established the prerequisites for the action of centuries, such as the continual Italian campaigns of the German emperors all the way up into the high Middle Ages. It was at this time that German politics took on its orientation toward the South (see pp. 282–83), just as at this time the presuppositions for the papal claims of power during the Middle Ages were created.

5. THE CAROLINGIAN AGE

The last years of Pepin's life were occupied with military campaigns. He fought against the Saxons, and eight times in fulfillment of his promises to the pope he moved into Italy which he increasingly came to control. He also extended his reign over Bavaria. When he died in the year 768, his kingdom was divided among his sons Charlemagne and Carloman in such a way that each of them received an equal amount of Roman and Germanic territories. Thus, it was evident that the rule of the Carolingians had been decisively strengthened under Pepin. When his father Charles Martel died, Pepin had to overcome strong opposition and spend several years putting down revolts. Now the sons assumed power without trouble. Revolts occurred only in the newly won Aquitaine, the area bordering on Spain, but they were quickly suppressed. Carloman died after only a three year reign, so that internal struggles were avoided which, according to the laws of the time and the rules applying to the Frankish rulers, would otherwise have been inevitable.

The Kingdom of Charlemagne

After assuming his rule, therefore, Charlemagne did not have to drain his energy with internal conflicts, but could immediately devote it toward the outside. In powerful military campaigns he extended Frankish rule in all directions. Sometimes he achieved only partial results; for example, the campaign against the Arabs in 778 in Spain had only limited success. But nevertheless, Frankish rule could be advanced across the Pyrenees, and the Spanish march protected the kingdom from further incursions of the Arabs and of Islam. As a result of internal disorders within Islam, it happened that Charlemagne was even given a sort of protectorate over the holy places in Jerusalem. This shows the reputation of the Franks even beyond the actual area of their own rule. The tone was set for the future. At first, however, the most important thing was the redirection of Frankish power toward the East. For a long time the Frankish rulers had been attempting to press beyond the previously conquered Frisian territory, but the results were always extremely limited. Not until Charlemagne did Saxon territory all the way to the Elbe River come firmly under Frankish authority.

That Charlemagne's campaigns against the Saxons lasted thirty-two years—Charlemagne really fought war after war against them from 772 until 804—is explained by their form of organization. The Saxons were divided into four sharply distinct tribes: the Engerians along the Weser River, the Westphalians, the Eastphalians, and finally the Albingians in the North. These four tribes were further divided into numerous districts which were independent of one another. Only in times of war were they united under one leader, when one of the district princes would be commissioned a duke with the responsibility of waging war and exercising a type of supremacy over at least a large portion of the Saxon tribes. This sort of organization did limit the capacity of the Saxon tribes to resist, for all the Saxons were never united at one time in total resistance against the Franks; each time some tribes or districts did not participate. On the other hand, this meant that each victory of the Franks was only a temporary one. The same thing happened over and over again: the Frankish army appeared in Saxony, occupied certain territories, and forced the inhabitants of these territories to render tribute and give up hostages. But no sooner would it depart than tribes in another part of the Saxon territory would arise, considering themselves not bound—in fact, not even affected—by the agreements. As soon as the Franks thought they had won the war, it began anew. Thus, Charlemagne had to take the field over and over against the Saxons, until the resistance of the Saxon people was exhausted and a generation had grown up that accepted the Frankish domination, that had in fact grown up with it.

This was true not only for Frankish rule, but also for the Christian faith, because the struggle of the Franks against the Saxons was not only a political struggle, but also a struggle of different kinds of faith. The Saxons were not just confronting the sword, but the cross as well; we can no more blame them for fighting against this combination with all their might, than we can blame all the other people who have done the same over the course of history. This does not change the fact that the Saxons, once won for Christianity, united political conquest and forcible Christianization when they later moved against people in the East, just as the Franks had done.

In the Franks' struggle against the Saxons, we find forcible mission employed for the first time in the history of the Christianization of the Germans. During the Third Reich, this was played up as the oppression of noble Germanic blood by sinister foreign rule. The fact that here Germans were fighting against Germans—the Franks were just as much Germans as the Saxons were—was deliberately suppressed. "Charles the butcher of the Saxons"—that was the name given Charlemagne at that time, because at Verden an der Aller he had 4500 Saxons put to death, if the tradition is accurate. The tears shed about the blood spilled at that time were truly crocodile tears—let us not forget, for example, that according to reliable reports, Heinrich Himmler liked to sign death warrants while breakfasting, and these were not simply individuals, but entire groups of people who were being wiped out with a stroke of the pen, and their numbers were a hundred times greater than the 4500 Saxons at Verden an der Aller. Naturally that does not excuse the action of the Franks and Charlemagne; but it can be explained by the presuppositions of the time and the special circumstances of the Saxon wars, which we have treated relatively thoroughly because just a few decades ago they were the center of discussion.

The first campaign against the Saxons began in the year 772. At that time Charlemagne moved through the southern part of the territory of the Engerians. He captured the Eresburg, he destroyed the Irminsul, and thus the campaign was successful in every respect. But when Charlemagne moved toward Italy, leaving Saxon territory behind him, the Saxons took their revenge by invading Frankish territory. Charlemagne retaliated with a campaign in 775. It was impossible to resist the Franks in a pitched battle, so the Saxons surrendered. But when Charlemagne departed, a new revolt broke out. In 776 Charlemagne returned again, and not only he, but the entire Frankish army was filled with mounting bitterness because of what appeared to them to be the Saxons' deceit and breach of faith. From campaign to campaign the bitterness on both sides increased, as is seen in the severity of the Frankish measures taken against the Saxons and the severity of the Saxon reaction, who ravaged the Frankish territory just as the Franks ravaged theirs.

For the first time, at the diet of Paderborn in 777 the Saxons formally accepted the permanence of Frankish domination. At that time, subjugation and baptism were virtually identical with each other. In greater numbers the Saxons converted to Christianity; we hear about mass baptisms. Plans were laid for the final missionary thrust into Saxon territory. Charlemagne withdrew, as satisfied as he could be. But while he was in Spain a new revolt broke out far surpassing all the previous ones, because now, for the first time since they began, all the strength of the Saxon tribe was united under one energetic leader.

It was Wittekind who stood at the head of the Saxon army, which advanced as far as Coblenz and devastated the Rhineland, so that the first thing Charlemagne had to undertake after returning from Spain was the pacification of the Saxon territory. At that time the so-called *Capitulatio Saxonica* ("Saxon Capitulation") was promulgated, a law which was intended finally to regulate affairs in Saxon territory, especially ecclesiastical questions. It stated: Wherever a Christian church is built in Saxony, it shall have not lesser, but greater and higher honor than the shrines of the idols. And further: Anyone who forces his way into a church and steals something from it or sets the church on fire is to be punished by death. That too is something understandable. But the provisions go even further: Whoever disdains Christianity and thus does not observe the forty-day fast and eats meat, shall be punished by death. Whoever cremates the body of a dead person according to pagan custom, shall be punished by death. Any unbaptized person attempting to hide among the Saxon people shall be punished by death. On the other hand, however, it stated: If anyone who has committed a capital offense flees on his own accord to a priest, confesses his guilt, and repents, his life shall be spared. On Sundays no assemblies may take place, all children must be baptized within a year, and all pagan priests must be delivered to the Christian churches.

At that time these provisions were introduced for the Saxons along with the payment of the tithe, which previously had been completely unknown to them. This caused a new Saxon revolt. In the year 782 a Frankish army was destroyed at Süntelberg. Now when Charlemagne moved once more with an army against the Saxons, he was determined to break their resistance permanently. It was at this time that the 4500 Saxons were executed at Verden an der Aller. This background does not justify the bloodbath, of course, but does serve to explain it. Understandably enough, this forcible measure did not pacify Saxony; rather, the Saxons rose up anew. The Frisians, who long since had appeared subjugated, joined this uprising as well. But resistance to the Frankish army was impossible. The Frankish troops drove as far as the Elbe, and Wittekind himself despaired of the possibility of further resistance. He submitted, and in 785 he was baptized along with many of his warriors.

But even this did not finish the revolt. Over and over again renewed battles broke out, although now of local character. Again and again between 792 and 799 Charlemagne marched into Saxony, and then for the last time in 804. As early as 795 he began to transport thousands of Saxons and their families from their homeland and resettle them in other parts of the kingdom, while Franks in turn were settled in the Saxon territory—and also Slavs in Holstein. In this way, which as a whole was truly not pleasant, in 804 the subjugation and also at least the external Christianization of the Saxon kingdom was completed.

The Saxon territory was firmly incorporated into the kingdom of the Franks, but this was not the end of the Franks' drive toward the East. Between the Elbe and the Saale dwelt the Sorbs; between the Elbe and the Oder, the Wilzen; in Mecklenburg, the Abodrites; and finally in Bohemia, the Czechs. All of them had suffered under the Saxons and therefore were quite willing to participate in a military campaign against them. They now came to realize that, in comparison to the domination of the Franks, that of the Saxons was a harmless matter, for in several campaigns Charlemagne now pushed beyond the boundaries of the Elbe, Salle, and Danube. At this time the fortifications near Magdeburg and Halle were constructed. Military resistance was broken everywhere. Charlemagne did not actually incorporate the conquered territories into the Frankish kingdom, but was satisfied with bringing them into a loose relationship. The symbol of this relationship was the payment of tribute. Whenever a tribe tried to withdraw from this relationship, its attempt was put down by a military expedition. Here criteria for the future were established. By his conquest of the Saxon territory, Charlemagne created the prerequisite for the establishment of a German people and a German kingdom. He refrained from taking advantage of his ultimate opportunities; if he had wished, he could also have incorporated into his domain the territories all the way to the Oder. But he laid the foundations for future developments.

The Relationship with the Papacy

The coronation of Pepin created an alliance between the Frankish rulers and the popes, and under Charlemagne this alliance was decisively expanded. Both times this took place initially because of difficulties confronting the popes, who feared the Lombards would destroy not only the States of the Church, but themselves as well. The Frankish rulers responded to the popes' cry for help and intervened in Italy—partially because they could not ignore an appeal from Peter's successor, but also partially out of very real considerations for power politics.

In his day, Pepin was summoned by Pope Stephen II. When Charlemagne moved southward in 773, this was at the request of Hadrian I (772–95). By 774 the Lombard kingdom was already subdued. Charlemagne assumed dominion over it with the title of King of the Lombards and annexed the area to the Frankish kingdom, just as he had done with the territories beyond the Elbe. At first this did not go very far beyond what had taken place at Pepin's time. Pepin had already used the title of *Patricius Romanorum* ("Protector of the Romans"), which Charlemagne now added to that of King of the Franks and the Lombards. But in contrast to Pepin, Charlemagne gained a footing in Italy, and this changed the situation for the papacy. When the pope called for the Franks, he really wanted nothing more than for them to do away with the dangerous Lombards. We know that Hadrian I was not very happy that things worked out differently. Charlemagne did not stop with the campaign of 773–74, but repeatedly marched into Italy until the land finally was virtually a portion of the kingdom of the Franks—except for the South, where Byzantium firmly retained the territories it dominated, and except for Venice, which indeed was conquered at one time by the

Franks, but, in an attempt to reach an agreement with the Eastern Empire, was then returned to Byzantium. (At this time the basis was laid for the independent and influential position Venice assumed in the Middle Ages.)

These Italian campaigns brought the outward culmination of Charlemagne's position. In the year 800 he was crowned emperor by Pope Leo II in St. Peter's Church; in the year 812 we find Byzantine ambassadors in Aachen honoring Charlemagne as *imperator* ("emperor") and *basileus* ("emperor"). The Germanic Middle Ages have reached their high point. Once before, at the time of the migrations, the Germans had dominated the Western world. But those Germans were not united; their tribes stood next to one another without unity, indeed frequently enough with animosity toward each other. Now dominion over the entire Western world was firmly in one hand, and this dominion of the Franks over the Western world was recognized by the East.

In all of this it is very difficult to determine Charlemagne's relationship to the papacy. Charlemagne was in Rome for the first time in 774, apparently in order to clarify the relationship between papacy and monarchy. We see him exhibiting the same attitude of devotion toward the pope and the Roman church as Pepin had in his day. Charlemagne approached Rome on foot, he kissed the steps of St. Peter's Church before entering, and only within the church itself did he walk hand in hand with the pope, and he and his Frankish companions prostrated themselves before the Confession in St. Peter's Church. Before visiting the churches of the city, he requested the pope's permission. Charlemagne formally renewed Pepin's donation. But if we view things only from this aspect, we get an incomplete picture. Even the timing of Charlemagne's visit to Rome is characteristic. It is noteworthy that the news of Charlemagne's coming filled Pope Hadrian with consternation. Charlemagne was coming to see the pope before the struggle against the Lombards had been concluded, thus at a time when the pope had not yet succeeded in having the Lombard danger removed, something he had been seeking with all his might. Charlemagne indeed stood under the spell of the numinous character, the religious influence of Rome, but nevertheless did not for a moment lose sight of the practical necessities his political goals demanded. At any rate, his position in the church would not suffer because of his devotion to the pope and the Roman church. Here Charlemagne obviously felt he was the superior. He dealt with appointments to ecclesiastical positions in Italy and supervised the lives of Italian clergy just as he did in the Frankish kingdom. At that time Rome was a Frankish city; there they prayed for their ruler Charlemagne.

When Leo III (795–816) assumed the papal office after Hadrian, he sent Charlemagne not merely an announcement about the election which had taken place, but also the minutes of the election itself for his examination, as well as the keys to Peter's grave and the banner of the city of Rome. Thus, from the very beginning he acknowledged Charlemagne's dominion in an emphatic way. He even dated his documents according to the years of Charlemagne's reign. In the year 799 he personally appeared at the Frankish court in Paderborn to request help, this time not against external enemies—external danger had passed since the defeat of the Lombards—but against internal enemies. A revolt against Leo had taken place in Rome. He had been taken prisoner, and only with the assistance of the Frankish representatives in the city had he regained his freedom, and only under the protection of the Frankish royal herald could he travel to the North. At first his appearance there made a great impression. But the splendor of his presence was soon dimmed considerably by the arrival of his accusers, who brought such massive charges against him that it was decided that the disputed questions could be investigated and decided nowhere but in Rome itself. Under heavy Frankish guard the pope was brought back to Rome, and the archbishops of Cologne and Salzburg, together with five Frankish bishops and three Frankish counts, undertook an investigation in Rome. What they uncovered appears to have been so highly unpleasant that Charlemagne himself felt it necessary to go to Rome in the year 800 to direct the investigation personally. Apparently this investigation ran a very stormy course. We know nothing about its content, for at its conclusion all the documents as well as the minutes were destroyed. In any case, Pope Leo had to take a formal oath of purification in St. Peter's Church with the book of the Gospels above his head, something that freed him from the charges made against him. This was something unheard of; nothing like this had ever happened since the time of the Goths.

It is in this context that the coronation of Charlemagne took place. Two days after this oath of innocence by the pope, while Charlemagne was attending Christmas mass in St. Peter's and rising from prayer before the Confession, Leo placed a crown (which was held ready) on Charlemagne's head. The people acclaimed him emperor, the new Augustus, and the pope rendered him *proskynese* ("worship") according to the Byzantine practice. Subsequently Charlemagne gave rich gifts to the Roman church and punished Leo's opponents.

As Pepin's coronation had at the time (see pp. 252–54), this imperial coronation has the character of a reciprocal exchange: Charlemagne helps Leo out of his personal and official difficulties; in gratitude for this Leo crowns the emperor; and then in response Leo's opponents are silenced. Apparently they were right, but all their accusations were invalidated when Leo took his oath of innocence; if the pope swore he was not guilty of the charge, the accusers could not be right. All of this took place merely in theory, however; only when they were silenced—forcibly—was the situation really settled.

Now we read in the *Vita Caroli* ("Life of Charles"), Einhard's biography of Charlemagne, that Charlemagne was not only surprised by Leo's action, but also was displeased by it. According to reliable tradition, Charlemagne declared that if he had known about the pope's plan, he would not have gone to mass that day. Thus, the only solution left is that Charlemagne was indeed agreeable to the fact of the imperial coronation. It accorded with his plans and wishes; he probably sought it for the same reasons Pepin sought the royal office in his day. Not until he received the office of emperor did his reign have complete legitimacy, just as had happened with Pepin's coronation as king. The imperial office not only documented the fact of Charlemagne's dominion over the Western world, but added the higher consecration of this office to the power he already possessed. But apparently what displeased Charlemagne was the way in which this imperial coronation took place. There is a parallel to this coronation of 800. In the year 813, Charlemagne's son Louis, later Louis the Pious, was crowned emperor. This did not take place in Rome, but in Aachen. Charlemagne took part in this coronation in his imperial regalia, while the crown lay ready on the altar. The father first addressed his son about the duties of his office and had him swear an oath to uphold them. Then he let Louis take the crown from the altar and place it upon his own head, after which came the acclamation of the people.

Perhaps, or probably—here we are in the realm of speculation—Charlemagne was here silently correcting what had taken place in St. Peter's Church at Christmas 800. What took place in 813 could possibly have been the form Charlemagne desired for his own coronation. Obviously the pope would have had to take part in it, but the act would not have been exclusively on his initiative.

When we disregard the motives and limit ourselves to the facts, the attitude of the emperor and pope to each other is clear, at least in Charlemagne's time. We see Leo in the role of the emperor's dutiful servant, who would not even leave Rome without advance imperial permission. Charlemagne also demanded a loyalty oath from the inhabitants of the States of the Church and received it, just as in his other territories. In the States of the Church the Frankish royal heralds were also the supreme temporal authority, just as in all other portions of the empire.

The Relationship Between Church and State

It is disputed how Charlemagne conceived of the relationship between state and church, a relationship which was above that of his to the pope. Some have spoken about the emperor's theocratic consciousness. Undoubtedly it is true that Charlemagne was filled with the consciousness of a God-given task. Even with Pepin we find the beginnings of the idea that the king is appointed only by God's grace and is subject only to it, not to temporal authorities. The *dei gratia* ("by the grace of God") in the titles of kings and emperors down through the centuries to our own day began very early: this is definitely how Charlemagne viewed himself. There is no doubt that he believed he held the chief position in the Frankish kingdom; there is no doubt that he viewed the pope only as the chief bishop in this kingdom of the Franks. That is the one side. On the other side, however, the devotion not only to the apostle Peter but also to his successors is unmistakable. And this sentiment probably prevented Charlemagne from documenting very clearly the position that he did in fact take, that is, supremacy over the pope which the events of the years 799 and 800 not only made possible, but really demanded.

Some have also spoken about a state church under Charlemagne. But this is certainly not quite correct. It is undoubtedly difficult to give a correct definition of the way state and church worked in and with each other during the Carolingian age—it is best to say that church and state were closely intertwined. The state indeed deserves the primary position in this relationship, but it is always limited by the devotion which it renders to the Christian faith and its representatives. The decisive position occupied by clergy in the Carolingian empire is quite remarkable: the imperial chancellery, that is the supreme temporal law court, was staffed with clerics. Even the clergy at court, the so-called imperial chapel, who were there really to perform exclusively spiritual functions, were involved in carrying out political tasks. This, some have thought, shows the preponderance of the clergy in the Carolingian empire. But that is certainly not correct; the preeminence of the state is not contradicted because a preponderance of clergy occupied all the significant offices. Even though the imperial chancellery was almost filled exclusively with clergy, there were completely different reasons for this than ecclesiastical and spiritual ones. Charlemagne wanted to have trustworthy people governing his empire; for all practical purposes, this meant Franks. But if he wanted to have Franks in these positions, then normally he would have to use clerics, for they were the only ones who possessed the educational prerequisites for these offices. The art of writing and reading had been mastered by the Frankish nobility only to a limited extent, so that only a very small number of this group was suitable for high offices; this explains the large number of clerics in higher temporal offices.

These clerics had a spiritual office (they were abbots or something similar), and they also stood firmly within the structure of church life at that time. But not infrequently these clerics differed considerably from the way we would picture them. For example, the abbot Angilbert played a decisive role at Charlemagne's court and to a large extent defined Carolingian politics. But under the eyes of the undisputedly morally strict emperor, the abbot lived with the emperor's daughter in a relationship whose only relative platonic character is documented by the fact that two sons issued from it. No one found that at all unusual. Not only was the imperial chancellery filled with clerics, but we also find them among the leading officials of the empire—what we would call ministers—among both the counselors Charlemagne chose freely, as well as the royal heralds, who were sent out annually to visit certain territories, to represent in their person the authority of the king and in his name and authority to make necessary decisions.

Naturally these clerics took part in the imperial assembly, while on the other hand the king, the royal heralds, and the temporal courts had the making of ecclesiastical laws as well as the supervising of the entire church firmly in their hands. The king named bishops and appointed abbots without considering, for example, the right of election existing anywhere. He dealt with the church's property the same way he did with his own. It was self-evident that the clergy, particularly the higher clergy, were subject to the civil courts, so that, if we look at things from this perspective, it appears that the state possessed absolute supremacy over the church. On the other hand, we see Charlemagne paying meticulous attention to ecclesiastical concerns in connection with his civil measures. He attempted to maintain the health of the church's finances: everyone, even in the newly subjugated Saxon territory, had to pay the tithe. It is true that the clergy were subject to temporal courts, but on the other hand the state carried out punishments imposed by the church; crimes against the church and violations of its regulations were punished severely.

That civil points of view and interests were ultimately decisive in the way state and church worked in and with each other is shown by the fact that Charlemagne did not permit the church to have a metropolitan constitution, or did not let more than the initial forms of one develop. This was probably out of concern that the metropolitans could place themselves between the clergy and the ruler and disrupt the direct relationship between them. Instead of this, the position of the bishops was decisively strengthened. The bishop had supreme authority in his diocese; the monasteries were also subordinate to him. But this bishop found himself directly subject to the king, who on his part now carefully, permanently, and emphatically took the responsibility for the welfare of the church into his own hands. Synods were held regularly in order to guarantee and strengthen the internal continuity of the dioceses, just as regular visitations were held to examine the clergy's level of education and performance. It was considered important for preaching to take place regularly—in the vernacular—each Sunday and festival. Charlemagne was concerned about improving the conduct of the worship services; Alcuin's revision of the lectionary demonstrates this. The sanctity of Sunday was supported with severe measures, the legal regulations for the Saxon territory were characteristic (see pp. 257–58). On Sunday everyone had to attend worship service at which the congregation was not only supposed to join in saying the Creed and the Lord's Prayer, but to participate actively in the liturgy.

The Internal Life of the Church

The life style of the clergy was not only regulated by visitations, but was also supervised by other measures. Their level of education was examined when they entered office. The canonical regulations were strongly impressed upon them. In all the larger churches they were to live in community with one another. Thus, Charlemagne not only took great care with external matters but also the internal life of the church, and he continued the work begun by the Scotch-Irish and Anglo-Saxons so that the situation in the Christian church in Frankish tribal territory as well as in the newly added territories was incomparably higher than ever before. This concern for the church was at the same time a concern for learning. Here too the efforts of the Scotch-Irish and Anglo-Saxons were continued, and here also a zenith was reached. When we speak about the "Carolingian Renaissance," this word is fully justified. It had its effect in all areas of culture and left impressive traces behind in grand buildings and artistic monuments. It was decisive for the stimulation of academic work that a decree of Charlemagne required the establishment of libraries and schools of higher learning at all cathedrals and monasteries. Thus, centers of learning arose everywhere in the Carolingian empire where, alongside Alcuin, numerous Anglo-Saxons, Scotch-Irish, and Lombards were active—the most significant of these among the Lombards was Paul the Deacon (ca. 720–95).

The Anglo-Saxon Alcuin (ca. 730–804) played the decisive role. He had a similar significance for the elevation of general education and the development of learning in the Frankish empire as Melanchthon later had in the Reformation age. It is true that Alcuin was not really a creative figure, and his commentaries as well as his chief dogmatic work *De trinitate* ("On the Trinity") were no original academic achievements, no matter how much that age may have regarded them as such because it initially had no way of comparing them. Alcuin's decisive accomplishment, as well as his real significance, consisted in bringing the educational level of the Anglo-Saxon church—or, put more precisely, the educational level of York from which he came—into the kingdom of the Franks. A number of generally edifying tracts from his pen helped the court and the higher clergy to make contact with the academic work of that time. Now the theologians of the Frankish empire began to study the church fathers; Jerome and Augustine, and Chrysostom as well, took on significance for them. At that time not only was a revision of the lectionary carried out, but Alcuin could even begin with a revision of the Vulgate, something that was generally considered necessary.

It cannot amaze us that these Frankish theologians began to take an active part in the dogmatic disputes of the time. As early as Pepin we find the initial beginning of this. That is not surprising, for we see parallels between Pepin and Charlemagne—what happened at that time might be termed a prototype of what we observe under Charlemagne. A genuine need as well as an attempt to demonstrate to others the position which the Frankish empire had recently attained played a role in their involvement in the dogmatic disputes. Their participation in the disputes of the time was not only part of these Frankish theologians' attempt to prove themselves, but they also believed they had to triumph. If theological means were not sufficient, they still had others available—this is what they thought and accordingly how they acted. At first some disputes were created; for example, the so-called Adoptionist controversy would really not have been necessary. In Spain, Bishop Elipandus of Toledo and Bishop Felix of Urgel held Christological views which had been usual in Spain since ancient times. Here the liturgy spoke about Christ as the *filius Dei adoptivus* ("adopted son of God"), something that can be explained by the fact that Spain had been isolated from general ecclesiastical and theological development for a long time. Thus they could preserve formulas there that long since had become impossible in other places. Now that the Franks had become a part of the world of general theological learning, they felt themselves obligated to take offense at this. Adoptionism (see p. 190) was a heresy which had been condemned by the church centuries ago. The Frankish empire now had to catch up as rapidly as possible. They proclaimed this at no fewer than three synods: Regensburg in 792, Frankfurt in 794, and Aachen in 799, and each time they formally condemned Adoptionism—Rome could do nothing else but follow along. Here the enjoyment with which the Frankish theologians played the role of preservers of theological orthodoxy over against Rome and the world is obvious.

The presuppositions were different with the next disputes, the Filioque controversy as well as the Iconoclastic controversy. The Filioque controversy originated in a way that might be called coincidental. In the year 808, Frankish monks at a worship service in a monastery on the Mount of Olives used the Nicaeno-Constantinopolitanum with the addition of *filioque* ("and the Son") to which they were accustomed, that is, in the customary form of the symbol used in the mass within the Frankish empire, what was said was *processio spiritus sancti ex patre filioque*, that the Holy Spirit proceeds from the Father and the Son. That had been said earlier in the church of the West; we find this formula in Augustine, and even as early as Tertullian. However, it was foreign to the Greek church. In 381 at the Council of Constantinople the Nicaeno-Constantinopolitanum had said that the Holy Spirit proceeds from the Father (see p. 196). The most the Greeks would say is that the Holy Spirit proceeds from the Father through the Son, but definitely nothing more than this. Thus, the Franks with their doctrine of the *processio spiritus sancti ex patre filioque* were regarded as opposing not only the formula, but also the intent of the Greek church—and not just the ancient Greek church, but also that of subsequent centuries. If the Holy Spirit proceeds from the Father and the Son, the relationship of the three persons in the Trinity to one another would change. This is how the formula, as well as the concept which lies behind the *filioque,* has come to be one of the most decisive points of difference between the Eastern and Western church down to the present day. The official church in the West, that is, the Roman church, was not yet using the *filioque* at that time. When the Franks appealed to the pope in this controversy, they put him in somewhat of a dilemma. He conceded the validity of the *filioque,* even its necessity, but not its inclusion in the symbol. Rome could regard this controversy with some objectivity, for at that time the Nicaeno-Constantinopolitanum was not a part of the formula of the mass. Not until 1014 when the Nicaeno-Constantinopolitanum became the symbol used in the mass, did the Frankish standpoint finally triumph, for it was virtually self-evident that this Roman Nicaeno-Constantinopolitanum included the *filioque.*

They fell into this controversy by chance, because they had no conception of the implications of this *filioque.* Nevertheless, they pursued it emphatically. When those Frankish monks on the Mount of Olives (their very existence there shows the change that the church of that time was undergoing) used the symbol with the *filioque* in 808, what resulted was violent arguments and opposition of the populace toward the Franks. Because they did not know the historical and theological background, the Franks regarded this as an attack not only against their monks but also against their church, an act of animosity against the Frankish empire, and therefore they felt compelled to take energetic countermeasures. Here we see the sensitivity of this young empire which cannot endure even a tiny reduction of its authority. Therefore, in 809 a synod in Aachen set forth not only the justification, but also the necessity of the *filioque,* following which an embassy was sent to Rome where things developed as we have described.

The participation of the Frankish theologians in the Iconoclastic controversy undoubtedly had a political component as well. The Iconoclastic controversy as such was an intra-Byzantine affair (see p. 204), but the West—and thus the Franks—was twice involved in it. When first the anti-icon party triumphed, Rome and Pepin united against iconoclasm. Then the situation reversed; in 787 at the second Council of Nicaea the demand for veneration of icons was legitimized, and this time two papal legates participated. In the Frankish empire they were not now disposed to recognize the decision of this council. Here as well six ecumenical synods were considered valid. They were all in the past and did not limit the claim of Frankish sovereignty. But now when the Eastern church thought it could make decisions about the faith which were supposed to apply to the Frankish empire as well, the Franks believed this could not be accepted. Thus the Frankish theologians wrote the *Libri Carolini* ("Books of Charlemagne"). In this extensive work the standpoint of the ancient church was assumed: icons should not be destroyed, they also should not be venerated, but they should be piously used. This did not speak to the subject at all, and it also did not prevail. The reason was that the pope, because of his legates' participation and agreement there, was bound to the decisions made by the Council of Nicaea in 787. Thus, he could not obey the emperor's wishes without further ado, even if they were presented most forcefully (which Charlemagne had not neglected to do). He vacillated until he could harvest the (apparent) fruits of his vacillation after Carolingian power had dwindled (for the decisions of the second Council of Nicaea really did not agree with the position of the Roman church).

The *Libri Carolini* undoubtedly had a certain enlightened aspect about them. In addition, it is apparent that they were merely initial attempts. The Frankish theologians were trying for the first time to present an extensive theological system, and they were not equipped to do so. That is the only way we can explain the fact that the *Libri Carolini* proceeded on the basis of a confession of faith they called a work "of the fathers," while in reality it came from Pelagius, who again and again had been condemned as a heretic. This confession of faith of Pelagius was written at the time of Innocent I and for him. There are various reasons why the Frankish theologians could accept it as orthodox. In formulating a confession, anyone in danger of losing not only his position, but also his freedom and his life, as Pelagius was, as much as possible would have placed in the foreground that which united his faith with the larger church, what he had in common with it and not what separated him from it. And when he then did speak about what separated him, about his specific views, he would express things in such a way that his difference from the faith of the community would appear as little as possible. So what Pelagius declared at that time does sound very close to the view of the larger church. That is the one thing.

The other reason why the Frankish theologians did not see that the confession of faith was not orthodox, but came from Pelagius, is because to a great extent the Frankish church still stood under Scotch-Irish influence. They could accept the confession of Pelagius, because they— along with the Catholic church in general at that time—only quoted Augustine and praised Augustine, but in reality the most that can be said is that they stood at a point between him and Pelagius; the entire

Catholic church, as we have already emphasized (see pp. 211–12), was dominated under Augustine's name either by an out and out Semi-pelagianism or a Crypto-Semipelagianism.

It was characteristic of the level of theological learning and church life attained in the Frankish empire that the theologians were not satisfied with remaining with these Semi- or Crypto-Semipelagian views dominating the church, but that what could occur was a reaction against this half or whole Semipelagianism, a reaction comparable to that which had once taken place at the conclusion of the Pelagian controversy (see pp. 211–12). Now the relatively complete or original Augustinianism appeared in the Frankish empire as well. First in Fulda and then in the diocese of Reims, the monk Gottschalk, on the basis of a thorough direct study of Augustine's writings, taught the Augustinian doctrine of predestination with a sharpness unheard of at that time. He even did what the so-called Augustinians themselves did not dare to do at the time of the Semipelagian controversy—speak about *praedestinatio gemina*, about double predestination, about God's election of people from the very beginning either to good or to evil. And he was also not the only one who held views of this sort, but a whole series of important theologians of that time, such as Bishop Prudentius of Troyes, formulated them as he did and expressly joined with him.

This Predestination controversy was not imported from outside as were the other theological disputes, but originated in the Frankish church itself. It proves that the Frankish church, which had been so far behind the other provinces of the church, had not only reached their level but even risen above it. This controversy passionately moved the Frankish church. Yet it concluded in the only way that could have been expected: radical Augustinianism did not win out. Rather, Gottschalk finally was condemned and imprisoned in a monastery in 849 where he had to spend the next twenty years until his death. Rabanus Maurus and Hincmar of Reims were the leaders of the opposing side which held an attitude we previously met with Gregory the Great (see pp. 211–12), one which at that time seemed adequate to the church and to Catholicism in general: a truncated Augustinianism which removes decisive things from the Augustinian doctrine in order to incorporate Augustine and his theology into the solidified Catholic church. But not just this Predestination controversy troubled the Carolingian age; there were other disputes which were just as native to it as the Predestination controversy. The Eucharistic controversy between Paschasius Radbertus and Ratramnus was fought just as passionately. From it came the first writings about the

Lord's Supper in the West, additional proof that the Frankish church not only has learned from others, but that it is now in a position to make its own contribution, one which goes beyond what we find in other places.

The literary productions of that time were considerable. Rabanus Maurus (ca. 780–856) and Walafrid Strabo (d. 849) at Reichenau show the sort of significance that monasteries attained as centers of learning in the meantime. Not only did Reichenau, Fulda, and St. Gall produce this sort of thing, but numerous other monasteries furnished authors of high rank: Notker Balbulus ("the Stammerer"), Regino of Prüm, and many others. The overwhelming portion of these highly educated theologians came from the West of the empire, the later France. But we cannot fail to recognize the vitality and success of theological endeavor in the East as well. The Old Saxon biblical poems originated at this time: the Saxon Genesis, the Heliand, the gospel harmony of Ottfried of Weissenburg— a result of the attempt to nourish the vernacular not only in worship services, but also in the entire life of the church. The most significant theological figure of that time was certainly John Scotus Erigena, an Irishman (d. after 877), who now assumed a full position in theological and academic life (even being translated into Greek). He translated writings of Dionysius the Areopagite, Maximus the Confessor, Gregory of Nyssa, and others, thus laying the cornerstone for the level of learning in the high Middle Ages. Erigena prepared the way for scholasticism in the Frankish empire.

All which we have reported belongs to the ninth century or to the period up to the threshold of the tenth century. The cultural, theological, and academic flowering in the Frankish empire lasted beyond the death of Charlemagne (d. 814). The Frankish church was filled with a vital life. It also continued missionary activity. Naturally there are various ways to evaluate the life of a church, but one of the most significant (and not merely in earlier times) is that of the missionary activity proceeding from a church. This Frankish church missionized in the North, especially in Danish territory—this is the age of Ansgar and the missionary bishopric of Hamburg—and this church also proclaimed the gospel among the Slavs (at this time Christian churches were established around Lake Balaton, as well as in Bohemia). The vital life of the church continued. On the other hand, the power of the state was quickly exhausted.

The Demise of the Carolingians

Not even Louis the Pious, who assumed the reign after Charlemagne's death in 814 (the other sons died earlier), was in a position to continue to expand the empire and in fact was not even in a position to hold the massive territory together and to restrain, or at least coordinate, his sons' claims to power. As early as 817 he had to issue a law regulating the succession among his three sons, proof of how weak his position was. At that time it provided that the oldest, Lothair, would receive the imperial crown and the supreme authority, while the other two sons would get portions of the empire. That accorded with Frankish law. Under both the Merovingians and the Carolingians the empire was the personal possession of the ruler. He (just like all other classes) was not only entitled, but required to give his sons equal portions of property at his death. Not until later, when the king was no longer born to office but elected, did this change and the empire become indivisible and had to be passed on in its original size to a successor. Thus under Louis a threefold division of the empire was anticipated, something that was already complicated enough. When a fourth son was born to Louis in a second marriage and provision also had to be made for him under the Frankish law of inheritance, things became even more complicated.

The result of the controversy was that Louis the Pious was deposed from his throne for the first time in 830 by his sons, who fought among themselves but were united in their opposition to him. Lothair assumed the position intended for him. That lasted only for a brief time, since the other sons then became concerned about their brother's supreme authority, and the father again regained his throne, but only for a short time. In 833 they finally—as they thought—deposed him and attempted to prevent his return by having him do public penance. Despite this, Louis came to power a third time. It is obvious that what resulted from this going and coming, from the struggles of the sons among themselves and against their father, was a significant weakening not only of the central authority, but of the empire as a whole. In addition, in 834 the raids of the Normans, against which there was no defense, began in increased measure.

The Frankish armies were invincible on land, but their power ended at the coastline. Charlemagne had therefore begun to build a fleet. But this came to a standstill before it had hardly begun, so that the Franks were virtually defenseless against the Normans coming from the sea who could invade the empire sometimes here, sometimes there (and, following the rivers, could indeed drive deeply into the country). The empire was in danger from within, and the danger from without increased. But there still remained from Charlemagne's time a strong party which wanted with all its might to preserve the unity of the empire. That would at least prevent the worst from happening. But in the long run the dissolution of the Carolingian empire could not be prevented, for the longer time went on the more the German and Roman elements contained in it diverged from one another. The more their own history developed, the stronger grew the consciousness of independence and the centrifugal forces.

When Louis the Pious died in 840, the struggles broke out anew. They grew into a war between the brothers, until the Frankish kingdom was finally divided in the Treaty of Verdun in 843 into three domains: in the West the kingdom of Charles (II) the Bald arose, in the East the kingdom of Louis (II) the German—his name is already characteristic— and between these two kingdoms lay the narrow strip of a middle kingdom, Lotharingia, Lothair's kingdom, which extended from the North Sea to Italy and included, along with the possession of Rome, the imperial office. Only here were Romans and Germans joined in one state. This division did not last long, for Lothair died early (855). He divided his possessions among his sons and thus weakened the otherwise threatened artificial construction of this middle kingdom even more. To a certain extent, the large kingdoms in East and West were compelled to appropriate pieces from this middle kingdom for themselves. In 870 it was divided by the Treaty of Mersen. The imperial crown was given to Charles the Bald in the Western kingdom.

That these struggles among the rulers meant a strengthening of the pope's position is self-evident. As early as the time of Louis the Pious the pope appeared in Germany in order to make peace between the opponents. In 870 when the imperial crown was at stake, the pope could appear as an impartial arbitrator. But with the Treaty of Mersen the end of the development was not yet completed. The weakening of the portions of the empire proceeded apace. When Louis the German, the ruler of the eastern Franks, died in 876, there was a danger that the Eastern kingdom would disintegrate into various segments, since he had three sons, and each of the three would have received a part of the kingdom. But two of the sons died early, so that the unity of the Eastern kingdom was preserved. Unfortunately, the one of the three sons who was the most incapable was the one who lived the longest. Charles III, known as the Fat, was even able to reunite Charlemagne's kingdom almost completely in his own hand. There were disruptions not only in the Eastern kingdom, but also in the Western kingdom, and there the powers feuding among themselves invited Charles III into the country. But the position we see Charles III assuming is deceptive. More and more the kingdom was endangered from outside. In Italy the Arabs were advancing, and the raids of the Normans were devastating West Franconia and Lotharingia, so that Charles III was finally toppled because of his demonstrated incompetence.

In his place a Carolingian was installed once again, but one who might be called a Carolingian of the left hand, Arnulf of Carinthia (887–99), an illegitimate son of Carloman, the brother of Charles III. Arnulf was summoned, however, only by the tribes of the Eastern kingdom. In the other portions of the empire either a rival triumphed or their feeling of independence was already so strongly developed that they no longer wanted to participate in the question of succession anywhere else. What finally resulted was five portions of the empire: East Franconia, West Franconia, Italy, and the two Burgundies. Yet the remembrance of a common history and the greatness of the past was not completely extinguished. There were still powers everywhere which either wanted to restore the original unity or at least preserve as much of it as possible. Therefore Arnulf could still exercise a sort of supremacy over all portions of the empire. West Franconia was so hopelessly sunk in party strife that there Arnulf was almost automatically accorded a position as arbitrator. And all other portions of the empire also oriented themselves more or less toward him, for Arnulf was successful: he could defeat the Normans, and he could meet the invasions from the East. Twice he went to Italy in answer to appeals for help from the popes, so that he also was able to establish a reign over northern Italy at least, although a rather unstable one. He was also crowned emperor, but these beginnings of a possible renewal of Charlemagne's domain could not be developed. This is because when Arnulf died in 899 his son Louis was only six years old, and therefore incapable of ruling. Others ruled in his name, and they did not even give a thought to strengthening the kingdom as much as possible, not to mention restoring or strengthening the old unity. Now the same situation developed in East Franconia as in the West: the local powers emancipated themselves from the central authority, and in addition initiated a struggle against the bishops for power in their territories which lasted, with some interruptions, for generations. The destructive forces from outside could thus do their work more and more strongly. A large part of the southeastern territory fell to Hungary, so that when Louis the Child died in 911 at the age of eighteen, East Franconia was seriously endangered from within as well as from without. The Carolingians suffered an undistinguished demise like that of the Merovingians.

After the death of Louis the Child, Conrad of Franconia was chosen his successor in 911. The idea of summoning the French Carolingians to lead the Eastern kingdom was not even considered. The development of the two kingdoms had diverged too greatly to let them find their way back together; in the meantime they had become virtually separate nations.

And thus we are at the end of the Germanic Middle Ages. Naturally Germany also plays an extraordinary role in the coming centuries. A whole line of great rulers exercised significant political influence even beyond the German borders. Nevertheless, I would claim that we can no longer speak about the Germanic Middle Ages. The age of the Germans has passed. They still exist, but no longer are they a force dominating central Europe as in the preceding centuries. The empire of the Franks no longer exists. It has divided into Roman and Germanic territories which have developed their own life and their own identity. Thus we can no longer include what is now going to be presented under the heading of the Germanic Middle Ages, but if we have to use one title for the following centuries, we must speak about the Catholic Middle Ages. The Catholic faith is the single bond uniting all the peoples of Europe, and the struggle with the papacy which is striving for world dominance is the characteristic mark of these centuries.

II

The Catholic Middle Ages

1. THE PAPAL CLAIM TO SUPREMACY

The papacy's path toward supremacy was initially very difficult. It had inauspicious beginnings, and along the way the papacy also suffered the severest reverses. Under the leading rulers of the coming centuries we see the situation which prevailed under Charlemagne being restored over and over again; again and again state and church relate to one another in the same peculiar way and penetrate one another as they did at that time (see pp. 264–65).

It is impossible to overlook the fact, however, that from the very beginning the papacy clearly strove to attain the goal—even though as a rule it probably was unconscious of what it was doing—which it finally achieved under Innocent III. Again and again popes pushed forward in this direction. In a moment we shall speak about Nicholas I, who is one of those popes who resolutely attempted to bring the papacy along the path to a position alongside—and even above—the empire. These popes indeed failed. But a successor soon arises who in the meantime picks up, as if nothing had happened, at the place where his predecessors had had to stop.

As early as Hadrian I (772–95) such an attitude is apparent. The legend about the Donation of Constantine (see p. 163) which originated at that time was no coincidence, but is evidence of the forces dreaming about an independent position for the church, even one of a place of supremacy. They did that although there was nothing in the political situation of that time which promised any possibility for realizing these dreams. Then when the imperial power grew weaker, this group grew not only in size but also in the claims it made. They were documented by the so-called Pseudo-Isidorian Decretals, a forgery like that of the Donation of Constantine. Characteristically, they originated in the ninth century in the Frankish kingdom, in that area where state and church had apparently achieved the closest alliance with each other.

To the extent that the Carolingian state became weaker, it succumbed to the wishes and demands of this party which supported a strong church. For all practical purposes, Louis the Pious had already created a position for the pope next to himself. In the meantime, devotion and ecclesiastical piety had become so strong that the political components, which in Charlemagne's time had remained within bounds, vanished. The goal set for the empire was lost from sight, and decisions were made on the basis of personal piety, which, viewed from the ruler's position, could not be justified. Thus Pope Nicholas I (858–67) made demands which accorded completely with those of the high Middle Ages. The church should be free from temporal authority, it was said. Temporal authority had no legal claim over possessions of the church but rather had to serve the church. Its laws were valid only to the extent they did not contradict ecclesiastical regulations. The emperor was a vassal of the apostle Peter, that is, a vassal of his successor as well, a vassal of the current pope. That was the program of Nicholas I, one that corresponded exactly with the program of the great popes of the high Middle Ages. Even they could advance it only with great difficulty. It was self-evident that Nicholas I had no hope of doing so in the ninth century. He failed as soon as he raised his claims over against the Greek church, which he included in his claim to supremacy, just as he did the state. Patriarch Photius (858–91) in Constantinople proved himself a match for Nicholas, so that at the conclusion of the controversies the papacy was compelled to surrender because it needed the East's help.

Pope Nicholas's claims to supremacy over the entire church virtually turned the bishops into employees working for the pope and the synods into courts where the pope's decisions were proclaimed (as actually happened later under Innocent III [see p. 329]). These claims grew out of the weakening of the temporal authority. This is the only way their origin can be explained at all. But it proves—and this is a phenomenon that occurs again and again throughout the entire Middle Ages—that the decline of temporal power which generated these claims simultaneously made those claims impossible. At least in its initial period, the decline of the German kingdom did not ultimately have the effect of strengthening the papacy's position, but was a catastrophe for it. This was because the pope was involved in internal Italian struggles as a result of his possession of the States of the Church. As soon as he no longer had a strong central authority behind him, he became subject to internal Italian powers. Over and over again at regular intervals, the papacy, which ultimately destroyed the empire, was helpless in the face of local

Italian forces. This was the law that now went into effect: instead of being subject to the emperor's authority, the pope became the plaything of the Italian noble families. Instead of benefiting from the weakening of the empire, which we might have assumed was inevitable, the papacy suffered a great fall.

It is quite characteristic that, following Nicholas I, seventeen popes succeeded one another in the period from 867 to 914. As soon as the central authority disintegrated, anarchy broke out in Italy. In the Western kingdom there had not been a strong government for a long time, so that what is today France was unable to have any influence beyond its borders. In what is today Germany a similar development also took place. The weaker central authority became, that much more were territorial powers strengthened. They raised greater and greater claims, which we must acknowledge had a certain validity. When the central government disintegrated, they were the ones which had to fight to preserve the German nation—if we can now use that term—against the forces on all sides which were seeking to take over portions of this German state. The Hungarians crossed the Danube, the Slavs advanced as far as the Elbe and the upper Main, and the north Germanic peoples occupied the territories around the estuaries. Thus, there was an acute danger that Germany might also fragment. To a certain extent this could be controlled, for in Germany, in contrast to Italy and France, there was still an alliance between the central authority and the episcopacy. In Germany the bishops were the born opponents of the territorial princes, whom they feared were not only a danger to their property, but also to their position.

2. CHURCH AND STATE UNTIL OTTO THE GREAT

Thus Conrad I of Franconia (911–18) allied himself with the bishops in his struggle against the tribal princes. The bishops were attempting to extend the demands of the papacy over the monarchy. They made the pope's demands their own. We hear them using the same words the curia did. What they meant, however, was something completely different. The bishops were demanding freedom from temporal authority, but they did not intend this to strengthen the papal position, as the pope did when he raised this demand. Instead they intended it to strengthen their own position, for the territorial princes were the temporal authority for them. The effect of this was to strengthen the position of the papacy, and not—as intended—that of the position of the king.

Conrad was able to prevent a complete catastrophe for the kingdom. But his efforts still had no permanent results. At the end of his life, when he installed the strongest of his opponents, Henry the Fowler, as his successor, that was an admission not only of personal defeat, but also defeat of the entire Carolingian system—or we should say the temporary defeat of the entire Carolingian system, for we soon see it growing into a new power under Otto I.

When Conrad made the strongest of his opponents his successor, he clearly recognized that the single possibility for keeping the kingdom together lay in placing the strongest of the powers available at its head. This shows Conrad's personal greatness. Henry I (919–36, the first of the Saxon line of kings and emperors) ran the government, in accordance with his presuppositions, as a representative of the local powers. But the territory over which he reigned bordered on that of the Slavs. In order to preserve the territory he personally possessed, Henry had to fight again and again against the Slavs, thereby strengthening, without intending to, not only the existence but also the consolidation of the kingdom. His struggles against the Hungarians were also not without result. Thus, viewed on the surface, the rule of Henry I does indeed appear to be a weakening of the monarchy. But, practically speaking, here is where the prerequisites for the rapid rise of central power under Otto I were created. Even the fact that the kingdom did not fall apart at that time should be seen as Henry's significant contribution. He created the foundations on which his son Otto I (936–73) could continue to build.

Then under Otto I a fundamental change suddenly occurred—as happened several more times during the period we are considering—in the presuppositions as well as the objectives of the reign. Henry I ruled on the basis of the territorial powers and from their perspective. In contrast, Otto I sought to restore the central authority. Thus, conflicts rapidly developed with the tribal dukes. But because Otto I had inherited a strong territory of his own from his father, he was victorious in these conflicts. He conquered one territory after another and by giving the newly won principalities to members of his family at least indirectly restored the unity of the kingdom. This increase in power then enabled him also to expand the dominion of the kingdom. He could move against the Slavs and force the territory all the way to the Oder to pay tribute. Monasteries and bishoprics were founded in the middle of the Slavic territory as bases for Christianization (although they were also regarded as bulwarks of temporal dominion). Havelberg and Brandenburg were founded at this time. The newly won power of the kingdom also extended in other directions. For the first time Otto could move into Italy. But when it came to this point, the chain of his successes was suddenly broken. In 953 a revolt led by Otto's own son broke out. This shows that the local forces indeed were repressed but had not become powerless. Otto saw that he was in a very difficult situation, one that was made that much worse because an invasion of the kingdom by the Hungarians occurred at the time. A catastrophe appeared imminent. But because the opposition allied itself with the Hungarians and openly favored them, the attitude in the kingdom changed so that Otto could suppress his opponents. When the Hungarians invaded the kingdom anew in 955 he defeated them decisively near Augsburg (at the Lechfeld), finally taming the Hungarian danger. Otto pursued the fleeing Hungarians all the way to the border of the kingdom. From then on their power was exhausted. They settled down so they were no longer a danger to the kingdom, and now missionary work could even begin in their territory. Nevertheless, Otto had to admit that his first attempt at accomplishing this had been a failure. He had been able to establish himself, but at the end of the conflict the strength of the local forces was just as strong as at the time he took over the reign from his father. In light of this situation, Otto now undertook a complete change in his politics.

His father Henry I had been very cool toward the church. He had even rejected anointing and coronation. Otto had been anointed and crowned, but under the father's influence still conducted himself very cautiously toward the church. Now he entered into a close alliance with the church which he had previously ignored. And this alliance between monarchy and church not only became the basis of Otto I's politics, but the basis of German politics of the next centuries.

When Otto turned to the church, the church willingly received him. Not only was the position of the monarchy in danger at that time, but also the position of the bishops and the church in general. The tribal dukes wanted to limit the central authority and enrich themselves at its expense. The lay nobility wanted to do the same thing at the expense of church possessions. Thus a creeping secularization had taken place in the preceding generations. The lay nobility took larger and larger portions of the church's property; the bishops had no means of opposing them, for the monarchy neglected its connection with the bishops. Now Otto's intervention ended this situation. In addition, Otto increased the property of the church by numerous gifts. This took place for two reasons: one is that territory given to the church was not lost to the monarchy in the long run, since these fiefs could not be inherited. In giving royal possessions to the church there was no danger that new local powers might arise, as was the case in secular proceedings. This is because fiefs given to laity could be inherited, and the heirs often enough sought to build them into a position at the expense of the monarchy.

That is the one aspect. The other is that placing territories in the hand of the church guaranteed a much more profitable use of these areas then if they were in temporal hands. At that time the church enjoyed not just a higher level of culture, but also a much higher economic level than the state. The king or other important secular personages could take only very limited advantage of forests or wastelands, but the church was in a position to multiply this advantage—we need only remind ourselves of the way monasteries cultivated vast areas. From this point of view the king supported the extension of the church's possessions and also encouraged their economic development. He gave episcopal sees not merely the right to hold markets, but also the right to mint coins; in this fashion the economic conditions and the living standards of the land began to improve considerably.

Otto I allied himself with the church, that is, he allied himself with the bishops and made this alliance the foundation of his dominion. If this was to bring the desired advantage to the king and the kingdom, the essential presupposition for this was that the king also actually ruled the church and that the bishops in turn felt themselves unconditionally subject to the king and that all other authorities took second place to the authority of the ruler. That was the case under Otto I. The higher clergy of the German church oriented themselves toward the king and felt they were state officials. The bishops and abbots of the kingdom were named by the king, synods took place only with his permission, and so on. The church became not only a financial, but also a political power.

This alliance had decisive advantages for both sides. But it also contained a great danger. The moment the church diverged from the state, when it reflected upon its autonomy and when it saw its supreme authority not in the king or emperor but in the pope, it was not merely the dominion of the king or emperor, but the entire empire that was in deadly danger. Thus the presupposition of Otto's rule and of all the emperors following him was not only the close connection with the German episcopacy, but also dominion over the papacy. Pepin and Charlemagne were still acting freely when they turned toward the South of Europe. From Otto I onward that was no longer true. Pepin and Charlemagne extended their domain over the South in order to round out their area of influence and adorn the rule they were exercising in practice by being consecrated to the royal or imperial office. The German kings from Otto onward acted under necessity. They had to direct their politics toward the South; they had to rule Italy with as strong a hand as possible if they did not want to endanger their own land.

In the past severe criticisms have been raised about the political moves toward the South made by medieval German emperors, but we forget that these kings and emperors had no other choice at all. We should not criticize the Italian politics of the German emperors, but if we want to be critical we must go more deeply and criticize the alliance between the monarchy and the episcopacy. That we can do very easily. This alliance between the bishops and the king was contrary to nature and contradicted the task of the bishops and the position of the church as well. A great deal could be said about this, but as justified as this criticism is, it is just as inappropriate. We must consider the presuppositions of that time and can criticize its special structure only on that basis. And here there is nothing else that can be said except that not only the king, but the bishops as well, had no other choice. If the bishops had refused to ally themselves with the monarchy, not only the external existence but also the internal existence of the German church would have been in great danger. Undoubtedly the autonomous episcopal church, as we may call it, was to a certain extent dominated by the secular points of view. The bishops regarded themselves not only as princes of the church, but to a large extent and sometimes primarily as princes of the empire. But the possibility of real action in the church would certainly have been very much less for them if they had refused the alliance with the monarchy. Then they would have had to use up their power in fighting the lay nobility, and thus would not only have seriously endangered the property of the church, but a creeping secularization would also have done the same for its internal structure.

Under Otto I the supremacy of the monarchy over the papacy posed no difficulty. During his second Italian campaign he received the imperial crown in 962. At that time the pope swore fealty to him, and he did this not only for his own person, but in the name of the institution of the papacy. Not only would he never fall away from the emperor, he declared, but he promised the same for his successors as well. At that time it was established that the consecration of a pope would take place only if he had previously sworn allegiance to the emperor. That was maintained during the entire period Otto ruled. In 967, during his third Italian campaign, his son Otto II was invested with the imperial crown. This son, Otto, was wed to a Byzantine princess. This reflects the heights of power and esteem the German empire reached under Otto I. This height of power and esteem is comparable to that of Charlemagne's time. At this time the German imperial court was one of the centers of the world, at least the center of Europe.

3. THE DEVELOPMENT UNDER THE SUCCESSORS OF OTTO I UNTIL HENRY III

The influence of the German state reached in all directions: to England, to France, to Byzantium, and now in connection with all these new interests—this is the greatness of Otto I—the old responsibilities and the presuppositions behind both were not forgotten. Otto turned toward the South, but in doing so did not neglect the East. By 960 he had already completed the subjugation of the territory as far as the Oder. When he founded the archdiocese of Magdeburg in 968, he was following an ancient dream. But even here he did not ignore the goal at which his politics were aimed, for this new archdiocese of Magdeburg was to be the headquarters for mission among the Slavs. It also pursued this task until Otto's successors decisively limited it. As early as Otto II and much more under Otto III, significant presuppositions of the previous politics were forgotten. The orientation toward the South came more and more sharply into the foreground. By the time of Otto II (973–83), Italy was equal to the actual heartland, and under Otto III (983–1002), the South even had the preeminence. Otto III dreamed—there is no other way to describe it—about the *renovatio imperii*, about the restoration of the empire. But this empire was not the German empire as existed under Charlemagne, for example, but the old Roman Empire. For Otto III the center of his domain was not Germany, but Rome, which he wanted to make the center of the world once again. He dreamed of the emperor, allied with the pope, exercising dominion over the world. That ignored the real possibilities of imperial politics, as well as the structure of the world at that time.

Under Otto II the perspectives by which the ruler conducted his politics had already shifted, and Otto I's system had been weakened. This continued under Otto III. In addition, there was the fact that both rulers reigned for only a brief time. Otto II was only eighteen years old when he came to the throne, and twenty-eight years old when he died.

At that time Otto III was three years old and at first was under the regency of his grandmother and mother; when he acceded to the throne he was fifteen, and when he died he was only twenty-two. Neither ruler was able to attain his own development. If Otto II had been granted a longer reign, the judgment about him would undoubtedly have been positive. In contrast, with Otto III we must judge that it was a blessing to Germany and Europe that he was unable to pursue the realization of his dream any longer than he did.

Otto II remained within the realm of possibilities with his politics, yet under him the beginning of the decline became apparent. In 983 a revolt of the Slavs broke out. This destroyed the basis laid by Otto I for a peaceful penetration and conquest of the eastern border territories, and this applied not only to the empire but also to Christianity. The situation reverted to that of the time before Otto I when Germanic tribes in the Eastern border areas regarded the Slavic territory only as something to be plundered. They continually undertook campaigns in the territory of the Slavs, just as the Franks had done earlier among the Saxons. And unfortunately these campaigns were not just carried out with the sword, but under the auspices of the cross as well, so that the bitterness of the Slavs increased not only against the German state, but also against Christianity which they met in the same way the Saxons previously had (see p. 256).

When Otto III died the situation was even more catastrophic. Characteristic of that were the severe battles that had to be fought in order to bring his body back to Germany from Italy. At that time the East had become virtually independent. Otto III had given the East a certain justification for its drive toward independence, for he had founded the archdiocese of Gniezno, thus removing the East from the ecclesiastical supervision of Magdeburg. The territorial powers renewed their strength. And finally the German bishops had also joined with the secular rulers in opposition to him. This was because Otto III had departed from the fundamental principles of Otto I's politics by abandoning the system of alliances with the church of the bishops and going over to the reform party. He died without issue, so that the power of the empire was weakened additionally by the struggle over the succession, from which Henry II (1002–24) finally emerged victorious. At that time the situation which we observed at the end of the Carolingian rule returned: in Italy anarchy ruled, and Germany was dominated by the struggle with the territorial powers which stood against the central authority. If Henry II could at least to some extent restore the position of the empire, the credit was due to the bishops' church of the Ottos. It had enabled Henry II to win out over the candidates of the lay princes and the other powers who were clamoring for attention at that time.

The support given by this bishops' church of the Ottos received only limited thanks from Henry II. He did reign in the old relationship with the church and the bishops. In fact, he made vigorous use of his authority over the church. In three Italian campaigns he also extended the emperor's dominance over the South. In externals, he followed entirely the course set by Otto I, but in truth drew away from it as he became more and more closely connected with the reform party. And the more the German clergy saw him doing that, the more they came to distrust him. We shall have to say more about the reform party later (see pp. 293–96), for it and its activities come to our attention in wave after wave. If we observe its formation and growth piecemeal, we will lay the basis for a summary evaluation of it in the section dealing with the internal life of the church (see pp. 330–36).

At first we find the reform party in the monasteries. It began by reorganizing them, by strictly subordinating monks to the abbot, and by cleaning out the secularization which had taken considerable hold in monasteries at that time. After reforming the individual monastery, what was achieved here was applied to the relationship between the daughter monasteries and the mother monastery which held strict control over them. Subsequently—this is the third stage of the development—the reform movement took on a direct relationship to the pope, disregarding the episcopacy, so that the monastery of Cluny, where the entire reform movement originated, was subjected to the pope from the very beginning. And what had at first been demanded from the monks was now demanded from the clergy: a life style that accorded with ecclesiastical regulations, chiefly celibacy of the priests. This clerical celibacy was the rule in Germany, but things looked quite different in Italy where marriages or relationships like marriage were the rule at least among the higher clergy. After the demand for clerical celibacy came that for strict morality of life, and the third demand—which from now on came increasingly to dominate the controversy—was for the abolition of simony. This word comes from Simon Magus in Acts 8, who wanted to give the apostles money in order that his laying on of hands might also mediate the Holy Spirit and his power. At first the accusation of simony referred to someone who had obtained a spiritual office by means of a monetary payment. But the word very rapidly took on a broader meaning. It then referred to the lay investiture, that is, practically speaking, the appointment of bishops by the king. The appointment of bishops was traditionally connected with the payment of a fee to the crown. This was important for the empire which was continually suffering from a lack of funds, while the church, as a result of its economic activities, had them available in rich amounts. This payment of a fee, however, had only a secondary significance. This is because the bishop received his office not because of it, but as a result of his fitness or because he displayed other characteristics which recommended him to the king. Although this payment of a fee when one assumed the episcopal office was not really the significant thing, the term simony now came to be used increasingly, in this characteristically broad sense, to apply to the installation of church officials by a layman, the so-called lay investiture. And this catchword possesses the dangerous power of being used in a demagogic way, just as catchwords through all the centuries have. The reform party saw the influence of the state over the church incorporated in this "simony" in a way that the new piety could not endure, and thus anyone fervently condemning "simony" received corresponding approval. That the leading advocates were striving not only for the church's freedom from the state but also for its dominance over it, was something that only later became visible (see p. 290).

We see Henry II open to the influence of the reform party and together with the pope advocating its demands. The surprising thing in this is that it was not the pope but the king who was the real advocate of this demand. The pope did not bring the king along with him, but on the contrary it was the king who was leading the pope—at that time it was Benedict VIII (1012–24), a man who was quite dominated by secular points of view. In this way Henry II still acted as if he were personally captivated by the new piety of the reform party with its ascetic fundamental principle. The German clergy observed this development with the greatest discomfort. Thus a serious feud with Henry II occurred, in which the German bishops were led by Archbishop Aribo of Mainz. They did not fight against the new piety as such, but against its practical results for the structure of the German church. They wanted to have exclusive jurisdiction over their territory and therefore attempted with all their might to deflect any assumption of influence by the papacy. Appeals from Germany to Rome were forbidden, no one could go to Rome without his bishop's permission, no one could absolve anyone from penance imposed on him by a bishop. This was the situation at the conclusion of the rule of the Saxon emperors.

Conrad II, with whom the Franconian (Salian) emperors begin, brought new points of view to the political controversy. He brought into play a third force, which previously we have been able to observe occasionally, but one which so far had been without great significance. Previously the territorial princes and bishops stood in the foreground, but now Conrad II relied on the lower nobility, the so-called deputies. Thus he could observe a certain degree of neutrality in the controversy among the powers struggling against one another. He was not as dependent upon the episcopacy as were his predecessors and thus achieved a new position of power. Henry III (1039–56) utilized this new orientation of the forces under Conrad II. Seen externally, Henry III's reign was successful. Germany became a part of the world of international commerce. Bremen became a center for trade with the North, and Cologne a center for trade with England. Other cities also began to flourish. Henry could extend the domination of the empire over the Hungarians. But even though he was in command of an astonishing amount of strength, he used this strength much more uncertainly and reluctantly than his predecessors had done. Thus an opposition could arise which extracted various concessions from the king. For example, they declared they would accept the bestowal of royal office on his son only if he promised to be a just king, that is, to carry out politics which accorded with their wishes. Thus, Henry III was not able to take advantage of the opportunities offered him.

Because the king was chiefly oriented toward the South, the North developed independently. This was the time of Archbishop Adalbert of Bremen (1043/45–72), whose extraordinarily successful mission was carried out under the banner of independence. He strove for a Northern church which would be independent and led by its own patriarch (that is, naturally, by himself). As far as Finland and Greenland, as far as Iceland extended the activity of the missionary work initiated and led by Adalbert of Bremen.

But also in the South, Henry III could not achieve everything that was possible, although the papacy at that time was filled with unsatisfactory or even completely unworthy ecclesiastical officials. Benedict IX (1032–44) was deposed in 1044, and Silvester III took his place. He was only in office for a few weeks when he had to give way to the returning Benedict. But Benedict did not feel secure in his position, so he transferred his office for one thousand pounds of silver to a confessor, who now assumed the papal throne as Gregory VI (1045–46). It was not that Gregory had raised the thousand pounds of silver by himself, but nevertheless he was closely associated with this payment—simony in the real sense of the word. And it was precisely this pope—from now on the name Gregory refers to a program—who made himself the spokesman of the reform party whose influence became stronger and stronger. This was revealed when Henry III wanted to move into Italy in 1046. In this connection he found that one of the abbots refused to swear loyalty to him. When he proceeded against the bishop of Ravenna, the objection was made that the king was not authorized to render judgment over a bishop. It was true that the clergy owed the king allegiance, but obedience they owed exclusively to the pope. Henry indeed took care of these difficulties without further ado, but that they could even be raised is characteristic of the way things were changing.

Henry III was also under the influence of the new piety. On the way to Rome he first had a synod called in Pavia. This synod passed resolutions against simony and threatened those who practiced it with removal from office and excommunication. That was not the truly remarkable thing which took place, rather it was the fact that Henry, in whose empire the investiture regularly occurred—and in which, therefore, according to ecclesiastical understanding, simony was continuously practiced—expressly renounced any future demand for lay investiture. Under the influence of the renewal movement in the church, the king voluntarily surrendered a decisive portion of the foundation of his own position. Then at a synod in Sutri in 1046 there was an attempt to solve the question of the pope. First Silvester was deposed, then Gregory VI. Gregory went into exile, accompanied at that time by the monk Hildebrand—later Pope Gregory VII—who now enjoyed a continually increasing influence on papal activity. Shortly afterward, Benedict IX was also deposed. There can be no doubt that this was justified at the time. It was more difficult to install a new pope, for the king wanted a candidate from the German episcopate. Finally the bishop of Bamberg was elevated to the papal throne as Clement II (1046–47). It was self-evident that the new pope should crown the emperor, who then, as a result of the situations in Rome and Italy, attained real influence in filling the papal throne. Again and again in the rapidly occurring vacancies of the see, the Roman populace requested the king to name a pope or to confirm the election of the pope which had taken place. That there were energetic representatives of the demands of the reform party among these popes could not be prevented from happening; and the king also did not want to prevent it, for he belonged inwardly to this reform group. Thus Leo IX (1049–54) could obtain the office of the papacy along with confirmation from the king, although from the very beginning there was no doubt about how Leo IX understood the office of the pope and the position of temporal authority. He made the very acceptance of the office dependent on confirmation by the Roman clergy and populace. Consequently, immediately after his accession he began the attempt of building up not just the ecclesiastical, but also the temporal power of the pope.

A fact that should not be overlooked is that in this age it was precisely those popes who took their office seriously who were most involved in politics. The representatives of the reform movement, who wanted to renew the church from within and who were motivated by the ascetic attitude of the time, were precisely the ones who at the same time were striving with all their might—and often with all sorts of means as well—for the increase of the papacy's temporal power. Inwardly that was just as impossible and just as easy to criticize as the connection between the bishops' church of the Ottos and the state. No matter how justified this criticism, it is just as clear that in the final analysis it ignores the presumptions of the age. For these popes, temporal authority unalterably went along with spiritual office, and it was what finally gave that office its full splendor. It was many centuries more before this concept was abandoned, and then it was not done voluntarily but only because of the duress of external circumstances. Even the modern papacy spent many decades before coming to terms with the fact that dominion over the remainder of the States of the Church had been taken from it in 1870 at the unification of Italy. At any rate, we cannot reproach the Middle Ages and their popes for attempting with every means available to establish an empire for themselves in Italy. For them, it was simply part of the complete existence of the papacy and the complete task of the church for the pope, for the church, to exercise dominion over the world as well.

It was only a natural consequence of Leo IX's presumptions for him to make an attempt to extend his dominion over southern Italy. If the pope had realistically evaluated the chances, it would have been clear that attaching southern Italy to the papacy's sphere of dominion would be possible only if an arrangement could be reached with the Normans who at that time ruled southern Italy. The Norman princes were also prepared to subject themselves to the papacy. As we frequently find again during the late Middle Ages (see p. 326), they offered to give the pope dominion over their territory, with the understanding that they would immediately receive it back from him as a fief. Leo IX's concept of himself, however, made it impossible for him to agree to this. Thus, what developed was armed conflict with the Normans and an unavoidable catastrophe for the pope. The emperor did send an army to assist him, but the major portion of this German army did not even reach the area of battle. Under the influence of the German episcopate, which had absolutely no intention of supporting, let alone strengthening the pope's claim to temporal power, the army turned back. The result was a defeat of the papal troops by the Normans. Leo IX was even taken prisoner. Instead of extending the power of the church, he had only reduced it and, in addition, at the same time brought about the catastrophe of an official schism in the church.

At that time southern Italy was territory temporally subject to the Normans but ecclesiastically subject to the Greek Orthodox church. When the pope attempted to extend his temporal authority over southern Italy, that meant he was simultaneously attempting to put an end to the previous position of the Orthodox church there and bring the churches back to Roman Catholicism. The Byzantine church retaliated to the threat to its churches by closing all the Latin churches and monasteries in Constantinople. Thus, a heated controversy developed, until Leo finally sent a delegation to Constantinople. At first it attempted to resolve the conflict by negotiations. When that proved impossible, the papal legates placed a bull of excommunication upon the altar of the church of Santa Sophia in Constantinople on July 16, 1054. It was self-evident that the patriarch of Constantinople retaliate by excommunicating the pope. The Eastern churches followed the lead of the Greek patriarch so that communion between the churches of the East and the church of the West was ended.

This separation has proved to be permanent. It is true that in the following centuries negotiations about union frequently took place (see pp. 402-3). But they were all without results, for underlying them was the presupposition of an immediate threat to the Eastern empire. In the East they were prepared to enter into negotiations about reunion only if they offered some promise for real assistance in the political area. It was political, not ecclesiastical or even spiritual concerns which dominated these negotiations about a possible union. It is true that during the Crusades the West could extend its dominion over the East not only politically, but also ecclesiastically, but this "reunion," which was achieved by force of arms, does not deserve to be called that; moreover, it did not help communion between the churches, but only hurt it. It is from this period of the so-called Latin empire (see p. 328) that we can date the passionate bitterness of the Greek Christians toward the West, which—in a manner of speaking—offered them Catholic Christianity at the point of a sword.

Viewed outwardly, Henry III—to return to him—possessed an extraordinarily powerful position. Nevertheless, it was under his reign that the foundations for the conflict of the next generations were laid. The fact that he also died early, at age thirty-nine, also played a role in this. Again and again the rulers of that time were removed very early before completing their work. His son, Henry IV (1056–1106), was six years old at the time, and therefore there would be a long period before he would assume the reign for himself. Henry IV's mother Agnes and Bishops Anno of Cologne and Adalbert of Bremen together led the government, but sometimes were also at odds with one another. It is self-evident that the fact that the empire was without a real ruler could not help but have an influence on the position of the central authority and the empire. Nevertheless, Adalbert of Bremen was able to maintain the position of the monarchy to a certain extent until the time (about 1070) when Henry IV himself reached for the reins of authority. At that time he immediately steered things back into Otto I's track—this reveals the greatness of this man, the most significant ruler since Otto I. Under him politics took a similar radical swing as they had done with Otto I in comparison with his predecessor Henry I. In addition, Henry IV energetically attempted to advance the position of the king in the direction of an absolute ruler, virtually an absolutistic one. In doing so he first built his support on the lesser lay nobility, just as Conrad II had begun.

Naturally the principalities did not bow to Henry IV's claims, especially because their strength had increased significantly during the time which had passed without a ruler. Thus Henry IV was involved right at the beginning of his reign in a feud with Otto of Northeim. In 1073 the first plot against him took place. It originated in Saxony which Henry regarded as the center of his domain. Here he regularly resided. Here he had fortresses built in order to strengthen his position of power.

According to ancient imperial law, the forces occupying these fortresses had to be provisioned by the populace of the surrounding area. Whenever the king needed money, the screws of taxation were therefore first tightened in Saxony. In order to secure his possessions and his sources of income, he also passed up no opportunity of confiscating estates which had no heirs to claim them. Thus the Saxon nobility, whose bitterness had increased from year to year, revolted. Henry had to flee from this revolt. He found very little support among the princes to whom he went. That is not surprising, for the princes' position was affected just as much as that of the nobility by Henry IV's turn to absolutism. So again and again Henry had to vacillate. At first he could not even count unconditionally on the bishops, for Otto I's system had been too neglected for too long before Henry directly assumed the sovereignty. Only when the bishops were frightened by actual or threatened revolts of the people against their rule did they join more closely with Henry. This enabled him to suppress one opponent after another. He was already beginning to secure the succession of his son Conrad when the conflict with the papacy broke out.

This conflict goes back to the beginning of Henry's reign, when he was still without potential of his own. When Henry IV began to act on his own, in political matters he still followed a course set not by himself but by the influence of the German bishops. Above all, Henry IV, who was not inconsiderably influenced by secular ideas, had no conception of the difficulty of the undertaking on which he was embarking. He failed to see that he was fighting not only against a pope, but attacking an institution, and that he was in opposition to the piety which controlled church and state, that is, the law of the age. This was because Otto I's establishment, which he restored when he took over direct rule, could not endure in the long run. When viewed from the nature of the bishop's office, this connection between the ruler and the episcopate was contrary to nature at that time. As soon as new religious powers awakened, as soon as the church began to renew itself from within, this establishment fell by itself. Any empire which in the age of the reform movement based its real support on the alliance with the episcopate was doomed to lose the battle with the papacy of the high Middle Ages, as long as that papacy could rightly interpret the signs of the time.

4. THE STRUGGLE BETWEEN PAPACY AND EMPIRE UNDER HENRY IV AND HENRY V

In 1057 Pope Stephen IX was already elected without regard to the civil authority, even though the king was subsequently notified of the election. At the court of Stephen IX we also find the two possibilities of opposing the empire represented. Two cardinals, Peter Damian and Humbert of Silva Candida, used their writings and speeches to present the two ways the church could oppose the rulers. In this respect Peter Damian was still relatively restrained. He viewed empire and papacy in the context of the two swords of Luke 22:38, that is, for him papacy and empire were two powers that still stood alongside one another. He did not elevate the pope above the emperor, even though he believed the pope could administer the empire if the throne were vacant. It is understandable that he polemicized against simony. But he was opposed only to simony in the real sense, that is, against the purchase of an office, not against lay investiture as such. The longer time went by—as we see again and again in the course of history—the more this moderate opposition was displaced by the radical one represented by Humbert. In his programmatic writing, *Libri tres adversus Simoniacos* ("Three books against the simoniacs"), he presented the demand for freedom of the papacy from the monarchy and that of the dominion of the church over the world. The installation into an ecclesiastical office—the investiture—could be carried out only by the church, by the church which signified the soul of the world while the monarchy only represented its body. Simony was thus the greatest evil, and not just a narrowly defined simony, but one that was broadly understood. Not just the purchase of an office should be condemned, but installation of a cleric by a layman in general. Lay investiture had brought the church immeasurable damage, for offices conveyed by means of this lay investiture were incapable of mediating the Holy Spirit. The present situation was thus intolerable and had to be changed by any means possible.

Supported by the monk Hildebrand, who had now returned from the exile in which he accompanied Gregory VI, this standpoint of Humbert became more and more firmly established under Stephen IX. As much as lay in his power, Stephen IX attempted to build up his position—not just his spiritual position, but also his temporal one. That this claim of the papacy could not yet be established permanently, is shown by the fact that Stephen IX was followed by a pope (Benedict X, 1058–59) who was installed by Roman nobility who were just as opposed to the papacy's claims as was the German monarchy. The triumph of Nicholas II (1058–61) over this pope was a sign that the temporal power had not read the signs of the time correctly. Although Nicholas II clearly stood under the influence of Cardinal Humbert as well as Hildebrand (who was now gradually rising to a leading position in the curia), the state agreed to his election and not that of Benedict X, and established his rule in Rome with the force of arms.

Under Nicholas II the papacy could decisively strengthen its position. He was now able to find political support in southern Italy. The alliance with the Normans, which Leo IX had angrily refused, was now concluded in the way originally proposed: the Normans surrendered their territory to the pope and immediately received it back as a fief. In this way the papacy now obtained political support in the South. It also quickly found it in the North with the help of the movement of the so-called Patarenes who rose up against the secularized northern Italian episcopate. These Patarenes were a lay movement, and their name was originally an insult which the Patarenes then took over as a title of honor, as has happened again and again throughout history: "Lutherans" and "Pietists," for example, were also originally used by their opponents and had negative connotations. "Pateria" was likely the original name of the quarter in Milan where the ragpickers' market was located. The movement of the Patarenes was motivated not only by social ideas, but primarily by those of the reform movement.

The bishops of northern Italy were not only completely oriented toward Germany, but their entire life style was an offense to the pious. The bishops of Lombardy attempted as best they could to oppose the Patarenes; for example, they excommunicated the insurgents. But their measures had no real success, for there were legates of the pope in the camp of the rebels so that the Lombard bishops finally had to submit to papal authority. Thus strengthened, the papacy could proclaim its claims in their full extent at the Lateran synod of 1059. Here the earlier decrees against marriage of priests were repeated, and then they were strengthened by forbidding the laity to hear mass said by a married priest— something that was in no way a rarity in Italy at that time, evidence of the secularization of the Italian church. In addition, the clergy were forbidden to receive an office from a layman, that is, the synod attacked the lay investiture. Above all else, the synod proclaimed a papal election decree that was intended to exclude foreign influences from the election of a pope. According to the synod's decree, a candidate for the highest office in Christianity had to be elected exclusively from among the cardinal-bishops. Thus a very small circle would carry out the papal election, and even the cardinal-presbyters and cardinal-deacons (that is, the majority of the cardinals) would have only indirect influence. All they could do would be either to accept or reject the candidate elected by the cardinal-bishops. Clergy and people came into the picture only in the third place; their approval was a pure formality. It is obvious that this papal election decree was directed principally against the German king, even if it provided that honor due the king was to be maintained. But it was not only directed against the king, but against the Italian nobility as well. It is characteristic that this papal election decree, which expresses in purest form what we would call papalism, was not only altered immediately but was also not employed by the church in the next generations. It is understandable that the imperial side attempted to alter the papal election decree. A forgery providing for the emperor's participation was inserted in the original text; the way it now read was that the emperor was to be present at the papal election. But the curial side also forged it, since the majority of cardinals felt their rights were limited and altered the text to say that the papal election was to be carried out by all the cardinals.

It is obvious that the German church would not consider acceding to these wishes of the papacy—what the synod decided was certainly nothing more than that. The papal legate sent to the German court was dismissed, and a synod in Worms in 1061 declared the pope deposed. That was the answer of the church of the German bishops which was united against the papal claims. At that time it would still have been possible to enforce the German claims to their complete or virtually complete extent. But as a result of a series of inexcusable omissions, the German church and the German monarchy did not exercise the influence in Rome they could have. After Nicholas II's death, the nobility which had become embittered at the curia because of these events, requested the German government to name a pope. However, nothing was done in Germany. Subsequently Hildebrand, whose influence had become greater and greater, caused Alexander II (1061–73) to be chosen in circumvention of the recently proclaimed election decree, an election that could be established only with the help of the Normans. The circle of reformers in the curia—this is the weakness, indeed the questionableness of their position—did not even consider holding to what they had just decided, but acted purely opportunistically and seized whatever measures appeared suitable to them in achieving their goals.

As a response to this election of Alexander II, the Lombard bishops installed an antipope, Honorius II (1061–64). He was able, with the assistance of an army raised in northern Italy, to enter Rome. In the light of this double election, it was decided in Germany to send an embassy to Italy under the leadership of Anno of Cologne's nephew. This delegation did not now decide as it could have done, or rather as it really should have done, for Honorius, but under Anno's influence, who was dominated in turn by the new piety, for Alexander. Although he could not have expected any support from the German bishops, he was brought with military support to Rome. In view of the conflicts which now ensued between the two popes, even the reform party finally sought the intervention of the German state. Anno of Cologne could appear as an arbitrator at a synod in Mantua where the German and Italian episcopates were assembled. But Honorius refused to appear unless his rights and position were approved in advance. Thus Alexander could dominate the synod. He swore an oath of atonement and was recognized by all the assembled bishops, while Honorius was excommunicated. Nevertheless, the antipope could still maintain his claim, so that now all sides wanted the king to come to Rome. But this did not happen, since the jealousy of the regents for the still underage king took over, and Bishops Anno of Cologne and Adalbert of Bremen, who were struggling with each other for the decisive position in Germany, prohibited Henry IV's journey to Rome.

Honorius died, but Italy did not quiet down, for the pope now experienced difficulties with the Normans. For the third time they wanted the German king to take a hand in Italy, but once again it did not happen. Thus a long series of possibilities for the German monarchy was simply not utilized. When the mistakes that had been made were realized, it was too late. What now happened was that the reform party proceeded against the German episcopacy, which had just rendered it inestimable services. Not only Anno of Cologne, but also the archbishop of Trier, the archbishop of Mainz, and the bishop of Bamberg were cited to Rome, and there were forced to answer the charge of simony. They either had to swear a purification oath that would release them from the accusations made against them, or they could formally promise never again to be guilty of committing simony. The right of the king to name bishops was not just basically disputed, but practically abolished, when the bishop of Constance, for example, who had been named by the king, could not maintain himself against the curia's objection.

The conflict between the German church and the curia beame sharper and sharper. In connection with the dispute over filling the archdiocese of Milan, five Lombard bishops and five councillors of the king were finally excommunicated at a Roman synod. That was the last act of Pope Alexander II. On the very day after he died, Hildebrand was named by acclamation of the people as Pope Gregory VII (1073–85), and this took place with complete disregard of all the regulations applying to the papal election, including the papal election decree recently enacted by the curial party. Only after his election did he obtain the approval of the cardinals. That he took Gregory as his papal name signified that he intended to carry on a program as Gregory VI's successor. Thus from the very beginning his course was clear. Yet it is not true, as the usual understanding has it, that Gregory VII and Henry IV were opposed to one another from the very beginning. On the contrary, both of them, king and pope, attempted to live together peacefully. Gregory VII informed the king of his election and the king raised no objection to it, although—especially according to the papal election decree—that would have been possible. They wanted to get along with one another; it was the way the two, king and pope, understood the inherent opposition of their offices that first led to an increasingly sharp controversy. At least at first, Gregory was also not motivated by real political aspects, but the contrast to the monarchy became apparent to him as a result of his passionate attempt to realize his understanding of his office which presupposed the absolute supremacy of the pope over the church.

At first that was possible only in Italy. If he wanted to see his wishes carried out in Germany, appropriate decrees of a German synod were needed. Gregory therefore attempted to convene a German national council. But the German bishops prevented this with the most varied means. When Gregory wanted to establish his wishes for reform in Germany, he therefore had to go over the heads of the German bishops. First, Gregory assumed a contact with the German churches in continually stronger measure and investigated complaints of clergy directly, for example, without regard to the legal chain of appeal. Second, he proceeded against the German bishops. He continued the practice, begun under Alexander II, of citing German bishops to appear in Rome to answer charges of simony. This happened with the bishops of Mainz, Bamberg, and Augsburg, only the result was now different than previously. The bishops refused to appear before the papal tribunal. Thus, at the Lenten synod of 1075 four German bishops were summarily suspended, and in addition the councillors were excommunicated. The opposition came to a head. Gregory's previous measures were not sufficient to attain his goals, so he used his final weapon and attempted to demolish the foundation of the German bishops' position by moving the frequent condemnations of lay investiture, from what previously had been an essentially theoretical forum, into the arena of practice. He had to do this if he wanted to subordinate the bishops to the papacy in the only way he felt appropriate. Previously they had been installed by the king, and only if this were done exclusively by the pope could they become a constituent part of the new order of the church he envisioned. In this way Gregory's struggle against simony now became a struggle against the king's influence over the episcopate in general. We must add that this direct struggle was not begun by Gregory, but by Henry IV, who was probably not acting completely of his own volition. Rather, it was directly or indirectly forced on him by the German episcopate which was embittered against Rome. Henry probably also did not understand the situation completely. He thought he was fighting against a person. But he was fighting, as we mentioned above (see pp. 292–93), not only against a person at all, but against the institution of the papacy represented by Gregory—and also not just against the institution as such, but the papacy that was supported by the piety of that time. In the last analysis he was fighting against the movement of awakening which permeated the church of those generations, to which any influence of the state over the internal affairs of the church was intolerable, and which moreover felt it essential for the church and people's salvation that this church's influence extend as far as possible, even over temporal affairs.

Henry IV could not have anticipated the full extent of this, for the "high church" *(Hochkirche)* had not yet developed as much in Germany as it had in other lands. Even the German branch of the Cluniacs, who led the "high church" in other places, restrained itself here. Here what was needed was a new wave of awakening—the activity of the Hirsau congregation—to bring about the change in Germany which long ago had occurred in other places. The direct struggle began when Henry responded to the pope's measures in a similar fashion. When the pope attacked the German church, Henry did the same with the Italian. He filled the vacant Italian episcopal sees with German bishops. And he even sent a count, who had been excommunicated by the Lenten synod, into Lombardy to support the bishops there in their struggle against the Patarenes, something that could not help being regarded in Italy as an open provocation. In response, Gregory threatened him with excommunication. The Synod of Worms in 1076 replied to this threat of excommunication by deposing the pope. That took place in a way that was exactly paralleled 230 years later in the struggle of Philip IV of France against Boniface VIII (see pp. 344–45), but this does not make it any more believable. Cardinal Hugo appeared in Worms. He had supported the election of Gregory at the time and was one of the prominent representatives of the reform party, but then had fallen out with Gregory. Now he made himself the leader of Gregory's opponents and appeared at the Synod of Worms accusing the pope of dogmatic as well as moral offenses which were so extravagant that no rational person should really have believed them. However, the synod did believe, or at least gave the appearance of doing so. Thus, the pope was declared deposed and a Lombard synod accepted this decree. Now Henry sent a letter to Gregory which made a reconciliation impossible. That was the letter "to the false monk Hildebrand," which concluded with the famous words: *Descende, descende,* "come down, come down" (from the throne).

When something like this is decided and something like this is written, one must be aware of the consequences. This sort of message could be delivered to Rome at that time only at the head of a substantial army. Henry evaluated the situation completely incorrectly, however, and sent only two legates. They were imprisoned and tortured, and Henry was excommunicated. Not only was he forbidden to rule, but his subjects were released from their oath of allegiance to him. Something like this had never before taken place; although a whole series of popes had been deposed by the German king, never had the pope done the same thing to the king. Not only had the pope's position of power changed decisively, but also the attitude of the time.

Previously the German church had stood united on the side of the king; not only the bishops but even the Cluniacs took up his support. The decision in the controversy between king and pope was brought about by the German princes. When he began, Henry IV had attempted to reign independently, to set up a strict central authority, and to steer an absolutistic course. At first the princes could not defend themselves against this. They had to submit, but they were only waiting for an opportunity to restore and extend their own privileges. After the excommunication of the king and the release of his subjects from their sworn oath, they saw that this opportunity had now come. To what extent this action of the princes was religiously motivated is difficult to determine. Perhaps religious motives played a subordinate role, but obviously what was decisive for the princes' action was their drive for autonomy. They now were participating in the development in which the civil authority in general was becoming emancipated from the church as an institution. This had to do not with an increasing secularization—not with the civil authorities becoming more worldly—but solely with the fact that they were becoming conscious of their autonomy, their "worldliness." They were emancipating themselves as an institution from the influence of the papacy—from the influence of the church—and were proclaiming the autonomy of their position while their personal piety could remain unaffected. This began with the monarchy but then was continued by the nobility of the country. First, the king proclaimed his immediate connection with God: he was installed *gratia dei* ("by the grace of God"), independent from the pope and on his level. Then step by step the princes of the country adopted the same position in reference to themselves.

The territorial principalities turned away from Henry for the reasons we have described. The results were immediately evident. Henry called an assembly of princes in Worms, but hardly a single one of the princes answered his call. In the same way, a diet which Henry summoned in Mainz was attended almost exclusively by bishops. Instead, the princes organized their own diet in Trebur in 1076, and the papal legates participated in it. That appeared to be showing a clear partisanship for the princes and perhaps was also supposed to look that way. But ap pearances were deceiving, for at the same time the legates had a com- mission from the pope to negotiate with Henry and to present the king with a proposal for absolution if he dismissed his councillors who were under the ban, that is, if he changed his policies and his autonomous position, thus—practically speaking—acknowledging the dominance of the church. Henry agreed. He promised to dismiss his councillors, he also promised to write an apology to the pope, and primarily he prom- ised to be obedient in the future. How seriously he took these promises is another question, but in a formal sense they ended the conflict between king and pope.

However, when the German princes invited the pope to come to Germany in order to adjudicate their controversies with the king at a diet, Gregory could not resist the temptation. He withdrew the absolu- tion of the king, which really had been required by the agreement reached between the legates and Henry, and departed for Germany in order to assume what appeared to him to be the promising post of official arbitrator for Germany. When he reached northern Italy, Gregory heard that Henry was coming to meet him. In line with the thinking of the time, the only way he could understand this was that the king wanted to confront him with force. He therefore took refuge in the fortress of Canossa. But what took place was something no one had reckoned with: Henry pleaded for the church's absolution. In spite of several attempts at mediating the matter, Gregory felt he was strong enough to refuse the offer. Thus, Henry used the most powerful means available at that time: on January 25, 1077, and for several days follow- ing, he appeared outside the fortress in penitential clothing. We should not understand this as meaning that Henry stood for days on end in the snow, for this was only a demonstration: several hours a day or at appointed hours of the day he appeared in the garb of a penitent. By doing so he forced the pope to negotiate, for Gregory was not just playing politics, but unveiled power politics. Still Gregory was not merely a politician; he was also a priest. We might even say that it was because he was a priest that he was a politician and power politician, for according to his understanding the exercise of power belonged to the priesthood. But the new piety not only led him to these demands, it also obligated him as well. When approached in this way, the priest saw no alternative but to grant Henry the absolution previously denied, although the politician in him may have rebelled at the compulsion imposed on him by the king's action.

There has been a great deal of dispute over Canossa, and it has been seen as a humiliation of the German monarchy. To a certain extent that is true. But when we view things from the perspective of that time they look considerably different. At any rate, the pope did not regard the episode as a victory, or at most only a victory won very reluctantly, for in it he was robbed of the fruit of his previous politics. Therefore, we must see Henry succeeding in the events surrounding the self-humiliation of the ruler at Canossa. He was set free from the ban. Negotiations also took place in which the pope recognized Henry as the ruler and in which he was even promised support in his struggle against the princes. On the other hand, Henry IV promised only that he would either deal with the princes according to the pope's advice or that he would render satisfaction to him within a limited period of time. By his actions at Canossa, Henry was able to destroy the alliance between papacy and lay principalities. He did that as a precisely considered and calculated action— so much for the explanation of Henry's action. I believe we cannot say that at Canossa, Henry was under the influence of a piety that was forcing him to take an action directly contrary to his office and its demands. He was not acting out of humility in having the representative of the highest temporal authority subject himself to spiritual authority but was really directly attacking the mentality of the other side. And he triumphed, although only for a short time, since the lay princes did not even consider submitting to the papal decision, proof that ultimately they were controlled by secular points of view.

Since their hope of seizing power from the emperor with the pope's help was not fulfilled, the princes now attempted to accomplish this on their own, completely disregarding the situation then existing in the empire which really should have demanded that the princes again be subjected to the king. In 1077 they called their own assembly of princes in Forchheim and deposed Henry on their own authority. In his place they selected Rudolf of Swabia. Significantly, only a few bishops were present at this assembly of the princes, but it was just as significant that papal legates were there. This was because Gregory was trying to escape what he had been forced to concede at Canossa. The legates did have instructions not to take part in the deliberations of the princes, but characteristically they were also instructed to undertake nothing against what the princes decided. Gregory was probably quite pleased with the decision of the princes, for what they did was formally reestablish the position he had held before Canossa. After the priest had triumphed over the politician at that time, the politician was now triumphing over the priest, and this likewise was happening without regard to the real situation in the empire. The princes had gone beyond the law not only by holding the election, but also by making Rudolf recognize certain provisions: in the future the crown was to be passed on by free election, and so on.

Gregory conducted himself cautiously at first. Apparently it was not easy for him to act against that to which he had agreed at Canossa. But as the struggles in Germany went increasingly against Henry, Gregory gradually turned his support more and more openly toward the opposition king. When both kings, one after another, asked the pope to excommunicate their opponents, the pope decided, after some hesitation, to excommunicate Henry. Not only did he excommunicate the king, but he now even went so far as to prophesy his imminent death.

All the old demands were renewed: lay investiture was forbidden, and the election of bishops was to be arranged by the pope or the archbishop. If the election were irregular, the pope or archbishop had the right to name the candidate. Rudolf of Swabia was recognized as king but significantly only as king of Germany, not as king of Italy, which the pope reserved for his own influence.

However, things did not turn out as Gregory wished and as he— ridicuously—had prophesied. The German church appeared to be little impressed by the pope's action. It continued to stand by Henry IV and replied to the deposition of the king by deposing the pope at several synods and finally placing an antipope, Clement III (1080–1100), in opposition to him. Six months after the pope imposed the ban and prophesied Henry's death, a new battle occurred between the king and his opponent. Henry was defeated, but because Rudolf of Swabia was wounded the situation changed. Rudolf of Swabia lost a hand—it is still displayed today in the Merseburg cathedral—and he died of the wound. Thus Gregory's prophecy did not come true, but the conflict was not yet over for Henry. Now it was carried on under a completely new aspect. Three times he took an army to Rome, and the third time—that was in the year 1083—he was able to capture the city. He now concluded a dual treaty with the Romans: an official one which provided for an armistice and the convoking of a synod. At this synod the dispute between the king and the pope was to be smoothed over. That was the official treaty. In a secret agreement, however, the Romans promised to compel the pope to crown the emperor. In case the pope refused, they declared themselves prepared to elect an antipope. The synod met. At first things went according to the official agreement, but Gregory refused to withdraw the ban. He would crown Henry only if he first did public penance. That was a flat rejection. Now the secret agreement came into play. Almost the entire curia turned against Gregory, and almost the entire city administration forsook him and declared itself for Henry. In 1084 a Roman synod declared Gregory VII deposed and once again chose Clement III as pope. Clement III performed Henry IV's coronation, while Gregory VII withdrew into the Castel Sant'Angelo.

Here Gregory was certainly safe, for no one was in a position to storm this strong fortress, but still he had to look on helplessly at what was taking place around him. With the help of the Normans he attempted to regain power. At first he was successful, for when confronted with the approach of the strong Norman army, Henry had to abandon Rome. But it was the appeal to the Normans which sealed Gregory VII's fall. The Normans conquered the city and conducted themselves so horribly in it that Gregory VII, when the Norman army withdrew, had to leave with it if he wanted to remain alive. Gregory died on May 25, 1085, aware of his total defeat. Until his dying day he tirelessly attempted to stir up new opponents against the king, but to no avail. It is true that the struggles in Germany continued, for the princes did not abandon their cause. When Rudolf of Swabia died, they chose a successor for him. But step by step Henry's influence grew and the position of the princes became weaker. In this he was supported by the people's longing for peace. Germany had been heavily afflicted by the continual struggles. Not just the political, but the ecclesiastical dividedness as well, no longer appeared endurable, for in the meantime most of the dioceses had been filled by both popes with two bishops who were passionately fighting each other, similar to the situation we see later in the Great Schism (see pp. 350–51). Thus Henry, when he proclaimed the *Treuga Dei,* the peace of God, could be certain not only of everyone's sympathy, but of their support as well.

Henry appeared to be the victor and the princes finally destroyed, when Henry's son Conrad suddenly went over to the side of the rebels and the pope. Henry also defeated this opponent. Again victory appeared certain for him. But now another son, the later Henry V, rose up against him and found support with a number of German bishops. Henry V's revolt was based on the premise that no one was bound to obey someone whom the pope had banned. But despite this ecclesiastical motivation, it became clearer and clearer that those who exercised temporal authority were acting on the basis of nonecclesiastical points of view, and only using churchly arguments when it appeared to them to serve the purpose of attaining their goals. The armies were mobilized against each other. However, a battle did not take place, because Henry V declared he would subject himself to his father if he made peace with Rome. The father promised to do so, and both armies were disbanded. Apparently in agreement, father and son set off for Mainz until Henry V had his father taken prisoner by his entourage while underway. Here we can see how modern the twelfth century already was—how unscrupulously they acted in disregarding oaths and all similar promises. But even this apparently final defeat could not suppress Henry IV. He regained his freedom and successfully followed the path to dominance a fourth time. He had triumphed against all opposition by the time death took him in the year 1106. The church's hatred followed him to the grave, however. Henry IV had wanted to be buried in Speyer. At first he was buried in the place where he died, but at the command of the papal legate the coffin was exhumed and placed in an unconsecrated chapel. There it remained until Henry V had it brought to Speyer. Not until five years after his death did Henry IV find his final rest in the cathedral there after a turbulent and varied life.

One would like to believe that it would be impossible to surpass what we observe during Henry IV's time. Yet it happened with Henry V (1106–25). Under him the investiture controversy, the struggle between kingdom and papacy, came to an end. The battles had gone on so long and so much devastation had been caused, that the desire for peace spread more and more widely and forced compromises from the representatives of the struggling temporal and ecclesiastical powers. But before that happened we see the struggle still raging at its height. Once again both sides proclaimed their radical claims and defended them to the end, so that it seemed as if no way out could be found. But—a law which we observe again and again in history—this flare-up of the opposing sides obscured the real situation; in it only the final powers were exhausted, and suddenly it was apparent that the struggle had reached the stage of agony.

Henry V's position at the beginning of the conflict was not very strong. He had contributed decisively to the fact that the territorial princes had finally become an autonomous force. Successful governing could now be carried out only if the king developed a positive relationship to the territorial princes, on whom he was principally dependent when he had to fight against an external opponent. However, initially Henry V was not prepared to give in on the question of investiture. He demanded the participation of the king not only in the election of bishops, but also in their consecration. The investiture with the regalia, the insignia of temporal office, he declared to be the king's exclusive right, which he was free to exercise in any way he chose. The church and pope were accorded only the purely spiritual side. On the other hand, the current pope, Paschal II (1099–1118), twice forbade investiture until—after Henry invaded Italy and triumphed everywhere—he made a proposal to the king which, if adopted, would have meant a turning point in the history of the church.

The pope, supported and influenced by that piety which wanted to remove the church from the world, proposed that the crown completely renounce the investiture of bishops. The spiritual office should be filled and administered solely by the church. In return for this, the church would give up all positions in the kingdom which it had held as fiefs since Charlemagne. The only things that would remain in the hands of the bishops would be private donations, the right of the tithe, and the personal property of the dioceses. Obviously excluded from this would be the States of the Church, which had already been deprived of temporal power under Henry IV. The pope promised to crown Henry V as emperor and to force the bishops under threat of excommunication not only to recognize him, but also to observe this treaty, while the king on his part swore not to encroach on the dignities, freedom, and life of the pope.

That is the treaty of February 4, 1111. If it had been put into effect, the papacy obviously would not have become a purely spiritual power, for the papacy still retained the possession of the States of the Church. And the bishops also would not have become purely spiritual rulers, for they still would have retained vast temporal possessions. Nevertheless, at least the clergy—but probably the church as well—would have been directed back to their real spiritual task by this treaty. This would have given a completely different course to the history of the church. By concentrating its power on its real task, the church would have been able to exercise a completely different sort of control over souls than it did in the following age, and it might have been spared a great deal of painful history. But Paschal II, who took what he proposed seriously, did not understand the situation. As highly as his proposal was regarded and as nobly as it was made—seen from the church's point of view—it was also just as much a utopian solution when considered from the realities of that time. It was impossible to realize such a proposal. It would be passionately opposed by the bishops as well as all the temporal powers. If the possessions which had come to the church during the course of the last four centuries were to be given back to the state, the king and the central authority would attain a completely new position. Not only would the bishops have lost their previous position of power, but the territorial princes would also become powerless, first because of the new strength of the king and then also probably because the demand for return of royal fiefs would probably not cease with those of the bishops, but would extend to those of all other estates.

Apparently Henry saw that quite clearly from the very outset. Accordingly, he arranged a way of placing the pope in an untenable situation. He summoned an assembly in St. Peter's Church. Outside the assembly stood troops, which shows how carefully Henry had calculated the situation. He not only wanted to put the pope in an untenable and impossible situation, but at the same time he also wanted to use the opportunity to bring the church under his power. The reason for the troops' presence sounded plausible. A rumor had been spread that a coup d'état would be attempted, and the troops were necessary to protect the assembly from the coup. The king first delivered an address to the assembly, formally guaranteeing the church all its property. Obviously he did not mean this speech seriously; it was only intended to provide the necessary background for what followed, for when following this speech the treaty with the pope was read, all the guilt for what was agreed upon there—all the blame for transferring the property and the power connected with it—was ascribed to the pope. It was not only the bishops, but also the princes who were extremely irritated, even enraged. It was impossible for them to accept this edict; just to be sure, they immediately declared it heretical. Henry thereupon took the full right of investiture upon himself, as well as the coronation promised by the pope. The pope refused to comply with this. Thereupon the king declared that the treaty had been broken and was invalid, and he had the pope and cardinals seized by the waiting troops.

At first the pope steadfastly refused to do what was demanded of him, but what choice did he have? He agreed to crown the emperor, he permitted the emperor to continue practicing lay investiture as before, and finally he had to make the suicidal promise that he never again would impose a ban upon the emperor. Only after that did Henry free him. It is true that at the same time he promised obedience to the pope, but with the significant limitation that this would be only insofar as such obedience did not violate the laws of the empire. Henry triumphed completely through the coldbloodedness, not to mention the untruthfulness, with which he acted.

At any rate, he should have been aware that this victory could not endure and that this was not only because of the means he used, but also because it conflicted with the constellation of powers as well as the "spirit of the time." As soon as Henry left Italy, a Lateran synod in 1112 declared the agreement between pope and emperor invalid. Other synods at that time even excommunicated the emperor. At first the pope acted somewhat hesitantly because of the promise he had given. Not until Henry again moved into Italy, did the pope seize his final weapon and punish Henry V by excommunication, which now was partially recognized even in Germany. The contrasting positions were once again carried to their ultimate extremes; each side adopted the most radical stances, and both used the sharpest means against the other, until all at once it became clear that all of this was nothing but a desperate attempt to impose their own desires in the hope that what was really impossible could still be made possible. At the same time they were already aware that this would not work and that they would have to seek a compromise. In the year 1122 they met at a synod in Worms, and at this synod the controversy was solved by a compromise. An armistice between Henry V and the German princes had preceded this synod, so that the emperor was aware that he had a united empire behind him. On September 23, 1122, he renounced—this is the Concordat of Worms—the investiture of bishops. However, it provided that the election would take place in his presence or in the presence of his representative, so that the king would still have indirect influence on the conduct of the election. If the election were disputed, he would undertake the function of an arbitrator and award the office to the party who appeared to be in the right. Those were the provisions concerning the election. Then with his scepter the king would invest the one elected with the regalia signifying his temporal possessions. In Germany that would take place before the ecclesiastical consecration, so that the king received a second opportunity to exercise his influence over the filling of the office. In Italy and in Burgundy the investiture would take place after the bishop's consecration, and here the king's position was accordingly weaker. In addition, the States of the Church were excluded from the agreement altogether.

There all the rights of investiture were in the hands of the pope. This was the solution which was adopted for Germany. Shortly before, in France and England similar agreements had been reached; in England the king retained the feudal oath and in France approval of the election by the temporal power became the rule. But there the autonomy of the ecclesiastical office was also recognized, along with the church's unlimited right to do as it pleased with its offices. This was the way that time came to terms with the realities of the age.

Seen through the eyes of Gregory VII, this was a severe defeat for the papacy. For Gregory VII and all who were influenced by his spirit, the pope was the spiritual ruler of the world, and here the emphasis lay upon "ruler," for it was necessary that the temporal authority be subordinate to the spiritual. The pope was the ruler of the world, the supreme authority, even more than the supreme authority, for it was he who established authority. The successor of Peter was the one who proclaimed the divine will which could brook no opposition. The successor of Peter was holy and as unerring as the church itself. From this comes the right—indeed the obligation—of the pope to appoint princes, to depose rulers, and to absolve subjects of their allegiance if he considers it necessary. That was Gregory VII's demand, not because Gregory VII was striving primarily for political power, but because—just to repeat it—his understanding of the spiritual office had no room for any other conception. Gregory VII failed with his claim; not until Innocent III was it achieved. It is correct that this success of Innocent III was possible only against the background of a very special constellation in the German kingdom (see pp. 315–18). But that does not change the situation that in fact Innocent III acted not only unrestrictedly as a spiritual ruler but also just as unrestrictedly as ruler over the principalities of the world, which unresistingly accorded him this supreme position.

5. THE COLLAPSE OF THE GERMAN KINGDOM AND THE RISE OF THE PAPACY AS A WORLD POWER

With Henry V the line of Franconian emperors came to an end. Henry's successor was Lothair of Supplinburg (1125–37), who was a representative of the Saxon line which had been the chief contender against Henry. Lothair triumphed over Henry V's candidate, a Hohenstaufen, and at this time began the opposition between the Welfs and Hohenstaufens which lasted for generations. Not until after Lothair's death could the Hohenstaufens come to power with Conrad III (1138–52). Lothair already clearly stood under the influence of the new piety which was exemplified at that time in the personality and activity of Bernard of Clairvaux (1091–1153). The church had the decisive influence in Conrad's election—not the autonomous church of the bishops any more, but the high church which had become newly conscious of its independence and power. It was the church's doing that the Hohenstaufens achieved dominion in the person of Conrad III, for he had been completely under its influence. If he is also known as the priests' king, that is not to be regarded as negatively as it sounds today. For example, when he became acquainted with another type of government in the East during the Second Crusade, Conrad attempted to make himself more independent of the church's tutelege. But he was unsuccessful in this because of the distribution of power at that time.

It is characteristic of the piety of Conrad III that he entered into correspondence with Hildegard of Bingen, a leading representative of German mysticism (see pp. 390–92), and also characteristic that, when he left Germany for the crusade, Archbishop Henry of Mainz was not only given the formal authority over the government, but that he actually administered it as the ruler of Germany.

Conrad could not triumph over the superior influence of the church. He was also incapable of opposing the power of the Welfs which at that time was extending farther and farther toward the East. Although Henry the Lion was only ten years old when his father died, the Saxon dominance could be secured for him, that dominance which under his leadership led to an increasing opposition of the Welfs and Hohenstaufens. Conrad III's successor, Frederick I Barbarossa (1152–90), was also selected as a result of a compromise between the Hohenstaufens and the Welfs. He was Conrad's nephew, therefore a Hohenstaufen, but at the same time a cousin of Henry the Lion, thus united by blood with both the houses struggling for power. And—this third consideration was the decisive one—he appeared to be continuing Conrad's ecclesiastical line. Thus, Frederick I Barbarossa came to the throne. But to everyone's real surprise, Frederick broke radically with the inherited traditions. He did not accept the agreements made at Worms but attempted to turn the clock back to the time before Worms—although things had changed considerably since then—by exercising direct influence over filling the bishops' thrones. For example, an expression of this was the way he established his candidate in Magdeburg, Archbishop Wichmann, despite resistance. He also based his rule on a completely new foundation by attempting to increase the power of his house in Italy. Here in Italy the essentials of an independent position of the empire had existed since the time of Charlemagne. The German king still possessed extraordinary possessions and rights in Italy, that is, opportunities for extraordinary income. In the meantime these possessions and rights had been alienated from the monarchy in various ways; if the monarchy could regain them, it would not only achieve independence from the powers in the empire, but also attain a position over them. On the surface, with his Italian campaigns Frederick Barbarossa appeared to be continuing the line which we have observed since Otto I. But the motives which impelled him were completely different from those of his predecessors, and the same thing was true of his successor. At that time the German kings were just as oriented toward the South as the previous ones had been, but the idea that the king had to dominate the papacy, which had earlier been the decisive consideration, now had only a subordinate significance.

When Barbarossa marched into Italy for the first time in 1154, he did so at the request of the pope. The papacy, which had already made such high claims under Gregory VII, now came into a difficult situation because of the very powers which enabled it to make those high claims at that time. The ascetic concept which had made the church great—which not only had made it capable of combating the empire, but had even compelled it to—this ascetic concept now began to turn against the church. Even while the church was in the process of triumphing over the central authority—and totally thereafter—the church itself became secularized and denied (even fought against) the ideals which earlier had motivated it. We have seen that it was precisely the strongest popes—the popes who made the demands of the reform movement their own—who strove for temporal authority in a special way (see p. 290). They did not do this for the sake of temporal authority as such, but because authority over Italy (authority over Europe) seemed to them an unalterable component of their office. But after the papacy achieved authority, it was overcome and corrupted by it. Now the pious no longer protested exclusively against the emperor. Naturally they continued those protests whenever and wherever they felt the emperor was interfering inadmissibly in the church, but they now also protested against the secularized papacy.

The leader of this attitude at that time was Arnold of Brescia (ca. 1100—55). He declared that the church should renounce earthly possessions. The clergy should seek their example not in the rulers of this world, but in the life of Jesus and the apostles who were poor and possessed nothing. A priest had nothing except such a claim to obedience; but obedience should be refused to an unworthy priest. These were precisely the demands of the ecclesiastical reform movement, but now they had turned 180 degrees and were aimed at the church. Arnold wanted to restore the greatness of Rome, but not with the church's help, rather as a leader of the people not only in opposition to the emperor, but also to the pope and the church.

The movement initiated and led by Arnold became so strong that the papacy could ward it off only when Hadrian IV (1154–59) imposed an interdict on the city of Rome, that is, prohibited all ministrations of the church. Because of this Arnold had to leave the city, but the danger that was inherent in the movement was not yet tamed. It was hoped that Frederick Barbarossa would do that, and therefore the pope summoned him to Italy. At first he did what was expected of him and delivered Arnold to the papacy for execution. In gratitude for that he was crowned emperor. But he prematurely discontinued his Italian campaign before completing the subjugation of all of Italy which was expected of him, and returned to Germany. He was still at the beginning of his reign and first wanted to secure his position there. He did this in various ways. First he married the heiress of Franche-Comté, not only increasing his territory but also securing the empire against the West. He could also strengthen the position of the empire in the North and East. The Danish king received his domain from him as a fief, the separation of Silesia from Poland was initiated, and Bohemia was more closely connected to the empire. Only when the stability of the empire was thus assured did Barbarossa again turn toward Italy, this time motivated by the conflict with the papacy.

This is because a serious conflict had arisen at the diet of Besançon in 1157. Here a papal legate, the later Pope Alexander III, appeared and delivered a letter from Pope Hadrian IV to the emperor. It was read (that is, translated into German) by Frederick's chancellor, Rainald of Dassel. In the pope's letter it was said that the pope had conveyed to the emperor the plentitude of power and the crown. Then it spoke about the *beneficia* which the papacy had given the emperor. The term *"beneficium"* was ambiguous; it could mean "blessing," but it could also mean "fief." Rainald of Dassel now translated it not as "blessing," but as "fief," and intentionally so. What occurred was a repetition of what we observed as early as Henry IV and then especially under Henry V. The Middle Ages were already operating with a cunning and with methods that instinctively appear to us to be the province of the modern world.

An uproar arose, and one of the princes stepped before the legates with an unsheathed sword. But although a member of the papal delegation even shouted: "From whom does the emperor get the *imperium* ("empire"), if not from the pope?" the worst could be avoided. All that happened was that the delegation was sent back to Rome and the visitation it was supposed to carry out was prohibited. This time Henry IV's mistake was not repeated (see p. 300), for the emperor immediately set out after the expelled delegation at the head of an army. He also carefully prepared propaganda for his expedition and had letters circulated which made the king's attitude toward the relationship of both powers clear to everyone. It was only necessary to state what had already been proclaimed at the election: *regnum* ("kingdom") and *sacerdotium* ("priesthood") were on an equal level, papacy and monarchy both traced their origin directly to God. The *imperium* ("power") was not based upon a grant by the pope, but on an election by the princes. The pope attempted to play the German bishops off against this, but to no avail. They only forwarded his letters to the emperor, and their attitude mirrored only this understanding: the crown is a divine gift; the coronation signified nothing except an additional sacred act and not something fundamentally new. Accordingly, the pope changed his mind and declared with (apparent) indignation that he was amazed at the general excitement. When he had spoken about *beneficia,* it was self-evident that he had meant "blessings," and the papacy had certainly bestowed them upon the kingdom in great measure.

He had also spoken about giving the emperor the crown. That was certainly correct, for he had placed it on his head—that was all he meant. The pope had given in when confronted with Frederick's army against which no resistance was possible. Northern and central Italy were tightly incorporated in the empire at that time. When Pope Hadrian died, it was not by chance that a double election occurred. The majority chose Alexander III (1159–81), the legate of Besançon, about whose position we need to say nothing more in the light of his activity there. A minority chose Victor IV (1159–64), who was supported not only by the emperor but also by a large synod at Pavia. But England and France declared themselves in favor of Alexander so that the emperor could not ultimately triumph over the pope. His Italian expedition was indeed a success, but the goals involved in it were not completely attained, precisely because of the opposition of England and France, which now appeared as major European powers alongside Germany and exercised influence not only on Italian affairs but even on German affairs themselves.

Frederick's Italian politics, which previously had been so successful, were now pursued less energetically and produced correspondingly weaker results. Frederick had to abandon his fourth Italian expedition because malaria broke out in his army, also claiming Rainald of Dassel as a victim, a severe loss for imperial politics. The next Italian campaign, at least on the surface, turned into a disaster, for at the battle of Legnano in 1176 Barbarossa was defeated for the first time. His army was too weak, for Henry the Lion had not sent the contingent of troops he had promised. Frederick had to return to Germany and initially spend time correcting the reasons for his defeat. Previously the Welfs and Hohenstaufens had lived alongside one another. The Welfs could pursue their Eastern politics because they were certain of the emperor's support if needed, and the emperor could pursue his Italian politics because the Welfs supported him. Now that was at an end. Henry the Lion attempted to test his strength. Things went as might be expected, and he had to submit to the emperor in 1181. Nevertheless, the power of the emperor was not what it used to be and his possibilities were fewer, for it took Frederick a long time before he could make up for the blow at Legnano.

Only gradually had his position in Italy risen to the point where it resembled what it had previously been. But then he met his death on a crusade he had undertaken. He died in 1190 while riding his horse across the Calycadnus River. That was the end of an entire epoch.

His son Henry VI (1190–97) at first was confronted with many difficulties, for Henry the Lion had not abandoned his opposition and was supported by England. In addition, there was the fact that Henry VI emphasized the central authority too strongly when he assumed the reign (just as Henry IV had done in his age), so that the territorial princes hesitated to support him. If Henry VI had not had the extraordinary good fortune of having the English king Richard the Lion-Hearted imprisoned in Germany, his reign probably would have been less successful. Richard the Lion-Hearted had undertaken a crusade, but the crusade failed. In returning to England he had to traverse German territory because England and France were irreconcilable opponents. He attempted in vain to cross Germany without being recognized. In spite of his disguise he was recognized and kept prisoner until Henry VI had attained all his goals. This took place so cold-bloodedly, so cynically, indeed so completely unconscionably that we are apt to think we are in the modern age. But we have previously met the modern cold cunning which does not accord with the romantic image of the Middle Ages (see p. 305). The age of chivalry, if it ever existed, was long past on all sides. Rather, power politics was being played here, with all the marks that apply to power politics. First, Richard the Lion-Hearted had to pay an immense ransom. Then he had to receive his country from Henry VI as a fief. Finally he had to compel the German princes, who were closely or loosely allied with him because he supported their opposition to the central authority, to submit to the German emperor. With the help of this one prisoner, whom he himself had not even captured, Henry VI could achieve such an extraordinarily strong position in Germany. The same applied to Italy, for the second Italian campaign brought results for Henry which went far beyond those which Frederick Barbarossa had ever achieved. Henry drove far into the South, he conquered Sicily and had himself crowned king of the Normans.

These successes in Italy in turn strengthened his position in Germany, so that Henry VI ultimately possessed an astonishing position of strength. He declared that he could dispose of the heritage of the Normans, that is, he assumed rights of ownership in Africa and sections of the Balkans. He planned campaigns against France and Spain, and his plans even included a campaign against Byzantium. But these plans, which are reminiscent of Otto III's ideas of world dominion (see p. 284), cannot merely be described as flights of fancy and delusions of power, for all of them were not without certain possibilities of being realized. A crusade was supposed to prove the dominant position of Henry VI, but his sudden death in the year 1197 after only an eight-year reign brought all of this to nought. The domination of the world which the German emperor thought within his grasp was now assumed by the pope—by Innocent III, who ascended the papal throne on January 8, 1198, and under the auspices of the church could accomplish everything which Henry VI had planned. This was because Germany was incapacitated by a dual monarchy for nearly twenty years after Henry's death. The North spent its powers in the battles between the two kings, behind which stood the ancient antagonism of the Hohenstaufens and Welfs. It is true that a year before his death Henry VI already had his son elected the king of Germany. But no one seriously considered him for the succession, although according to the law of inheritance he should have been the legal successor. The one group which wanted a Hohenstaufen as king advanced the twenty-year-old Philip of Swabia as king. And the followers of the Welfs chose Henry the Lion's second son, Otto IV of

Brunswick, as king, although he was only sixteen years old at the time. Behind the Welfs and Otto of Brunswick stood England, which since Henry the Lion's time had been seeking an influence in German politics, and in a corresponding way Philip of France stood behind Philip of Swabia. Philip was practically under the ban, but that bothered no one. When the papacy took up Otto IV of Brunswick's side, it did not do so on that account, but because of the reasons expressed in Innocent III's *Deliberatio* ("Deliberation") which he presented before a secret consistory of the cardinals. Innocent III opposed Philip of Swabia because he belonged to the line of the persecutors—because he was a Hohenstaufen. Again and again the Hohenstaufen kings and emperors had opposed the claims of the papacy, again and again they had brought the papacy to the brink of disaster, so the papacy almost automatically turned to the opposition candidate, who Innocent could say was loyal to the church and came from a line loyal to the church and the papacy. In fact, Otto IV also responded to the pope with expressions of deepest respect, and it appeared as if the papacy had made the proper selection.

But the papacy had made a mistake. The Hohenstaufens were indeed exponents of the antipapal politics of the Middle Ages, but their politics were not specifically characteristic of the Hohenstaufen house. The politics the Hohenstaufens played and the attitude they took was occasioned by the requirements of the central authority; any other ruling family would have acted in exactly the same way. It is significant that Otto IV, as soon as he was freed from the necessity of subjecting himself to the pope, followed the same political course as the Hohenstaufens. If the papacy persecuted the Hohenstaufens with bitter hatred to the very end and used all the means at its command—including illegitimate ones—the explanation for this is that the Hohenstaufens at that time were the strongest power in Germany. But if the papacy's action against Philip of Swabia was caused because he belonged to the house of persecutors, then the bearers of the papal office were looking only at the surface, not at the powers which were really at work.

At first Innocent could restrain himself, for Otto IV was successful. But the tide soon turned. Philip gained decisive military advantages in the year 1204. In addition, he had himself crowned by the archbishop of Cologne at Aachen in 1205. That was extraordinarily important for that time, since Aachen was the proper site for the coronation, and the archbishop of Cologne was the proper man to perform it. Thus the coronation took place at the right place and in the right way. At that time Otto IV, who urgently needed support, had to pay the price demanded by the papacy. He acknowledged all its possessions, including Sicily, though obviously not with the intention of holding to this promise, but rather because he had no other choice but to do so and wait for the moment when he would obtain a free hand to pursue the politics which appeared to him to be his only chance—politics which agreed completely with those of the Hohenstaufens.

That moment occurred a few years after Otto's cause appeared to be lost, when the victorious Philip of Swabia was murdered by Otto of Wittelsbach in the year 1208. At that moment, to the dismay of the curia which believed it was safe from him, we see Otto IV setting off on the old course of the German emperors. He marched into Italy and drove as far as Sicily, doing this not at the pope's behest and in his name, but subjugating these areas in his own name just as his predecessors had done. Consequently, Innocent III excommunicated Otto IV and, contrary to all his principles and the politics of all his predecessors, turned to the Hohenstaufens, despite all the ill feelings which had grown up toward them. Henry IV's son, Frederick II (1212–50), was now put forth as king in opposition to Otto IV. Frederick II obviously had to promise the church everything it wished, despite the fact that he later revealed himself as even more emancipated from the church—indeed virtually from Christianity—than all of his predecessors. But he had no difficulty in doing this. Frederick II even went so far as to employ the state in the service of persecuting heretics. With cool calculation he arranged this with the church, which apparently signified nothing to him. It is said that Frederick II spoke about the *impostores tres,* the three deceivers: Moses, Jesus, and Mohammed. At least Gregory IX (1227–41) claimed that this expression came from him, but he was probably incorrect; this claim was only one of the public relations and propaganda attacks of the time against Frederick II. Yet it is certain that he felt he was independent from the church in a way that none of his predecessors did. For the time being, however, this was not evident, but rather everything happened in such a way that the papacy could not be dissatisfied. The establishment of Frederick as the opposing emperor forced Otto IV to abandon Italy in order to defend himself in Germany against the Hohenstaufens. At first he was successful. But when his wife, a Hohenstaufen princess, died, he was abandoned by all the adherents of the Hohenstaufens who previously had supported him, because his only connection with the Hohenstaufens had been through his wife. Frederick was now the legal ruler for them. In the year 1212 Frederick was elected king in Germany, so that all Otto IV could do was hope for

England's victory in its struggles with France, for England supported the Welfs and France the Hohenstaufens.

But France triumphed, so that Otto IV remained powerless until his death in the year 1218. At that time we see the church in Germany being emancipated even more than before from the influence of the central temporal power, completely in line with Innocent III. In the year 1220 the royal rights over the spiritual territories were limited even more, so that the spiritual princes (this expression was now used for the first time) now stood alongside the temporal princes. Purely externally, the situation was thereby restored to what had prevailed among the bishops at the time of the Ottos. The bishops were not only spiritual, but temporal rulers at the same time. But in contrast to the age of the Ottos, they now were completely independent of the king. Frederick II could also agree to this, for his political interests lay essentially in the South.

When we observe the map of central and eastern Europe at that time, things appear somewhat different, for despite this orientation of Frederick II toward the South, the empire was growing toward the East. This was not Frederick II's doing, but that of Archbishop Engelbert of Cologne, who functioned as regent for Frederick II during his absence from Germany. This is the time of the Order of the Teutonic Knights which was then embarking on establishing its power in Prussia, so that not only was German rule advanced farther toward the East, but Christianity as well (at least in principle).

Frederick's interests and goals, as we said, lay in the South. It was inevitable that his Italian politics would lead to a confrontation with the curia. Yet because of the cold-blooded calculations which dominated his politics, Frederick II could postpone this confrontation for a considerable time. Innocent III, to whom Frederick already had had to promise a crusade, died in 1216. We find his successor Honorius III (1216–27) in astonishing agreement with Frederick II, simply because Frederick conceded a relatively great amount to the church, and the real goals of his politics, as well as the fundamental direction of his attitude, had not yet become fully apparent. The pope even negotiated when Frederick took the field against the northern Italian cities. But gradually the demands of the papacy for the frequently promised crusade became so insistent, that under threat of excommunication Frederick had to promise to undertake a crusade against the infidels in 1227 in order to recapture the Holy Land. Before that date came, Honorius died and Gregory IX (1227–41) succeeded him. The name selected by the new pope expressed his program, and his attitude toward the emperor corresponded with it. Frederick began virtually on time, but while underway his army suffered an epidemic, and he therefore turned back. Because of this he was excommunicated by the pope. Things now developed in a way that was a tragedy from the church's viewpoint, and one that would be termed grotesque by secular standards. When Frederick again set off on the crusade, the pope did not lift the excommunication, but instead Gregory IX now forbade the crusade which he really should have welcomed with enthusiasm. Now all methods were fair game for the papacy in seeking to triumph over the German central authority and establish the church's supremacy. Even Gregory VII was still at least influenced by his priestly responsibilities in the measures he employed against the German monarchy. Now that appeared to be over. The papacy had fallen prey to unscrupulous power politics and thereby had step by step destroyed not only its dominance over the world, but its position in the church as well. Only in this way can we explain the fact that a few generations after Innocent III the papacy suddenly collapsed when it advanced the old claims and applied the old methods (see pp. 337–52).

The crusade, as we have said, was expressly prohibited by the pope. But that did not stop Frederick from setting off for Palestine with an army. And this crusade was one of the most successful, if not the most successful, of the Middle Ages since the First Crusade. By means of negotiations, without any bloodshed, the excommunicated king and the army, which consequently was also under the ban, obtained the surrender of Jerusalem, Bethlehem, Nazareth, and a strip of land connecting them with the coast—achieving the goal of all the crusades. It was possible to perform the coronation of the emperor in the Church of the Holy Sepulchre. But all this, which should have been greeted by the church with services of thanksgiving, made no impression on the curia; rather, the curia imposed an interdict on the territory of Jerusalem immediately after it had been reconquered for Christianity, that is, it prohibited worship services and ecclesiastical rites in the reconquered holy sites—thus pronouncing its own verdict in the face of public opinion.

Moreover, the curia also employed all its methods against Frederick II. In Germany as well as in Italy, all subjects were relieved of their obligation to the emperor. However, this was effective only as long as the emperor and his army remained in Palestine. When Frederick returned to Europe, all the opposition to him quickly collapsed. The pope saw that he had been abandoned by everyone and was forced to release

Frederick II from excommunication in 1230 and conclude a peace with him. Frederick triumphed over all opposition. His son Henry attempted a revolt against him but was captured and died in prison. Austria had joined the revolt against Frederick, and it was made a part of his hereditary domain. His nine-year-old son Conrad was elected king of the Romans and future emperor, so that it appeared that Henry had done everything necessary to assure the dominance of his house and the continuation of a strong central authority.

When Frederick again moved into Italy, the conflict with the curia flared up again, for this campaign dealt with the claim to territory which previously had been considered within the papal sphere of influence. Frederick gave Sardinia to his son Enzio, and the pope thus excommunicated him again in 1239. This time that had very little significance, for the more frequently the weapon of excommunication was wielded against rulers, the blunter it became. More significant was the literary feud which now broke out. It was obvious that the pope, taking his cue from the Apocalypse, would compare the emperor with the beast from the bottomless pit. But the emperor repaid the pope in kind and also labeled him the beast from the bottomless pit. Indeed, he went even further and summoned people to fight against Babylon, the great harlot. In the Revelation of John this image was used to represent pagan Rome, and now it was applied to the Rome dominated by the pope. Peter had once given up all he owned in order to follow Christ, said the imperial polemics, but the present pope sits on a pile of gold. These polemics reached wide circles and struck a responsive chord, for the piety which had been changing the church inwardly ever since the ninth century had by no means exhausted its power. The ideal of poverty not only affected Francis of Assisi and the Franciscan order, but countless clergy as well, and reached to the remotest corners of the church. The more the official church contradicted this ideal of poverty, the more it lost its power and influence among those who really believed. The way which finally led to the Reformation began very early, and the papacy helped as much as it could to prepare that way, even when and sometimes precisely because it appeared to be at the summit of its power.

But let us return to Gregory IX. To sharpen the struggle against Frederick, the pope wanted to assemble a council. The participants in the council from France and other countries had to travel to Italy by sea—because the emperor controlled the land routes to Italy—and Frederick had the ships captured and the council participants imprisoned. Frederick stood before Rome, and in the city street fighting

between the supporters of the pope and the emperor was a daily oc-
curence. Frederick's victory appeared at hand when Gregory IX died.
After a few weeks of Celestine IV's pontificate (1241), the next papal
election was possible only after a lengthy vacancy. The new pope, who
assumed office in 1243, significantly called himself Innocent IV
(1243–54). The animosity did not become less during the vacancy, but
the struggle between the two powers was at least interrupted. Negotiations began and at first appeared successful, until the animosity again
attained its old severity. The pope now gave up his hope of being able to
establish himself against Frederick in Italy, and fled to France. There he
summoned a council in Lyons in 1245 which deposed the emperor and
threatened the bishops supporting the emperor with all the punishments
of the church. The Franciscan and Dominican orders were commanded
to undertake passionate propaganda against the emperor. All financial
means of the church were placed at the disposal of the struggle against
the emperor. Finally, in the year 1246, they went the reliable route of
setting up an opposition king, the Landgrave Henry of Thuringia, who
was able to defeat Henry's son Conrad, but otherwise achieved essentially no results. When he died after only a year, a successor, Duke
William of Holland, was chosen. But all the means they tried achieved
nothing, and Frederick continued his reign without interruption, even
when they captured his son Enzio and took their vengeance on him: for
twenty-three years until his death in 1272 he was kept in prison. However, when Frederick died on December 13, 1250, the catastrophe began
not only for the Hohenstaufen house but for the central authority in
Germany altogether.

In Germany and in Sicily, Frederick had appointed his son Conrad as
his successor, and he now set off for Sicily in 1251. However, he died in
1254. When the opposition king William of Holland also died in 1256,
Conrad's son Conradin would have been the normal successor. But no
one supported him. After long deliberations they proceeded with a new
election, which revealed the agony the empire was experiencing. The
dual election which occurred should have been enough to demonstrate
the central authority's powerlessness. But this fact was even underscored
by the fact that the two men chosen were not even Germans. One party
proposed an English ruler, Richard of Cornwall, for the German king;
and the other, what would today be called a Spaniard, Alfonso of
Castile. Alfonso was never even in Germany at all. Richard was crowned
at Aachen in 1257 but he remained in Germany only for a year and a
half and then returned to England, visiting Germany again only three

more times for brief periods. Either Germany was not being ruled at all, or, if it was, it was being done from afar.

With this began the Interregnum, "the terrible time without an emperor." Its official end came when Rudolf of Hapsburg ascended the throne in 1273. Because one of the representatives of one of the strong territorial powers of Germany had taken the throne, it appeared that this was a new beginning of the establishment of a strong central authority. But the princes jealously took care that this did not happen, and so rulers from various houses succeeded one another until the year 1347: first Rudolf of Hapsburg, 1273–91; then Adolf of Nassau, 1292–98; again a Hapsburg, Albert I of Austria, 1298–1308; then Henry VIII of Luxembourg, 1308–13; and finally Louis IV of Bavaria, 1314–47 (who significantly had to contend with Frederick of Austria as opposition king until 1330). The situation now seemed to improve when a line of Luxembourg emperors unbroken until 1437 came to the throne. But appearances were deceiving. Although the same house furnished a ruler for a hundred years, no strengthening of the central authority took place. This did not happen until 1438 when the Hapsburgs finally took control.

We shall mention all these rulers only occasionally when they especially participate in ecclesiastical issues or if state and ecclesiastical matters come into conflict during their reign. Naturally empire and church remained closely united, but this was a union of things that were separated. *Imperium* ("empire") and *sacerdotium* ("priesthood") were now divorced from one another, while before one could not be described without the other. Both temporal and spiritual princes not only carefully guarded their autonomy and developed the consciousness and understanding of their own office, but now they also began to rule the empire through their representatives, the electors. If a ruler wanted to attain a strong position in the empire for himself, that was possible on the basis of his own possessions or the development of sufficient power in his own hereditary lands. All the ways which the rulers of the Middle Ages had previously pursued and all the systems of government they had organized now belonged to the past and could not be restored. As we mentioned above (see p. 300), this has to do not with what one might term a secularization or profanation of the empire, but we have to say that both—king as well as territorial princes—had now become aware of their special nature, their "worldliness." The kings as well as the individual princes were nevertheless connected with the church. But this tie was an external one, as far as its effect on the institutions was concerned.

Naturally the princes were numbered among the faithful of their time. But their personal piety—at least usually—had no influence on their action as temporal rulers. Thus we are entering a new age, especially since the general political situation had also changed. Germany is now just one power alongside others and frequently not the strongest one. The importance of England and France continued to increase, and France's influence on the church especially grew.

Then when the papacy was finally able to stamp out the Hohenstaufens, it did so only with France's help. It is true that William of Holland had triumphed significantly in the North, but the Hohenstaufens were still in the South in Sicily where they were defending the remainder of their domain on which they hoped to rebuild the old greatness of their dominion. The pope at that time, Urban IV (1261–64), was French. He offered the crown of Sicily to the brother of Louis IX of France, Charles of Anjou. His successor, Clement IV (1265–68), was also French.

The connection between the curia and France became closer and closer. In 1264 Charles of Anjou landed at the mouth of the Tiber and in a battle in 1266 defeated and killed Manfred, who was fighting in Conradin's name for the Hohenstaufens in Sicily. Thereupon Conradin hastened to the South. Italy fell to him. He was greeted enthusiastically everywhere, for the people of Italy were tired of both papal and French rule. In 1268 he entered Rome, and it thus appeared as if the great days of the Hohenstaufens had returned. But after initial successes in a battle with Charles of Anjou, Conradin was defeated and compelled to flee. He was betrayed during his escape and delivered to Charles of Anjou, who beheaded him in Naples on October 29, 1268, along with Duke Frederick of Baden. Thus ended the Hohenstaufens.

But if the papacy believed that it was going to be free from the yoke that had oppressed it for centuries, it was making a decisive mistake. It had thrown off one yoke but at the price of obtaining a new and more oppressive one. The papacy had fought against the Hohenstaufens because the Hohenstaufens had extended their dominion over Italy and surrounded the States of the Church, the foundation of the papal existence, by Sicily on the South and their northern and central Italian possessions on the North. The situation had not changed. Charles of Anjou had taken over Sicily with papal support, and France ruled Naples. Once again the papacy was surrounded on both sides, and this time by a country that was geographically just as close as Germany and, more importantly, one that was more politically unified and provided fewer opportunities within it for playing off rival powers against one another—thus internally weakening it. The consequences which ensued from the defeat of the Hohenstaufens and the destruction of the central authority had a much greater effect on the papacy and the Catholic church than all the influences which had stemmed from Germany. Consequently the papacy, which had first summoned France into the country to fight against the Hohenstaufens, soon had to defend itself against the French and become involved in continual attempts to escape the fact that it was surrounded by them. But the papacy paid for its successes in this struggle with losses which were immeasurably greater than its apparent gains. After long struggles, it was able to throw off the French control. But this was possible only with Spain's help. And Spain inflicted an even greater and more oppressive dependence upon the papacy than had France.

The tragedy of the medieval papacy consisted in its desire to hold on to temporal power next to the spiritual power which everyone acknowledged it had. For this reason it was continually in danger of losing both. That went on for centuries, even up to the time of the Reformation. At that time the papacy was confronting Spain which was threatening its temporal position. Consequently it continually allied itself with France. This then made it impossible for the emperor to proceed against the Reformation as forcefully as he would have wished. He spent his time and strength in the continual war with France. At that time four wars were fought between the two countries in almost unbroken succession from 1521 until 1544. At that time the emperor was compelled to neglect Germany, so that the German territorial princes had many more opportunities to pursue their territorial and religious objectives than they probably would have had if the pope had not been playing his anti-Spanish, anti-imperial, and actually anti-Catholic politics.

Thus, there is the question of whether we should really so admire the world supremacy of the papacy in the Middle Ages as we often do. The dangers associated with this world dominance—and therefore both for the external and internal maintenance of Catholicism—are frequently obscured for the general viewer by the splendor of the papacy's world dominance. The representative of the papacy's world dominance and its claims is Innocent III, about whom we shall speak more thoroughly at the end of this chapter, although in our chronology we already have proceeded beyond his age and already have spoken about his participation in the events in Germany (see pp. 315–18). All the reservations we have about this claim to world dominance as such and about the way

Innocent III presented those claims can nevertheless not detract from our admiration of this man and his achievements.

It is naturally true that Innocent was only the one who put into practice what others before him had thought and others before him had desired. The line which reached its culmination in Innocent III extended back as far as Hadrian I, the pope of the Carolingian age (see p. 277), in fact, even back into the ancient church. Many popes since Hadrian I had attempted to establish the papacy's claim to world dominance: Nicholas I (see p. 278), Leo IX (see pp. 289–90), Nicholas II (see pp. 294–96), then Gregory VII (see pp. 297–304), and finally Alexander III (see pp. 312–13). They all demanded the same thing as Innocent; they were all motivated by his spirit. But they had all made this claim against strong rulers, sometimes even against a superior empire, while when Innocent III came to power he found a divided central government after Henry VI's sudden death. On their part, Germany's political powers rose up and exhausted one another in striving for the upper hand. And when Innocent died, Frederick II was still beginning to take control. There were still two kings contending with one another in Germany, and thus the central authority was weakened. We may therefore ask whether one of the popes of an earlier time might have achieved the same things as Innocent III if he had reigned under the same circumstances. On the other hand, we may ask whether Innocent III would not have failed if Henry VI had lived longer, for example, or if he had had to deal with those strong rulers who were the downfall of his predecessors. These are questions which arise—here as well as other places in history—but questions—here as well as other places in history—which are ultimately moot, since no answer can be given to them.

Innocent III (1198–1216) was thirty-seven years old, the youngest of the cardinals, when he ascended the papal throne and first set out to realize his objectives. At first he strengthened papal authority in Italy. He began in Rome, where the imperial city prefect, who had no way of resisting because of the disunity in Germany, had to swear allegiance to him. Then he extended his dominion over central Italy and finally also over Sicily. Here Constance, Henry VI's widow, was ruling because her son, Frederick II, was still a very young child. Constance had no other choice but to install Innocent as regent over Sicily, recognize that the country was a papal fief, and finally even make Innocent guardian over the young Frederick. Then Innocent could make use of the animosity between Otto IV and Philip of Swabia to get Otto to promise him everything he considered necessary or desirable, so that Innocent was convinced he had created the basis for a permanent establishment of the present situation in Italy and Germany.

In France, Innocent was also able to accomplish his will. Here the king, Philip II, had divorced his wife. With the help of an interdict, the pope was able to force him to take her back. Now this had no real influence on the actual government of the country, but it was still a significant moral triumph. It demonstrated to all the world that the pope was supreme over the monarchy. In Portugal and Aragon it was even possible to get both rulers to receive their land as a fief from the pope, and now the same thing happened—which was more important—in England. Here the conflict began with a dispute over filling the see of the Archbishop of Canterbury. The pope put forth his own candidate, Stephen Langton, in opposition to King John's candidate, and forced the king to concede by placing the country under an interdict. Thus, no worship services and no ecclesiastical acts were performed any longer. The pope then excommunicated the king and relieved his subjects of their obligation to him—an act that had been successfully tried in Germany. Anyone who was even close to the king, and every single person who now associated with him, was also placed under the ban. Not only did he declare that the king himself had forfeited the crown, but Innocent invited the French king to take over the now vacant English throne. For a long time England and France had been waging war, and that was the reason this invitation possessed such explosive power. Moreover, Innocent declared that anyone taking part in the struggle against John and anyone assisting in the conquest of England would be considered a crusader and would participate in all the merits promised to those who went to war to free the Holy Land from the infidels. Thus, Innocent III, heedless of the final consequences, used all the weapons of the church.

Innocent could triumph over King John of England because John was not supported by his nobles, who long had been dissatisfied with him and his way of ruling. When John gave his land (that is, England and Ireland) to the pope as a fief—from which the nickname "John Lack-land" comes—we must not necessarily read into this that the king inwardly agreed with the papal claims. This was probably a precautionary measure taken by the king. By doing this he kept other claimants from attempting to take over: when he gave the pope the country as a fief, he was preventing an invasion by the French king as well as the rise of an opposition candidate whom the barons might propose. But if John thought this would satisfy the claims of the pope, he was mistaken.

Rather, he was forced into deep personal humiliation by the pope. John now had to plead for forgiveness in public before the Archbishop of Canterbury, Stephen Langton, whom he had not been willing to accept, and grovel in the dust at Langton's feet, before the pope would free him from the ban. The triumph of the pope and the church could not be surpassed.

To the knowledgeable it was already clear at that time that Innocent had extended himself too far. The further this triumph of the church went, the more expensive it became. Next the barons rose up against John and in 1215 forced him to sign the Magna Charta which decisively curtailed the rights of the king. Naturally the pope declared this agreement invalid. It was evident that he was powerless against the barons; he excommunicated them several times, but could not compel them to submit. Archbishop Langton, whom the pope had installed in office over the king's opposition, refused to excommunicate the barons, so Innocent deposed him at the Lateran Council. The opposition to Innocent III could not be forestalled. This was not just an opposition to the concrete measures taken by the pope, but it was also an opposition that was beginning to take shape against the increasingly excessive claims of the papacy as such. This opposition continued to spread. It first took hold among the English nobles, then among the English populace as well. When the demand for the secularization of church property in England struck such a responsive chord in England a hundred years later (see pp. 360 61), and when Wycliffe very quickly turned from initial political demands to their ecclesiastical, nay, even theological consequences (see pp. 361–62) and large portions of the populace followed him, these were the result of those actions taken by the church of the high Middle Ages.

However, Innocent III's time only saw the success in England, not the negative consequences. Other spectacular successes in eastern Europe followed it. In the Balkans at that time the Catholic church exercised an influence as never before. A Bulgarian king was crowned by a papal legate. The pope's legates presided over Serbian reforming synods. The high point of Innocent's triumph was the extension of Catholic dominance over the area of the Orthodox church as well. Paradoxically, this took place against the pope's intention. What Innocent was striving for was a crusade to the Holy Land, for the crowning achievement for an emperor as well as a pope was success in the struggle against the infidels. This crusade, which Innocent passionately demanded and promoted, however, ran a completely different course than the pope had intended. Venice provided the ships for it. In lieu of the costs of the voyage, which the crusading army was unable to pay, the Venetians obligated the crusaders first to conquer the city of Zadar in Dalmatia, that is, to further their own political interests. Then they were able to get the crusaders to take a hand in the dispute in Byzantium, where quarrels had erupted within the imperial family. Isaac II Angelus had been deposed and blinded by his brother Alexius III; with the help of the crusaders, Isaac and his son Alexius IV Angelus were restored. But they could maintain their position for only a brief time. Even while they were being restored to power by the Latins, their opposition quickly regained the upper hand. Alexius was taken prisoner and finally murdered. The crusaders regarded that as a challenge and again marched to Constantinople, conquering it on April 13, 1204—accompanying their conquest with gruesome pillaging and destruction of the most valuable art treasures—and establishing the so-called Latin empire. A Venetian became the Orthodox patriarch, all the archdioceses were filled anew, and all Orthodox clergy, if retained in office at all, had to swear an oath of obedience to the Roman church. The possessions of the Orthodox church were redistributed, and above all, the newly established military orders took vast territories for themselves. Innocent, as we have said, initially had regarded this undertaking with aversion and mistrust. But when it was successful, he welcomed it wholeheartedly. Reunification appeared to be achieved and in the only form in which Rome at that time—and for a long time afterward as well—could conceive of reunification of the churches, namely, in such a way that the papacy triumphed and achieved all its demands.

This Latin empire lasted only for sixty years. No matter how splendid it may have appeared at that time, we must regard it very critically today. This Latin empire decisively reduced the political power of Byzantium by dividing the empire into various territories. In addition, it not only considerably weakened the Greek church, but also decisively deepened the animosity between East and West. Not only the permanent bitterness of the Greek people against the West, but also that of the entire Eastern church against that of the West dates from this. From now on the Greek church was willing to talk with the church of the West only when the most extreme circumstances compelled it and when it saw no other way out. In the future, the very fact that discussions about union took place signified an absolute calamity for the Eastern church. Seen from the perspective of that time, however, the crusade appeared to be a powerful success. Similar crusades took place against the East in northern Europe, in Latvia and Lithuania. They were also successful. Thus the Fourth Lateran Council in 1215 could display in splendid fashion Innocent III's position of dominance as well as the powerful position of the Catholic church in the world in general at that time. Four hundred twelve bishops, eight hundred abbots, and representatives of all the princes of the lands within the papal sphere of influence were present at this council, which did not deliberate, but only acknowledged the pope's proposals, not to mention the decrees. Enthusiastic support was expressed for what the pope demanded of the council. The way the papacy here presented itself to the church and the world accorded with Innocent III's conception and with the wish and aspiration of the papacy in the high Middle Ages in general.

The way Innocent conceived of the relationship between spiritual and temporal power can be studied in the example of England. In the arguments first with John Lackland, then with the Archbishop of Canterbury, and finally with the barons, Innocent declared that the pope possessed both swords—the spiritual one which he wielded himself, and the temporal one which was bestowed by him upon princes. Since this temporal sword really belonged to him, he not only had the right, but the duty as well, to correct the wrong decisions of princes. The pope was high priest and king in one person, just as Melchizedek in the Old Testament. Even Peter was given supervision over the world of humanity, as the New Testament account of Peter's walking on the sea proves. Here the sea signifies the world of humanity, and Peter's walking on the sea signifies the dominance of Peter and his successors over this world of humanity. The rights which Peter possessed have been given in their full extent to his successors, so that if one wishes to describe the position of the pope, one can only say that the pope stands between God and man. He was indeed less than God, but still more than a man, for God was working and acting in him. From this the pope derived his claim for absolute obedience to all his regulations.

We would fundamentally misunderstand this and similar declarations if we were to think of them as the proclamation of a modern sort of drive for power. What Innocent here declared and demanded was only something that naturally flowed out of his understanding of his office, and his understanding of his office was also a result of his entire understanding of Christianity and his personal piety. Over and over again Innocent's theological writings and sermons express the idea that everything he does is motivated by his faith and that he acts in humility before God. And what can be said about Innocent also applies to the popes preceding him. Certainly at times all of them fell prey to a purely secular claim to power; their success forced them to it. But they acted out of duty, and they all felt that they would have been guilty of decisive omissions if they had acted differently than they did. This claim to power of the church— even the claim to secular power of the church—is a result of the way that age understood the church. And precisely this understanding is what contributed decisively to the destruction of that church.

6. THE INNER LIFE OF THE CHURCH

In the above, the epoch of the Catholic Middle Ages was dealt with essentially in terms of the events and considerations of political history, because that was what the internal structure of the time demanded. I believe it is evident that the forces affecting Christianity during this epoch did not come off too badly in such a presentation. Because of the close connection between political and ecclesiastical events, one must speak about this external history, even if one proceeds from a different perspective than we did here. In this way we meet all the popes and synods, to the extent they can be dealt with in such a survey presentation.

Questions of ecclesiastical structure were also discussed in connection with the developments which the episcopal office experienced during the four centuries we considered here. But what is chiefly apparent—at least I hope so—is what sort of importance piety had during the centuries of the Catholic Middle Ages: one that reaches directly into the political arena. Ever since the monastery of Cluny was founded in Burgundy at the beginning of the tenth century, a reform movement proceeded from it which is known as the Cluniac Reform. We have spoken about its individual phases (see p. 286). The monasteries were renewed from within and their real purpose reasserted, and from them this aspiration spread throughout the entire church. It was also brought back to its original purity and strictness. This began with the way the individual priests led their lives and performed the duties of their offices; then the demand spread further and further and higher and higher, extending to the bishops and reaching the pope. But if these offices were to have their full authority and the church were really to be the church, it had to be free from foreign influences; it had to be free from the state. That the German king influenced or even participated in filling episcopal offices—indeed, the highest office in the church, for example—was something that contradicted its nature.

This great renewal movement was determinative for the Catholic

Middle Ages. We can see how strong it was in the fact that it even took hold among the German rulers and compelled them to take actions which not only were contrary to tradition, but also to the responsibilities of their office. It prepared the way for the church to triumph over the German empire—this church which ever since Charlemagne's time and even centuries earlier had been striving for equal rights with the state, even dominance over it. At first this aspiration of the popes for dominance was not favored by the new piety. But if faith were the supreme possession of the human race, the church as its guardian and representative also deserved the supreme position. If the church were ranked above the state, it could also guide it to a new, higher position of honor.

But as soon as this happened, the victorious church, freed from the false influence of the world, opened itself to that world and increasingly succumbed to it and denied the ideals of the new piety and its fundamentally ascetic attitude, so that the new piety first became doubtful and then suspicious of this church and its representatives. First it registered protests and attempted to direct the secularized church back into the right path. When that did not succeed, it initially withdrew into itself and then finally sought its own way alongside the official church until it finally opposed it directly. The beginnings of this situation were reached at the conclusion of our epoch.

Something like the establishment of the Franciscan order is clear proof for this. February 24, 1208, is dated as the "day of St. Francis's marriage to poverty." Later that same year, Giovanni Bernardone (1181/82–1226), the son of a wealthy cloth merchant of Assisi, together with a few companions, began to imitate the life of Christ and the apostles in complete poverty. He felt compelled to do that after hearing a sermon about the gospel's demand for poverty, which is what had moved Anthony the Great (see p. 183) to withdraw from the world. The ascetic Christianity they preached—and more importantly which they lived—at first experienced a powerful response in Italy so that the order quickly spread throughout the land and beyond its borders. In addition to the Franciscans, a whole series of other mendicant orders arose in the thirteenth century: The Humiliati in 1201, the order of the Dominicans in 1216 or 1220, the Carmelite order in 1238, and the order of Augustinian Hermits in 1256, just to mention only the most important. They all wanted to live a life without property—not only the individual monks but the orders themselves, which rejected houses for their orders as well as other real or personal property and certain financial income. As individuals and as a community they lived from the gifts of the pious.

These so-called mendicant orders quickly experienced an extraordinary growth; for example, a few years after its organization the Dominican order already had sixty monasteries in eight provinces. They were also not limited to men, but the Dominican and Franciscan orders quickly organized branches for women. All of this shows the strength of the ascetic concept in the thirteenth century, as well as the silent protest against the world that was inherent in it, just as had happened with monasticism in the ancient church in the third and fourth centuries (see pp. 183–84). And the church of the Middle Ages reacted in exactly the same way as the ancient church had done. It did not perceive the latent protest that was hidden in the new phenomenon, but viewed it with amazement as a vicarious achievement. When Francis was canonized in 1228, two years after his death, this was characteristic (Dominic was also raised to sainthood right after his death), as was the alarm which the saint expressed in his testament about the way the order was diverging from the original ideals. It was self-evident that in the long run the mendicant orders could not keep from establishing either permanent houses for their orders or accumulating possessions, something that soon led to considerable conflicts among the Franciscans (see pp. 355–56).

All of these establishments, even that of Francis of Assisi, were strongly controlled by the church, and the Dominican order even became the elite group of the church. Founded initially to bring back the heretics to the church, it soon assumed the task of the inquisition and became the most frightful instrument with which the church persecuted every real or imagined divergence, and the state—not just in Germany—soon placed its support at its disposal. That happened after the experience of the twelfth century, when the movement of the Cathari (the Greek *katharos* means "pure," and it is from this that the German word for heretic, *Ketzer,* is derived), fed from secret sources which have not been explained to the present day, took root especially in southern France, as well as everywhere else in Europe. Divided into the small circle of apostles, the "Perfect," and the larger circles of the "Faithful," they practiced a severe asceticism and condemned significant portions of the doctrine and practices of the church—the sacraments, as well as altars, pictures, and veneration of the saints and relics. Here in the "Faithful," who also remained members of the official church, we see how the ascetic piety was already beginning to move outside the church.

The significance monasticism had for the Middle Ages was demonstrated in its first centuries by the Scotch-Irish. They were the ones who created the foundation for a renewal of Christianity and the church in the Frankish kingdom. They had their roots in the Benedictine order, that last great monastic movement of the ancient church which went back to Benedict of Nursia and the beginning of the sixth century. When the time we are now considering brings forth a number of new monastic orders, what might be called the second wave in the history of monasticism, it thus shows its internal strength. In many places the eremite ideal in its strict form arose anew, for example, in Italy in the Camaldolese congregation, and in the Carthusian order in France. We have spoken about the mendicant orders. The Cistercian order (founded at Cîteaux in 1098) was just as strongly opposed to the world, something that is demonstrated by its buildings which not only refrain from using church towers, but also any sort of decoration. But it had a considerable influence in the world through its agricultural activities, which especially in Germany included large waste areas. Its establishments were located everywhere and contributed to the elevation of the economic level of the country. In Bernard of Clairvaux the Cistercian order had one of the most significant and influential figures of our age. We have already spoken above about the influences coming from Cluny (see pp. 330–31), and especially significant for Germany was the monastery at Hirsau which was reformed in 1069. Its monks, who developed a widespread activity, contributed significantly to the strengthening of the high church spirit. Finally, the Premonstratensian Canons (founded at Prémontré in 1120) can be compared to the Cistercians in their extent and significance.

The final group of orders which were founded at that time were the hospital and military orders. They originated in direct connection with the crusades. In addition to the monastic vows of poverty, chastity, and obedience, those who entered the military orders took a fourth vow to fight against the infidels. The flowering of European knighthood occurred under the white cross of the Hospitallers or the red cross of the Templars. Their establishments in the Holy Land created a bulwark for Christianity. Certainly some nontheological motives played a role in the crusades: desire for adventure, enthusiasm, hope for plunder and wealth, aspiration for power, securing trade outposts, and so forth. But decisive for the crusaders, surpassing all other motives, however, was the religious one; at that time the thought of the holy places of Christianity being in the hands of unbelievers was unendurable. *Deus lo volt,* "God wills it," shouted thousands at the Synod of Clermont in 1095 when the First Crusade was initiated. Again and again the armies of the crusaders set off (First Crusade, 1096–99; Second Crusade, 1147–49; Third Crusade, 1189–92; Fourth Crusade, 1202–04; Fifth Crusade, 1228–29; Sixth Crusade, 1248–54; Seventh Crusade, 1270). Only in the First Crusade could Jerusalem be conquered for a longer period of time, and the Kingdom of Jerusalem was established along with the Principality of Antioch and the Counties of Edessa and Tripolis. After Islam retook Jerusalem in 1187, the city was regained in the Fifth Crusade under Frederick II and then finally lost to Christianity in 1244. All in all, the results of the crusades had absolutely no relationship to the efforts expended. Infinite blood was spilled and infinite suffering caused—we need only remember the Children's Crusade of 1212. Thousands of boys and girls from the lower Rhine Valley and from France set off at that time to free the Holy Land without force—only by the power of their prayers. If they even got as far as the port of embarkation at Marseille, they ended up in Alexandria in slavery and in the brothel.

Certainly in Asia Minor, especially in the Fourth Crusade, significant territories were freed from Islamic control, and certainly some significant conquests took place on what might be called the fringes of the crusades (Lisbon in the Second Crusade, for example). But seen as a whole, their objective was not achieved. It is characteristic that the Sixth and Seventh Crusades did not even have the Holy Land as their objective, but Egypt and Tunis, and both failed completely. What endured were the military orders holding islands in the Mediterranean as advanced outposts against Islam up into the sixteenth century. But even the order of the Teutonic Knights, originally founded in 1190–98 in order to fight in the Holy Land, no longer had any task there and returned to Europe. Under its leadership, the crusaders received a new objective in the thirteenth century in the area of the Baltic Sea where the East Prussian state of the Teutonic Knights arose.

In these cases we can still present things under the aspect of the expansion of Christianity (even if considerable portions of the populace had already been Christianized). And we can even apply the original objective of the crusades to the Albigensian War in southern France (1209–29)—although only to a considerably limited degree—since the purpose of the campaign was to exterminate the (real or alleged) heretics. But, for example, when the papacy even earlier (under Innocent III) proclaimed a crusade against England because the pope had excommunicated King John (see p. 326), or a crusade (under Boniface VIII) because two cardinals and their supporters had had a falling out with the pope, this was obviously a misuse of the concept of the crusade and perverted the institution of the crusades into a pure means of power for the papacy.

It is difficult to say what sort of harm the crusades' failure did to piety, the authority of the papacy which supported them with all its might, and the rulers who were forced to participate in them under threat of excommunication. There is insufficient evidence on which to make a judgment, so the opinions differ widely. There can be no doubt that the degeneration of the crusades into an extended arm of papal power politics had negative effects—and they extended far beyond the areas affected by them. However, it is certain that the piety of the Catholic Middle Ages was still intact at their close.

At that time Christianity was a force encompassing all of Europe, and it reached into the details of intellectual life. Art, poetry, and learning were in its service. The magnificent cathedrals of the Middle Ages, as well as countless smaller church buildings, bear witness to this, just as do painting, sculpture, and artistic endeavors. Although the art of poetry began in the twelfth century among the troubadours and minnesingers who made use of secular material, the entire educational system was oriented toward the church. That had been the case in England, Scotland, and Ireland since the sixth century, and on the continent since the Carolingian age, even extending down into the schools for the populace. In a way that had never happened before and has never happened since, all knowledge at the time was brought together in a unity under theological and ecclesiastical auspices. No one but Origen in the third century had ever been able to do anything like this, but his was the accomplishment of an individual—or at most a school—whose possibilities for influence were restricted to the church and had only a minimal impact on the Roman Empire that was then dominated by paganism. Now around 1200 we find universities first being established in Italy, France, and England (the oldest German universities of Prague and Vienna were not founded until the middle of the fourteenth century). At least they stood under the influence of theology—canon law played a decisive role even in the "lay" law school at Bologna—for they received their rights to grant degrees from the pope. We are accustomed to regard scholasticism as a special discipline of systematic theology, and we usually regard it negatively and forget that it achieved a unified summary of all the world's knowledge under a theological perspective.

Anselm of Canterbury (1033–1109) was the forerunner of the attempt to bring knowledge, thought, and belief into a unified whole, and Abelard (1079–1142) developed the dialectic of the scholastic method with its increasingly subdivided system of question, subquestion, and answer. In this way Christianity assimilated the foreign concepts of Aristotle—characteristically by way of Arabic and Jewish sources. It is significant that the monastic orders, which were detached from the world in their origin as well as their objective, provided the most important representatives of scholasticism: the Englishman Alexander of Hales (d. 1245), as well as the Italian Bonaventure (1221–74), and the Scot Johannes Duns Scotus (ca. 1270–1308) were Franciscans, and the German Albertus Magnus (1193–1280) and the Italian Thomas Aquinas (1225–74) were Dominicans. The church has honored all of them with the most mellifluous honorary titles: Alexander is the *Doctor irrefragabilis* ("irrefutable teacher"), Bonaventure the *Doctor seraphicus* ("seraphic teacher"), Duns Scotus the *Doctor subtilis* ("subtle teacher"), Albertus the *Doctor universalis* ("universal teacher"), and Thomas the *Doctor angelicus* ("angelic teacher"). All this was justified; yet after 1286 a sharper and sharper opposition between the schools developed: at that time the Dominicans pledged the members of their order, under penalty of excommunication, to Thomas Aquinas, who has played a dominant role in Catholic theology from then until the modern age, while the Franciscans are likewise obligated to Duns Scotus, so that their original unity gave way to a feud that became sharper and sharper. But this is now part of the conclusion of the Catholic Middle Ages and the factors paving the way for its demise, which we shall consider in the following section. We can certainly understand why Romanticism of the nineteenth century, as well as wide circles within Catholicism, for example, can lament the passing of the Middle Ages in which the world was still a unity: in language, culture, learning, government, faith, and church. But this beautiful picture is deceptive. Along with all these, the destructive power which would destroy this unity was already present— and in all areas. We shall have to deal with it in the next section.

III

The Conclusion of the Catholic Middle Ages and the Development to the Threshold of the Reformation

1. THE DECLINE OF THE PAPACY TO THE GREAT SCHISM AND THE COUNCIL OF PISA

It would be an absolutely incorrect conclusion if someone, building on the preceding chapter (see p. 325), were to think that Innocent's claims were something extraordinary and applied only to his own person. Rather, Innocent was only developing the natural consequences of the legacy left by his predecessors. He was representing the claim the Catholic church had been making for many centuries, the fundamental origin of which can be set as early as the fifth century. Boniface VIII (1294–1303) reigned only seventy-eight years after Innocent III. He held exactly the same concepts as Innocent III and raised exactly the same demands. The one had ruled the world with them, but the other not only suffered a deep personal defeat, but even demonstrated the impotence of the papacy and its demands to all the world. The reason that an epoch of humiliation for the papacy and an utter disunity of the church that was far worse than anything that could have been imagined began with him, lies in the fact that structural changes, which had already been initiated, rapidly developed further in the time between Innocent III and Boniface VIII.

If we want to observe Boniface VIII's claims and those of the papacy at that time, we must study the bull *Unam sanctam ecclesiam* ("One holy church") of 1302. It presents the classical formulation of the papal claim to supremacy of the preceding centuries, as well as of the following centuries. The papacy did not abandon this claim to supremacy voluntarily, but only when any hope of realizing it was completely gone. This bull *Unam sanctam ecclesiam* stated that the church, which was the one and only church, had only one body and one head—Christ and Christ's vicar, Peter and Peter's successors. Peter was the bearer of Christ's promise; the pope had succeeded him—not just as Peter's successor, but as the vicar of Christ. No one in the world can claim to be a Christian if he does not belong to the church which is subject to the pope. It said: "Therefore, if the Greeks or others say that they were not committed to Peter and his successors, they necessarily confess that they are not of Christ's sheep."

It spoke about the two swords in the usual fashion: "We learn from the words of the Gospel that in this church and in her power are two swords, the spiritual and the temporal. . . . Both are in the power of the church, the spiritual sword and the temporal. But the latter is to be used for the church, the former by her; the former by the priest, the latter by kings and soliders but at the will and by the permission of the priest." From this comes the hierarchy: "The one sword, then, should be under the other, and temporal authority subject to spiritual." Since spiritual power exceeds the temporal in honor, no explanation is necessary to justify the use of spiritual power against the temporal, and it must judge it if it is in error. If the spiritual power errs, it will be judged by a greater; if the supreme power (that is, the pope) errs, he can only be judged by God, not by man. "For this authority, although given to a man and exercised by a man, is not human, but rather divine. . . ." Whoever therefore resists the pope, resists the ordinance of God. "Furthermore we declare, state, define and pronounce that it is altogether necessary to salvation for every human creature to be subject to the Roman pontiff": *Porro subesse Romano Pontifici omni humanae creaturae declaramus, dicimus, diffinimus et pronunciamus omnino esse de necessitate salutis.* So much for Boniface VIII's bull *Unam sanctam ecclesiam* of 1302. It was formulated within the context of the disputes we shall now discuss; it was not motivated by them, however, but only expressed the attitude which controlled Boniface VIII's action from the outset.

In Boniface VIII's attempt to realize his claims of supremacy, it quickly became apparent that he was not even in a position to accomplish anything in the internal Italian disputes. At that time Venice and Genoa were warring against one another. The pope attempted to end the war, but without success. When the two states finally did make peace, it happened without papal mediation. Boniface wanted to conquer Sicily, but even though he was supplied with troops from various sources he was unsuccessful. Again and again he used the weapon of excommunication, but Sicily nevertheless maintained its independence. In Florence two factions were fighting, the so-called "Whites" and "Blacks." The "Whites" sent Dante to the papal court in order to win over the pope for their side, or at least bring him to a more understanding position, but he was unsuccessful. Embittered, Dante left Rome. All attempts to accomplish what the pope considered pacification of the city were fruitless, and his attempts only succeeded in the loss of all sympathy for him in Florence.

In southern Italy and portions of central Italy his intervention was more successful. But more important and more impressive to his age was the fact that in Rome itself a dangerous opponent arose against the pope. The leaders of the opposition were the Colonna cardinals, uncle and nephew. Boniface now used all his means against this opposition, finally proclaiming a crusade against them. It was successful in itself: the lands of the Colonnas were captured, and the cardinals could not maintain themselves and had to leave the country. But, understandably enough, the sensation that this crusade caused was overwhelming, for participation in it was also accompanied by the extraordinary ecclesiastical promises which applied to crusades to reconquer the Holy Land—the churchly guarantee of salvation for anyone who participated in it. After the Seventh Crusade failed in 1270, people had become accustomed to crusades against the heretics or having crusades proclaimed in order to conquer territory for the church. But now when a crusade took place against two cardinals, this was something previously unknown. It demonstrated how far the internal dissolution of the church had proceeded. Its external appearance must have appeared questionable precisely to those who wanted to be Christians. It was no coincidence that the two cardinals called a general council at that time. That happened even more frequently in the subsequent time: the papacy lost its position not only as the temporal, but also as the supreme spiritual authority, and the council gradually replaced it as the highest tribunal of the church.

In Germany, where the rulers rapidly followed one another because the jealousy of the territorial princes prevented any continuing central authority from forming, Boniface VIII's successes were greater. As a result of the disputes over the throne there, he was able to get his view recognized, "that the apostolic see had transferred the Roman Empire from the Greeks to the Germans and granted the electors the right to select the Roman king," as Albert I of Austria formulated it. But this success was only on the surface. This formulation was only conceded to

the pope because the monarchy urgently needed his help against the
territorial powers. The pope had no opportunity to turn his theoretical
success into a practical one. As soon as the situation in Germany was
less urgent, not only the central authority but the territorial principalities advanced a completely different position, which we shall meet
below (see pp. 353–58).

Boniface VIII's claims in Hungary and Poland collapsed completely,
although he made use not only of the ban but the interdict as well; a
portion of the Hungarian bishops replied to Boniface VIII's measures by
even excommunicating him. All of this, however, was only a preface to
what Boniface confronted in his conflict with England and France, that
is, the great powers of the time. Here the subject of contention was
whether the state was justified in taxing the possessions of the church to
pay the nation's debts. In the development of a monetary economy, the
state had become more and more attracted to the huge source of income
that was potentially available to it in the property of the church. Taxing
churches, monasteries, and the clergy previously had been prohibited to
it, even though practically it had been taking place here and there for a
long time. In England taxation of church property had quietly been
practiced for a long time, and France was planning to initiate it when
Boniface VIII issued the bull *Clericis laicos* ("[because] the laity [are
enemies] of the clergy") on February 25, 1296. It forbade the taxation of
church property by the state in a blunt way: only the pope, so it
proclaimed, could order and approve ecclesiastical expenditures. Clergy
who paid taxes demanded by the state without the express permission of
the pope were to be punished by the interdict and the ban, just as were
the states who seized money from the churches without papal approval.
At first this bull was successful, for the spiritual authority of the pope
was not yet exhausted. The English clergy ceased paying taxes to the
state until they received papal authorization. It was characteristic that
this did not deter the action of the English king, Edward I. He withdrew
the protection of the royal law courts from the clergy who refused to pay
taxes and threatened to expropriate the temporal fiefs which had been
given to the church.

In France, Philip IV (the Fair), who quickly developed into Boniface
VIII's real opponent, acted more radically but more elegantly. When he
forbade the export of gold and silver from the kingdom in August, 1296,
and simultaneously expelled all foreign merchants, this appeared to be
avoiding any measures against the church. But in reality the church was
seriously affected by this. It had developed a monetary economy much

earlier than the state, and therefore was also much more dependent on its financial sources than the state, which was largely still tied to an agricultural economy. Thus this blocking of his income from France forced Boniface VIII into action. He declared that bishops and orders should make voluntary payments and acknowledged that the king had the right to tax the church in emergencies. When the pope spoke about "voluntary payments," it appeared that he was attempting to save face. That this practically involved a capitulation was apparent in the fact that the pope added an explanation that the king himself could determine what were emergencies in which he could undertake to tax the church. This willingness to oblige was not sufficient for Philip IV, however; not until the pope installed bishops who favored the royal right of taxation did Philip lift the ban on exporting money. Boniface had suffered the first great defeat. Here it became clearly evident that times had changed.

The controversy which followed the one with France demonstrated that anew. In 1298 Edward I conquered Scotland. Boniface immediately declared himself opposed to this; ever since the time of the treaty with John Lackland, Scotland had been a possession of the Roman church, and the king had therefore acted against a papal possession in attacking Scotland and must answer for that before the pope's judgment seat. Edward I presented the papal bull to parliament, and parliament declared: "Scotland has never been a fief of the Roman church; the king will therefore not appear before your judgment seat, and even if he wished, we would not suffer it." Here we see how far the states of Europe had departed from a recognition of the claim to temporal supremacy made by the papacy and the church. The papacy was not struggling against the encroachment of individual rulers, but against what we might call the "spirit of the time," against an attitude which dominated people at that time, and thus it inevitably suffered defeat. If we compare this situation with that of the high Middle Ages (see p. 299), the tremendous change which has occurred since then is apparent.

The year 1300 was a turning point in these controversies. In that year a jubilee indulgence with special promises (similar to those for participating in a crusade) was issued for the first time. Accordingly, huge throngs of pilgrims streamed from all European countries to Rome. Not only did this bring the curia an extraordinarily large income, but it also conveyed the impression that the position of the pope was still the same as it had been in earlier times. The piety of the time was still largely intact; Boniface thought that this devotion to the holy places and recognition of ecclesiastical promises also included recognition of the demand for a special position of the pope above the rulers and states of the age. Thus he revived the controversy with England as well as France, and in so doing brought about his personal catastrophe as well as demonstrating the impotence of the papacy. France was a much more dangerous adversary for the papacy than the German empire had once been. The French state, as mentioned above (see pp. 323–24), was a much stronger one than the German state had ever been. Here nobility and clergy were closely related to the king in a way that we see only for brief periods in Germany, at the time of Otto the Great, for example. In addition, France had the possibility of influencing the curia directly because of this, since it was much more strongly represented in the College of Cardinals than Germany had ever been. These French cardinals were always conscious of their heritage and at least subordinated the pope's temporal claims to those of their own king and nation. Finally, the French kingdom was internally free from ecclesiastical influence in a way that only infrequently existed in Germany. If we want to compare Philip IV's internal position with that of a German king, the best example we can take is Frederick II; other parallels are nonexistent.

Where Boniface VIII stood in these controversies which were now beginning needs no explanation after his bull *Unam sanctam ecclesiam.* It was, as we have said, proclaimed later (see pp. 337–38), but expressed only what Boniface felt and demanded from the beginning. On the other hand, Philip the Fair of France not only felt himself confirmed and strengthened in his position and claims by the preceding controversies about taxing the clergy and the church, but at that time he apparently was toying with much more far-reaching plans. We know of a memorandum given him at that time which sketched ways and means the king could use in subordinating Europe to himself. In reference to the States of the Church and the pope's position, it stated that it was the task of the pope to pray, to preach, and to forgive sins, not to assume temporal authority, so the next step recommended to the king was to secularize the States of the Church. This memorandum did not come from the king, so we need not identify him with its opinions, but it is certainly characteristic that a memorandum of that sort could originate at that time and be presented to the king without his refusing it.

Apart from this, the attitude in France toward the pope was antagonistic enough. The Colonna cardinals, after they had first attempted to stir up opponents against Boniface VIII in Italy, had gone to France and offered sufficient material to those circles demanding greater freedom from the church for the French state. Then came Boniface's blundering actions. He sent the bishop of Pamiers, Bernhard de Saisset, as a legate to Philip IV in order to remind him to carry out a crusade which the king had promised. At the same time the legate had a commission to inform the king that the tithes which were being collected in his land for the crusade could really be used only for preparations for it and not for other purposes (which Philip as well as the rulers preceding him had in fact been doing).

This message in itself was already a challenge. In addition, the choice of the messenger also provoked the king. Bernard de Saisset stood in open opposition to the court. He felt himself strengthened in his position by his appointment as a papal legate and accordingly acted quite provocatively. As long as he remained at court he was unharmed, but as soon as he returned to his diocese (that is, when he was now just a French bishop again and no longer a papal legate), Philip had him brought to Paris and put on trial for high treason and lese majesty. The tribunal pronounced Bernard guilty and demanded his deposition and imprisonment. That took place promptly. He was handed over to the archbishop of Narbonne as a prisoner. One might perhaps believe that here Boniface was only acting undiplomatically. But that is not so definite, for Boniface appears rather to have chosen Bernard consciously as his legate and entrusted him with this commission, for as soon as Boniface learned of Bernard's imprisonment and his deposition, he addressed the bull *Salvator mundi* ("Savior of the world") to the king on December 4, 1301. This bull not only demanded the immediate release of the papal legate so that Bernard could travel to Rome to report to the pope, but it also renewed the old prohibition of taxation and thus revoked all the pope's concessions to France. On the very same day Boniface, in order to make his demand complete, ordered the heads of the French clergy—all the bishops, doctors of theology, representatives of the cathedral chapters, and so forth—to come to Rome in order to advise him in matters concerning the French church. In a special bull Boniface informed the king of this action. Here not only did he severely reprimand him personally, but demanded that he appear in person before a body assembled by him or send his plenipotentiary. As the vicar of Christ, the pope was set over kings and kingdoms and had not only the right but the duty to deal with grievances and to regulate what was useful for a good administration of the French realm.

That was an open declaration of war, for Boniface VIII accompanied this demand with the threat of excommunication. Philip did free the bishop of Pamiers, but expelled him from France a few days later along with the papal nuncio. He summoned a diet for Paris in April, 1302, at which not only nobility and clergy were to be represented, but for the first time delegates from the cities as well. The papal bull was presented to this diet—not the genuine one, but a forged one which abbreviated and sharpened the original text of the papal bull in the way Bismarck did in 1870 with the so-called "Ems dispatch." In this abbreviated form the bull was even more insulting and provocative than its original text had been. Accordingly, the nobility and cities declared that the king was in a justified struggle against the pope's attacks and that they were prepared to stand with him in this fight. There was no alternative left to the clergy but to express themselves in a similar fashion. Yet they asked to be permitted to journey to Rome in order to take part in the meeting announced by the pope. Naturally this request was refused without further ado. The public was informed of this, and in fact a forged answer of the king in a form which was never sent to the pope was made public. It began: "Your great foolishness (*Tua maxima fatuitas,* instead of the usual formula: *Tua maxima Sanctitas* ["your great holiness"]) should know that we are subject to no one in temporal things," and then continued in that vein. The still unsophisticated public, which believed it impossible that anyone would work with forgeries—since the royal authority really stood behind this wording—was extraordinarily impressed at that time. The opposition against Boniface VIII and thus against the papacy, and accordingly the emancipation of the French church from Roman influence, made significant advances at that time.

In reality the king's position toward the church was not as strong as he thought, and the pope's position not as weak as it appeared from the course of these events. That was evidenced by the fact that despite all prohibitions by the French crown, thirty-seven French bishops appeared at the Roman synod. It was then at this synod on November 18, 1302, that the bull *Unam sanctam ecclesiam* was proclaimed. The bull was personally drafted by Boniface VIII and not produced by curial functionaries.

Both parties had taken positions which could not be reconciled. When Boniface finally sent a cardinal legate to France in April, 1303, with a message to the king that Philip should regard himself excommunicated, Philip summoned an Estates General at which he opened a counterattack. Here an indictment against Boniface was read which said that the church no longer had a legal head. Boniface occupied his office illegally; he had obtained his office surreptitiously and after seizing his office had profaned the see of Peter with numerous crimes. In twenty-four points these crimes were detailed. Boniface was not only accused of promoting worship of idols, but he was declared guilty as well. He trafficked with demons and not only was guilty of simony, but also sodomy and similar things. That was expressly certified by declarations of cardinals and other high clergy, just as were accusations against Gregory VII by Cardinal Hugo under Henry IV (see p. 299). Although these indictments were not even worthy of discussion (since it must have been clear to an impartial observer from the outset that they were essentially fabricated), this indictment had its effect. From all sides came declarations of support for the king's actions. It was apparent that a whole series of them was what used to be called "spontaneous declarations of support," that is, ones that originated under gentle or heavier pressure. But there are not a few of these declarations that do give the impression of being made voluntarily. They assure the king of all support in his just struggle against the destruction of Christianity. Therefore Philip could at least indulge the idea that the public approved of his action.

Naturally such an indictment, which self-evidently appealed from the pope to a general council, was only a demonstration. Nothing which was decided could be put into effect unless accompanied with concrete measures. In earlier times the king would have marched to Rome at the head of an army. This age reacted differently. Only Philip's vice-chancellor, William de Nogaret, journeyed to Italy, but he was furnished with liberal supplies of money. He easily found support among the Italian nobility unfriendly to Boniface, especially since a member of the Colonna family accompanied him. And with the help of his money he could assemble mercenaries and wait for a time to strike. The necessity for that soon appeared, for Boniface, who at that time was in Anagni, was preparing a bull of excommunication against Philip. The document was already signed and was to be proclaimed officially in the church of Anagni on September 8, 1303. But on the morning of September 7, William de Nogaret with his companions and a few hundred mercenaries forced their way into the city, whose gates were opened by citizens who had been bribed. They attempted to negotiate with the pope, but without success. To his credit, Boniface refused to make any concession. He therefore was taken prisoner. He was imprisoned only for two days, and in his palace at that, when the citizens rose up against the invaders, and Nogaret and his soldiers were forced to flee. Boniface was freed and could return to Rome. But he died soon thereafter on October 11, 1303.

In that age the capture of a pope was a demonstration of his catastrophe, and the pope's death soon afterward obviously underscored that for the ordinary person. However, Boniface VIII's real defeat lay not in his imprisonment, but in the fact that the means he had used, not merely against the French king but against the French people as well, had had no effect. Even the popes of the high Middle Ages often experienced a lack of success with their measures against the German rulers. But almost always they had supporters for their demands in Germany or in other places so that an opposition party formed against the king. At least a sizable minority always declared itself in favor of the pope, so that the emperor experienced difficulties and not infrequently very substantial ones. However, in France there was no opposition party to the king which declared itself in support of the pope. This was the real defeat of the papacy.

Still the papacy's lowest point was not reached under Boniface. Boniface's successor, Benedict XI (1303–04), gave in to Philip's demands on every point. He released Philip from the ban without even being asked. He granted the king all the financial demands. He even amnestied the French soldiers who were involved in the attack at Anagni. Only the Italians and the leader of the whole thing, William de Nogaret, were (temporarily) excommunicated. With its absolution of almost everyone who participated in the attack and its concessions, the papacy demonstrated its subjection to the monarchy. But even that was not the final stroke. The next pope, Clement V (1305–14), could be elected by the cardinals only after eleven months of deliberation, and then only as a result of the support which Philip gave him. He was of French origin (previously he had been archbishop of Bordeaux) and in 1039 at Philip's instigation moved the seat of the curia to Avignon in the center of French territory. With this the papacy was completely in the hand of the French king. It is true that Avignon later became a papal enclave in France so that the pope could declare he was on the territory of the States of the Church just as before. But even if Avignon were not situated opposite a royal fortification, the guns of which directly threatened Avignon and the palace of the popes, the submission of the papacy to French control would have been clear to everyone with the removal of the seat of the curia. This so-called Babylonian Captivity of the church lasted from 1309 until 1377. The pope, the curia, and the church were thus ruled by France during almost the entire fourteenth century. The number of French cardinals now rose from one-third to two-thirds. In this way the pope and the church were irresistibly bound to the French king. Philip's chief means of applying force against the pope was to demand a heresy trial for Boniface VIII. With that he achieved virtually everything, since every pope would want to do everything possible to avoid this final humiliation. The bull *Salvator mundi* ("Savior of the world") was withdrawn, the Colonnas got their cardinalate back, and France received a special privilege in regard to the bull *Unam sanctam ecclesiam* ("One holy church"). The claims made in it were indeed valid, it was declared, but they had never applied to France. Finally the pope even had to sacrifice the Templars because the order was in the king's way. It disturbed him in his drive toward centralization and attracted him because of its wealth. The widespread possessions of the order in France stood outside the royal domain, neither the king's police nor courts had any say over them, and they paid no taxes to the crown. Both of these combined to cause the king to take action against the Templars. This occurred just as it had erected a bulwark in Cyprus which would have been able to prevent, at least for a period of time, the further advance of Islam which at that time was destroying one Christian fortress after another. But on October 13, 1307, this possibility was destroyed in France when all the members of the Templars were simultaneously arrested.

It was officially stated that this arrest took place on the order of the inquisition, but in reality it was the king who had asked for authority from the inquisition to carry it out. In addition to the accusation of heresy against the Templar order and the individual Templars, serious moral indictments were raised, similar to those accusations against the male Catholic orders which the Third Reich exploited for publicity reasons. It is certain that there were some things at that time which were not right among the Templar order. It was unable to maintain its original religious and moral level (just like the other orders). But what the Templars were accused of and what they were forced to admit under torture was completely improbable from the outset. The trial of the Templars was a scandal of injustice which hardly has its equal in history. Not only did it seriously burden Philip IV, but undermined the moral position of the pope even more than had previously been the case. This was because the pope not only had agreed to the action against the Templars, but now he also turned to the bishops of Europe, demanding that they proceed similarly against them as France was doing. From time to time the pope came to his senses and attempted to deter the sharper and sharper measures. But the French king was able to ward off the pope's every attempt at resistance. For example, he was presented with seventy-two members of the order who under torture had confessed everything they wanted to hear, and out of fear of having the torture repeated, renewed these confessions in his presence. Thus we see the action against the Templars spreading from France throughout all Europe. Wherever torture was used, the same confessions were obtained; wherever they acted according to law, the innocence of the order in all significant points of the accusation was established.

But the Templars' power of resistance was broken. When fifty-four knights of the order, after being summoned from the agonies of the torture chamber, declared that they had made their statements only under torture and revoked their confessions, they were burned as relapsed heretics. Thus no one attempted to offer resistance any longer. The single body which sided with the order was the Council of Vienne, which in 1311 almost unanimously declared that the order was not guilty of the heresy of which it was accused and that it should at least be allowed to defend itself. That was not very much, but a great deal in comparison to what otherwise was said from the ecclesiastical and governmental side.

The pope did not listen to the voice of the council, but dissolved the Templars on his own authority. The single thing that he still did—characteristically—was to try to save the property of the order. He transferred it to the Hospitallers, something that usually could be accomplished only against opposition—in France only partially, and not at all in the Iberian peninsula—for one of the decisive motives of the king in his action against the Templars was the desire for their property. But this attempt to preserve the temporal property changed nothing in the internal catastrophe of the papacy which had also acquiesced in the demands of the French king when everyone—and really even the pope himself—was clearly aware of the injustice of the crown and the miscarriage of justice committed by the king. The papacy had submitted to the king, even against the decision of the Council of Vienne, and this simply made its guilt that much greater in the eyes of the world. Boniface VIII's bulls were now annulled; in the papal registers (that is, in the papal chancellery) all files pertaining to the actions and measures of Boniface VIII against Philip IV had to be removed. Now even William de Nogaret was absolved. The papacy had finally capitulated.

The next pope, John XXII, could be elected only after a bloody two-year conflict between the French and the Italian cardinals, and then only because they hoped his reign would be short because of his age—at the time he was seventy-two years old. Contrary to all expectations, he reigned very long, from 1316 until 1334. John XXII steered the course of the papacy and the church further toward its self-destruction. He was indeed able to accumulate extraordinary means and thus make the papacy the primary financial power of Europe. But that was possible only by further destroying the fiber of the church, for the twenty-five million gold gulden in the papal treasury (about which the legend speaks) could be assembled only if the bestowal of every office were accompanied with increased monetary payments to the curia and if the system of monetary payments for all sorts of purposes—legitimate, but chiefly illegitimate—were continually developed down to the last detail. At that time the church became virtually a collection agency; in this way it sustained damages that were that much more consequential because everyone immediately recognized them. At that time opposition against the secularized church became popular everywhere. At that time the public complaints about papacy and church began—the demands for reform of the church in head and members—which were expressed in a number of reformatory writings, until this reforming literature was finally crowned by Luther's *To the Christian Nobility of the German Nation* of 1520.

The longer the "Babylonian Captivity" lasted, the stronger became the pressure from the cardinals for a return of the curia to Rome. But this initially had no success. John XXII refused to leave Avignon. Urban V attempted to return to Rome in 1367, since the protests—coming chiefly from Italy, but also from other areas of the Catholic church—against a continued stay in Avignon were too strong. However, he remained in Rome for only three years and in 1370 returned to Avignon because conditions in Rome were too bleak. In the pope's absence, the States of the Church had become the plaything of the Italian nobility. Everyone had enriched himself as much as he could. Urban despaired of the circumstances which confronted him. In 1376 a new attempt was made. Gregory XI (1370–78) returned to Rome, since the Italian people were threatening to desert the pope if he did not resume his seat in the Holy City. When Gregory died, Urban VI was elected as his successor. The election had taken place with the Roman people forcing their way in to express their desire for an Italian pope. Despite this formal deficiency, they treated Urban VI as pope and enthroned him. But when it became apparent that he was concerned with reforming the curia and would attempt to do away with the basic causes which had led to the serious damages in curia and church, the majority of the French cardinals rose up against him and in September, 1378, elected Clement VII who returned again to Avignon. Gregory XI was greeted with rejoicing by the Italian people when he returned to Rome. Clement VII enjoyed the acclamation of the French people and the jubilation of the cardinals who had not even made the journey to Rome but had remained in Avignon.

If we observe Boniface VIII's failure and the history of the papacy in the fourteenth century, an additional destructive force becomes apparent alongside all the factors mentioned. At that time it was not only in the temporal sphere where centrifugal forces were active. There the territorial princes attempted to build up their position without regard for the results that ensued from the weakening of the central authority. The same thing was true in the ecclesiastical sphere for the cardinals. They were not interested in having strong popes ruling, but instead they chose candidates who appeared to them to best guarantee the continuance and increase of their personal influence as well as the protection of their personal interests. This explains why sixteen popes ruled during the less than eighty years which separated Innocent III and Boniface VIII. Naturally there could be no guarantee at a papal election of how long a pope would rule and what sort of attitude he would take. But if the cardinals chose an aged pope whose health was not too strong and who had demonstrated in the way he had previously performed his duties as a cardinal that he was not an overly energetic person—and one who had clearly recognized obligations (and there were many who met these criteria)—that could be a sort of guarantee for the egotistic interests of the cardinals. Sometimes they were mistaken, as with John XXII. But frequently they were correct.

As soon as Urban VI proved that he was a reforming pope by attempting to limit the power of the cardinals, he was deposed. He attempted to repress the excessive power of the French cardinals by naming Italian cardinals, and because of this the French majority turned against him. What resulted was the Great Schism which lasted from 1378 until 1415. This schism began with a war between the two popes, which was won by Urban VI at a battle near Marino, and concluded with Western Christianity being divided into two churches vehemently feuding with each other. The pope in Avignon was supported by France, Sardinia, Sicily, Scotland, Savoy, Castille, southwestern and western Germany, and a portion of the Hapsburg lands, while the pope in Rome was supported by central and northern Italy, Flanders, England, the remainder of Germany, and the northern and eastern lands. The world was divided into two camps; the church was split. In the lands which did not unanimously declare themselves in favor of one or the other pope, the situation was especially difficult. That was true in Germany, for example. Here dioceses were often torn apart. Two bishops contended for the same territory, a situation which had happened before during the high Middle Ages, but only in isolated and primarily temporary situations, while this schism lasted for almost forty years. Again and again whenever a pope died, the hope of ending the schism mounted, but again and again this hope was unfulfilled. This was because the cardinals immediately elected a successor and the new pope followed the politics of his predecessor. Even the orders at that time were divided into national groups, and the universities organized themselves into two parties according to the origin of their students. The financial pressure, which had already seemed unbearable under John XXII, even increased, for half the world now had to provide the same amount as all of Christianity had done previously. So the evils of the financial mismanagement were multiplied. Each of two popes was nothing more than a pawn in the hands of the temporal powers. But both advanced the same spiritual claims as the popes of earlier time. It was almost self-evident that one pope declared the other the antichrist, and that each pope imposed the ban not only on his opponent but also on his supporters, so that finally all of Christianity was living in excommunication.

All of that is easy to relate. But we must attempt to imagine what it meant for people of that time—especially for those who really took Christianity and the church seriously, but even for those who lived within the traditional ecclesiastical piety. Only then can we view these events in any sort of perspective. Attempts at reform naturally were not lacking. Again and again the cardinals attempted to secure a pledge from the pope before his election that he would reach an agreement with his opponent about ending the schism. Again and again the popes before their election promised this and everything else that was asked of them. But as soon as they were enthroned, everything was forgotten. The very claim to absoluteness which each pope held really excluded any negotiations with the other. Each one considered himself the representative—the embodiment—of the one true church and all the claims that that involved.

When these attempts failed again and again, the cardinals saw they were compelled to act independently. At first the French cardinals renounced obedience to the pope, and then the cardinals of the pope residing in Rome agreed with the French cardinals and summoned the Council of Pisa in the year 1409. On March 25 the council opened, deposing both reigning popes, Benedict XIII and Gregory XII, and electing a new one, Alexander V. In this way they believed they had corrected the damages of the past and united the church. But the sole result was that the church now had three instead of two popes as before and was now divided into three parts fighting against each other instead of two as before. This was because both popes deposed by the Council of Pisa were not impressed by that decision. When the newly elected pope, Alexander V, died after a ten-month reign, no improvement happened, for John XXIII was immediately elected as his successor. This is how Christianity appeared at the beginning of the fifteenth century. The destruction of the church appeared complete; one hundred years had sufficed to accomplish it.

2. INCREASING NATIONAL CONSCIOUSNESS AND ITS EFFECTS ON THE SPHERE OF THE CHURCH

Perhaps a chapter with this sort of title might seem foreign because it appears to deal with secular factors when what is called for is a discussion of the reasons for the internal decline of the church. But I would believe that it is only on the basis of national consciousness that we can really comprehend the powers which brought catastrophe upon the papacy in those one hundred years and determined the development of the coming generations. It is self-evident that we should not observe this national consciousness in isolation, but only in connection with the presuppositions of that time, that is, in close connection with the piety of the now beginning late Middle Ages. It is not sufficient to talk about an emancipation of the states from the supremacy of the church, since at that time this emancipation had long since been achieved, as we have seen (see p. 300). What we now observe is that the national consciousness is directed not only against the pope's claim to supremacy, but also against the previous construction of the church, and provides a new ideal of the church and ecclesiastical life. In this connection, the real religious criticism itself and the theological formulation frequently grow out of the national protest.

That the papacy contributed to its own demise and was largely guilty of its own catastrophe needs no further detailed discussion (see pp. 347–49). It had used all means, legitimate and illegitimate, to destroy the German kingdom, and beheld the moment of its triumph when the last representative of the despised Hohenstaufen line died at the executioner's hand (see p. 323). This victory was possible only with France's help. Charles of Anjou brought catastrophe upon the Hohenstaufens in

Italy. Thus they were allied with an opponent who soon revealed himself as much more dangerous than the German kingdom.

On the surface, France possessed the same position as the German kingdom had at the height of its power, but inwardly France was more united. The church had no opportunity to stir up opposition to the French king within his own land. And the papacy also found no other support.

It had indeed been able to achieve the destruction of the central authority in Germany. The individual states which resulted were no longer any danger, but they could also provide no help. The same was true for Italy, which now was splintered into numerous individual states which as such could not threaten the papacy, but they also could not provide help when the danger of the high Middle Ages appeared in a different guise. In taking action against the Templars (see pp. 347–48), the papacy itself had helped to destroy the final obstacles which opposed the king's central authority in France. Thus, nowhere could help be found, and the deeper the papacy sank and the more it prostituted itself, that much more did it strengthen the national powers. Not only did it justify their actions, but even challenged them to go farther and farther. The self-destruction of the papacy affected not only its temporal, but also its spiritual position. When conciliarism now became stronger and stronger, this was an outgrowth of the self-destruction of the papacy which had been discredited as the supreme spiritual authority and now attracted the sharpest attacks from all sides—not only from the side of the growing national consciousness, but also from the side of piety.

Germany

Even in Germany, which was experiencing a deep period of weakness at that time, the criticism of the papacy was extraordinarily strong. Despite the weakness of his position, Henry VII (1308–13) could count on the support of many. The intellectual power of the time joined behind him. Whether we read Walther von der Vogelweide or Dante, it is apparent in both cases how strong the powers were which turned against the church and its temporal claims and supported the emperor. Even in the *Divine Comedy* Dante's hatred of the papacy of that time was clear. For example, the nineteenth canto described how Dante wandered through the landscape of hell with his guide. Here they found the popes in unusual circumstances. One, who was head down in a fissure in the earth with his legs pointing upward, motivated the passersby to ask: "O wretched soul, whoso thou art, that keepest upside down, planted like a stake, say a word, if thou canst." The text continues: "And he cried out: Art thou already standing there, Boniface?" This was the way a pope was being punished; he was waiting for his successor Boniface VIII to push him more deeply into the fissure of hell in which his predecessors were already placed.

When Henry VII died in 1314 a dual election occurred, as had happened so often in the preceding generations: Louis IV of Bavaria and Frederick the Fair of Austria were rivaling each other. The double monarchy was ended in the year 1322 by the battle of Mühldorf: Frederick was defeated and taken prisoner. Now the old drama between the German king and the pope repeated itself. In many respects this conflict is reminiscent of the struggle between *imperium* ("empire") and *sacerdotium* ("priesthood") during the high Middle Ages. But only the external circumstances are similar; the considerations under which they existed have fundamentally changed. When John XXII declared that the throne was vacant without papal confirmation and demanded that Louis give up the crown and turn over the administration of the empire to him, the king appealed from the pope to a general council. We now find the same thing happening in Germany that already had taken place earlier in France in Philip IV's time and in Italy at the time of the Colonna cardinals (see p. 339). The papacy had lost its supreme dignity—its supreme ecclesiastical and spiritual dignity as well—because for the very powerful forces of that time the supreme authority of the church resided in the general council. As in earlier times, the pope applied the ban to Louis and freed his subjects from their obedience to him. But now in the Sachsenhausen Appellation of May 22, 1324, Louis declared that the pope was a heretic who wanted to destroy the empire and an opponent of Christ because he had raised up his statutes against evangelical poverty. The king was also not alone with his Appellation, but enjoyed the most powerful support from all sides. Behind him stood the leaders of the strict branch of the Franciscan order, Bonagratia and Cesena; behind him stood William of Occam, the most significant philosopher and theologian of the fourteenth century; behind him stood a widespread public relations campaign. This revealed a complete change in theological thinking. The *Defensor pacis* ("Defender of peace"), which Marsiglio of Padua and John of Jandun published, was the most important writing in this context, since here the thoughts which we otherwise find only in preliminary form were most sharply formulated and most thoroughly developed. Here the sovereignty of the people was proclaimed. The people themselves had all power, and the ruler only exercised power because the people had delegated it to him. Only the civil law applied in the execution of governing power in the state; the law of the church had no influence because it was not valid on this earth, not until the life to come. Thus the church was not identical with what it was generally considered to be, namely the external institution. Rather, the church was represented by the Christian people. There could not be a hierarchy in the church; one office could not be above another. Neither did the pope stand over the bishops, nor the bishop over the clergy of his diocese. All of them were without external authority; all of them were equal to each other; all of them had to act solely with intellectual and spiritual means. They had to proclaim the evangelical law and administer the sacraments. The external means this church needed for its existence were received from the Christian people or their ruler. The state regulated all external affairs of the clergy. The supreme authority and the supreme power in Christianity was not the clergy, certainly not the pope, but the general council. This general council represented Christianity and thus not only had to include clerics, but Christian laity had to belong to it as well. The general council interpreted Scripture, which alone was infallible. The pope had no claim to do so. He was Peter's successor, but not by virtue of divine right, rather only as a result of historical development.

This *Defensor pacis* was accompanied by a great number of tracts of a similar nature. It undoubtedly is of quite extraordinary significance for intellectual history. But we should not exaggerate its significance for that time and the writing's contemporary effect, as is sometimes done. The radicality of its position anticipates the time, and it was certainly circulated only within small, if influential, circles. Here seed was being planted for the future. At the time the *Defensor pacis* was not as significant as something like the activity of Occam (d. after 1347 in Munich), who made himself the spokesman of the Spiritual Franciscans, that is, the branch of the order which wanted to take Francis of Assisi's ideal of poverty with radical seriousness and turn it into the religious ideal of the age (see p. 331). Not even Francis of Assisi could maintain his original radical demands in general. The longer the order existed, the more it was drawn into the general trend of the church, and the more it accommodated itself to the development in the other orders. Contrary to Francis's desire, the order increasingly obtained property. Thus, it was soon forced to make compromises and not just on the subject of property but in many other things. Because of this the radical branch of the order appeared, the so-called Spirituals, who with the support of the

355

papacy and the official church were now gradually suppressed in the order until John XXII, in accordance with the general line of his reign, finally condemned the Spiritual Franciscans. However, they did not submit, but with the help of the emperor and the state now fought for the concerns of the piety of that time against the papacy and official church.

Under the auspices of national consciousness or with its help, the real ecclesiastical challenges were presented, first in Germany, then in England, and finally in Bohemia. In his writings Occam proceeded on the basis that the pope was a heretic, since John XXII had made decisions in the question of the church's temporal property and its ordinances that clearly declared him to be one. If the church were to continue to exist and enjoy protection from the heresy which had broken out in it, it had to turn to the emperor and to the state. Whoever wanted to fight for the church had to stand on the side of the state. That was the conclusion which Occam and many in his age drew.

Fundamentally, Occam understood the relationship between the state and church in this way: papacy and empire stood independently alongside each other. These stood under different auspices, they had a different structure, they were subject to a different legality, and they had to rule according to their own laws. But this equality and independence applied only as long as both were intact. If one of them were in trouble or even in danger of internal collapse, the law of fairness would compel the other to come to its aid. If the state were in danger of collapsing, the pope would therefore be justified in deposing princes and transferring their authority to others. That was the medieval concept. But now something new follows: if the church were in danger of destruction, then not only the princes but even any ordinary layman could exert his claim over it, assuming that he held the true faith. Christ did not promise that the pope or the clergy would always remain in the true faith, but promised only that the true faith would always remain in the church. In this way the laity are not excluded, but rather are expressly included. If the church is in danger, the princes and the Christian laity not only have the right but even the duty to exercise influence over the church in order to safeguard the true faith.

These concepts had an extraordinary effect and exercised a significant influence for generations, precisely because they were not formulated as radically as those of the *Defensor pacis*. If we read Luther's writing, *To the Christian Nobility of the German Nation,* we find a very similar position at its very beginning. Luther demanded that the nobility (that is, practically, the princes) take a hand in the church by calling a general council. The church was destroyed and in danger of more and more disintegration. It could not avoid this disintegration itself; therefore the believing Christians must intervene, especially those among them who because of their position have the ability to do so, that is, the Christian nobility, the princes as the chief members of the church. This Luther wrote at the beginning of his work. That sounds very similar to what we have reported, and in the course of this chapter we shall emphasize many similar parallels which in different ways lead again and again to the threshold of the Reformation. Because of this a preliminary remark is necessary. One after another, we shall discuss Wycliffe, then Huss, then the Renaissance and humanism, then internal criticism in the church, mysticism, and the reform movement within the church. Again and again in doing so, actual and apparent echoes of the Reformation will be heard, so that some might perhaps get the idea (which played a great role in past generations) that the Reformation was really only the result of the various movements of the late Middle Ages and that to a certain extent we can explain it as either an addition or a subtraction to the things which we find appearing in church and world in the preceding centuries.

That is not the case. Rather, with the Reformation something entirely new begins. Even when Luther talks the way people talked before him, as he does, for example, at the beginning of *To the Christian Nobility of the German Nation,* he takes a completely different position (as is immediately shown in the way he continues; he demolishes the "three walls of the Romanists" on the basis of the universal priesthood of Christians [see Vol. II]; his basic presuppositions are competely different. All the sections which now follow cannot be discussed under the heading of "Reformation of the church." They do not even deserve the title of "Pre-Reformation," but rather "Catholic attempts at reform." This is because all of these movements, as significant as they may be, remain within the sphere of the Catholic church. Even Wycliffe's radical criticism does not extend beyond that boundary. All attempts to explain the Reformation on the basis of the age before it—for example, the convinced groups of Marxism, following Marx and Engels, believe that Luther borrowed his decisive material from Wycliffe and Huss—end in a dead end. Undoubtedly, the *success* which the Reformation enjoyed is also (nothing more) to be understood on the basis of the presuppositions of the late Middle Ages, but not the Reformation as such.

But this is only a general remark; now back to our theme: what we observe here in Germany must be even more impressive in view of the weakened condition of the land. Even this internally divided Germany, which at that time was in last place among European powers, roused itself to make decisions such as that taken by the electoral assembly of Rense in 1338. Here, in opposition to the claims of the papacy, the electors declared that the person elected king of the Romans did not need to be confirmed and proclaimed by the Roman see. At the Diet of Frankfurt in 1338 this decision was elevated to the law of the empire: imperial power comes from God; whoever is chosen by the electors is emperor and king solely on the basis of that election. And even in its weakness, the German monarchy held tightly to this; even a king like Charles IV, who with certain justification was nicknamed the Priests' King, held to it. Despite all the defeats which the empire experienced in the high Middle Ages, despite the weakness of the central authority, the principle of the state's freedom from the church's influence also triumphed in Germany, in opposition to the popes' continually renewed claims.

France

In France things were completely different. Here in the sphere of the church the national consciousness really dominated completely, and since being located in Avignon the curia had become virtually a French institution. The pope was French, as well as a majority of the cardinals, and all of them were almost unrestrictedly subject to the wishes of the French king. But despite the injuries to the church which they saw clearly, they really offered relatively little criticism against the existing situation. Not until it came to a schism were the first critical voices raised. Then when a great deal of effort was expended on ending the schism, it was done to improve the ecclesiastical circumstances, but above all to restore the original influence of the French state. It is no coincidence that the University of Paris became the leader of the conciliar group and the instigator of all measures to end the schism. When negotiations accomplished nothing, a French national synod enacted the total subtraction of taxes and provisions, that is, simply put, the cessation of all payments to the curia. In this way they hoped to be able to compel the pope to give in and submit. But they soon saw that these measures were contrary to French interests, since they affected only the papacy at Avignon; hence they pursued other ways. In the year 1407 the original decisions were modified. Not only did they repeat the earlier demands, but now proclaimed the fundamental independence of the

French church. The so-called ancient liberties of the Gallican clergy would be restored, they stated, which meant that within certain limits a French national church was now proclaimed. In the year 1408 they finally separated themselves from the pope in Avignon, henceforth regarding him as nonexistent, and conveyed the administration of his affairs to the provincial synod. This French provincial synod now made laws in the name of the pope, distributed benefices, and so forth. But when the other side enacted similar measures, that is, first withdrew financial support from the pope—this time the one in Rome—and then revoked their obedience to him, the foundations were given for the Council of Pisa about which we have already spoken (see pp. 351–52). In principle, that council acted correctly; it erred only in its choice of means, and above all it acted too quickly. Thus a further division of the church ensued. But despite its lack of success, the Council of Pisa strengthened conciliarism, which was what in fact was finally able at Constance to end the division of Christianity. Through the crisis of the papacy, the self-consciousness of the state in France and the already extraordinarily strong position of France over against the church were only strengthened. The action of the centrifugal forces which would pull the French church away from its subordination to the papacy and lead to independence increased at that time.

England: John Wycliffe

In England things developed similarly. The personal attitude of the kings toward the papacy varied; sometimes they withdrew their obedience toward the pope, and sometimes they drew closer to the papacy. These zigzagging politics apparently were dictated by the piety of the kings. Again and again they submitted themselves to this pope and this papacy despite all its weaknesses, because for them it was an institution established by Christ, because the pope was the vicar of Christ. But in the last analysis it was not the personal attitude of the kings which was decisive for the development of things in England, but rather that of parliament and the representatives of the nobility who assumed an attitude similar to the one we observed in France. Here we find a party continually increasing in strength which raised an alarm about the papacy's dominance over England and demanded a national church. This opposition to the dominance of the papacy was provoked by the political presuppositions of the time.

Since the year 1339, England had been engaged in a war with France which really lasted without interruption until the year 1453 (the so-called Hundred Years' War). In it France was making continually new attempts to free itself from English dominance. At that time England not only occupied strongholds on the channel coast, but above all, areas in southwestern France, and at times, depending on the fortunes of the fighting armies, considerable portions of France. This war made quite extraordinary demands on English finances, so that it was necessary to seek new sources of income. In this context it was easy to tax the church (which possessed between a fourth and a third of England's land) more heavily than before. In addition, there was the fact that the papacy, supported by the French and the curia, even though in a papal enclave, was for all practical purposes located on French territory. Payments from the English church to the curia thus at least indirectly meant a strengthening of France. The stronger anti-French passion was, that much stronger became the demand for action against the church's property, even extending to a demand for complete secularization.

The leader and spokesman of this group was John of Lancaster, Duke of Bedford. Very soon we see Wycliffe taking his side. He became known to a greater public for the first time in 1374 as a member of a commission sent to Brugge to settle the disputes between England and the pope. It was led by the Duke of Bedford. Wycliffe apparently took part in it not because he had previously been involved in the dispute, but as a theological expert. The negotiations did deal with political and financial problems, but the theological questions were not therefore in the background, for the way they were decided frequently laid the foundation for everything else. From then on Wycliffe began to adopt the demands made by Bedford and his party. Wycliffe began with the national consciousness; his rise as well as his demands cannot be understood except on the basis of English church politics and the history of the English church. Only gradually, under the pressure of the schism and the pressure of the ecclesiastical measures against him, did Wycliffe go beyond the national demands to their specifically religious and theological consequences. If the heading of this section and its subject material still needs any justification, it is provided anew by Wycliffe. Here the transition from one to the other is tangible. The national consciousness, about which we spoke in the title of this section, cannot be understood in the modern (that is, secular) sense, but only under the presupposition of that time. This is because the national opposition at that time was simultaneously (or, put more precisely, initially) an opposition against a church which was departing from its origins. It grew out of the piety of that time. If the church were measured against its ideal, against its past, against Scripture—this did not come from the national consciousness, but from piety in the way we have described. An explanation for what was happening in the same way in quite different places can be found, it seems to me, only in the way of looking at things which we have followed here.

Wycliffe was born about 1320, in or near Wycliffe, thus his name. He was a descendant of Anglo-Saxon nobility. His heritage as well as his studies at Oxford and above all his accomplishments there, prepared the way for him. As early as 1365 he was the warden of Canterbury Hall at Oxford, although not for a long time, for in connection with its financial politics the curia was compelled to take a hand in the filling of positions in various ways. If they were to maintain as high an income as possible, they had to try to obtain as many positions in the church as possible for themselves. The more the curia were able to remove a person from his office because of more or less appropriate reasons and then fill that office anew, that much higher would be the income. The newly appointed person naturally had to pay fees to the curia, so the more frequently an office changed hands the better it would be for ecclesiastical finances. Thus Wycliffe was suddenly removed, and someone else took his position as warden of Canterbury Hall. Any resistance was of no avail; Wycliffe had to yield. He received a position as rector in the vicinity of Oxford and also remained a teacher at the university. Even when he received the lucrative parish of Lutterworth in 1374, this did not change.

His activity took place through teaching, lecturing, preaching, and writing. From 1376 on he published a series of tracts in which personal experiences undoubtedly played a role. In them he initially supported the demands of the Duke of Bedford and his party. Here taxation of the clergy in order to reduce the burden on the state was demanded, and moreover a secularization of the church's property. With this he had already abandoned the national arena and moved into the ecclesiastical and theological one. This secularization was essential, Wycliffe declared, not only for the welfare of the state but also for that of the church. Since the essence of the church was poverty, the king was superior to the pope in temporal affairs, and so forth. These ideas, which Wycliffe also presented in sermons in London and other places, enjoyed a powerful echo. The attempt of the bishops to take action against this had little success. Wycliffe was summoned before the episcopal court, but when this first countermeasure was attempted the actual distribution of power immediately became clear. This was because Wycliffe did not appear alone before the episcopal court, but was accom-

panied by the Duke of Bedford and other high officials of the kingdom—
and he was followed by a great crowd of common people. Thus all the
trial produced was strong arguments, but no results. Later the orders
took Wycliffe to court in Avignon. This accusation brought results.
Gregory XI, who in the meantime had returned to Rome, directed
several bulls in 1377 to temporal and ecclesiastical superiors in which
eighteen theses from Wycliffe's writings were condemned. But renewed
trials before the episcopal court produced no results, since now not only
the Duke of Bedford but also the Queen Mother openly declared
themselves in favor of Wycliffe, so that no one dared do anything more
than admonish him.

When we observe these events from the outside, it appears that the
church's action against Wycliffe was without result. In reality, it had
extraordinary consequences. Wycliffe, similar to Luther later, was
driven farther and farther along his way by the action of the opposing
side. Wycliffe had already crossed the boundary earlier into religious
and theological argumentation, but in a way which could be termed only
incidental. Now he did it in a fundamental way and in ever increasing
measure. Now the activity of Wycliffe begins which, if we wish, can be
termed reforming or prereforming. Within two years, from 1378 to
1379, he published a whole series of tracts in which he more and more
developed his theological system. Scripture, he declared here, is the
basis and rule for all things. Scripture contains the complete truth
because it is given by God. It cannot be understood by everyone,
however, but must be interpreted by theologians. These theologians
have significance not only for the spiritual but also the temporal sphere,
since Wycliffe conceived of Scripture as the law of God which is applicable to all, not only as the basis for faith and the church but also for the
world and the daily life of all people. Therefore, the king, the supreme
governor, needs theologians who provide him the necessary conclusions
from the contents of the divine law and show him the means by which
this divine law can be made to apply to daily life as well as the life of the
state. Wycliffe found such a special position of theologians depicted in
the New Testament; it approximates that of the prophets in the Old
Testament.

Theologians, therefore, are really the highest court in the church.
Usually pope and cardinals were considered the representation of the
church, but according to Wycliffe that was a mistake. The church is a
communion of those elected to salvation from all eternity. Thus not even
the pope can be sure that he belongs to the elect or that he is even a

member of the church at all. For this reason the position which he claims to hold as the supreme head of the church does not really exist. With these ideas Wycliffe appears close to the Reformation on many points. But the appearance is deceiving. For example, Scripture is the basis for everything, says Wycliffe, and thus appears to be anticipating the Reformation principle of Scripture. In reality, however, he is decisively distinct from the Reformation on this point. This is because Scripture is the *law* of God for Wycliffe, while for Luther it is the *gospel* which proclaims the justification of the sinner. The situation is similar in other respects. Wycliffe most sharply opposes the pope, as Luther does too. But when we observe Wycliffe's attacks on the papacy, it is apparent that Wycliffe never attacks the papacy as an institution. Wycliffe addresses himself solely to the degenerate papacy which had developed since the Donation of Constantine; he addresses himself against individuals who held the office. The papacy has to be reformed because it has departed from apostolic poverty; it has to be brought back to that. Thus Wycliffe could call an individual pope the antichrist, but as soon as a pope like Urban V undertook reforms in the church, Wycliffe greeted him with enthusiasm. Quite differently, Luther could say rather favorable words about individual popes (even those who were in office at his time!), but for him the papacy as an *institution* was the antichrist, because it had destroyed the faith and destroyed the church—statements that were impossible for Wycliffe to make.

Wycliffe fought against the orders, even the mendicant orders, and declared that the church needed no new sects. But he did this only because the mendicant orders had declared that they supported the cause of the orders which held property. The mendicant orders, which strove for the original ideal of poverty, Wycliffe characterized as an institution worthy of honor, while Luther attacked monasticism as such. Luther also said that there had always been and could always be specially chosen individuals who really were able to fulfill the monastic vows. But monasticism as such was an institution of the devil, because it destroyed faith with works, because here a person rejected God's promise and placed himself in his place, just as the papacy had done in the church. Thus we come again and again to the same result on the basis of different theological presuppositions—that is, that the commonality between Luther and the "Pre-Reformers" was only on the surface and appearances are deceiving. And what is true of Wycliffe—to say this in advance—is also true of Huss and later of humanism.

We need only compare Luther's doctrine of the two kingdoms (see

Vol. II) with Wycliffe's demand that supreme authority in state and church belonged to the king in order to see that the two men's views cannot even be brought together externally, let alone stand in inner dependence on each other. The position of the king, said Wycliffe, was based in the New Testament and confirmed by the church fathers. His power in state and church had no limits. Obviously it was not absolute, for even the king would have to render account in the final judgment about how he had used the power entrusted to him. But until then no limits should be placed upon the king—with the silent presupposition that he was correctly advised by the theologians. Even over the clergy, Wycliffe declared, the king exercised evangelical authority. He called them to order and summoned them to account if they neglected their office. And if the king took a hand in the structure of the church and took temporal property from the clergy—here we return to Wycliffe's old line—then the king was indeed acting properly and for the welfare of the church, since worldly possessions were not something for the clergy. If the clergy opposed the king—under the influence of the pope, for example—then the clergy had to be punished, for the dominion of the king over the clergy and accordingly over the church could be limited by nothing, certainly not even by papal instructions.

These were the basic principles Wycliffe developed in his tracts at that time. Then when he was disappointed in his hope that the church would purify itself, he proceeded to take practical measures. That took place as soon as Urban VI, who began his pontificate with reforms, not only failed with these reforms but was also rendered powerless by the opposing pope (see pp. 349–50). At that time, in the year 1380, Wycliffe first provided for the translation of the Bible into English. In connection with this, he began sending out his own priests, "poor priests," according to the example of Matthew 10. In their person they were to exemplify the apostolic ideal and with their sermons call their hearers to follow it. With staff in hand these priests went across the country two by two, clothed in dark red robes, proclaiming the law of God in every place. Even when their sermons were completely without polemics, their demand for poverty already signified a sharp attack against the clergy and the papacy of that time. Initially Wycliffe limited himself to sending out clerics, but later we also find laity in the role of priests and those caring for souls. At first all of this happened without any opposition to Wycliffe by the church or state.

In the year 1381 that changed. In that year a peasants' revolt broke out in England. Wycliffe had nothing to do with it; in the areas where he was influential the revolt caused less harm than it did, for example, in the areas of his patron and promoter, the Duke of Bedford. Nevertheless, the English upper class did not regard the peasants' revolt as the inevitable consequence of a faulty economic policy that had been practiced and continually increased for generations, but they believed this revolt of the peasants was the result of Wycliffe's activity. Thus among the nobility a group of Wycliffe's enemies formed, now allying themselves with the clergy who had long been opposed to Wycliffe—the external parallels to the Reformation age are obvious (see Vol. II). The year 1381 can certainly be compared to the year 1525. Just as the English upper class made Wycliffe into the intellectual originator of the peasants' revolt, so the Catholic princes at the time of the Reformation claimed that Luther was guilty of the peasants' revolt. The one as well as the other ignored the facts of the situation but did not prevent the corresponding consequences. At any rate, a new synod could meet in London in 1382 and take action against Wycliffe. It condemned twenty-four of his statements, but—in order to be safe—without mentioning Wycliffe's name. At the beginning of the synod an earthquake occurred which should really have been interpreted by popular belief, and by clergy as well who were under its influence, as a sign of God's wrath upon the synod. However, the archbishop skillfully knew how to counteract this mood, declaring that this earthquake foretold that the kingdom would be cleansed of the unworthy and thus was a sign of God's approval and not of his wrath. The House of Lords, dominated by the wealthy classes, agreed with Wycliffe's condemnation by the synod, but the House of Commons characteristically rejected it. Nevertheless, the first measures against Wycliffe and his friends were now taken. Wycliffe did not feel this limited him in his activity. He preached just as before, even with greater and greater clarity, and when he was summoned to appear before a synod in Oxford in 1382 he appeared unbroken and vigorously defended his views before it.

Until his death in the year 1384, Wycliffe in fact did remain untouched. In his final years he developed his theological system more and more and drew dogmatic consequences which brought him into sharper and sharper opposition to the church of that time. But after his death his friends were not able to carry on his work totally, especially since the opposing forces had become stronger and stronger and finally the state even allied itself with the church. In the year 1400 Henry IV, who needed the church's support, placed the civil administration of justice at its disposal. Now pyres on which Wycliffe's followers were burned were erected everywhere in the land. Even Wycliffe himself was condemned posthumously and the Council of Constance ordered his writings to be burned. In the year 1427 his bones were exhumed, burned, and the ashes cast into the River Swift. But all this had only a symbolic significance. Wycliffe's intellectual legacy could not be stamped out despite all the terror. In conventicles his thoughts were passed on. Above all, Wycliffe's seed meanwhile took root in another place. In Bohemia, in the Hussite movement initiated by John Huss, Wycliffe attained an influence that was far greater than anything he ever accomplished in England.

Bohemia: John Huss

It is true that John Huss did have predecessors in Bohemia: Conrad of Waldhausen, Jan Milíč, and others. But it is quite characteristic that Huss, despite the similarity of his ideas to those of someone like Conrad of Waldhausen, was hardly influenced by them, but almost exclusively by Wycliffe. Huss indeed always declared that he had not adopted everything from Wycliffe, for only Scripture deserves unconditional respect. He did in fact make some reductions, chiefly in the area of dogmatics. For example, he did not adopt Wycliffe's severe attack on the Catholic doctrine of the Lord's Supper. While in prison he did indeed agree with the administration of the Lord's Supper in both kinds, but this was far removed from adopting Wycliffe's dogmatic position. Huss was selective in choosing certain of Wycliffe's views and writings, therefore, but in all substantial matters he was completely dependent on him. Huss's dependence upon Wycliffe went so far that sermons that really came from Wycliffe circulated for centuries in Bohemia under Huss's name. When Huss went to Constance he took along three speeches defending himself and his teaching. To a large extent they were assembled from Wycliffe's writings, and even where they were not literally dependent upon Wycliffe's work they made use of his way of thinking. Huss saw his task and the task of his people as making Christianity aware of Wycliffe's thoughts and demands. Huss was not really an independent, productive thinker. His accomplishment consists in the way he selected and adapted Wycliffe's writings and sermons. Huss took Wycliffe's thoughts and formulations and assimilated them to himself or assimilated himself to them. He furnished what he had taken over from Wycliffe with his own experiences; he accommodated it to the presuppositions and demands of his country and time—this is where new material originates—and then welded everything together into an extraordinarily effective whole. In

1402, when Huss began to preach in Czech in the Bethlehem Chapel in Prague, the church soon could not accommodate the crowds of his hearers. The message which Huss presented was just as effective as the form he gave to it. In this way, within a few years he became the spokesman of the Czech portion of the people.

John Huss was born in 1369 or 1370 in Husinec, whence his name. He came from ordinary circumstances. If we are to believe his own account, he then studied theology without any passion for it. He declared that he was attracted to the career that was available to him there. In fact, Huss was not really a man of learning, but a man of action. It goes without saying that he was a Master of Arts. But in theology he obtained only the baccalaureate, that is, the lowest degree. When he became dean of the faculty of philosophy in 1401, that did not signify a great deal. Then as today, the bestowal of that honor might mean only an inevitable event, above all when certain constellations come together. Even when Huss subsequently became rector of the university, that was not a special recognition of his academic achievement, but it was a result of the political presuppositions of the time and Huss's attitude toward them, as also frequently happens today.

Huss proclaimed Wycliffe's national ideas. But when that was done in Bohemia, it was not the same as in England. This was because in Bohemia Germans occupied the decisive positions in the governmental administration as well as in the clergy and in intellectual life, since normally they were superior to indigenous applicants in knowledge and ability (*Fähigkeiten*). The Czechs were indeed in the majority, but the higher one went in state, church, and culture, that much less were they represented and that much more were the Germans. The inferiority complex of the Czechs was accordingly large and their national passion correspondingly strong. In addition, there was the fact that the land at that time was experiencing an economic boom. Not only did the upper class live in luxury, completely oriented toward the world, but the clergy were also caught up in this attitude, so that the Czech populace had some cause for criticism of the clergy. This criticism, which was basically an innerchurchly one, was heightened by the national opposition to the Germans, and thus received its special flavor. When Huss preached the ideal of apostolic poverty—indeed as a repetition of what Wycliffe had said—and when he attacked the claims of the clergy to temporal power and temporal influence, these demands took on a special impact and a special explosiveness. The national opposition between Germans and

Czechs gave Huss an effect that was a great deal stronger than Wycliffe had ever had.

The political situation—and the political situation within the church—was what brought Huss to the head of the university of Prague. We are in the time of the Great Schism, in the period of the so-called second neutrality (see p. 359). Powerful forces in East and West came together at that time and by withdrawing their obedience sought to force the two reigning popes to resign. The Czech king joined this so-called second neutrality (that is, he abandoned both popes), while the archbishop of Prague did not follow the king's lead, but adhered to Gregory XII, as did the majority of students at the university. The university of Prague was organized into four so-called nations, according to the origins of its students. The Bohemian nation was the weakest, while the German nation had an especially strong position. The three foreign nations, along with the archbishop, supported Gregory XII. The king therefore found support for his attitude at the university only among the Bohemian nation which was led by Huss. In order to subject the university to his demands, the king altered the university's constitution (quite parallel to later developments, even down to the present day). The Bohemian nation, which was not only in the absolute minority as far as numbers were concerned but above all as far as influence was concerned, was now given three votes, while the foreign nations together received only one. What resulted was the withdrawal of the German professors and students from Prague and the founding of the University of Leipzig. The University of Prague, which until then had been one of the leading universities of Europe, now declined to a national Czech institution of higher learning. Nationalism and political opportunism had triumphed and caused immeasurable damage, as always happens when they come to the fore. That was of no concern to nationalism (as to all isms); on the contrary, it spoke—as always happens in such cases—of its great success. But when one closes one's eyes to the damage that has been done, it does not disappear from the world and certainly is not healed. As a result of this conflict and the supposed triumph of the Bohemian nation, Huss became rector of the university.

The situation soon changed. After the Council of Pisa (see pp. 351–52), the archbishop supported the newly elected pope, Alexander V, as did the king. Thus, in the future the archbishop not only obtained the king's support, but also special preference from the new Pope Alexander V. As a reward for his attitude, he received from the pope the authority to proceed against Wycliffe's adherents. First the archbishop demanded the surrender of Wycliffe's writings for examination. Naturally Huss protested against this, and naturally the university dominated by Czechs followed his lead. Huss and his followers were therefore excommunicated. The external circumstances had brought Huss to the height of his position. But the external circumstances had now changed; what previously had advanced Huss now worked against him. At any rate, Huss's position was not seriously impaired at first. When the archbishop now turned against Huss, the populace reacted passionately to that and emphatically rallied behind their national hero, behind the spokesman for their feelings, behind the representative of their desires. It is true that the archbishop was a spokesman of the church, but at the same time he was a representative of the hated Germanism, so that his authority was impaired from the very outset.

The situation became critical. At that time John XXIII proclaimed a crusade against Naples. Wycliffe had also experienced a crusade, the one against Flanders. Thus Huss could use Wycliffe's sermons in support of his position against the newly proclaimed crusade. No pope and no bishop, Huss now proclaimed, was entitled to take the sword, even in the name of the church. The task of the church as a whole was no different than that of the individual Christian: it dare not fight against its enemies; it must pray for them. According to Christ's command the pope has to bless those who curse him. The forgiveness of sins cannot be bought by money and good works, only by true repentance. The indulgence which according to old custom was promised to the one who participated in the crusade was of no effect, for it could only help the one who was elected to salvation, the one who was predestined. This the pope did not know, so thus the indulgence which he promised was useless from the beginning. The pope was acting contrary to Scripture, and when the pope acts contrary to Scripture he must be resisted.

Thus, conflict with the entire church was unavoidable, going beyond the previous one with the archbishop of Prague. In addition, because of the new political constellation, this conflict had to become not only a conflict with the church but also a conflict with the state. The longer time went on, the more the king turned against Huss. The queen, considerable circles at court, and above all the nobility of the land were dominated by the Czech national consciousness and did not follow the king's attitude. But that did not change things, for now the state in its official representation stood together with the church in its official representation against Huss and the new Hussite movement. Thus, the initial countermeasures occurred. When the sermons of the clergy who proclaimed the pope's indulgence were disturbed by hecklers who said that the indulgence was a fraud, the hecklers, if they were apprehended, suffered the punishment provided for disturbing a worship service, which at that time was normally execution.

Huss's arguments with his opponents, whose number became greater and greater, constantly became sharper. His opponents among the Prague clergy united and accused Huss before the pope. A council in Rome not only excommunicated Wycliffe but also included Wycliffe's followers in its condemnation. Even though Huss and the Czechs were not expressly named here, it was clear that they were meant. That made little impression upon Huss. He appealed from the secret gathering in Rome, as he said, to Jesus Christ, the supreme judge. But Huss had to leave Prague and stay at a fortress in the vicinity of Prague. The nobility supported him, because for the most part they considered the national attitude against the Germans and Germanism as the decisive thing in the Hussite movement. In fact, at that time Huss was the leader of the majority of the Czech people. When he declared at the Council of Constance that he had come voluntarily, and if he had not wished to, no one could have forced him, that agreed with the facts, since his party members in Bohemia were numerous and powerful enough to protect him against all hostility of the state and the official church. Huss was not summoned to the Council of Constance as an accused man who had to defend himself there; instead he went there voluntarily, after challenging his opponents with an open announcement: whoever wished, should come to Constance and there accuse him of false doctrine. Huss acted this way because he thought he could convert the council to Wycliffe's and his view. That was how convinced he was of the righteousness of his cause and the victory of his just cause.

It is true that Huss possessed a letter of safe conduct, which promised him personal safety, from King Sigismund. But when he arrived in Constance, accusations were immediately raised against him by the Czechs. They managed to have Huss thrown into prison and proceeded so far with the trial against him that the German king, when he finally came to Constance, could not undo the events which had already occurred. Sigismund saw that if he wanted to achieve the goal of the council, and indeed if he wanted to preserve the unity of the council at all, he would have to sacrifice Huss (and breach his promise to him). Huss was imprisoned at length and questioned repeatedly. But he could never really present his case in these hearings, so great was the bitterness against him. A real debate with him did not take place; the sentence was pronounced upon him—we can pointedly say—in the moment he came to Constance. On July 6, 1415, in the Constance cathedral he was formally condemned to death by fire and following that burned at the stake. And the second leader of the movement, Jerome of Prague, who was really responsible for the connection between Wycliffe and Huss, was also burned at the stake in the spring of 1416. Jerome had studied at Oxford and had brought Wycliffe's writings from there, and it was probably through him that Huss became acquainted at all with Wycliffe's views.

As soon as the news of Huss's death at the stake reached Bohemia, the Czechs rose up. Riots first occurred in Prague. The residences of priests who were known to be his opponents were stormed. The Czech nobility united in a Hussite brotherhood and was quite openly supported by the queen. This brotherhood demanded free preaching of the gospel in all estates; the bishop was to be obeyed only in matters which were clearly dealt with and decided by the Bible. Thus obedience was practically withdrawn from the bishop and, in the further development of things, also from the king.

The Catholics attempted to oppose this, but without great success. Even the interdict imposed upon Prague had no significant effect. On July 20, 1419, the indignation broke out in full force, demonstrated— apparently this is the custom in Prague, for the Thirty Years' War also began in this way (see Vol. II)—by throwing the city councillors who opposed Huss out of a window. The reason for this is not completely clear, but they probably had ridiculed a passing procession of Hussites from these windows in the city hall. Shortly thereafter, King Wenceslaus died of a stroke. His successor, the German king Sigismund, could not enter his inheritance, since all of Bohemia was in revolt. An attack on monasteries and churches had driven monasticism out and taken temporal property away from the church. It came into the hands of the nobility. All of Bohemia declared itself for Huss and against the decision of the official church in Constance, and soon also against the state because it adopted the decision of the church.

The Hussites were divided into two groups, the Calixtines or Utra-quists, also known as Pragites, and the Taborites. The former were called this because their chief demand was to receive the Lord's Supper in both kinds (*calix* = chalice; *sub utraque specie* = under both forms), or Pragites, because they had the largest number of their adherents in Prague and at its university. In the Prague Articles of 1420 they announced their program: free preaching of the Word of God, the Lord's

Supper in both kinds also for the laity according to the New Testament institution, abolition of temporal authority and the earthly possessions of the church. The law of God had to be the rule in all things; government stood in the service of this law of God and had to strive to carry it out. That was the program of the moderate Hussites. The radicals called themselves Taborites after their center, the fortified mountain settlement of Tabor (the name comes either from the Old Testament or from the ecclesiastical tradition that says the transfiguration of Jesus took place on Mount Tabor). They demanded the implementation of Wycliffe's teachings in their full extent. The divine law was the guiding principle for everything; only what was expressly prescribed in it was valid. Everything not found in it was to be condemned. The cult of the saints, the veneration of images, the oath, auricular confessions, indulgences, the sacrament of confirmation, the sacrament of extreme unction, along with many other things belonged in this category. Earthly splendor was to be banished from all churches. The occupants of the pastoral office were not to be appointed, but elected. According to divine law, even laity could fill the office of the ministry; it could even be bestowed upon women. The kingdom of God, which is ruled by divine law, was not limited to Bohemia, but had to be brought to all people. After the Old Testament model (that is, with the sword), the kingdom of God had to be extended and its enemies had to be annihilated.

Naturally king and pope tried to subdue the Hussites. But their attempts were fruitless. All armies sent against the Hussites were defeated by them, although the power of the Hussites was seriously limited because of the split among them. When they united and in 1427 turned from defending themselves and took the offensive, this happened with massive force. Neither state nor church was able to stop the Hussite armies. Thus the pope finally agreed that the Council of Basel could begin negotations with the Hussites (see p. 398). These negotations, in which the Hussites appeared as full partners, ran a stormy course and produced no agreement. When the council continued its efforts and sent an embassy to Bohemia, it could not come to agreement with the Hussites as such, but it could with the moderate group among them, the Utraquists. At that time the so-called Compactata of Prague were concluded, giving the Hussites their chief demand, the chalice for the laity, and also, although in limited form, the demands of the Prague Articles of 1420.

The agreement with the Utraquists was possible because they believed they had accomplished their objective and because they were tired of the war. The Taborites refused to assent to the agreement. Accordingly, the Utraquists, who wanted to achieve an end to the conflicts, allied themselves with the Catholic party, and their united forces enabled them to defeat the Taborites decisively. Only because of the disunity of the Hussites was it possible to end the Hussite disputes, for not even the combined forces of pope and king would have been able to prevail against the Hussites if they had been unified among themselves.

The Hussites regarded themselves as cheated out of their deserved reward, for when no immediate danger existed any longer—really as soon as the Compactata of Prague were conceded—attempts began to revoke the concessions. Thus Bohemia remained full of unrest. It is true that the religious force of the Hussites weakened; the Taborites drew closer to the Utraquists, and the Utraquists on their part drew closer to the Catholic church. However, the Reformation, with which the Hussites sought a connection after the Leipzig debate, brought an influx of new strength, so that the ferment did not cease during the entire sixteenth century. At the end of that century the increasing pressure of the Counter-Reformation led to more numerous and increasingly sharp clashes, until finally in 1618 not by chance did the Thirty Years' War begin in Bohemia.

Italy: Renaissance and Humanism

In Italy the strengthening of national consciousness led to the Renaissance; humanism was the learned achievement that flowed from this movement caused by the strengthening of national consciousness. In this period Italy had degenerated into a number of small states. The powers which previously dominated the land were no more: first the empire had become impotent, then the papacy as well. In the fourteenth century the papacy was first in "Babylonian Captivity" in Avignon (see pp. 346–49). Then when it returned to Rome it divided first into two parts and finally into three (see pp. 349–52), and the doubling and tripling did not increase, but catastrophically reduced the strength of its individual parts. The land was divided in an infinite manner, and countless forces struggled with one another, so that one could almost say that everyone was fighting against everyone else. In Italy the representative of that age became the *condottiere,* the mercenary leader, who took part in the numerous struggles among the individual powers—sometimes here, sometimes there, according to which side promised him more advantages. The more important of these mercenary leaders attempted with the help of troops, which they had attracted to themselves by their ability, the success of their weapons, and their unscrupulousness—that also was not lacking—to establish a powerful position for themselves, in order to add another new one to the countless small powers in Italy. The present situation was in a shambles. Thus they looked with ever increasing nostalgia toward the past, the greatness of which they took as a model, searching for means to reestablish this past and its greatness.

Characteristic of the *condottieri* of that time was Cola di Rienzi, one of the most important of them. He was the son of a washerwoman and by occupation a notary. As a mercenary leader he was extraordinarily successful, so he thus attained a higher and higher reputation, and the more important his position became, that much higher did the goal become toward which he aspired. In 1347 he could achieve dominion over Rome as tribune of the people. At that time the city had been abandoned by the popes, and the noble houses of the Colonnas, the Orsini, the Caetani, and whatever their names may be, were constantly struggling with one another and thus paralyzing their strength. Cola di Rienzi was able to put an end to the chaos in Rome. After achieving that, he wanted to proceed from there to free Italy.

Finally his plans went even further; after the suffering of the present in Italy was replaced with something new and better, he would set out to establish the dominion of Jesus Christ over the entire world. Just presenting these plans—here the desires of the age are reflected—is sufficient to indicate that their realization was impossible; that they dealt with a utopia needs no explanation. Cola di Rienzi was not even able to maintain dominion over Rome for long. As soon as the disunited noble houses found their way back together, his power in the capital was at an end after a few months. But that did not prevent him from pursuing his plans. He went to Charles IV (1346–78) in Prague, in order to place himself at his disposal. Together with the emperor, Cola di Rienzi would undertake the attempt to renew the world.

All of that happened with a nostalgic look at the greatness of the past. The attraction to antiquity did not happen for the first time in the Renaissance, but in the early Middle Ages. But in the Carolingian Renaissance, for example, that antiquity presented itself exclusively in the church fathers. In scholasticism the return to antiquity took place on a somewhat broader plane: now the philosophers of antiquity were also studied; but that still was done only to the extent they were helpful in constructing the scholastic system. Only gradually did other writings of ancient authors come into consideration alongside ecclesiastical authors and those writings which were important for the ecclesiastical doctrinal system—but only insofar as they were written in Latin or available in Latin translation. The contact with antiquity was decisively curtailed by the language barrier. Only in the course of the fifteenth century did this change. More and more Greek scholars came to the West even before the fall of Constantinople in 1453. As the catastrophe of the Byzantine Empire gradually became apparent, they fled from the approaching Turks and brought their most valuable possession: manuscripts of the ancient writers. In Italy each one of them became the center of a circle which devoted itself to Greek antiquity. And in this context a second change took place: previously the ancient writings were read for their content—first the theological, then the profane—but now the interest gradually turned from their content to their form as well.

The pioneer of the new way of looking at things was Francesco Petrarch (1304–74). He proclaimed the ideal of beauty of form, and poetry gradually became an independent element alongside the previous disciplines. The world can be led out of its present miserable situation, Petrarch declared, only with the help of the philosophy of Christ (that is, although transposed, the old position) and—here he adds something new—poetry. In order that this can take place, the old powers must be destroyed. Petrarch therefore severely attacked Aristotle and scholasticism and presented Plato and Platonic philosophy as the ideal in opposition to them, although he did not know Plato in the Greek original at all, and not even totally in Latin translation, only in the excerpts which he knew from Augustine's work. According to Petrarch's standard, Plato was the ideal of the philosophers and the philosophy of that time.

The medieval encrustation had to be removed—that was the slogan. The philosophical pomposity of the jurists, philosophers, and theologians of the time was countered with Christian simplicity. The return to pure and genuine antiquity would heal the damages of the time. This is what Petrarch declared, and his friends and pupils repeated it after him. The center of these views now became not Rome, but Florence. That was no coincidence. This is because in Rome the ancient traditions had been broken down or at least had become so weak that not until later, after renewed strength was introduced, could they again take effect. Not only was Rome largely destroyed externally, but also was it destroyed internally through the continuing struggles of all the powers among themselves which had now been going on for generations. In contrast, in northern Italy the cities, because of their location along the major trade routes, had not only accumulated wealth, but new centers of culture had also been formed here because they had been less affected by the struggles of the past.

This culture of the northern Italian cities was now characterized not only by the attraction to antiquity but also by the increasing emancipation from the church. Here not only was a new relationship to antiquity found, but also a new relationship to the world in general. Petrarch still believed that reading the ancient writers should serve to restore Christianity. In Florence, Christianity often was now only an outer form when compared to antiquity, and even this frequently was not done. That had its effect and was frequently imitated. Nevertheless, Italian humanism deeply permeated the church. We not only find the popes of that time being affected by the Renaissance and humanism, but everywhere in the church—with the bishops, even with the simple clergy—we see the thoughts of the Renaissance and humanism taking effect. That those who held ecclesiastical office frequently—at least the way we see it— were influenced by the worldliness of the Renaissance is another matter. At any rate, the views of the humanists conquered all of Europe with great rapidity. In this, humanism was assisted by the newly invented art of printing. Now the ancient authors and their manuscripts could be brought out from the dust of the libraries and become the common possession of educated people of the world. The ideas of humanism, which was not merely an academic movement but also a special *Weltanschauung,* spread with voracious rapidity. Alongside the nobility of blood, the nobility of the sword, and the nobility of wealth which had previously ruled the world, a fourth group now appeared: the nobility of intellect. In Europe a republic of scholars arose. Everywhere we find humanists who consider themselves representatives of the same concern and, no matter how miserable their external existence may be, feel themselves the equal of all those who, for whatever reason, possess status and a name in the world. Never did scholarship stand so important as at that time, never did such effective influences and forces proceed from it. The leading humanists were uncrowned kings. Erasmus enjoyed a position like that of no intellectual after him—it might be too much to say before him, since the leading scholastics did occupy a similar position, but among a much smaller circle than the humanists.

3. THE SIGNIFICANCE FOR THE REFORMATION

Now what is the significance that Wycliffe and Huss, humanism and the Renaissance have for the Reformation? Previously, it used to be considered very great. Wycliffe, Huss, and others about whom we must still speak (see pp. 391–92), were labeled prereformers, since it was thought they were not only forerunners of the Reformation but also had already adopted definite theological understandings of the Reformation. Luther was their heir: if one wished to understand him and the Reformation, one had to study these men. That view is obsolete. Nowhere is it held any longer; only in certain circles of Marxism is Huss still labeled as Luther's forerunner, who already recognized and proclaimed everything that was decisive. Practically speaking, Luther was the same as Huss and could be distinguished from him only by his greater success. That is still being repeated today, because Friedrich Engels or Karl Marx declared it a hundred years ago—exaggerating a widely held view of that time. But of all the theses that might be held, this is certainly the most nonsensical, for all the pertinent sources permit us to make a dependable judgment. Only after the Leipzig debate did Luther become acquainted with Huss's writings. As a result of the echo which this disputation enjoyed, and because of the fame which Luther had already attained at that time, the Bohemian Brethren turned to him and presented him with Huss's writings, which we know Luther read with great amazement. At that time Luther said these writings and this man were a miracle, for Huss had already anticipated everything which Luther taught. Luther made that statement in 1519/20. Perhaps we may explain the position of Marx and Engels on this basis, but not understand it. That is because Luther's remark about Huss parallels others he made about his predecessors and contemporaries, all of which—although literally authentic—miss the mark in exactly the same way in exaggerating the matter. In regard to Huss there can be no doubt. In the time he was developing into a reformer, Luther was unacquainted with him. Only after he had completed his decisive development—no matter what date we assign to the tower experience, in any event it took place a long time before the Leipzig debate—did he become acquainted with Huss and was surprised at the apparent agreements, just as he had been with mysticism, just as he had been with Staupitz, and just as he had also been with others— and in every case incorrectly. It is indisputable that Wycliffe, Huss, and all others whom we might consider Luther's forerunners were completely dominated by late medieval thinking. The Reformation not only developed independently of them, but the Reformation took place on a completely different level—and that is the decisive thing. We may sharpen this statement by pointing out that even where the statements of Luther and those of his predecessors are literally identical, in both cases something completely different lies behind them. This can be proved again and again.

At the beginning of this century, for example, a controversy developed over whether the *iustitia Dei passiva* ("God's passive justification"), the formula expressing Luther's decisive discovery (see Vol. II), could be found in biblical exposition before the Reformation. At that time the learned Dominican (and anti-Reformation agitator) Denifle published an entire book in which he assembled citations where he alleged that the *iustitia Dei passiva* was found in pre-Reformation biblical exposition. Here, he declared, the real substance of the Reformation's concern was already mentioned in numerous ways. Karl Holl, in a very learned exposition, attacked his position, and—surprisingly—did not employ the decisive argument: when the Reformation spread and also quickly took hold among theologians of that time, the commentaries and learned works on which Denifle based his claim were generally known. The Reformation experienced lively opposition from the very beginning and from learned Catholic theologians as well. If things had really happened the way Denifle claimed, then we certainly would have expected someone at that time to stand up and declare that Luther's fundamental view was nothing new, but an ancient element of Catholic tradition. That did not happen; rather it was considered not only by the laity and pastors, but also by the learned theologians as something completely new—as a way of looking at things they previously had not thought of or even believed possible. The texts which Denifle uncovered were either interpreted differently by Luther or they were read by him with closed eyes, insofar as he was even acquainted with them at all. This also applies to Luther's early lectures. There he said things which today look reformatory to the observer, and it is on this basis that the tower experience is dated so early. But Luther said them—this formulation may seem paradoxical—without really knowing what he was saying. That is because they dealt with things he only partially understood, the significance of which was not apparent to him and which so far he had not put together into a total picture. One might say that he had not yet really become conscious of them; the breakthrough in which that occurred did not take place until shortly before the second lectures on the Psalms. Thus, when Luther later reminisces about something which took place in that early period, it is not always useful and must only be used with great caution. If we take Luther's statements in isolation, Luther appears to be wrong, and the modern scholar who finds the decisive material as early as the early period appears to be right. But if we read the early lectures as a whole, we see that here indeed Augustine is dominant, that here indeed Paul is dominant, but this is not yet the Reformation in its entirety.

It is obvious that Wycliffe's work, the activity of Huss, and the work of the humanists are of decisive significance for the Reformation insofar as they prepared the ground in which the seed of the Reformation sprang up. In this respect, humanism, to return to it, quite considerably surpassed Huss as well as Wycliffe. The Reformation received much greater assistance from humanism than from Huss and Wycliffe. But nevertheless the Reformation and humanism belong to different worlds. And this is true, although Melanchthon was a humanist, and although Zwingli was dependent upon Erasmus in a decisive way. We can see this in the example of Melanchthon. Melanchthon the humanist could only grow into the Reformation; he could only become its spokesman after experiencing a radical change which took place in him soon after he assumed his position at the university of Wittenberg. The disagreement between the Reformation and humanism, which occurred in 1524/25 in the controversy between Luther and Erasmus, was inevitable. This is because the encounter, indeed virtually the association between humanism and the Reformation which existed during the initial years of the Reformation, rested upon a misunderstanding—principally a misunderstanding on the side of the humanists, but a misunderstanding on the side of the Reformers as well. In the initial period of the Reformation both sides believed they were talking about the same thing, but in reality they were only using the same words. They lived by a different spirit. Erasmus's writing on free will and Luther's reply De servo arbitrio ("The bondage of the will") revealed the depth of the contrast, one which extended to the initial presuppositions about knowledge and faith. It was no coincidence that the humanists who did not surrender themselves completely to the Reformation—there is no other way to express it— soon turned away from their initial friendly or neutral attitude toward the Reformation and found their way back to the Catholic church.

The importance of humanism in preparing the way for the Reformation, however, cannot be evaluated highly enough. Instead of speaking about this in general, we shall introduce three representatives of this humanism: Lorenzo Valla as one who represents early humanism and also Italian humanism, Reuchlin as a representative of German humanism, and finally Erasmus as the most important humanist and at the same time a representative of humanism which understood itself in international terms. In this way we shall achieve greater clarity about the accomplishments as well as the significance of humanism. Lorenzo Valla (1405–57) is undoubtedly one of the greatest critical spirits who ever lived. His writing of 1440 (first printed in 1517 through Hutten's efforts) which proved the Donation of Constantine to be a forgery destroyed one of the foundations for the existence of the medieval papacy. This work alone would suffice to make Valla's name immortal, although Valla—in a proper perspective—was not writing exclusively to uncover historical truth and to correct errors. Rather, his writing was intended to be an attack; he coupled these historical proofs with the most severe attacks against the pope, whom he demanded relinquish temporal authority and become the real vicar of Christ, holy father, father of all and father of the church—renewed evidence of how close a connection there was between the movements presented in this chapter and the internal criticism of the church. Let it be stated in passing: the vehement polemic against pope and curia did not prevent Valla from accepting a position there and did not prevent the pope from giving him that position and holding a protective hand over Valla, something which he continually needed.

Besides this writing on the Donation of Constantine, Valla wrote tracts in which he proved that Christ's correspondence with Abgar of Edessa was not genuine. In addition, he doubted that the Areopagite writings were composed by Dionysius of Athens, and finally he even declared that the Apostles' Creed could not have been written by the apostles. At that time all of this was a sensation; at the same time it anticipated the results of the intellectual endeavors of many generations. All of these understandings and proofs are part of the self-evident presuppositions of today's scholarship, the scholarship of all churches. In addition, there was the fact that Valla dealt in advance with things that did not attain their full significance until the sixteenth century. Among his works we find a work on free will, as well as a comparison of the Vulgate with the Greek original of the New Testament. The theme of free will took on a central importance for the sixteenth century. Valla's interest in the Greek text indirectly prepared the way for biblical scholarship of the sixteenth century, and directly as well, since his work served as the foundation for Erasmus's parallel undertakings.

This is Valla, whom we may regard as representative of early humanism in Italy. If we wish to do so, however, we must add that alongside these almost unbelievably learned deeds there are some things which do not reduce Valla's stature—the most decisive thing about people is the accomplishments they achieve; they survive the centuries, while their imperfections soon recede behind them—but do reduce some of our respect for him. We must only look a little more closely at the conflict in which he was involved with his colleague Poggio Bracciolini in order to see at that time—as so frequently during the subsequent time—that greatness of intellect and academic achievement could be coupled with some human weaknesses. The two poured buckets of filth upon each other, and feuded with all means available. Here the vanity of the humanists, something that was characteristic of them, as well as of the learned world in general, celebrated a triumph. Here is revealed their sensitivity, and here also is revealed their unscrupulousness in the choice of means in the controversy. Here is revealed the fact that the way they led their lives was frequently open to criticism, and many similar things, to put it mildly. And that applied not only to these two, but to most of the Italian humanists.

German humanism possessed a different character. Naturally it was also influenced by the South, but it was significantly different from it both in life style and in attitude toward Christianity and the church. Johannes Reuchlin (1455–1522) may be taken as its representative. He matched the ideal of that time, for he was a *homo trilinguis*, that is, a man who knew the three languages in which the wisdom of the ancients was preserved: Latin, Greek, and Hebrew. Reuchlin was the first person in Germany who really had a command of Greek, and he was the first (not just the most outstanding, but also chronologically first) Hebrew scholar of humanism in general. Reuchlin laid that age's foundation for the study of Hebrew, the knowledge of which he acquired by studying with the Jews (as he studied Greek with the Greeks). His book *De rudimentis hebraicis* ("On the rudiments of Hebrew") of 1506 with a lexicon and grammar provided the basis as well as the practical tools for this. That Reuchlin had an especially high regard for Hebrew can be understood on the basis of his joy of discovery; he declared that it was not only equal to Latin and Greek, but even superior to both languages in its good qualities. This high regard for Hebrew and his love of Jewish literature led Reuchlin into the struggle of his life.

At the beginning of the sixteenth century there was a young Jew in Cologne named Pfefferkorn who had converted to Christianity. He saw it as his task in life to bring his former religious comrades to Christianity. Thus, he published a series of missionary writings in which the usual accusations were raised against the Jews—the arguments of anti-Semitism have changed little in the course of time. The special thing about this, however, was that here it was a Jew who was writing and making these accusations against his comrades in blood and faith. In the year

1509 he obtained an imperial mandate which ordered the confiscation of the writings of the Jews. This is because Pfefferkorn believed the best way of overcoming the stubbornness of the Jews was to take away their writings. If they were not continually able to draw new strength from them, it would most easily be possible to lead them to Christianity. The confiscation of Jewish literature began. But resistance was encountered from various sides. That happened partially at the instigation of the Jews themselves, whose influence at that time was in practice very considerable despite all the periodically recurring persecutions, and also because the territorial princes believed the imperial mandate was infringing improperly on their own sphere of authority. Thus opinions were sought from the experts, among them also Reuchlin. In 1510 he declared that the mandate was wrong. Only the obviously libelous writings of the Jews against Christians should be confiscated; everything else must be left alone. The manuscripts of the Hebrew Old Testament were untouchable. The Jewish biblical commentaries were necessary for interpreting them, and the cabalistic writings were important for faith. The Talmud also contained some good material. But even that which did not fall within these categories—biblical manuscripts necessary for biblical interpretation and important for faith—should be preserved, according to the model of the ancient church which also had not destroyed pagan writings even though their contents were opposed to Christianity. And finally, Reuchlin said (even in a defender of Judaism and Jewish writings at that time anti-Semitic points could be found), one should not believe everything a baptized Jew said.

Thus Reuchlin challenged Pfefferkorn, who had now begun a literary war against him with his *Handspiegel wider und gegen die Juden* ("Hand mirror against and contrary to the Jews"). Pfefferkorn's argumentation was relatively primitive. Only one who was unacquainted with the Jewish writings, he declared, could deny their hatred for Christianity. Reuchlin denied the Jews' hatred for Christians, so therefore he could not have been the author of the learned works about Hebrew which appeared under his name. Reuchlin replied with the *Augenspiegel* ("Ophthalmoscope"). But now the controversy, which until then had been one of the usual literary polemics, took a decisive turn when an appeal was made to the theological faculty at Cologne, which was given the task of carrying out the inquisition. They examined the *Augenspiegel* and declared forty-three statements from the work heretical. Reuchlin was deeply affected. He humbled himself in Cologne in a way that was characteristic for the humanists (and for all the humanists, including even Erasmus, all of whom developed intelligence at the expense of character, something that intellectuals apparently have been inheriting ever since). But Reuchlin's submission was without success; the inquisition, strong in its consciousness of power, was not impressed. Pfefferkorn triumphed and published a *Brandspiegel* ("Burning glass"), in which he proclaimed his triumph to all the world. With that, Reuchlin's patience was at an end and he wrote his *Defensio contra calumniatores,* the "Defense against the slanderers," and now spoke in the crude language of that time. (When people continually accuse Luther, even to the present day, of using crude language, they forget that Luther was fundamentally no different than others of his time; it is true that he was crude enough, but others were just as crude, if not even cruder than he.) Here Reuchlin speaks about the asses, the swine, the children of the devil, the senile Cologne faculty.

Now he increasingly won confederates, for in the meantime the humanists had become aware of the controversy. It is true that they were little interested in Hebrew, not at all in the cabala, and even negatively interested in Judaism. Thus they were not fighting for Judaism, and not at all or only to a limited extent for Hebrew. But when freedom of scholarship was concerned—and this must be said to humanism's credit (and also to the credit of some of its successors)—then they abandoned their fear of men. Then the weakness which otherwise characterized them fell away, then they determinedly risked everything, even to sacrificing their own person (compare the way Hutten's life ended, for example) for what they considered right. The Cologne theological faculty now became for the humanists the embodiment of scholasticism, the heretic tribunal, ignorance, and the roadblock to scholarly investigation; thus, the attack against the Cologne faculty took on greater and greater depth and sharpness. Reuchlin was condemned at a trial in Mainz. He appealed to the curia, however, which delegated the investigation to the bishop of Speyer, and Reuchlin was declared innocent: the accusation of heresy was undeserved, unconsidered, unjust, and had taken place at the expense of silencing truth. Thus, we see how strong were the forces of humanism. But the Cologne faculty did not admit defeat. Hochstraten went to Rome in the name of his faculty and the inquisition and attempted to bring about a change in the verdict. In this he was supported by influential powers both inside and outside the curia, for in the meantime the controversy had involved all of Europe. Even crowned heads took a hand in it; it was characteristic that Emperor

Maximilian took Reuchlin's side, while King Francis I of France, as well as the later Emperor Charles V, sided with Hochstraten.

But although Hochstraten used all his means, and although he was able to win the papal confessor over to his side, in 1516 the papal commission with only one member taking exception decided that the *Augenspiegel* was irreproachable. Reuchlin and the humanists' cause triumphed anew. The judgment was not made public because they did not want to encourage the critics of the church and the critics of monasticism by officially absolving Reuchlin. Nevertheless, it became known; Reuchlin's victory was obvious. The defeat of his opponents became the talk of the town when the *Epistolae obscurorum virorum* ("Letters of obscure men") appeared in 1515, and its continuation in 1517. With this satire they were exposed to all the world, morally destroyed as it were. The drama began in the year 1514 when Reuchlin put into print the *Clarorum virorum epistolae,* that is, the "Letters of famous men," who had taken his part in the controversy. This collection of letters was intended to show the world that the academic world supported his party. Then when the *Epistolae obscurorum virorum* ("Letters of obscure men") appeared, everyone believed that here the opposing side was publishing letters by its adherents in order to strengthen its position and that the title had been chosen in contrast to Reuchlin's to show the humility of the authors of these letters. But when these letters were read, they produced hearty laughter on one side and hearty rage on the other, because the letters were fictitious, *Dunkelmännerbriefe* ("Letters of shady men"), as they soon were called. They were written in bad vulgar Latin, and uncovered—sometimes in what we must admit was extremely crude satire—the intellectual backwardness, the academic incompetence, the arrogance, and the immoral life of the Cologne faculty and Reuchlin's opponents. It goes without saying that the identity of the authors was painstakingly sought at that time, and the search has continued to the present, but final clarity cannot be achieved. The most that can be said is only that Crotus Rubeanus had a significant part in the first volume, and Hutten in the second.

The laughter generated in all of Europe made Reuchlin the final victor, although in 1520, when the verdict of the church was finally announced, he submitted formally. With this verdict of 1520 Reuchlin was not the only one to be affected, but Luther was affected as well, who in the meantime had become entangled in the matter concerning Reuchlin—indeed unjustifiably, for there was no real connection between Luther and Reuchlin. As had numerous others, Luther had written a letter to Reuchlin in which he took his side in the controversy with the Cologne faculty, and Melanchthon, a nephew of Reuchlin, had come to Wittenberg at his recommendation. That was all; Reuchlin had never had any personal association with the Reformation. Besides that, the verdict of 1520 came too late; in the meantime, the dispute about Reuchlin, which earlier had affected the entire world, had been forgotten. Now other problems were being considered, and the most that can be said is that the condemnation of Reuchlin affected Luther and his concern only peripherally.

Reuchlin was treated as a representative of German humanism. Desiderius Erasmus of Rotterdam (1466 or 1469–1536) represents a different type. He was Dutch by birth, but he lived in England, as well as in France, Germany, and Switzerland. He was a cosmopolitan. In him humanism broke free from its national attachment, which had been undeniable with Valla as well as with Reuchlin. Learning was international; the humanist belonged to no one people, but to all peoples—this was the attitude represented and lived by Erasmus. It is true that his chief area of activity was in Germany, which he called "his Teutonic land," but that no more removes his fundamental internationality than does the fact that on his deathbed Erasmus uttered his last words in his mother tongue.

If we wish to understand Erasmus, we must consider two facts. He was the son of a priest and a physician's daughter, and in fact the second child of this relationship which existed for some time. His ancestry thus was covered with stain. His mother and father died early, and Erasmus was orphaned. His relatives cheated him of his inheritance, and as a youth he entered a monastery. There he first became a monk and then in 1492 a priest. A summons into the service of the bishop of Cambrai freed him from this slavery, which is how Erasmus characterized life in the monastery. When he was ordered to return to the monastery he refused, thus violating ecclesiastical law. Not until the year 1517 did he obtain a dispensation for his disobedience. Erasmus, to put it bluntly, thus was a bastard and a renegade monk at the same time. We must consider this if we want to understand his attitude. He needed high patrons, for they were the only ones who could free him from his difficult situation. So Erasmus came to be dependent on the prominent people of that time, a situation—this must be added—which he otherwise would certainly have achieved anyway, for Erasmus needed comfortable living, the best wine, and the expensive furs—they were part of the presuppositions of his existence. In his letters he never tired of speaking about his weak

physical condition and of what his weak body needed for its maintenance, and he did so in a way which made it difficult (just as with
Lorenzo Valla) to admire the man in his learned achievement, no matter
how aware we are that in evaluating Erasmus we must look at his learned
achievement, not at the frail man.

When we now read Erasmus's writings, they immediately show the
twofold significance which humanism had for the preparation and development of the Reformation. Even Erasmus's nonpolemical writings are
concerned with attacking the piety of the time: the exaggerated importance of ceremonies, fasting, and all other externals—what Erasmus
called pharisaic Jewish works-righteousness. The ethics which Erasmus
attempted to enforce contrasted with those practiced by the church and
the faithful at that time. As soon as Erasmus began to polemicize, the
contrast could not be overlooked. In the year 1511 he published his
Praise of Folly, which made his breakthrough to the general public. This
book was virtually devoured everywhere. In it, Erasmus praised folly as
"the Alpha" (that is, the beginning of everything; alpha is the first letter
of the Greek alphabet) of all deities. Human beings owe their comfortable life to folly. That was explained in detail: first with philosophers,
with physicians, with jurists, with princes, but also with theologians,
monks, bishops, and popes; in fact, the representatives of the church are
treated worst of all. Erasmus continued this in his *Colloquia familiaria*
("Familiar colloquies"), which were couched in the form of practice
conversations. Here we find the sharpest attacks against life in the
monastery, against monasticism, against pilgrimages, and against fasting. We can read them only with great amazement and must ask ourselves how the church could tolerate something like them. That was
possible only because Erasmus very scrupulously observed the narrow
boundary between satire and seriousness. Each time he could retreat to
the excuse that he had meant it only in jest, or that it was formulated
only to be a practice conversation—exclusively for the educated class
which understood Latin, not for the broad masses. But that is not
sufficient as an explanation. The only way we can understand all of this is
by presuming that Erasmus himself, along with his readers, was not clear
about the final consequences of these attacks.

This criticism had an extraordinary effect. It was enthusiastically
taken up by the learned, and they also transplanted it into the circles
which were unable to use Latin. Because this criticism only gave names
to what all people in the church could observe with their own eyes—and
exceedingly accurate and impressive names—it unfolded into a destruc-

tive effect. That was one side of humanism. With its biting criticism of the Catholic church of the time, it most effectively prepared the way for the Reformation. But its academic work had preparatory character as well. Alongside Erasmus's controversial writings, of which numerous others could be mentioned, he published editions (and most of the time they were first editions) of the church fathers virtually on an assembly line: Origen, Basil, Cyril, Chrysostom, Irenaeus, Ambrose, Augustine, and so forth. At that time the libraries were searched, and new manuscripts which were previously unknown were constantly found. This explains Erasmus's long series of editions of the church fathers. In themselves they had significant importance, but they were far exceeded by the edition of the Greek New Testament which Erasmus produced in the year 1516. In itself this edition was not an act worthy of fame, for it was undertaken by Erasmus only in order to appear before the edition prepared in Spain by Cardinal Ximénez, which was much more thoroughly done than the one Erasmus and his publisher Froben put together in great haste. The Greek manuscripts of the New Testament, which Erasmus basically borrowed from the Basel library, were sent directly to the print shop as copy and were printed almost without editing, and thus had corresponding deficiencies. The conclusion of the Apocalypse was missing in the Greek manuscript. Erasmus therefore translated it back into Greek from Latin, making astonishing mistakes. This edition was thus only a very modest accomplishment. And yet, because it was the first edition, it decisively affected the sixteenth and seventeenth centuries and was used until the end of the nineteenth century.

When Erasmus's edition appeared, Luther had reached the ninth chapter in his lectures on the Epistle to the Romans, and from then on we see how he increasingly used the Greek text alongside the Latin one. Luther's translation of the New Testament at the Wartburg was based on an edition by Erasmus, and the translation of the New Testament into English goes back to a related edition. Thus, Erasmus indirectly has dominated the English-speaking as well as the German-speaking area of the church down through the centuries to the present day. In England the so-called Authorized Version (King James Version) still holds the standard position, despite all the modern translations which have appeared in the meantime, exactly the way Luther's translation does in Germany: its nucleus (even with numerous archaisms) has remained unchanged despite all the revisions of the nineteenth and twentieth centuries and was not thoroughly adapted to the modern age until 1975.

In addition, there is the fact that for centuries the literature of both the German and English languages has been deeply affected by these translations of the Bible which contributed decisively to the establishment of the literary languages in both territories.

4. CRITICISM WITHIN THE CHURCH

Enough for the Renaissance and humanism, whose dependence—to return to where we began—on the increase of national feeling and national consciousness cannot be overlooked. This national consciousness, as we have already emphasized frequently, is embedded in a religiosity which is indeed attempting to free itself from the tutelage of the church, but in a way that will lead this church back to itself, even against its own will, because it believes that it understands what is decisive about Christianity better than does the church itself. This attempt by humanism, Wycliffe, and Huss is most closely associated with the criticism within the church, a criticism which also occurs where no one has anything to do with humanism, Wycliffe, or Huss, nor with the various manifestations of the national consciousness. The real cause of the decline of the church ("church" understood as the external organization) in the late Middle Ages and for the destruction of the papacy's claims to power is to be found in the ascetic ideas in which the religious sensitivity of that time was concentrated. The ascetic idea, the real piety of the time, once helped the church and papacy win its victory over the empire. It wanted to free the church from foreign influences, from domination by the world. By it the papacy in the thirteenth century was brought to the height of its power (see pp. 330–31). But when the world and the foreign powers were forced out of the church, the church succumbed from within to the influence of that world. As the papacy and the church became increasingly ensnared in the world, the ascetic idea and piety turned against the church. They attempted to force the church back to the ancient ideal, and as soon as they despaired of that separated from it.

Thus originated the movements of the Cathari and the Waldenses, the best known of the so-called heretical groups of the twelfth century (see p. 332), which are mentioned as representative of the numerous similarly oriented conventicles at that time; thus originated the revolt of the so-called Spiritual Franciscans (see pp. 355–56). It is characteristic that the founder of the Waldenses, the merchant Peter Valdes, at the end of the twelfth century in Lyon gave up all of his possessions and chose to lead a life in accordance with Scripture, that is, a life of complete poverty according to Matthew 10. He founded a brotherhood to realize this ideal, and this brotherhood soon spread throughout France, Italy, Spain, and Germany—proof of the power this ascetic idea possessed, how widespread it was, and the receptive attitude of people toward the preaching of this apostolic poverty. Valdes wanted to remain in the church, since he wanted to reform the church from within by preaching poverty. But the church refused him the permission, which he sought, to preach, and he and his followers were finally excommunicated, thus forcing the Waldenses out of the church and turning them into a sect.

That also happened to the radical branch of the Franciscan order, the Spiritual Franciscans. Even the establishment of the Franciscan order as such was a protest against the worldly church (see p. 332). From the very beginning, Francis of Assisi and the Franciscans were on the attack against the development of Catholicism which was taking place at that time. Characteristically, the more the order came into the hands of the church, that much more did Francis of Assisi's influence recede. Again and again he attempted to oppose this development, but without success. Once again in his testament he protested against the development which the order was undertaking, against its turning away from the ideal of absolute poverty, and added that his testament had to be carried out to the letter. But that did not happen, and it could not even happen according to the law of that time. Thus, after his death the order soon divided into two groups the strict party which carried out the testament word for word and wished to live according to the order's original ideals in their fullness, and the majority party which wanted to adapt the order to the real circumstances in church and world. Even here the radicals were driven out of the order and out of the church. And the church did not stop there, but also applied all its forceful means against the representatives of the ascetic ideal, against the Cathari, against the Waldenses, against the Spiritual Franciscans, and finally also against the mystics.

In this the church was supported by the state, for in the year 1215, under Innocent III's influence, the Fourth Lateran Council expressly prescribed that the temporal authority was obligated to lend a hand to the inquisition. It was one of the tasks of the secular ruler, it prescribed, to exterminate heretics which the church identified for him. If anyone failed to perform this duty which was part of the ruler's office, the crusade that originally was to have been directed against the heretics should be initiated against him. In Frisia the Stedingers were now exterminated as Cathari by a crusade, just as the Albigenses in France had been exterminated by the crusades against them; thus we see that everywhere it is precisely those who seriously want to be Christians who are attacked by the Christian church in the name of Christianity. But the success of this struggle was limited. One can indeed destroy the organization of a group, but one cannot exterminate its teachings, and above all one cannot exterminate the ascetic idea which became even more impressive to many people precisely because of the martyr's death which many of its representatives suffered. The forces behind the criticism within the church were forced out of public view, but they remained alive in hiding, especially because they were marked by the influx of apocalyptic ideas—among the Spiritual Franciscans, for example. It is because of these forces that from then on the conception that the papacy was the antichrist was impossible to exterminate.

Mysticism was also a protest against the development of the church at that time whose voice could not be ignored. Just as with the establishment of the Franciscan order, from its very beginning mysticism had a character of protest which was undeniable. Naturally the mystics did not undertake a campaign to eliminate the evil situations in the church. The mystics did not even criticize the church overtly; rather, their criticism consisted of withdrawing from that church and creating a world of their own inhabited only by God and the soul, nothing else. To a certain extent the mystic lived within a glass jar from which the world was banished, from which the church was banished, and in which there was really nothing but a private conversation between God and the soul. Whoever was an adherent of radical mysticism—what we shall call God mysticism—needed no church, needed no hierarchy, and, strictly speaking, did not even need Christ. The soul had direct access to God, to him it ascended in ecstasy, with him it was united according to laws which— as must be added—were not limited only to Christianity, for this God mysticism has parallels in other religions. Characteristically, mysticism at that time within the Christian church developed out of acquaintance with Neoplatonism, which was encountered when scholasticism began to occupy itself with commentaries on Aristotle. Even theologians ran into difficulties when they wished to prove the necessity of ecclesiastical demands, (indeed of the church itself) over against the God mysticism. And as soon as mysticism passed from the theologians to the laity, the centrifugal forces became even stronger. Under the influence of mysticism, lay piety virtually automatically began to go different ways, away from the church—and, in the last analysis, I would believe away from

Christianity. That is because this radical mysticism—the God mysticism, which conceived of the connection between God and the soul without intermediaries—only nominally belonged within Christianity: only because here it was the Christian God to whom the soul was seeking its way, and here it was also the Christian mystic who was doing so. But nevertheless there was ultimately a contrast between this form of mysticism and Christianity which could not be surmounted.

It was different with Christ mysticism. At all times this mystically oriented piety possessed an extraordinary source of power. For example, when the Catholic church of the sixteenth century enjoyed such a steep rise after its deep fall at the time of the Reformation (see Vol. II), this was at least in part due to the fact that Catholic piety was nourished by the forces of mysticism which the Catholic church tolerated at that time, while Lutheranism furnished only weak possibilities for it. Then when pietism came along at the close of the seventeenth century, it provided a home for the forces of mysticism, while the Catholic church turned sharply against mysticism. Correspondingly, the situation of power between the churches changed.

At this time, as really at every time, God mysticism and Christ mysticism existed side by side and united with one another in the most varied ways. Even the laity, whom we saw at times in full retreat from the church, did not as a rule pursue to its very end the mystical path away from the church because of their late medieval connection with it. Thus we find mysticism in very different forms. Alongside the pantheistically oriented Brethren and Sisters of the Free Spirit, there were the *Gottesfreunde* ("Friends of God") and Meister Eckhart (d. 1327), Johann Tauler (1300–61), Henry Suso (1295–1362), and Jan van Ruysbroeck (1294–1381). Even mystical societies were formed, which in themselves were a contradiction, for mysticism is not a societal concern, but an individual one. Everywhere in Germany and in Europe at the close of the Middle Ages there were the mystics, the silent ones in the land *(die Stillen im Lande)*. Since each mystic had a large circle of followers, and since the writings of the mystics were read and had an effect where people were far distant from a direct contact with mysticism, that is, because the sympathizers were many times greater than the number of "actives"—as had been true with monasticism in ancient church history—mysticism at the close of the Middle Ages served as one of the determinative spiritual forces.

There appears to be a direct path from mysticism to the Reformation. In his letters of 1515–18, Luther frequently referred Spalatin to Tauler and the "ancient pure theology" which he taught. Luther twice published the *German Theology (Theologia deutsch),* once in an abridged form in 1516 and again in its entirety in 1518 (and both times as an *editio princeps,* that is, a first edition), and said that here the true, correct, pure theology was to be found. He said that everything he wanted had been said there. Thus we might suppose that German mysticism had a decisive significance in preparing for the Reformation.

This conclusion is based on a misunderstanding—shared by Luther himself—and ends in a dead end. We have already mentioned (see pp. 377–79), that Luther really deceived himself about his predecessors and his dependence upon them. Luther believed that everything he taught was already there in Huss, and several times he declared: "Everything I am, I owe to Staupitz." When Luther said that everything he wanted was already written in the *German Theology,* we must evaluate this in exactly the same way. All of these statements were possible only because Luther read his own theological ideas into these works, because he did not recognize that not only were they speaking from a completely different basis, but that they were set in a completely different world. After he became acquainted with mysticism, Luther had something like a mystically tinted way of speaking, but that is just as external and just as transitory as the humanistic flowery language which we find at the beginning of Luther's letters. Without doubt, Luther experienced a certain influence from mysticism. The Christ mysticism of Bernard of Clairvaux was not only of importance to him in his early period, but later as well. Staupitz, who was directly connected with mysticism, even exercised a substantial influence upon him, while the other representatives of a mystically colored piety—Thomas à Kempis, along with John of Wesel, Wessel Gansfort, John Pupper of Goch, and whoever the so-called prereformers are—had relatively little or no significance at all for Luther.

When we observe Luther's relationship to Staupitz more closely, then we find the validity of this thesis being confirmed. Undoubtedly Staupitz had spoken early about the effectiveness of electing grace alone. Several times Staupitz showed Luther the way out of deep conflicts and was a light in the darkness which surrounded Luther. It is on this basis that we must understand Luther's statement: "I owe everything to Staupitz." But it is just as clear from Luther's statements—and not just indirectly, but very directly—that Staupitz, despite all the help he gave Luther, could not comprehend what was going on in Luther's struggles and that he did not at all understand what importance his words possessed. For Luther,

392

Staupitz's statements served as a guide along his way, and he derived much more from them than they really contained because he understood them very differently and much more deeply. It very quickly became apparent that Staupitz fully comprehended neither Luther nor the Reformation. Staupitz was full of sympathy for Luther and he even had friendly feelings for him. He saw Luther as his pupil and supported him as much as he could. But as early as 1518 in Augsburg, when Staupitz was still completely behind Luther, we see that Staupitz could not keep in step with Luther. From the time shortly thereafter we possess a whole series of impassioned letters from Luther, in which he attempts to win Staupitz over to the cause of the gospel, which Staupitz, Luther says, was the first to show him. Staupitz not only very soon submitted to the authority of the Catholic church outwardly, but he also made his peace inwardly with it. That he could do, aside from a certain anxiety and lack of courage which played a role, only because he had not grasped the depths of the questions which were involved. With Staupitz it becomes clear how Luther was connected in a certain way with the age and men before him, but also how he had fundamentally separated from that age and its representatives.

5. THE REFORM COUNCILS

The reform councils manifested the will of the church to purify itself from the evils that had invaded it, and therefore they deserve a relatively thorough presentation. Nevertheless, if we want to understand them and their history properly, we must look at the way they conformed to the law to which they were subject. The reform councils were a decisive reduction of the papacy's position. Despite all the reduction of external power which the papacy experienced in this period of time, it could still always maintain its influence over things within the church. It is true that at the time of the schism each of the popes controlled only a portion of the original territory (see pp. 350–51), but nevertheless their ecclesiastical influence in that portion of the world was unbroken until the time of the reform councils. At that time it ceased. The reform councils challenged the papacy's claim of supremacy over the church and to a large extent assumed it themselves. Very quickly did the councils proclaim that they were the supreme authority in the church and that all significant decisions belonged to them. A legally assembled council was not subordinate to the pope, but superior to him. In fact, the reform councils did lead to the abolition of many errors: first, if only after repeated attempts, the abolition of the schism and then abolition of the worst abuses in the church. But to the extent they were successful and to the extent the papacy could be brought out of its previous period of weakness, a conflict between papacy and council had to occur. The councils promoted the strengthening of the papacy by abolishing what the time called the "cursed Trinity," so that once again the church had *one* head. But because of the law imposed upon him by his office, this one head of the church then had to proceed against the reform councils and attempt to exclude them from the church.

The epoch of the reform councils begins with the Council of Pisa of 1409, about which we have already reported briefly (see pp. 351–52). The very fact that this council could happen signified a revolution in the church. It was possible only because dissatisfaction and criticism within the church had grown so strong that it burst all bounds. This Council of Pisa came into being, although at that time there was not yet any conception of what a council was and what a council might do. The cardinals of both sides abandoned everything which heritage, devotion, and law imposed as binding upon them. They first assembled in a peace conference and in 1408 jointly called a council, although they really did not know how to justify that council, for at that time the conciliar theory was still in its earliest beginnings. Thus the cardinals initially thought about an assembly of bishops. Then, because they felt themselves unsure, they solicited theological opinions which unanimously recommended not an assembly of bishops, but a general council. The opinions came from very different sides: from theologians, from teachers of canon law, professors, clergy, and laity—and in extraordinary numbers. They urgently depicted the injuries to the church, especially the injuries to the curia, and not only called, but virtually screamed for a correction of these injuries to the church which, they declared, past experience proved could not come from the papacy which was much too deeply involved in the general ruin, but only from a general assembly of the church—from a council. Thus, it came to the Council of Pisa, thus it came to the development of the conciliar theory, thus it came to the fact that the council could declare itself the supreme representation of the church, with a demand that increased from one time to the next.

The Council of Pisa failed. It had to fail because sufficient experience had not yet been gained, and it therefore acted too quickly. Indeed, it did declare the two popes of the time (Gregory XII and Benedict XIII) deposed and chose a new pope (Alexander V). But these depositions were not efficacious, and after the council Christianity had three popes instead of two. The Council of Constance (1414–18) could put an end to this with the support at least initially of one of the popes reigning at that time, John XXIII. In Pisa, as mentioned, Alexander V had been elected. He reigned only a brief time, but this did not change anything concerning the number of three popes, for Alexander V had only been put forward by Baldassare Cossa, who dominated the curia and pope and, after Alexander's death, was chosen his successor as John XXIII in 1410, really against his own will.

John XXIII's past was, shall we say, not completely pure. We can express it this way: he had practiced the trade of war; if we want to describe it pejoratively, we would say he had been a pirate. Following that, he turned to a spiritual career, took a doctorate in canon and civil law, and quickly climbed the ecclesiastical ladder, distinguishing his career on every rung with energy and success. However, as soon as he reached the highest office, the previously so circumspect, farsighted, and energetic man suffered a certain paralysis. His position was weak: Rome was again conquered and sacked, his own plan for a council collapsed, and the king of Naples beseiged him. Therefore John XXIII agreed with the call of the council to Constance.

Hardly had he agreed to the council when he repented and wanted to change his mind. But Sigismund, the German king, and the cardinals held him to his word. John XXIII was present personally in Constance and announced to the council that he was even prepared to resign whether he did this under the influence of the paralysis we have mentioned, or whether (which is more probable) he believed that this would especially recommend him for the new election. When he realized that this would not be the case, he fled twelve days later under cover of darkness. He believed that in this way he could compel the council to disband. In reality he only forced the conciliar movement farther, for now in Constance they hastened to make a fundamental definition of what previously they had only done practically, and that signified a decisive step.

On April 6, 1415, the famous proclamation of conciliarism was enacted. It said:

> This holy council of Constance . . . declares, first that it is lawfully assembled in the Holy Spirit, that it constitutes a general council, representing the Catholic church, and that therefore it has its authority immediately from Christ; and that all men, of every rank and condition, including the pope himself, are bound to obey it in matters concerning the faith, the

abolition of the schism, and the reformation of the church of God in its head and its members.

The council succeeded not only in getting rid of John XXIII, but also in disposing of his two rivals. John XXIII made his peace with the church and became cardinal-bishop of Tusculum, dying in Florence in 1419. (For centuries the papal name of John was unused because of this. When Giuseppe Roncalli chose the name John XXIII at his election in 1958, that signified to the knowledgeable that an unusual pontificate was to be expected of him.) Of the two other popes ruling at that time, Gregory XII finally gave up in 1415 after the application of some pressure. Only Benedict XIII offered stubborn resistance. He demanded that King Sigismund personally negotiate with him. That took place. Nevertheless he refused to resign, probably because he thought, as the single one of the three previous popes who was still in office, that he had the greatest claim to the office. Finally he was deposed on July 26, 1417, and expelled from the church as punishment for his stubbornness.

If the three popes, Gregory XII, Benedict XIII, and John XXIII, held on to their office, egoism naturally played a certain part. Understandably, it was extraordinarily difficult for each of these popes to give up the high office and retire from power, even if it was only a divided power. But the attitude of the popes was controlled by other forces as well which can best be studied in the person of the newly elected pope at Constance, Martin V.

On the very day after his election (November 11, 1417), Martin V issued new chancery rules which set a new course. Six weeks later he prohibited appeal from a pope to any other court. It is true that he did not mention the council, but obviously it was what was meant. From the very outset, the papacy which was restored to its original position attempted, if not to remove the council and conciliarism, at least to limit it as much as possible. That took place on the basis of laws which were inherent in the papacy and the structure of the Catholic church. Martin V's attempts remained without success, however. The council continued to meet, and the reform commission assembled to deliberate on the agenda prepared for it. But now it ran aground—and with it the council—because the national differences within it became too strong. In Pisa the voting was still done simply by individuals; because John XXIII thought that would also be the case in Constance he had brought numerous Italians with him to Constance. In Constance that system was abandoned, and they determined to have the council vote according to nations, of which four were established, with a fifth vote given to the cardinals. This caused the collapse of the Council of Constance. In Pisa the French still had the decisive influence, while in Constance the strength lay with the Germans, or more precisely with the German nation, which obviously does not correspond to the modern division, for this "German nation" included all the people of central and northern Europe. The French felt their accustomed decisive position was limited. Therefore they asked whether the council, which met in the presence of the German king, was free at all. Thus the reform commission was weakened from within. The pope took advantage of this, proclaimed seven reform decrees, and postponed all further reforms to a future council. Within five years, this council should meet, he declared. In the meantime the reform measures should be more thoroughly prepared than apparently had taken place previously.

Thus the Council of Constance collapsed. The various nations still attempted, in concert with the pope, to rescue whatever could be salvaged from the ruins. In this the French were especially successful, next the Germans, and then the smaller nations came out much worse. Martin V had won a victory over the council and conciliarism. He also never recognized the dogmatic decrees of the Council of Constance. But, seen as a whole, he could not establish himself, since the council's attitude was too strong, and the confidence that the papacy could eliminate or even was willing to eliminate the abuses in the church was too weak. In addition, there was the conflict with the Hussites (see p. 372), who triumphed over all the crusading armies sent against them. Finally, even the schism continued, for Benedict XIII, who had twice been deposed and finally expelled from the church, achieved recognition in Spain, and after his death Spain and Sicily even chose Clement VIII as his successor. Thus Martin V could not postpone calling the promised council after five years, and it was summoned to Pavia. But here the plague threatened to break out. Thus the pope moved it to Siena. But when he determined that here the same sort of reform proposals were being made as in Constance, he dissolved the council with the excuse that it was too poorly attended. At a later time it was supposed to assemble anew in Basel.

Only one single decree with a few reform provisions was published by the pope, characteristically coupled with a reprimand of the cardinals and bishops who had participated in the council. But he was not able to stifle the demand for a reform council with this; instead, because of the pope's obvious obstruction, the demand for a council only became that much stronger. The pope attempted to take the wind out of the sails of this demand for a council by establishing a reform commission made up of cardinals, but to no avail. Stronger and stronger became the demand for a council, rising even to open threats against the pope. At length he finally sent a legate to Basel, Cardinal Cesarini, with a bull empowering him to open and preside over the Council of Basel, whose beginning had already been fixed for March 8, 1431, at Siena. But that was only the one bull the cardinal was given. Characteristically, at the same time the second bull authorized him either to transfer the council to a new place or to disband it entirely. When the first participants at the council appeared in Basel a week before its official beginning, nothing at all had been done yet in preparation for it. When Martin V died, his successor, Eugene IV (1431–47), issued a decree after only a few weeks, dissolving the council without giving even a single reason.

Despite all the obstruction of its work, the Council of Basel at that time already began with its first practical measures. When Eugene's decree of dissolution arrived, the council had already proceeded so far that the decree remained without effect. Rather, the council decided— and with the vote of the papal legate—that it was meeting under the assistance of the Holy Spirit and would work on its tasks until the reforms for which it was striving were achieved. This council, which began with such weak prospects and whose beginnings were confronted with so many difficulties, lasted longer than even the greatest optimists would have attempted to prophesy at its beginning, and had a greater importance than one would have considered possible in view of the distribution of forces at the beginning of the council. It even reached—in the first part of its session (1431–37)—the high point of the conciliar movement. It could win clear successes. When the discussions with the Hussites in Basel produced no results, the council did not give up but sent an embassy to Bohemia. It was able to negotiate a peace with the Utraquists (see pp. 372–73), and, allied with them, to destroy the radical party, the Taborites. Impressed by these results, Eugene IV had to withdraw the decree of dissolution. In addition to this, he had great difficulties in Italy, and France, Germany, and Venice as well continually put pressure upon him. Thus he now declared that the council had been meeting legally since its beginning. It must continue its work until it had accomplished its three great tasks: extermination of the heretics, creation of peace within Christendom, and general reform of the church in head and members.

The pope first made this declaration when he could do nothing else.

Indeed, he really made it too late, for he could not appease the secret opposition against him by reestablishing the council. A revolt took place against him in Rome. In 1434 he had to flee from the city; disguised as a monk, he made his way to Florence. This was a clear triumph for the conciliar forces. Nevertheless, with this, conciliarism furnished the first prerequisite for the collapse of the Council of Basel, for the pope who was driven from Rome now had to employ all his means in order, if not to do away with the council, at least to rob it of its power. Since his exile from Rome, Eugene IV had been fighting for his existence. And in the course of its further work the council also created conditions which would have compelled not only Eugene IV, but every pope to fight against the council, because in abolishing annates (see pp. 400–401) it removed the prerequisites for the papacy's external existence.

Next it was decided in Basel no longer to meet separately as nations—the dangers of such a way of working had been clearly evident at Constance—but rather according to deputations. According to a fixed formula the participants from various nations were equally divided into various deputations for faith, peace, reformation, and general questions, so that no longer could national opposition arise, but at most opposition between the deputations. A vast amount of material was presented for consideration: at first, the eighteen reform demands which had not been acted upon at Constance, as well as a reform proposal of the curia which contained a program of no less than sixty-two points. This memorandum came from the pen of the cardinals and was further developed by Cesarini. Finally the Council of Basel was presented with a profusion of reforms, since, following previous example, the chairman Cesarini had invited all to present the council with opinions about the situation of the church and proposals for the measures necessary to correct the abuses. Clergy, high ecclesiastical officials, and scholars from all nations accordingly presented reform documents. Their content does not need to be reported in detail here: it is sufficient to name a few of the reform decrees enacted by the Council of Basel, for in them the abuses of that time are mirrored. From them we can recognize the *via negativa* ("negative way") as it appeared in this church at the conclusion of the Middle Ages. Here it was prescribed that in the future offices could be bestowed only according to the provisions of spiritual law after orderly elections. Synods should take place regularly, diocesan synods every year, and provincial synods every two years. These synods should give attention to the conduct of the clergy, that worship services were taking place orderly, and that church property was being used in accordance with the regulations. Concubinage was prohibited for all clergy. In the future frivolous imposition of the interdict was forbidden, and it was forbidden to appeal to Rome without strong reasons.

These abuses were so great that the council felt compelled to occupy itself urgently with them and so clear that it unanimously determined to abolish them. For example, concubinage was in no way an exception, as we might suppose in light of the repeated prohibitions of it during the centuries, but it occurred frequently and with public approval of the church authorities. At all levels, beginning with the lower clergy and ascending to the bishops and cardinals, one could obtain the church's permission for it by paying an appropriate sum.

Obviously at that time the interdict was imposed for compelling ecclesiastical reasons as well. But that was virtually the exception, for in the course of time it had become more and more of a weapon in ordinary controversies: when a bishop had difficulty with his prince, when an abbot could not get along with the villages and cities which were subject to his monastery, whenever any kind of attack took place against a monastery or monk, an interdict was imposed. When church taxes were not paid promptly or in sufficient amount, an interdict was imposed. Indeed, an interdict was even imposed when the populace would not permit a monastery to have the exclusive right to brew beer, when they refused to drink the expensive and inferior monastery beer and brewed their own instead. This use of the interdict, that is, the suspension of all official ecclesiastical acts and worship services, not only paralyzed the life of the church, but certainly had to become a trial for the pious.

Finally, the council decreed the abolition of annates, that is, the fees that had to be paid to the pope when an office was filled. For higher offices, the income of an entire year had to be rendered (thus the name); with lesser offices, part of it. With the abolition of annates the council was in fact declaring war on the papacy—and at the same time laying the ax to the root of its existence. This is because their abolition endangered the financial foundation of the papacy at that time, and the pope was now compelled to proceed with all energy and means against the council. Eugene IV was certainly prepared to do that without further ado, but he probably would not have taken this route so radically and so quickly if the council had not forced him to by going beyond abolishing the annates and issuing a decree providing for securing the possession of benefices. Anyone who had held a benefice for three years without its being contested, should keep it and could not be removed from it, as had taken place again and again because the papacy was continually attempting to make its income as high as possible by frequently changing ecclesiastical offices (see Wycliffe, for example, p. 361).

Alongside these practical reform measures, the council worked further on the theoretical and practical foundation of conciliarism. The decree *Frequens* ("Repeatedly") was renewed: A lawfully assembled council could be dissolved only by a two-thirds majority vote. The college of cardinals was limited to twenty-four positions, and all nations should be given equal consideration in it. The jurisdiction of the papal court was limited, the curia's ability to fill benefices was restricted, and so on, until the conciliar idea was formulated again in three main sentences. First: The general council stands above the pope. Second: Without the council's permission, it cannot be dissolved, transferred, or adjourned by the pope. And third: Whoever rejects these provisions of the council is to be regarded as a heretic.

When the council achieved this formulation of the claims of conciliarism, its position was already seriously endangered. Eugene IV had first attempted to weaken the position of the Council of Basel by calling his own reform council. He was unsuccessful in that and accordingly decided to intensify the negotiations with the Greek Orthodox church which had already been going on for a long time. He was able to bring a delegation from the Greek Orthodox church to Italy for union negotiations. The history preceding this was not particularly praiseworthy. The council learned of the pope's negotiations with the Greek emperor and thus also sent an embassy to Constantinople. Thus, Venetian ships sent by the pope and Genovese ships sent by the council were anchored in the harbor of Constantinople. The representatives of the pope as well as those of the council simultaneously attempted to get the representatives of the Greek Orthodox church aboard their ships; by means of a stratagem the plenipotentiaries of the pope were successful. After they had brought the emperor and the ecclesiastical delegation on board, they set sail and the order was given to ram the ships of the council. Only through the intervention of the Greek emperor, who in this manner had the situation within Western Christianity demonstrated to him, could they be prevented from doing so.

The pope had brought the Greeks on board his ship; he had them in his hand and would not release them. The arrival of the Greek delegation in September, 1437, gave him the opportunity to demand first that the council move from Basel to Ferrara and second that it should no longer meet as a reform council, but, in view of the arrival of the representatives of the Orthodox church, should continue to meet as a union council. In this way Eugene IV was able to destroy the Council of Basel internally. Stormy debates took place in Basel. The pope's demand to move was indeed rejected. But the majority which decided this (among it was Enea Silvio de' Piccolomini, the later Pope Pius II) was not very large, and, in addition, the minority which followed the pope's summons, except for a single one of all the cardinals, included almost all the bishops and almost all the men of greater importance. Only a single cardinal remained behind in Basel. He was quickly made the president of the council, since the previous one, Cardinal Cesarini, had gone to Florence to the pope. Piccolomini, the secretary of the council, did defend its legitimacy in a special work, but that was not of much help to the Council of Basel. It did continue to meet from 1437 until 1449, also formally declaring Eugene IV deposed and choosing a successor for him, Felix V. But this only weakly disguised the impotence of the Council of Basel after 1437. It was transferred from Basel to Lausanne and spent most of its time and effort in negotiations with the secular powers, one after another of which abandoned the council and gave their support to Eugene IV.

The Council of Basel died of internal exhaustion even before it formally decreed its dissolution. In contrast, the union council, which first met in Ferrara and then in Florence, became stronger and more significant, and Eugene IV's position and influence increased accordingly. The union council was splendidly attended. It also appeared to offer promise for lasting success, for not only did the Greek emperor appear with an appropriate entourage, but at his side were the patriarch of Constantinople with a magnificent following, the archbishop of Nicaea, the archbishop of Ephesus, and so forth. The legitimacy of this delegation appeared beyond dispute. When the bull *Laetentur caeli* ("Let the heavens rejoice") on July 6, 1439, proclaimed the union with the Greek Orthodox church, the schism of four centuries appeared in fact to have ended, and it seemed that the final reunification had been achieved. But it only appeared to be so, and the attentive observer had to be aware that this union council was doomed before it began. This is because it came into existence under nontheological factors. The auspices under which this union council took place were not of an ecclesiastical or theological nature, and therefore its decisions had to remain without effect. And what applies to this council applies to all councils, to all church negotiations, no matter on what level they take place. If one acts on the basis of practical or even political considerations, if one acts on the basis of nontheological considerations of any sort, perhaps one can achieve outward successes, but nothing which will stand the test of time. Union negotiations between churches can only be successful if all sides enter into them with pure hands. Only when one acts on the basis of essential necessities and when the negotiations end not only with both sides declaring the subject settled, but when it really is settled—only then will the results endure.

At the Florence union council the nontheological motives on both sides were obvious. Eugene IV was intensifying the union negotiations because they promised him a strengthening of his position and a victory over the Council of Basel. The Byzantine empire was only prepared to negotiate with the Roman church because its power was declining more and more, and the Turks were drawing nearer and nearer. Thus it appeared to be agreeable to a union with the church of the West because it hoped that the West would send troops to support the battle against Islam. Both sides were acting under external pressure; both had to produce results. If the negotiations were without result, their existence was threatened: that of Pope Eugene IV by the council, that of the Greek emperor by the Turks.

Despite this pressure on both sides, the negotiations in Florence took shape with extraordinary difficulty. The difficulties began with the *fili-oque* ("and the Son") in the creed (see pp. 267–68) and continued in the discussion about the Lord's Supper. Then they could not come to agreement on purgatory, and finally the pope's claim to primacy forced extremely difficult negotiations, which could be terminated only by declaring the ancient privileges of the Orthodox patriarchs as inviolate. Finally, after all difficulties appeared to have been overcome, a conflict arose, which threatened to destroy the entire negotiations anew, over the words of institution in the mass. Finally, thirty-three Orthodox patriarchs, bishops, and prelates did sign the union document, since the pope had ceremoniously promised that in the future Constantinople would permanently be defended by soldiers of the West and that the West was prepared to proclaim a crusade against the Turks.

The rejoicing which spread in the Western world over the union which apparently had been reached between the churches concealed the true situation. More revealing was the fact that a whole series of Greek theologians had left the council before it came time to sign the union document. They did not want to take part; they did not want their names appearing on such a paper. Even some of the Greeks who were still in Florence at that time expressly refused to sign the document. Soon it became apparent that these theologians had recognized the actual situation, for when the Greek delegation returned to its homeland it was apparent that the Greek church and its congregations were not prepared to agree to the union with the West. They vehemently protested against it, despite all the promises the West had made them. Numerous participants at the union council who had signed the document could save themselves from the wrath of the Greek people only by claiming they had done so under duress. The chief proponents of the union could not remain in the Greek church. The archbishop of Nicaea, Bessarion, and Patriarch Isidore of Kiev had to flee and finally ended as cardinals in the Roman church. It soon was also evident that the pope had promised more than he could keep, in fact, even more than he wanted to keep. In the final struggle for Byzantium there was no help from the Western world. In the year 1453 Constantinople was conquered by the Turks, and all that remained of the union negotiations were only the accusations which had been made on both sides.

Nevertheless, the union council had given the pope the prerequisite for the final conquest over the powers within the church which opposed his claims and demands. At that time the pope triumphed over the council and the conciliar movement. He satisfied the claims of the secular powers through separate treaties. Once again, the most successful was France, which in 1438 proclaimed the Pragmatic Sanction of Bourges, a law which formulated the so-called Gallican liberties (see pp. 358–59). Germany also obtained concessions, as did other states as well. But because the curia agreed to all of these conditions only with extreme unwillingness and instantly attempted to nullify them, continual conflicts were unavoidable.

We can study how strong the laws are which control the papacy in this struggle against conciliarism in the change which the secretary of the Council of Basel, Enea Silvio de' Piccolomini, underwent in its second period. At one time he had expressly defended the legality of the council over against the pope. Finally he himself became pope as Pius II in 1458. As soon as he ascended the throne, he issued the bull *Execrabilis* ("Execrable"), in which conciliarism, which he had not only practiced himself but also expressly defended, was castigated as an unprecedented abuse worthy of condemnation. Councils meant, so it said, revolt against the pope. Even appealing to a future council belonged in this category. One did not do that, declared Pius II, for the sake of obtaining a fair judgment, but only because one wanted to avoid punishment for crimes one had committed. It would be ridiculous to appeal to something which has never been and which one does not know when it will be. That was abominable and erroneous and therefore was declared null and void. Whoever does so, whether emperor, king, or high ecclesiastical official, shall immediately be placed under the ban from which only the pope can free him and then only in anticipation of the sinner's imminent death.

The Council of Basel was the last of the reform councils. At that time the papacy triumphed over conciliarism. But it had not triumphed over the conciliar idea; that was kept alive among church people. It is true that through the council and also through the pope a great number of abuses were corrected. But in comparison to the number of evils in the church it was certainly very few. Thus the complaints did not cease, especially because the curia continually attempted to limit or even completely withdraw concessions made under the force of circumstances. At all diets the so-called *Gravamina* ("grievances") of the German nation were presented, and again and again up into the time of the Reformation tracts appeared promoting a reform of the church in head and members and demanding a council. Even strongly Catholic princes adopted the demand for a council (when they wanted to apply pressure to the pope). Even in circles where we later see the Reformation being passionately resisted, the demand for purification of the church and its inner renewal was very much alive. As we have mentioned several times (see pp. 376–79), the Reformation began as something new. But it also built on the demands for reform; the first part of Luther's writing *To the Christian Nobility of the German Nation* reads like a compendium of the reformatory tracts of the fifteenth century.

6. THE PAPACY AT THE CLOSE OF THE MIDDLE AGES

Even a generation ago this section would probably have been given a rather thorough treatment, since, like nothing else, a depiction of those who held the highest dignity in Christendom at the close of the Middle Ages is manifestly suited for proving the justification of and necessity for the Reformation. Pius II (1458–64) was the last pope we met in our previous presentation. The darkest picture can be painted of each one of his successors. In this regard, Paul II (1464–71) comes off the best, for Innocent VIII (1484–92) ceremoniously married his illegitimate children in the Vatican and had the Sultan pay him bribes to keep his brother in prison. Finally, we need only call Alexander VI (1492–1503) by his given name of Rodrigo Borgia to be reminded of the unholy trinity of father, son Caesar, and daughter Lucretia Borgia, who ever since that time have been regarded as the embodiment of depravity. That was different with the next popes, Julius II (1503–13) and Leo X (1513–21). But these two as well were everything else but shepherds of Christ's flock. Julius II was a warrior, and after his death the work *Julius exclusus e coelis* ("Julius excluded from heaven") could appear, ascribed to no one less than Erasmus: here the pope appears as a warrior before the gate of heaven, demands admittance, and is turned away by Peter. And Leo X was a humanist, completely oriented toward the world and without any understanding for what was going on in Germany in the initial period of the Reformation. As we said, the darkest picture can be painted on the basis of indisputable facts. But we shall consciously refrain from doing so, for the age of that sort of confessional polemics is over. In addition, a detailed presentation—even with superb examples—would only confirm what we have established again and again: the reform of the Catholic church was being demanded frequently at the close of the Middle Ages, but was in no way being carried out, aside from timid and absolutely unsatisfactory initiatives.

7. PIETY AND POPULAR FAITH AT THE THRESHOLD OF THE REFORMATION

In conclusion, when we now want to speak about piety at the close of the Middle Ages and at the threshold of the Reformation, we are fortunately in a different situation than our parents and grandparents. Then one could be certain after reading only a few pages of a work on this subject to which confessional body its writer belonged. Virtually without exception the Protestant depicted the religious and moral situation at the close of the Middle Ages as black as possible, in order to have the bright light of the Reformation appear in contrast to it. And the Catholic depicted the close of the Middle Ages in bright colors on a golden background, in order to have the destructive results of the Reformation, especially in the area of morality, appear in deepest black; not until the Counter-Reformation did the light reappear, blessedly terminating this dark epoch.

Fortunately it is no longer the case in the field of church history that one already knows before beginning to work how the result will appear. One rather attempts to determine what in fact did happen and lets one's attitude grow out of the result, not the result grow out of one's preconceived attitude. When we approach the closing Middle Ages in this way, then despite all the problems always inherent in forming a comprehensive judgment about the religious and moral attitude of an entire epoch, we must observe that the closing Middle Ages must look different—even on methodological grounds—than is often presented by the Protestant side. There can be no doubt about the intensity of religious life at the close of the Middle Ages, and only with this presumption can we understand the Reformation's success at all.

With what then did the Reformation have to do? It had to do with the justification of the sinner; it had to do with a new understanding of Rom. 1:17. And with this theological question—which, if we consider its details, was above all a very complicated one—a conflict was ignited, one which occupied not only theologians, but also ordinary people as well as the crowned heads, one that concerned all of Europe, and one that destroyed the old age and introduced a new one. If that is so, the question about justification—the question about a gracious God—must not only have been alive among people at that time, but it must have had a decisive importance for them as well. Only on the basis of this presupposition can we explain the echo which Luther's answer to this question experienced. If religious life was this vital, the situation at that time could not have been as dark as is often claimed.

If we want to summarize that age, perhaps this might do: That was an age filled with deep unrest and with striving for certainty of salvation. That unrest was not only apparent on the surface, but reached into the depth. That is apparent in literature; that is apparent in the art of the time, where we should not limit our attention to the large paintings which occupy prominent places in museums and in art histories, but we must above all look at the graphic arts. This is because as a rule the great artistic works of that time were created because of a commission from a rich patron, while those working in the graphic arts had to choose themes of general interest, for the artist naturally wanted to sell his works. When we look at the graphic arts of that time, we find certain themes over and over again. Again and again death is depicted on their pages, and not only in the heroic attitude in Dürer's well-known work in which a knight appears, threatened on the left by death and on the right by the devil, but continuing on his way undisturbed by either. Rather we find death everywhere: in the midst of people who are celebrating, he is not only looking over the shoulder of the elderly man, but also that of the young girl, the young man in the fullness of his strength, and the representatives of all occupations. The depictions of the so-called dance of death in the churches are one of the characteristics of the art of that time.

Not only the question of death affected people, but also that of sickness as well. In addition to plague and smallpox, which since ancient times had spread their scourge over humankind and against which everyone was helpless, another illness arose at that time, spread by the soldiers from Italy, which affected a person when he least expected it. But humanity was not only afflicted by death and illness, but also by apparitions. Dürer's notebooks are characteristic of this. Naturally, an artist was especially sensitive, but nevertheless here we find human beings of that age depicted in their insecurity, in their fear, and in their search for omens. They were all painstakingly recorded by Dürer. Although they sometimes appear remarkable to us, they nevertheless had an extraordinary meaning for the easily frightened person of that age. If somewhere a calf with two heads or a deformed child was born, we then find that immediately being presented in the graphic arts—certainly not because of joy over the abnormality, but because one saw a special significance behind it. That was true not only for Dürer's work, but for all artists of the time. If a comet appeared in the heavens, it frightened people deeply, just as did the mysterious appearance of bloody rain, something which happened repeatedly at that time.

At that time astrology played a role which it had previously done only in late antiquity (see p. 21). Naturally the emperor had an astrologer, but also the pope, and all public bodies, all the way down to the city council. The ruler inquired when it would be most profitable for him to take the field, the pope had the best time for the next meeting of the consistory fixed, and the city council asked about the most favorable date for its next session. This was because people believed that the stars had a direct influence on the fate not only of humanity in general but, in accordance with the constellations at one's birth, of every single person as well, and in this the powers for evil were stronger than those for good. They feared the end of the world. If Dürer frequently attempted to depict the Apocalypse in an artistic manner, it was because not only he but his age were concerned about the future, about the fate of the world, and about its end. At that time Professor Stöffler, on the basis of a conjunction of all the planets in the sign of Pisces, calculated that a deluge would occur in the year 1524. If we want to have an impressive picture of the effect of this prophecy we should read Bergengruen's *Am Himmel wie auf Erden* ("On earth as it is in heaven") or Alexis's *Die Hosen des Herrn von Bredow* ("The trousers of the man from Bredow"), in which the modern Bergengruen—let us note in passing—appears to be a repetition of the old Alexis. For example, here is related how

Elector Joachim I of Brandenburg, when a thunderstorm broke out at the time predicted, fled headlong with his court up Berlin's Kreuzberg hill, in order to bring himself and his courtiers to safety there (at an altitude of two hundred feet). But even the councillors of Charles V asked whether the army and the chancellery—the two most important components of power for them—should not encamp in the mountains. The abbot of Weingarten rented a room for himself on the uppermost floor of the Augsburg city hall, and the Wittenberg mayor took his beer into the attic for safekeeping. But not only on the Catholic side did people believe the stars foretold and controlled the future, but Melanchthon also practiced astrology and again and again felt he had to convince Luther to do or not to do something, to the good-natured ridicule of Luther who was not in the least inclined to follow him.

In this attitude also is revealed the unrest which was alive at this time of the threshold of the Reformation, the anxious longing of the creature who attempted in the most different ways to find certainty in its uncertainty. The demand for devotional literature, for works of comfort during sickness and in the face of death increased greatly. People began to read the Bible intensively—we are living in the time of the beginning of printing, which was the prerequisite not only for the success of humanism, but also for the spread of the Reformation—in which the decisive thing was that not only did the theologians go more deeply into the Bible in order to discover God's will in it, but also the laity. There was a whole series of printed translations of the Bible into German before Luther; in spite of their very high price, they quickly found readers. The veneration of saints increased. Exceeding all others was the veneration of Mary. The Cistercian order and the Franciscan order dedicated their churches to Mary, and the other orders followed this example, even including the Order of the Teutonic Knights, so that, for example, one finds one St. Mary's Church after another all along the Baltic coast as far as Riga. And this Mary was not someone who was distant, but one who was completely involved in ordinary life. When we look at the way Mary was depicted in the graphic arts of that time, not only do we find Mary in childbirth, but also Mary with the goldfinch, and so forth—a Mary, therefore, who was directly close to people of the time. From this Mary, who was so involved in human life, one could seek help in daily needs. And out of the cult of Mary at that time developed the cult of St. Anne, the mother of Mary. Numerous statues now show us the "St. Anne with two others": Anne, Mary, and the child sitting or playing between them. This Anne was what might be called the patron saint of miners. In the baptismal register of Wernigerode, one of the mining centers of the time, we can trace how her veneration increased. Up until the beginning of the fifteenth century the name very rarely appears. But from the beginning of the sixteenth century onward the name is the one most used for girls. At his experience near Stotternheim, when Luther called to St. Anne: "Help me, St. Anne, I will become a monk," that came from the piety of the miners' world in which he grew up. St. Anne, along with the fourteen saints of intercession whom we shall discuss more thoroughly below, was one of the saints who were newly coming into the foreground at that time. The relics of St. Anne performed sensational miracles. At that time the entire world was concerned with the skull, or, more precisely, with the piece of the skull of St. Anne at Düren. Originally it had been placed in the wall of the cathedral in Mainz. When the wall was repaired, a stonemason took the relic and brought it to his home town of Düren. But the people of Mainz discovered the theft and quickly sent emissaries to Düren, angrily demanding the return of their treasure. There they were preparing to return the stolen property, but the populace rose up and prevented it. Thus legal proceedings were initiated, and the case was carried as far as the diet and the curia. There it was finally decided that the skull of St. Anne should remain in Düren, for it had indicated by the miracles it performed there that it preferred Düren to Mainz, where it had not performed these miracles.

The pious attitude of that time was concentrated in the fourteen saints of intercession. It was not a coincidence that veneration of them originated in the fifteenth century. Balthasar Neumann's Baroque church of *Vierzehnheiligen* ("fourteen saints of intercession") was built on the spot where a shepherd in the middle of the fifteenth century was granted a miraculous apparition of the fourteen saints of intercession. They helped a person in all the needs of this life. They gave one the possibility of finding access to and immediate connection with a saint, not only in big problems, but those of everyday living as well, indeed involving the saint in one's life. This can be made clear with numerous examples. For example, the pinmakers chose Christmas as their guild's festival, because they believed Mary fastened Jesus' diapers with pins. St. Michael weighed souls in a balance, so merchants and apothecaries who also used scales chose him as their patron. St. Sebastian was pierced by arrows, so archers chose him as their symbol. St. Bartholomew, in the traditional representation of him, carried his skin in his hand because he had been flayed alive, so butchers and tanners chose him as their patron.

In these transpositions the most unusual interpretations came into existence. For example, it was generally believed that St. Blasius cured diseases of the bladder *(Blase)*. We find many similar sorts of things. It is easy to smile about these things. And it is also quite obvious what dangers accompany such an understanding and veneration of the saints. There can be no doubt that Erasmus's criticism at that time was justified: "We kiss the shoes and the filthy kerchiefs of the saints, and neglect their books, which are their relics that are most effective and deserving of veneration." All of that is true. But when we only look at things this way, we fail to understand the real concern of that age. This cult of saints can be understood correctly only from the presupposition of unrest—the uncertainty of people and their demand for something lasting, for certainty of salvation.

Not only did an increase in the cult of saints take place at this time, but also an increase in pilgrimages. Whoever could manage it financially made a pilgrimage to Palestine or to Rome. Ordinary people did not have this opportunity, so they made pilgrimages to the miracles of their own country. Colossal crowds of people were on the move at that time. On one day in Aachen in 1496 the doorkeepers counted 142,000 pilgrims who offered colossal sums of pious gifts. We must try to imagine this against the presuppositions of that time—the fastest means of transport was the horse, the most comfortable the cart, and the normal one the feet—and then we get some sort of indication not only of the privations and effort which pilgrims took upon themselves, but also of the force which drove them. They undertook pilgrimages to Trier to the exhibition of the seamless robe; they also made pilgrimages to Wilsnack. There in 1383 after a fire in the church the priests found three hosts on the altar, about which the report of their discovery says: *Apparebat quasi gutta sanguinis,* "something like a drop of blood," was contained in them. But that was sufficient to touch off these pilgrimages.

The veneration of relics which stood behind these pilgrimages led to new collections of relics in every place. In some places these relics congregated, such as in Annaberg, Wittenberg, and Halle. No less a figure than Spalatin once calculated in the book of relics of 1509 what indulgence could be offered by the relics collected by Frederick in the castle church in Wittenberg, and at that time it was 1,902,202 years and 270 days of indulgence which a person could obtain if he made a pilgrimage to them in the prescribed manner. At that time, in the year 1509, there were only 5,000 relics; ten years later it had grown to 20,000, and the size of the potential indulgence had risen accordingly. Albrecht of Mainz collected his relics in the cathedral church in Halle; they guaranteed an indulgence of 39,245,120 years and 220 days. We need to add nothing to this. This striving for indulgence, that is, for forgiveness of sins, shows how people attempted to obtain salvation and assure this salvation for themselves. The foundations of that time demonstrate this as well. For example, the time of building great churches was past. At that time all cities had more churches than they really needed, so they enlarged the churches and added to their interior furnishings. Each family that was somewhat well-to-do strove to provide its own altar in God's house, if possible its own chapel, in order to draw near to God not only by performing this pious act, but also to be physically close to him, for they had themselves buried in this chapel after their death, so that thereby they might be relatively certain about God and their salvation.

The worship services were continually increased. In Meissen the litany was sung day and night by more than one hundred clergy and choristers. After 1508 in the small town of Wittenberg there were almost 10,000 masses said annually. At that time Wittenberg had a diameter of a few hundred yards. If one walks from Luther's house to the castle church—even at the slowest pace it takes only ten minutes—one has traversed the Wittenberg of that time. In this nest "on the outskirts of civilization," as Luther graphically described it, there were, as we mentioned, 10,000 masses said in a year, while in Cologne (which was a metropolis for that time) more than 1,000 masses were said each day, that is, about 400,000 masses a year, and this was going on in 11 foundations, 22 monasteries, 19 parish churches, and 100 chapels. At that time the so-called Calends Brotherhoods were organized (so named because they met at the beginning of the month, the "calends"). They have been termed the "trade unions of piety," for in addition to holding convivial gatherings, their main purpose was to perform good works which accrued to the common possession of the brotherhood. Accounts were carefully kept about them. In Cologne the deposit of good works to the credit of the Brotherhood of the Little Ship of St. Ursula was more than 6,000 masses, more than 3,000 psalters, 200,000 Te Deums, 200,000 rosaries, and 630,000,000 Our Fathers and Hail Marys. The brotherhood had completed them as a group and obtained them so that each one who belonged to it could make use of this achievement at the time of death and appearance before God's judgment seat. Thus he could look forward to death with a certain amount of peace. And often a person was not only a member of one brotherhood, but of several at the same time in order to be very certain. For example, Pfeffinger, the councillor of Frederick the Wise, belonged to thirty-five brotherhoods at the same time.

All of these again are things which could easily be criticized as evidences of the decadence of Christianity. But when we once observe them from the other side, then not only are we deeply impressed with the unrest which pervaded that age but also with the sort of efforts people at that time expended in their search for salvation. Certainly then we also understand what sort of effect Luther's attack on indulgences had. This situation we have depicted explains the explosive effect of the Ninety-five Theses, which Myconius said were distributed through all Germany in two weeks as if they were angelic messengers, while Luther's theological theses a few weeks earlier, which dealt with the central questions and which he thought would have an extraordinary effect, attracted no attention. The Ninety-five Theses addressed questions which affected every Christian. At that time the indulgence was one of the most significant—if not the decisive—means of securing salvation, really *the* assurance of salvation for which people grasped in the midst of the unrest which surrounded them. Most of them certainly were not disturbed as deeply with the problem of justification as was Luther, who was brought almost to self-destruction by the question of a gracious God. But in all of them this question was very much alive; countless of them sought emphatically for an answer. What happened with them, although different in degree, was obviously the same as what happened with Luther, who could not find certainty the rest for his soul and conscience which he so desired—in the traditional and usual means. In the answer Luther offered these people they found the answer to their question; they found their search satisfied. This answer was different than had been given before—therefore its effect. This is the only way the explosive power of the Reformation message can be explained; this is the only explanation why at that time an entire world broke apart because of an exegetical discovery.

CHRONOLOGICAL TABLES

Political History	External History of Christianity	Internal History of Christianity	Intellectual and Cultural History
37 B.C.–A.D. 4 Herod (I) the Great			30 B.C.–A.D. 115 Powerful expansion of Roman Empire
30 B.C.–A.D. 14 Augustus			
4 B.C.–A.D. 39 Herod Antipas			
14–37 Tiberius	ca. 30 **Crucifixion of Jesus** on 14th (15th) Nisan, April 7	First Christian community, churches in Palestine and Syria, development of oral (and written) gospel tradition	
26–36 Pontius Pilate procurator	ca. 32/33 Conversion of Paul		37/38—beginning of 2nd cent. Josephus (*History of the Jewish War, Antiquities of the Jews*)
37–41 Caligula			After 40 Philo†
41–54 Claudius	ca. 45–57 Missionary journeys of Paul		
41–44 Herod Agrippa I		50–64 **Epistles of Paul** (earliest 1 Thess., latest the so-called prison epistles)	
54–68 Nero	64 Burning of Rome, persecution of Christians, death of Peter and Paul		65 Seneca and Lucan† (both forced to suicide by Nero)

416

68/69 Year of four emperors			
69/79 Vespasian	70 Conquest and destruction of **Jerusalem** by Titus; Jerusalem Christians move to Pella in Transjordan in 68; their significance soon declines	**Gospels:** Mark shortly before 70, Matthew shortly after 70, Luke around 80, John 90/95	
79–81 Titus		80–90 Acts of the Apostles	79 Eruption of Vesuvius, Herculaneum and Pompeii destroyed (Pliny the Elder†) Flourishing of silver age of Rome (Lucan, Statius, Martial, Juvenal, Quintilian)
81–96 Domitian	Persecution of Christians (in Rome)	ca. 95 Revelation of John ca. 95 1 Clement, oldest of writings of the so-called Apostolic Fathers (letters of Ignatius, *Didache*, letter of Barnabas, letter of Polycarp, 2 Clement, Shepherd of Hermas as last ca. 140/150)	From 90 Extension of the *limes*
96–98 Nerva			From 96 to 192 Adopted emperors
98–117 Trajan	ca. 110 Persecution in Antioch (ca. 117 Ignatius in Rome)	After 100 Latest portions of New Testament: pastoral Epistles, portions of catholic Epistles	Flourishing of pagan literature Tacitus (*Germania* 98, *Historiae* 100/105), Plutarch (ca. 46–120)

417

Political History	External History of Christianity	Internal History of Christianity	Intellectual and Cultural History
		Apostolic Fathers emphasize with ethics in theology	
	ca. 112 Persecution in Bythinia (letter of Pliny the Younger to emperor)		
117–138 Hadrian		ca. 135 **Gnosticism** flourishes; Basilides, Valentinus (both in Egypt, Valentinus ca. 138–68 in Rome)	138 Epictetus†
	135 after revolt of Simon ben Coziba (Bar-Cochba) Jerusalem becomes Roman military colony of Aelia Capitolina which cannot be entered by Jews, Christianity begins there anew as Gentile Christianity	144 Roman church rejects **Marcion**	
138–161 Antoninus Pius	154/55–166 Anacletus of Rome (155 Polycarp in Rome, question of Easter celebration) Persecution in Asia Minor (Polycarp†), Justin Martyr in Rome	ca. 150 Old Roman Symbol, preliminary form of Apostles' Creed ca. 150 **End of expecting the second coming** From 150 to 180 Writings of **Apologists** (Justin, Tatian, Athenagoras, Theophilus, Melito of Sardis, Aristides; the earliest as early as ca. 140: Quadratus)	In 2nd cent. Origin of numerous New Testament apocryphal writings

Emperors	Church	Culture / Learning
161–180 Marcus Aurelius	**ca. 156** Appearance of Montanus; development of **Montanism**, especially in Asia Minor (179 death of prophetess Maximilla) **Beginning of organization of early Catholic church** (canon, rule of faith, apostolic tradition and succession)	Celsus's *True Discourses* Learning flourishes: Ptolemy (100–178), Galen (126–ca. 200), second period of Sophism (Herodes Atticus, Aelius Aristides)
	166–175 Soter of Rome	
	177/178 Persecution in Gaul (Lyons and Vienne)	
	Canon of four gospels closed	
	178 **Irenaeus bishop of Lyons**	
180–192 Commodus	**ca. 180** First reports of Christians in Germanic tribes	**ca. 180** Beginning of Syrian and Latin Bible translations
193/194 Second year of four emperors	**189–198** Victor of Rome (**Quartodeciman-ian controversy** with Asia Minor under Polycrates of Ephesus) **ca. 190** **Monarchians** in Rome (Theodotus the Cobbler, Praxeas, Sabellius after 215)	Official appearance of Egyptian church (catechetical school, Bishop Demetrius of Alexandria, earliest witness ca. 125)
193–211 Septimius Severus	**ca. 200** Edessa Christianized (Bardesanes, first state church) **ca. 203** **Origen** (ca. 185–254) head of catechetical school in Alexandria	Lucian of Samosata Apollonius of Tyana

Political History	External History of Christianity	Internal History of Christianity	Intellectual and Cultural History
		ca. 207 Tertullian's conversion to Montanism	In 3rd cent. Increasing threats to Roman Empire from attacks of neighboring people
211–217 Caracalla	217–222 **Callistus** bishop of Rome	Before 215 Clement of Alexandria† (*Protrepticus, Paedagogus, Stromateis, Quis dives salvetur?*)	
	217 **Hippolytus** opposing bishop (†235)		
218–222 Heliogabalus		After 220 **Tertullian**† (born ca. 160)	Increasing oriental influence on Roman Empire: e.g., Heliogabalus priest of Syrian Baal cult
222–235 Alexander Severus		231 Origen moves to Caesarea (Palestine)	204–270 Plotinus (**Neoplatonism,** Porphyry publishes his *Enneads*)
235–238 Maximinus Thrax			233–304 Porphyry (writing *Against Christians*)
244–249 Philip the Arabian	248/49 **Cyprian** (–258) bishop of Carthage		248 Thousandth anniversary of Rome
249–251 Decius	250/51, 257/58 Decian-Valerian persecution		

251–253 Cornelius bishop of Rome	Schism in Carthage and Rome (Question about readmission of lapsed)		
251 Novatian opposing bishop			
253–260 Valerian	254–257 Stephen I of Rome	255–257 Dispute over validity of baptism by heretics	Main locations of empire protected by walls from external attacks, e.g., Aurelian wall around Rome
260–268 Gallienus		ca. 260 Dionysius of Alexandria (controversy of two Dionysiuses)	
270–275 Aurelian		**Forty years of peace**, internal development of church	
		276 Execution of Manes, founder of Manichaeism	
284–305 Diocletian (from 293, tetrarchy: Augusti Diocletian and Maximian, Caesars Galerius and Constantius Chlorus)	ca. 300 Armenia Christianized, state church	Before 300 **Antony** (†356) goes into desert as eremite	301 Maximum tariff in order to stabilize prices
305 Constantius Chlorus and Galerius become Augusti, Severus and Maximinus Daza Caesars, alongside Maxentius and Constantine as usurpers	303–311 (313) **Diocletian persecution**		

Political History	External History of Christianity	Internal History of Christianity	Intellectual and Cultural History
306–337 **Constantine the Great**	311 Toleration edict of Galerius	311ff. **Donatist Controversy**	**"Constantinian Age"** Numerous churches built, Christian art flourishes
312 Constantine's victory over Maxentius outside Rome at Milvian bridge, thus ruler over West	313 Edict of toleration at Milan (Constantine with Licinius, ruler of East)	313 (–339) **Eusebius** bishop of Caesarea (Palestine)	Age of **Arian controversy:** *anhomoios* (Arians); *homoios* (Semi-Arians, court party); *homoousios* (= identical essence, Athanasius and orthodoxy, West); *homoiousios* (= like essence. Neo-Nicenes, Cappadocians): until 381
	314–335 Pope Silvester	318 Alexander of Alexandria excommunicates Arius	
		ca. 320 **Pachomius** (292–346) establishes first monastery	
324 Constantine's victory over Licinius, thus ruler over entire empire		325 **Council of Nicaea** (*Nicaenum: homoousios,* condemnation of Arius; opposed by center party of Origen and Arians)	330 Dedication of new capital of Constantinople
		336 Arius†, shortly before his restoration to church	
337 Empire divided among sons: Constantius (East), Constantine II (West until 340), Constans (West until 350)			

350–361
Constantius sole ruler (anti-Nicene church politics: 353 and 355 synods of Arles and Milan, 359 of Rimini and Seleucia)

352–366
Pope Liberius

341
Eusebius consecrates Ulfilas (†383) as "bishop in land of Goths"[1]

342
Council of Sardica

The three **Cappadocians:** Basil the Great (ca. 330–379), Gregory of Nyssa (brother, ca. 335–394), Gregory of Nazianzus (329/30–390): Homoiousians

ca. 350 (–407)
John Chrysostom

After 341
Repeatedly renewed prohibitions of pagan temples and sacrifices

1) Christianization of Germanic tribes:

1. Mission begun by **Ulfilas** among Visigoths leads to Arian national churches among various Germanic tribes during time of migrations, until their dissolution in 6th cent.
2. Around 500, **Clovis'** conversion to Catholicism leads to Catholic national church of Franks, which becomes increasingly worldly.
3. After 600, numerous monasteries established on continent by thrust of **Scotch-Irish** (Columbanus); they strengthen existing Christianity and become centers for its missionary expansion; itinerant bishops. But independent organization alongside existing Frankish church, on whole of which they have no effect. Dispersal of monastery organization.
4. Around 690, organized work of **Anglo-Saxons** on continent begins under Willibrord, after Wilfrid previously lays foundation.
   a. Missionary activity in Frisia = present-day Holland (Wilfrid, Willibrord, Wynfrith-**Boniface**); thrust into Saxon territory (companions of Willibrord), after Hessen, Thuringia, Bavaria (Boniface, first period of life).
   b. Internal rebuilding of Frankish church (first synods 742/745), incorporation of territory won by mission (Boniface, second period of life) and close attachment of whole to Rome (Boniface, third period of life), Willibrord† 739–Boniface† 754.
5. After **Charlemagne** (768–814), expansion of Christianity among tribes in East: Frisians, Saxons, etc., in connection with forced subjugation (beginning of Saxon wars 722, end 804).
6. Around 1000, conversion of **Scandinavia.** Mission first beginning from Bremen, after 995 forcible Christianization of Norway by Olaf Tryggvason and Olaf Haraldson (converted in England), Iceland Christian around 1000, Olaf Skötkonung of Sweden baptized 1008.

Political History	External History of Christianity	Internal History of Christianity	Intellectual and Cultural History
		354–430 **Augustine**	
361–363 **Julian** ("the Apostate")			Revival of pagan worship
		362 Synod of Alexandria (approach of Athanasius to Homoiousians)	
		362 Condemnation of Apollinaris of Laodicea (ca. 310–ca. 390)	Age of **Christological controversy:** Apollinarian, Nestorian, Eutychian, Monophysite, Monenergistic, Monothelite controversy (extends into 7th cent.)
364 Valentinian I (West, until 375) and Valens (East, until 378) followed by Gratian (East, until 383) and Valentinian II (West, until 382)	366–384 Pope Damasus		
	374 **Ambrose** bishop of Milan (d. 397)		
		381 **Council of Constantinople** (*Nicaeno-Constantinopolitanum*, end of Arian controversy)	Ammianus Marcellinus, history of Roman Empire (extends to 378)
		386 Jerome (ca. 349–419/20) settles in Bethlehem	380ff. Edicts of Theodosius: Christianity declared state religion
		386 Augustine's conversion	393 Olympic games cease

Political / Secular	Church / Papacy	Other
394-395 Theodosius the Great sole ruler (previously since 379 ruler over East); further division after his death: Arcadius (East, until 408), Honorius (West, until 423)	395 Augustine bishop of Hippo Regius (Bône)	404 Ravenna becomes residence
408-450 Theodosius II in East	401-417 Pope Innocent I	
410 Rome conquered by Alaric (Visigoths)	410 Rufinus† (born ca. 345)	
	410 Pelagius and Celestius flee from Rome to Carthage, 411 beginning of controversy with Augustine	Outbreak of **Pelagian** (until 431) or **Semipelagian controversy** about Augustine's doctrine of grace, until 529 (Synod of Orange)
	411 Augustine's argument with Petillian of Sirte about Donatism (finally concluding with its being considered heresy)	415 Pagan philosopher Hypatia stoned by Christians in Alexandria
	412-444 **Cyril** bishop of Alexandria	438 *Codex Theodosianus* (first codification of church law)
418-507 Visigoth kingdom in Gaul	428 **Nestorius** patriarch of Constantinople	
429-534 Vandal kingdom in North Africa	431 **Council of Ephesus**	
	440-461 Pope Leo I	
	449 "Robber Council" of Ephesus	

Political History	External History of Christianity	Internal History of Christianity	Intellectual and Cultural History
451 Victory over Huns on Catalaunian Plains	444–451 Patriarch Dioscorus of Alexandria	451 **Council of Chalcedon** (*Chalcedonense*, doctrine of two natures), followed by Monophysite controversy	
476 Odoacer proclaimed king, **end of Western Roman Empire**			**Germanic dominance over entire Western Roman Empire** (until Justinian)
482–511 Clovis (Chlodowech)	484–519 First (Acacian) schism between Eastern and Western church	Christianization of Franks	
493–533 Ostrogoth kingdom in Italy	492–496 Pope Gelasius I (doctrine of two swords)	End of 5th cent.: writings of Dionysius the Pseudo-Areopagite	
493–526 Theodoric the Great	498–514 Pope Symmachus		
507–711 Visigoth kingdom in Spain	512–518 Severus patriarch of Antioch	519ff. Theopaschite controversy	
527–565 **Justinian I**	523–526 Pope John I	529 **Benedict of Nursia** (ca. 480–ca. 550) establishes Monte Cassino monastery	529 Platonic academy in Athens closed
		529 Council of Orange (end of Pelagian controversies)	

530–532
Boniface II (first pope of Germanic ancestry)

533/34–535
Byzantium defeats Vandals

534
Codification of Roman law: *Corpus Iuris*

535–553
Byzantium defeats Ostrogoths

537–555
Pope Vigilius ("Byzantine" pope)

538–594
Gregory of Tours

543
Origen and Antiochene school condemned (beginning of Three Chapters controversy, until 553)

553
5th ecumenical Council of Constantinople

568
Lombards in Italy (until 774)

ca. 570
Mohammed born (†632)

580–662
Maximus Confessor

589
Conversion of Visigoths to Catholicism

590
Columbanus founds monastery at Luxeuil

590–604
Pope Gregory (I) the Great

594
Gregory of Tours, *Gesta Francorum*

Political History	External History of Christianity	Internal History of Christianity	Intellectual and Cultural History
			End of idea of a Roman Empire
610–641 Heraclius (inauguration of Greek empire)		597 Beginning of mission to Anglo-Saxons	After 627 in Eastern Empire Greek replaces already declining Latin as language of administration
			From 635 on **Islamic conquests:** 638 capture of Jerusalem, 639–641 capture of Egypt and Persia, 698 Africa, 711 Spain, Constantinople twice unsuccessfully besieged (672/78 and 717/18)
	649–653 Pope Martin I	650–754 John of Damascus	Learning flourishes in Anglo-Saxon monasteries
		664 Synod of Whitby, finally joining Anglo-Saxon church to Rome (Wilfrid)	
		680/81 6th ecumenical Council of Constantinople (*Trullanum I*)	
After 687 Carolingian mayors of Frankish palace			

714–741
Charles Martel

717–741
Emperor Leo (III) the Isaurian

692
Trullanum II, *Quinisextum* (supplementing 5th and 6th councils)

719–754
Boniface in Germany

726
Beginning of **iconoclastic controversy** in Eastern church

ca. 720–797
Paul the Deacon

728–732
Rome's break with Byzantium

732
Victory of Charles Martel over Arabs at Tours and Poitiers

741–768
Pepin the Short (751/52 elevated to king)

752–757
Pope Stephen II (petitioner in Frankish kingdom in 754, anointed Pepin king)

756
Donation of Pepin (beginning of States of Church)

The Carolingians (until 911)

768–814
Charlemagne

Carolingian renaissance

Political History	External History of Christianity	Internal History of Christianity	Intellectual and Cultural History
772 Beginning of the Saxon wars (782 Verden an der Aller, 785 Wittekind's baptism, 804 last campaign)	772–795 Pope Hadrian I	780–795 Adoptionist controversy	781–804 Anglo-Saxon Alcuin in Charlemagne's services as advisor in spiritual and scholarly questions
		787 Second Synod of Nicaea (7th ecumenical council): allows veneration of icons	
		ca. 790 *Libri Carolini* (rejection of veneration of icons)	793 Art of making paper, discovered centuries earlier in China, reaches Baghdad, Cairo in 900, Spain in 1150, Italy in 1276, France in 1350, Nuremberg in 1390
800 imperial coronation (Dec. 25 in St. Peter's)	795–816 Pope Leo III	809 Synod of Aachen (*filioque*)	
814–840 Louis the Pious Norman raids after 820		831 Archdiocese of Hamburg established, entrusted to Ansgar (801–865)	ca. 830 *Heliand*
		843 Synod of Constantinople: final reintroduction of veneration of icons	840 Einhard† (*Life of Charlemagne*)

843
Treaty of Verdun, threefold division of empire: Louis the German (Germany; 854, German Carolingians until 911); Charles (II) the Bald (France, 877†, French Carolingians until 987); Lothair I (middle kingdom, 855†)

844ff.
First controversy about Lord's Supper: Paschasius Radbertus, Ratramnus

846
Sack of Rome by Saracens

847/852
Forgery of Pseudo-Isidorian Decretals

847–855
Pope Leo IV

848/849
Gottschalk's doctrine of predestination condemned

858–867
Pope Nicholas I

861
Paris sacked by Normans for third time (previously 845, 857; as well as numerous German cities: Aachen, Cologne, Mainz, Metz, Worms, etc.)

863/871
Gospel harmony of Ottfried of Weissenburg

After 863/864 Methodius and Cyril (Constantine) active among Slavs

867
Second schism (Photian) between Eastern and Western church

870
Treaty of Mersen (middle kingdom divided)

Political History	External History of Christianity	Internal History of Christianity	Intellectual and Cultural History
			Photius (820–897) and Arethas of Caesarea (†after 944), preservers of ancient ecclesiastical tradition, exponents of academic and cultural flowering in Byzantium from 9th until 11th cents.
		After 877 †John Scotus Erigena	
	From 896 to 963 Twenty popes in Rome, papacy in hands of nobility		
		909/910 **Founding of Cluny monastery,** Berno (†927) first abbot	
899–911 Louis (IV) the Child			
911–918 Conrad I of Franconia		Beginning of spread of Cluniac movement through France and beyond under abbot Odo of Cluny (927 to 941), zenith in 11th cent.	Beginning of German expansion toward East
The Saxon emperors (until 1024)			
919–936 Henry the Fowler			
933 Defeat of Hungarians at Unstrut			
936–973 **Otto I**			Beginning of imperial church politics of Ottos, dependence of bishops on ruler, thus necessarily leading to Italian politics of German emperors

432

955 Defeat of Hungarians at Lechfeld	955–964 Pope John XII (962 imperial coronation of Otto with oath of fealty)	968 Founding of archdiocese of Magdeburg (main effect in East, 1000 limited by founding of archdiocese of Gniezno)	End of 10th cent. Development of Mount Athos monastery (anchorites there since 850, already 300 monks by 1045)
973–983 Otto II		988 Vladimir the Great begins Christianization of Russia	Church building in time of Ottos: cathedrals in Magdeburg, Mainz, Augsburg, Regensburg, Worms, Bamberg, Münster, Paderborn, Eichstätt, Strasbourg, Merseburg
983–1002 Otto III	996–999 Pope Gregory V (Reform Party)		
	999–1003 Pope Silvester II	Increasing influence of reform party on monarchy	1022 Notker Labeo ("the German")† in St. Gall, translator of Latin and Greek texts into Old High German
1002–1024 Henry II		1033–1109 Anselm of Canterbury	

Political History	External History of Christianity	Internal History of Christianity	Intellectual and Cultural History
The Franconian (Salian) emperors (until 1125)			1037 Avicenna (Ibn Sina)†, Arabian physician and Aristotelian
1024–1039 Conrad II	1046 Synods in Sutri and Rome (three popes deposed, including Gregory VI) under emperor's influence, bishop of Bamberg chosen as Clement II in their place	1045 Adalbert archbishop of Bremen (mission in Greenland, Iceland, Finland, and East)	
1039–1056 Henry III	1049–1054 Pope Leo IX (Bruno of Egisheim)	1050–1080 Second controversy on Lord's Supper: Berengar of Tours, Lanfranc	
	1054 **Schism between Western and Eastern church**		
1056–1106 Henry IV			
1061 Normans conquer Arabian occupied Sicily from southern Italy			
1066 Battle of Hastings, William the Conqueror (duke of Normandy) wins English throne		Victory of Cluniac reform idea at curia (1059 decree on papal elections: election of pope only by cardinals, prohibition of lay investiture)	1066 Rebuilding of Monte Cassino monastery destroyed by Arabs
			In 11th cent. oldest Russian monasteries (cave monastery near Kiev), 1050 St. Sophia cathedral in Novgorod

1070
Hirsau reform (influence of Cluny)

1073–1085
Pope Gregory VII

1075
Lenten synod: prohibition of lay investiture

1076
Synod of Worms: deposition of pope

1077–1080
Rudolf of Swabia

Jan. 25–28, 1077
Henry IV as penitent at Canossa

Second flourishing of Byzantine literature and art under Comneni (1081 until 1185)

1079–1142
Peter Abelard

1083
Henry IV conquers Rome

1088–1099
Pope Urban II

1091–1153
Bernard of Clairvaux

1095
Synod of Clermont (prohibition of lay investiture, crusade indulgence)

Age of crusades (until 1270)

1096–1099
First crusade (Christian Kingdom of Jerusalem)

435

Political History	External History of Christianity	Internal History of Christianity	Intellectual and Cultural History
			Age of scholasticism
		1097–1141 Hugh of St. Victor (Areopagite mystic)	1097 Cathedral at Speyer (Romanesque)
			Nominalism (Roscellinus)
1106–1125 Henry V	1099–1118 Pope Paschal II		Realism (William of Champeaux) End of 11th cent. Bologna university
	1111 Treaty of Sutri	1098 Founding of Cistercian order (Citeaux monastery)	
		ca. 1100–1160 Peter Lombard (*Sentences*)	
	1122 **Concordat of Worms**	ca. 1120–1180 John of Salisbury	**End of investiture controversy between pope and emperor**
1125–1137 Lothair the Saxon	1130–1143 Pope Innocent II		Establishment of spiritual knightly orders: Knights Templar (Templars, 1118) Hospitallers (1113, Knights of Malta), Teutonic Knights (1190)
	1130–1138 Pope Anacletus II		Beginning of German colonization in East

The Hohenstaufen emperors (until 1254)

1138–1152
Conrad III

1147–1149
Second crusade

1147
Penitential preaching in Rome by Arnold of Brescia (1155 burned)

1137
Rebuilding of abbey church of St. Denis: beginning of Gothic

1140
Decretum Gratiani (Gratian† 1158) new collection of canon law, foundation of *Corpus Iuris Canonici*

1152–1190
Frederick (I) Barbarossa

1159–1181
Pope Alexander III

1170
Thomas Becket, archbishop of Canterbury† (murdered)

1167/68
Oxford University (exodus from Paris)

1176
Battle of Legnano

1176
Conversion of Peter Valdes (Waldensians)

1179
Hildegard of Bingen†

Since end of 12th cent. in Iceland collection of sagas of gods and heroes of 9th to 12th cents.: *Edda*

1181
Banning of Henry the Lion

ca. 1181–1226
Francis of Assisi, rule of Franciscan order in 1221 and 1223

ca. 1185–1245
Alexander of Hales

Political History	External History of Christianity	Internal History of Christianity	Intellectual and Cultural History
	1189–1192 Third crusade	1193 (1206/07)–1280 Albertus Magnus	ca. 1200 Origin of the *Nibelungenlied*
1190–1197 Henry VI			**Summit of papacy's position of power**
1198–1208 Philip of Swabia	1198–1216 **Pope Innocent III**	1201/02 Abbot Joachim of Fiore† (Joachimism)	1198–1228 Walther von der Vogelweide
1198–1215 Otto (IV) of Brunswick	1202–1204 Fourth crusade		1204 Moses Maimonides†
	1204–1261 Latin empire in Byzantium		ca. 1205 Wolfram von Eschenbach: *Parzival*
			ca. 1208 Gottfried von Strassburg: *Tristan und Isolde*
	1209–1229 Albigensian wars in France	ca. 1210–after 1291 Roger Bacon	1209 Cambridge University (exodus from Oxford, founded shortly before)
1212–1250 Frederick II		1212 Children's crusade	1209 Beginning of construction of Magdeburg cathedral (oldest Gothic cathedral of Germany)

1215
Magna Charta in England

1216
John Lackland† (king of
England after 1199)

1224
Mongols attack Russia

1227
Genghis Khan†, division of
Mongol empire (after 1206)

1241
Defeat by Mongols at
battle of Legnica

1227–1241
Pope Gregory IX

1228–1229
Fifth crusade (reestablishment
of Kingdom of Jerusalem,
finally lost in 1244)

1230
Beginning of conquest of
Prussia by Teutonic knights

Nov. 1215
Fourth Lateran Council

1216
Confirmation of Dominican order

1221–1274
Bonaventure

1225/26–1274
Thomas Aquinas

1232
Final establishment of Inqui-
sition (founded 1215 at Fourth
Lateran Council) in hands of
Dominicans

1234
"Crusade" against Stedinger
peasants

1220
Hartmann von Aue†
(*Der arme Heinrich*)

1220/35
Eike von Repgow: *Sachsenspiegel*

After 1226
Increasing establishment of
imperial free cities directly
subject to emperor

240
Caesarius of Heisterbach†

439

Political History	External History of Christianity	Internal History of Christianity	Intellectual and Cultural History
1242 Founding of Mongolian empire of "Golden Horde"			1241 Withdrawal of previously victorious Mongols from their advance toward West
	1243–1254 Pope Innocent IV	1245 Council of Lyons (struggle against Frederick II)	1248 Beginning of construction of Cologne cathedral on 9th cent. foundations
1250–1254 Conrad IV	1248–1254 Sixth crusade (unsuccessful)		
1254 Rhenish city league (until ca. 1450)			1257 Establishment of Sorbonne in Paris (uniting all educational institutions)
1256–1273 **Interregnum** in Germany			
After 1259 Under Kublai Khan (†1294) greatest expansion of power of Mongol empire, from China to Poland, from Siberia to Himalayas			1265–1321 Dante Alighieri
1268 Conradin executed in Naples, end of imperial domination in Italy	1270 Seventh crusade (unsuccessful)	1270 Jacob of Voragine archbishop of Genoa: Golden Legend	

1273–1347
Kings of various houses

1285–1314
Philip (IV) the Fair of France

1298–1308
Albert I of Austria

1291
Capture of Acre by Arabs,
Hospitallers and Templars move
their base to Cyprus
(Hospitallers to Rhodes in 1310)

1294–1303
Pope Boniface VIII

ca. 1270–1308
John Duns Scotus

Henceforth Dominicans = Tho-
mists, Franciscans = Scotists

1274
Second Council of Lyons (temporary union with Greek church,
regulation of conclave election)

ca. 1285
Mechthild of Magdeburg

1293–1381
John of Ruysbroeck

ca. 1270
Tannhäuser† (born ca. 1205)

1272 Berthold of Regensburg†

1274
Beginning of Marienburg
(completed in 1398)

1286
Bar-Hebraeus†

1287
Konrad von Würzburg†
(Der Trojanische Krieg)

1289
Founding of Montpelier
university (one of largest in
Europe in 14th cent.)

Political History	External History of Christianity	Internal History of Christianity	Intellectual and Cultural History
After 1301 Continual advances of Turks in Asia Minor		1300 First "holy year" with plenary indulgence	
	1302 Bull *Unam sanctam ecclesiam*		1303 Founding of Rome university
			1304–1374 Petrarch, beginning of age of Renaissance and humanism
			1306 Jacopone da Todi†
	1309–1377 Popes in Avignon (**Babylonian captivity of papacy**)		
	1312 Dissolution of Templars by Pope Clement V		
1314–1347 Louis IV of Bavaria		ca. 1315 Brethren and Sisters of the Free Spirit appear	1316 Raymond Lull† (born 1235)
1314–1330 Frederick the Fair of Austria	1316–1334 Pope John XXII		
		ca. 1320–1384 **John Wycliffe**	
	1323 Condemnation of doctrine of Christ's poverty, resistance from radical Franciscans (Spirituals)		1324 Marco Polo† (born 1254)
1324 Sachsenhausen Appellation (to a general council)		1324 *Defensor pacis* of Marsiglio of Padua and John of Jandun	

1327
Meister Eckhart† (born ca. 1260?)

1328
William of Occam (†1349), founder of new nominalism, flees to Emperor Louis IV, along with general of Franciscan order, Cesena

ca. 1348
Nicholas of Lyra† (*Postillae perpetuae*)

348–1352
Plague in Germany and Europe (almost half of populace said to have died)

348
Prague university

1328
Ivan I (1304–1341), grand prince of Russia, makes Moscow capital

1331
Swabian city league (until 1389)

1338
Electoral assembly of Rense: king chosen by electors does not need papal confirmation

1339–1453
Hundred Years' War between France and England

1346–1437 Luxembourg emperors

1347
Cola di Rienzi tribune of people in Rome

1356
Golden Bull (law establishing empire, election of king by seven electors in Frankfurt)

Political History	External History of Christianity	Internal History of Christianity	Intellectual and Cultural History
		1358 Gregory of Rimini†	1358 First designation of towns of Hanseatic League (beginnings in 12th cent., finally more than 200 cities)
		Second half of 14th cent. the *Gottesfreunde*	1359 Berlin member of Hanseatic League
		1361 Johann Tauler† (born ca. 1300)	
		1362 Henry Suso† (born ca. 1295)	1365 Vienna university
1370–1405 Mongolian empire of Tamerlane	1377 Pope Gregory XI returns to Rome (1367 Urban VI in Rome for a few years)	1369(?)–1415 **John Huss**	1373 Bridget of Sweden† (born 1303)
			1374 Konrad von Megenberg†
1378–1400 Wenceslaus (IV, king of Bohemia until 1419)	1378–1417 **Schism between popes in Rome and Avignon**	ca. 1380 Brethren of Common Life in Deventer, 1386/87 in Windesheim monastery near Zwolle (*Devotio moderna*)	

1381
Peasants' revolt in England (Wat Tyler), following one in France in 1358 (*Jacquerie*), first of series lasting until Reformation

1383
Wycliffe's Bible translation

1386
Heidelberg university

1388
Cologne university

1397
Union of Kalmar (three Scandinavian kingdoms united under Danish crown)

1399
Peter Parler†

ca. 1400
Theologia deutsch

1401–1464
Nicholas of Cusa

1405/07–1457
Lorenzo Valla (**Italian humanism**)

1409
Council of Pisa: three popes: Gregory XII, Benedict XIII (old), Alexander V (new)

1409
Leipzig university (exodus from Prague)

1410–1437
Emperor Sigismund (house of Luxembourg)

ca. 1410–1494
Gabriel Biel

1410
Battle of Tannenberg, defeat of Teutonic Knights

445

Political History	External History of Christianity	Internal History of Christianity	Intellectual and Cultural History
	1414–1418 **Council of Constance** (Pierre D'Ailly† 1420, Jean Gerson† 1429, leaders of reform)	June 6, 1415 Burning of Huss, followed by Hussite wars	1415 Rostock university (exodus in 1456 to Greifswald university)
	1417–1431 Pope Martin V		
1419–1436 Hussite wars (Utraquists/Taborites)	1431 Joan of Arc, the "Maid of Orléans," burned		
	1431–1449 **Council of Basel** (1437 divided, 1438 in Ferrara, 1439 in Florence under Pope Eugene IV)		1436–1476 Regiomontanus, astronomer
1438–1806 Emperors from Hapsburg house		1438 Pragmatic Sanction of Bourges ("Gallican Liberties")	
		1439 (Theoretical) union with Greek church at **Union Council of Florence**	1439 *Reformatio Sigismundi*
		1441 Thomas à Kempis (1380–1471): *Imitation of Christ*	1441 Henry VI founds Eton College

446

ca. 1444–1510
Botticelli (Alessandro Filipepi)

ca. 1450
Gutenberg invents **printing with movable type** (1453, 42-line Bible)

1452–1519
Leonardo da Vinci

1455
Fra Angelico† (born 1387)

1455–1522
Johannes Reuchlin (**German humanism**)

1463–1494
Giovanni Pico della Mirandola

1466(69)–1536
Erasmus of Rotterdam (**European humanism**)

1471–1528
Albrecht Dürer

1447–1455
Pope Nicholas V (first Renaissance pope)

After 1450
Via antiqua (Thomism and Scotism) beside and opposed to *Via moderna* (Occamism)

1452–1498
Girolamo Savonarola

After 1456
Gravamina of German nation

1466
First German Bible printed in Strasbourg: Johann Mentel

1453
Fall of Constantinople

1453
End of Hundred Years' War (England retains only Calais from its vast possessions in France)

1458–1464
Pope Pius II (Enea Silvio de' Piccolomini)

1462–1505
Ivan the Great of Moscow, married to niece of last Byzantine emperor, begins to make Moscow center of Orthodox Christianity

1464
Cosimo de' Medici†; after struggles, Lorenzo the Magnificent master of Florence in 1469

Political History	External History of Christianity	Internal History of Christianity	Intellectual and Cultural History
			1473 Copernicus born
			1475–1564 Michelangelo
		"Forerunners" of Reformation: John Pupper of Goch† after 1473, John Rucherat of Wesel† 1479/81, Wessel Gansfort† 1489	1477 Tübingen university
			1492 End of Arab rule in Spain
1485 Division of Saxony by princes Ernest (Ernestine, with Wittenberg and electoral dignity) and Albert (Albertine, with Leipzig)	1492–1503 Pope Alexander VI (Rodrigo Borgia)		1492 Columbus discovers America
1493–1519 Maximilian I			1493 Spain and Portugal divide the "New World"

Index

INDEX

Investiture controversy. *See* Lay investiture

Iona, 239–40

Ireland, 238

Irenaeus: as heretic fighter, 134; missionary work in Gaul, 50; origin in Asia Minor, 130; published by Erasmus, 387

Irminsul: and Charlemagne, 220; destruction of, 257; and Oak of Thor, 249

Isaac II Angelus (Byzantine emperor), 328

Isidore of Kiev, 404

Isis: Caligula's temple to, 10; central figure of mystery religion, 11; and resurrection, 24–25; Roman sanctuaries to, destroyed, 10

Islam: and Christianity, 221; spread of, 42

Italian politics: Frederick I Barbarossa, 314; Frederick II, 318; Otto I, 283

Italy: early establishment of universities in, 335; Paul's missionary activity in, 47

James, brother of the Lord and apostle: conversion of, 120–21; influence on Peter, 146

James, Epistle of: chronology of, 102; Luther on genuineness of authorship of, 103–4; on mention of Jesus' name, 106; origin of, 110; treatment of rich Christians in, 57

James, Protevangelium of, 129

Jan Milíč. *See* Milíč, Jan

Jehovah's Witnesses: as modern missionaries, 40; quoting Scripture, 116–17

Jerome: establishment of Hebrew text as basis for Old Testament, 108; as Semipelagian, 207; study of, by Frankish theologians, 266

Jerome of Prague, 371

Jerusalem: Charlemagne given protectorate over holy places in, 255; decline of the church of, reasons for, 125; as first Christian community, 45–46; and Frederick II's Crusade, 319; heavenly, 94; Kingdom of, established by First Crusade, 334

Jesus Christ: in Gnosticism, 95; preaching judgment, 33–34; and women, 61–62; words of, in Acts, 100; in the writings of the Apostolic Fathers, 98

Jewish Christian congregations, 121

Joachim of Brandenburg, 409

Job, 34–35

Johannine writings, 102

John I, 229

John XXII, 348–49; condemned Spiritual Franciscan order, 356

John XXIII (antipope): as Baldassare Cossa, 395; as cardinal of Tusculum, 396; elected pope by Council of Pisa, 352

John XXIII (Giuseppe Roncalli), 396

John, Epistles of, 110

John, Gospel of: difference from other Gospels, 106; evaluation by Dionysius of Alexandria, 103; Jesus' healing of the blind man in, 36; origin of, 99; promise of Paraclete, 94

John Duns Scotus. *See* Duns Scotus, John

John Lackland (king of England): and Innocent III, 326; Crusade against, 334

John of Jandun, 354

John of Lancaster (duke of Bedford), 360–62

John of Wesel, 392

John Scotus Erigena, 271

Jonah, 16–17

Joppa, 46

Judaea, as part of Roman Empire, 10

Judaism, as competitor of Christianity, 32–38